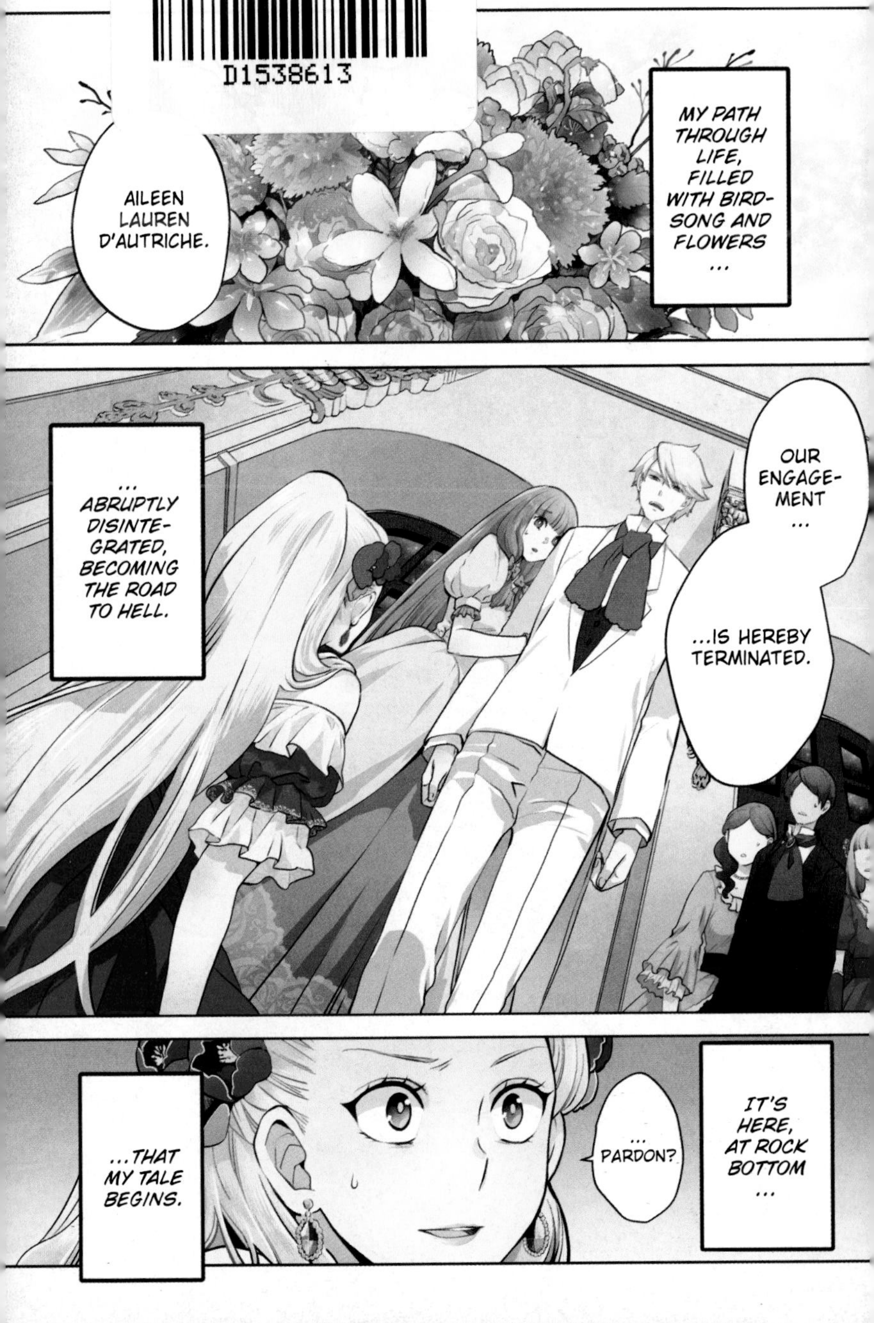
MY PATH THROUGH LIFE, FILLED WITH BIRD-SONG AND FLOWERS ...
AILEEN LAUREN D'AUTRICHE.
OUR ENGAGEMENT ...
...IS HEREBY TERMINATED.
... ABRUPTLY DISINTEGRATED, BECOMING THE ROAD TO HELL.
IT'S HERE, AT ROCK BOTTOM ...
... PARDON?
...THAT MY TALE BEGINS.

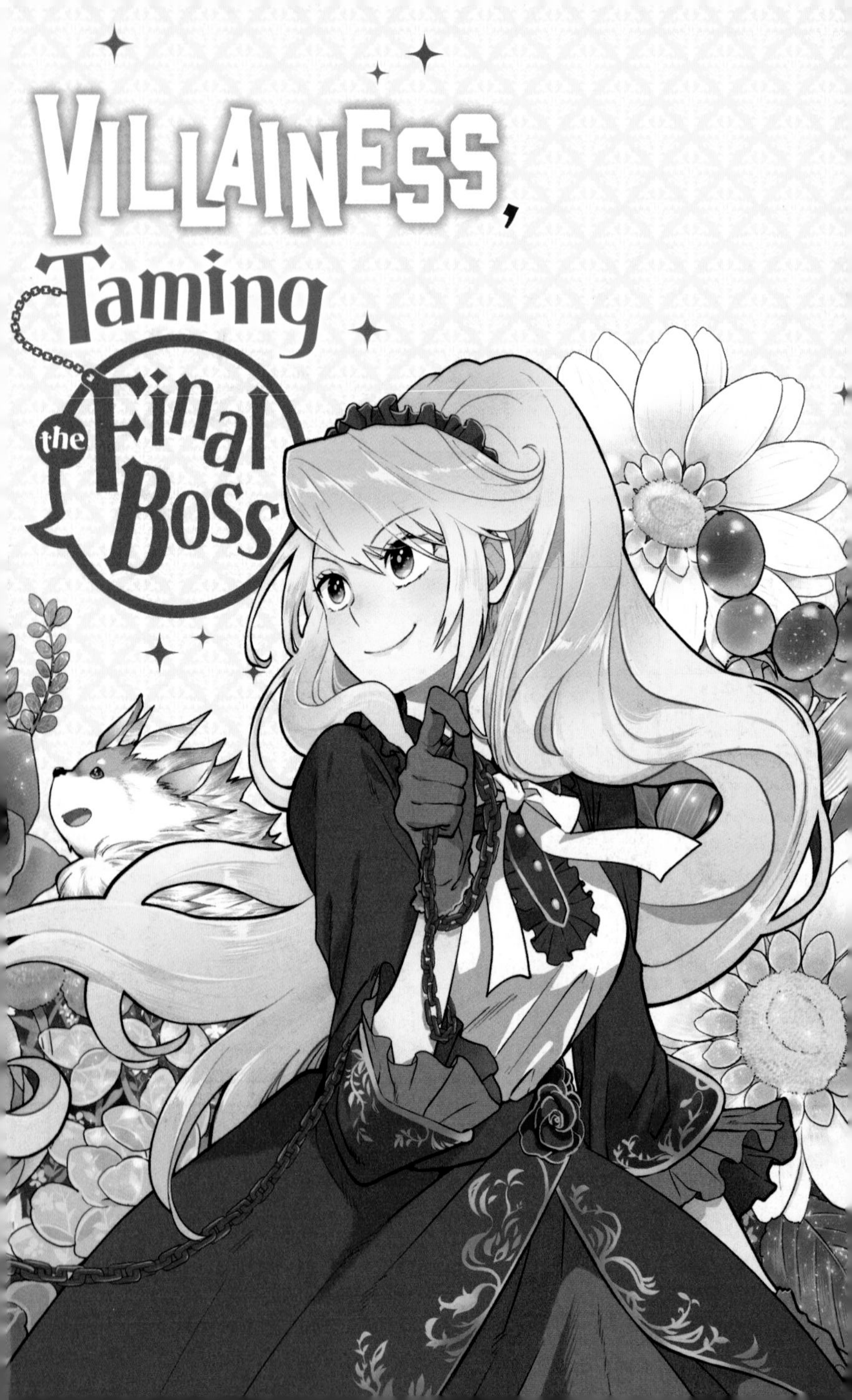
Villainess,
Taming
the Final
Boss

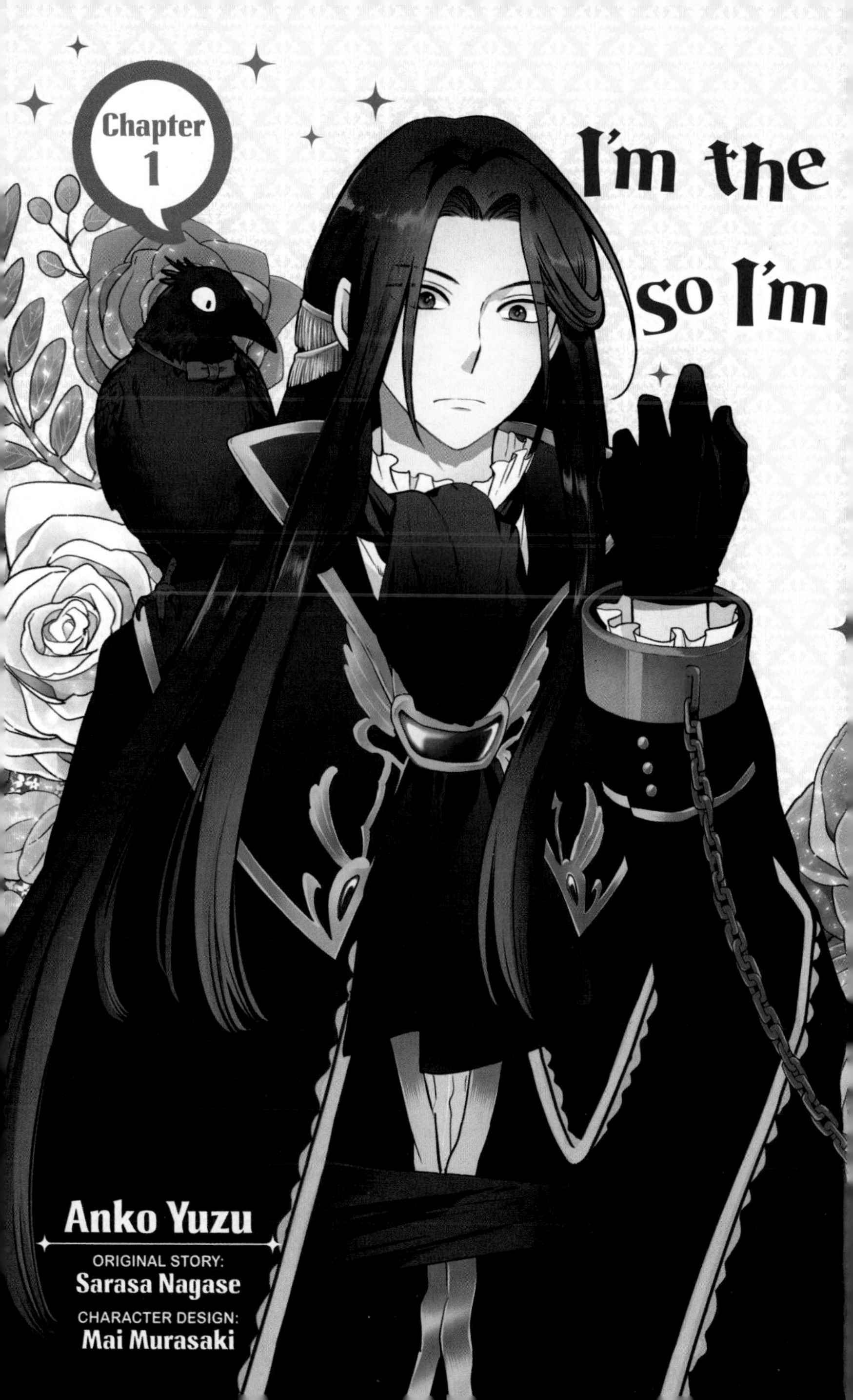
Chapter 1
I'm the
so I'm
Anko Yuzu
ORIGINAL STORY:
Sarasa Nagase
CHARACTER DESIGN:
Mai Murasaki

CONTENTS

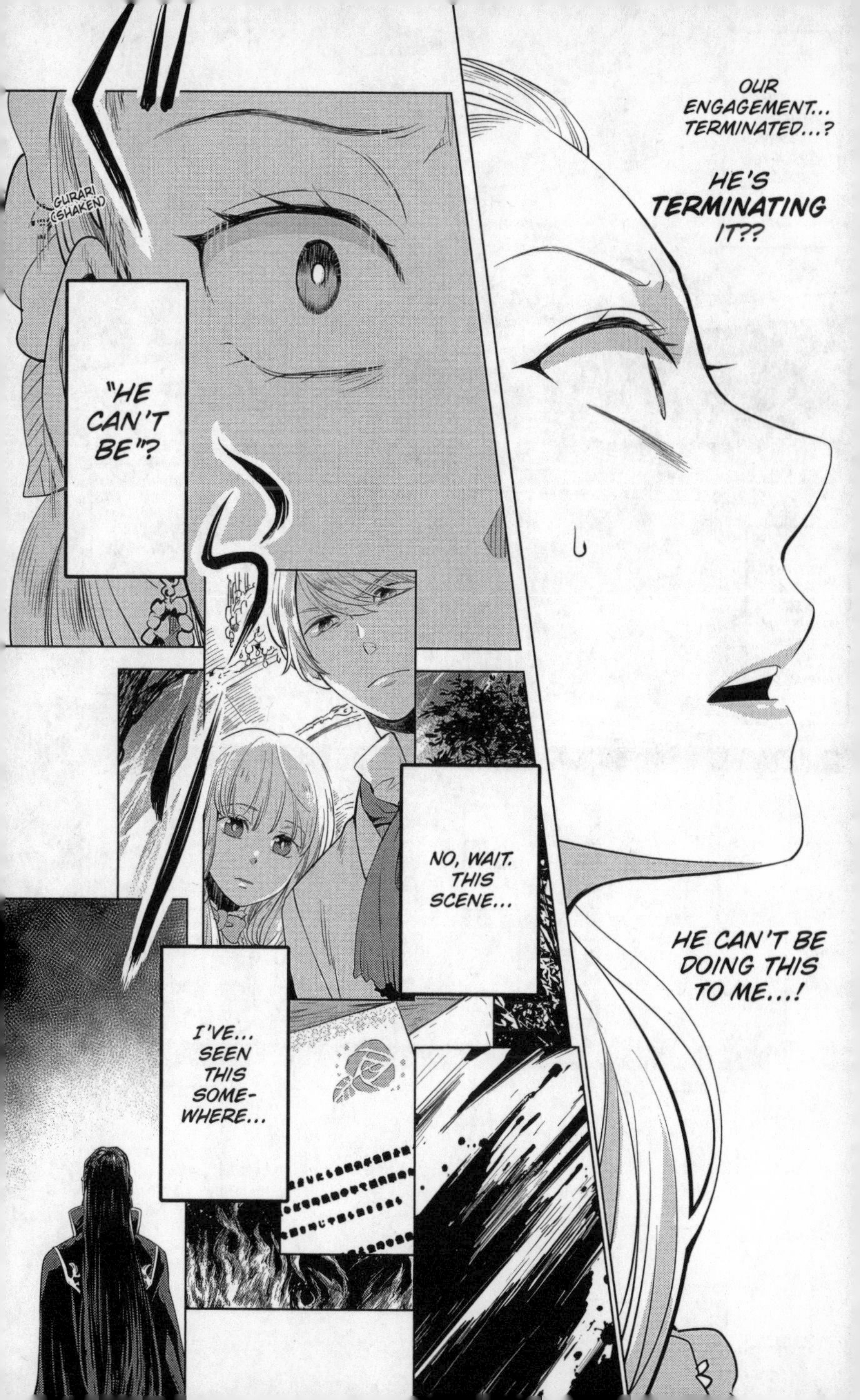
OUR ENGAGEMENT... TERMINATED...?
HE'S TERMINATING IT??
HE CAN'T BE DOING THIS TO ME...!
GURARI (SHAKEN)
"HE CAN'T BE"?
NO, WAIT. THIS SCENE...
I'VE... SEEN THIS SOMEWHERE...

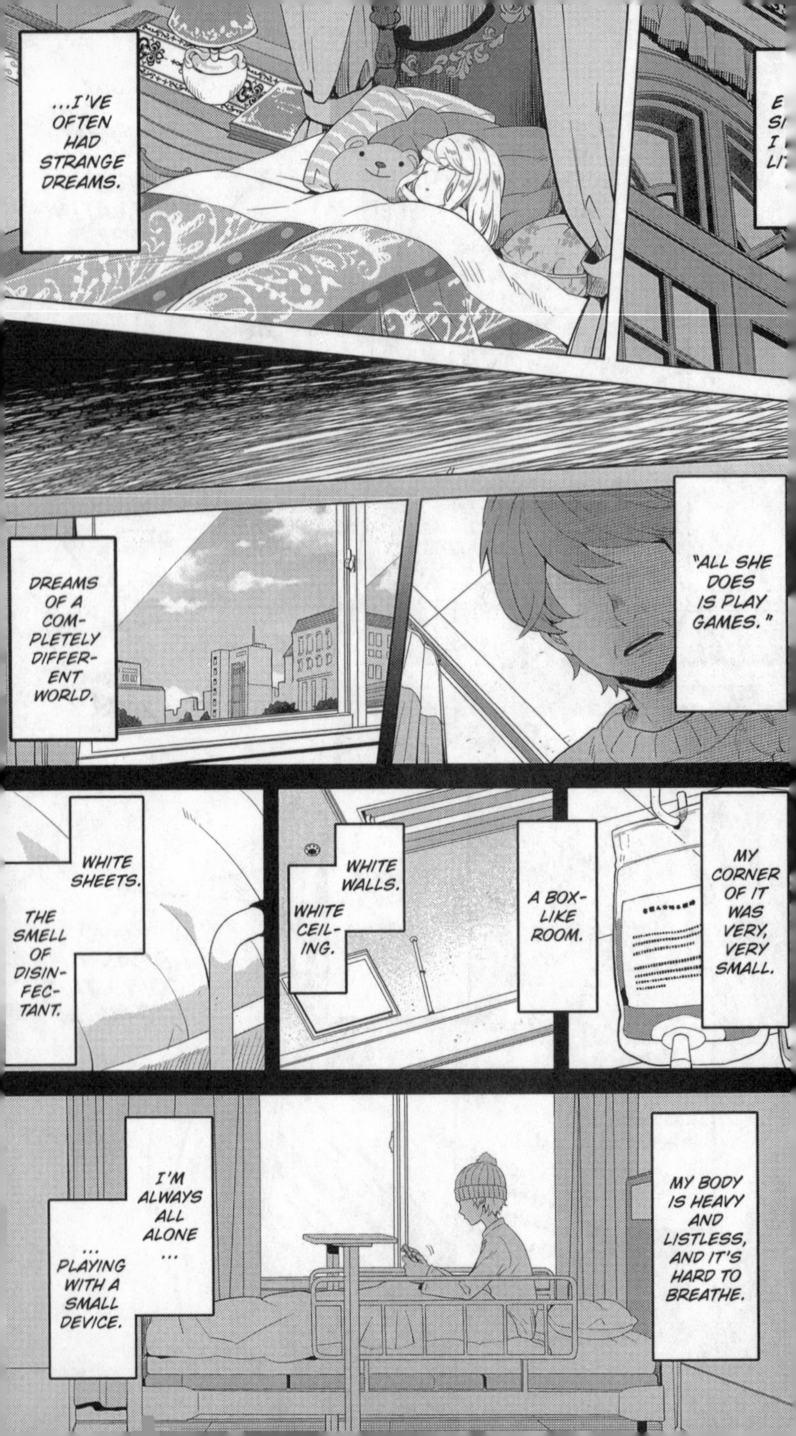
...I'VE OFTEN HAD STRANGE DREAMS.
"ALL SHE DOES IS PLAY GAMES."
DREAMS OF A COMPLETELY DIFFERENT WORLD.
MY CORNER OF IT WAS VERY, VERY SMALL.
A BOX-LIKE ROOM.
WHITE WALLS.
WHITE CEILING.
WHITE SHEETS.
THE SMELL OF DISINFECTANT.
MY BODY IS HEAVY AND LISTLESS, AND IT'S HARD TO BREATHE.
I'M ALWAYS ALL ALONE ...
... PLAYING WITH A SMALL DEVICE.

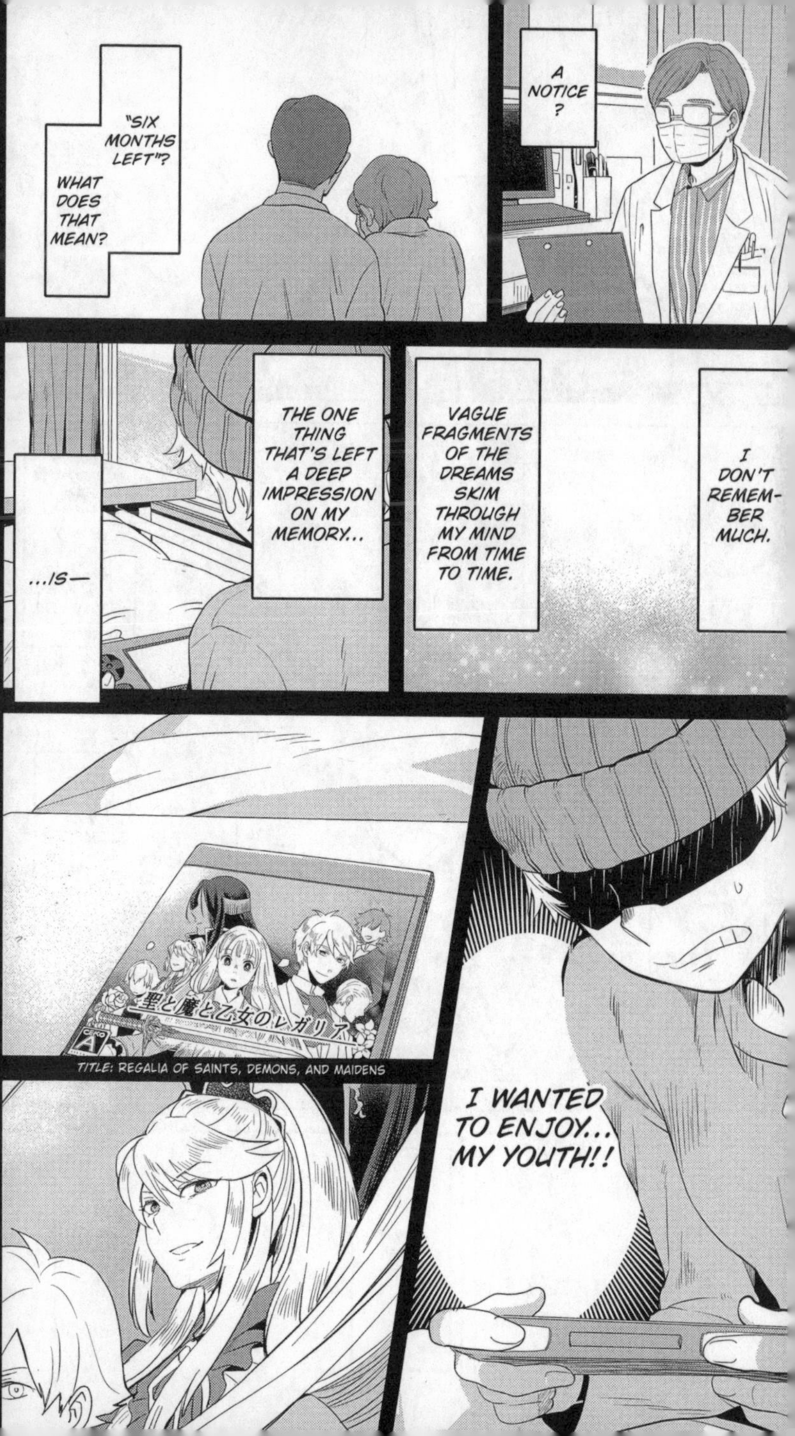
A NOTICE ?
"SIX MONTHS LEFT"?
WHAT DOES THAT MEAN?
I DON'T REMEMBER MUCH.
VAGUE FRAGMENTS OF THE DREAMS SKIM THROUGH MY MIND FROM TIME TO TIME.
THE ONE THING THAT'S LEFT A DEEP IMPRESSION ON MY MEMORY...
...IS—
I WANTED TO ENJOY... MY YOUTH!!
聖と魔と乙女のレガリア
TITLE: REGALIA OF SAINTS, DEMONS, AND MAIDENS

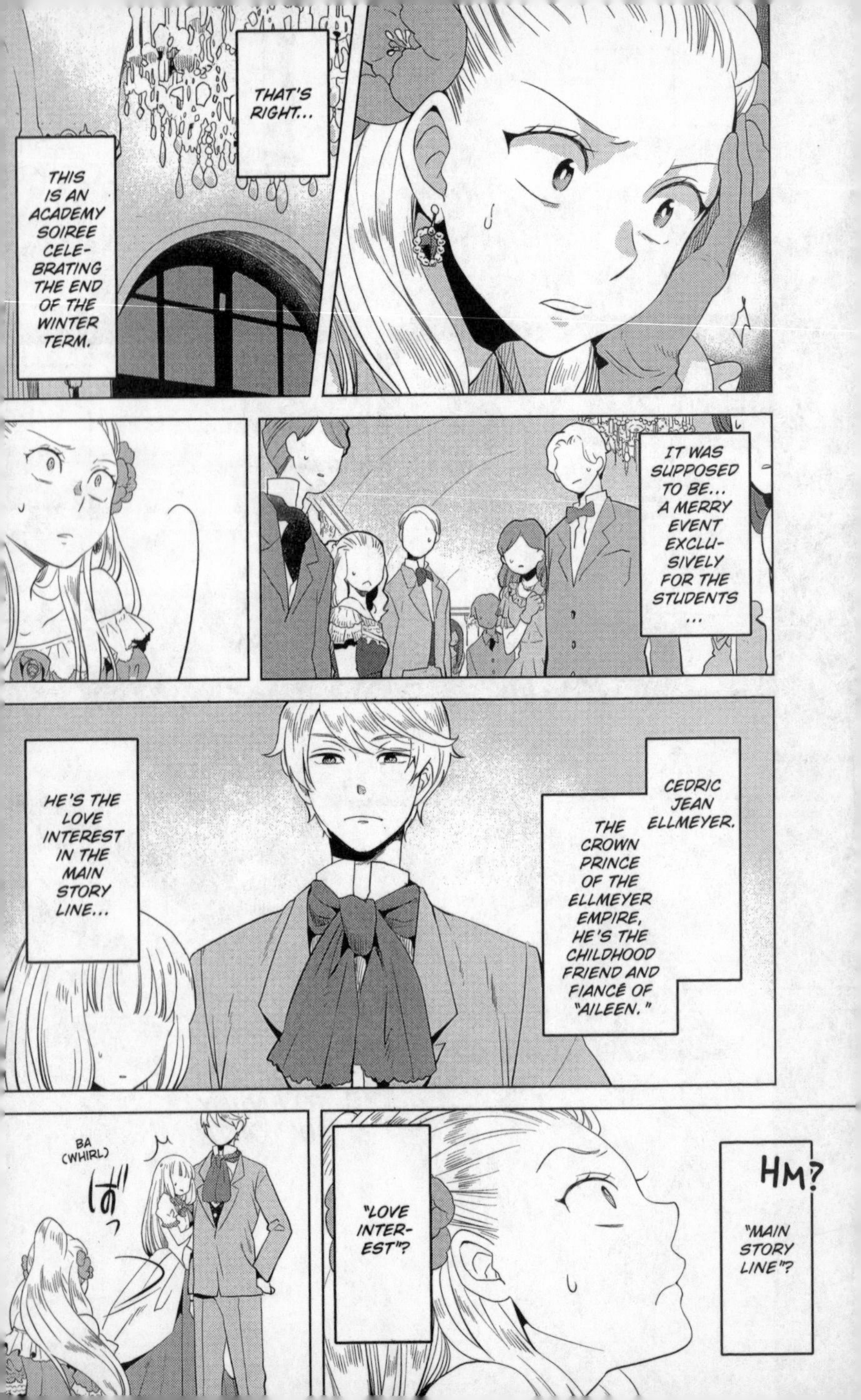
THAT'S RIGHT...
THIS IS AN ACADEMY SOIREE CELEBRATING THE END OF THE WINTER TERM.
IT WAS SUPPOSED TO BE... A MERRY EVENT EXCLUSIVELY FOR THE STUDENTS...
CEDRIC JEAN ELLMEYER.
THE CROWN PRINCE OF THE ELLMEYER EMPIRE, HE'S THE CHILDHOOD FRIEND AND FIANCÉ OF "AILEEN."
HE'S THE LOVE INTEREST IN THE MAIN STORY LINE...
HM?
"MAIN STORY LINE"?
"LOVE INTEREST"?
ばっ
BA (WHIRL)

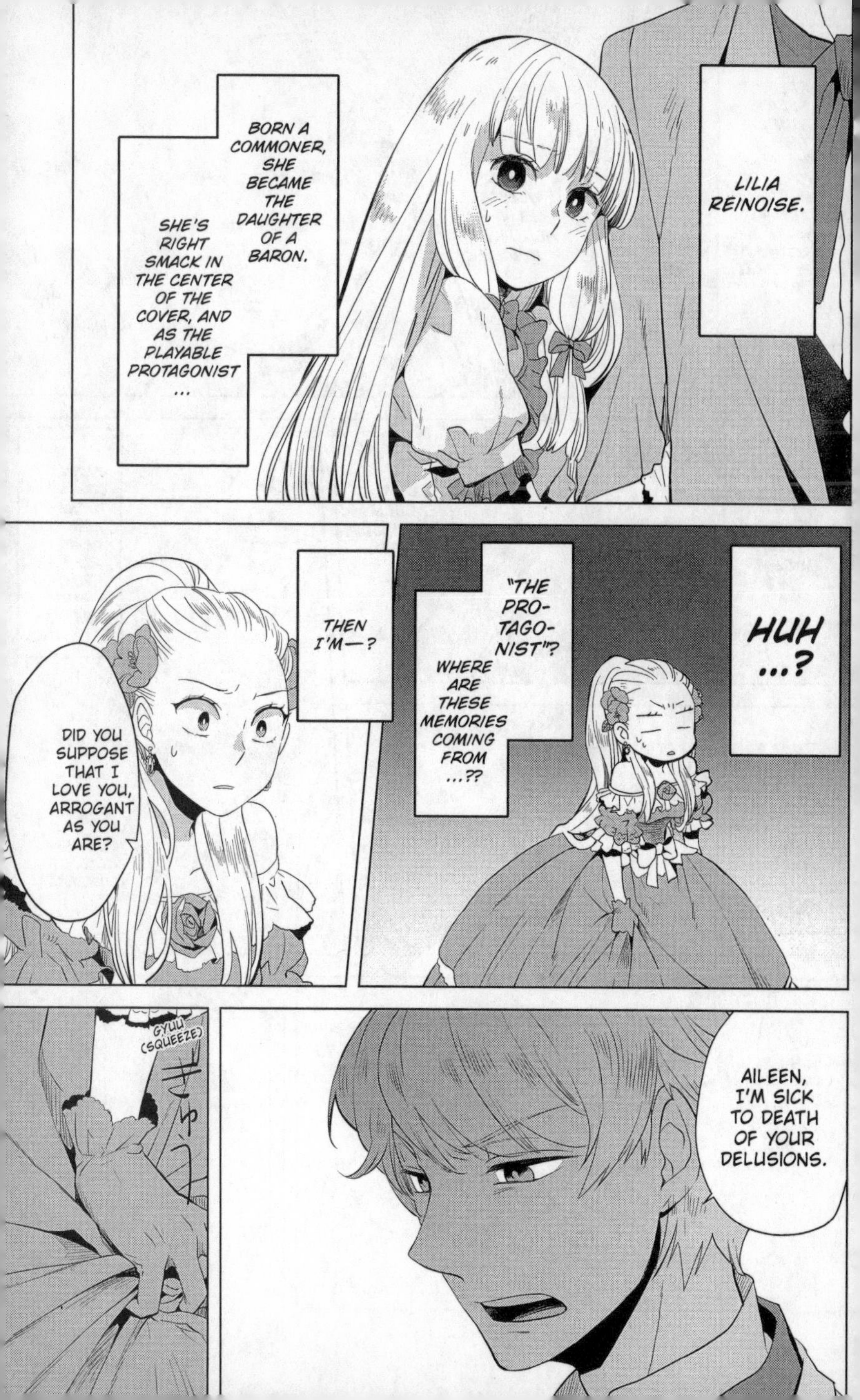
LILIA REINOISE.
BORN A COMMONER, SHE BECAME THE DAUGHTER OF A BARON.
SHE'S RIGHT SMACK IN THE CENTER OF THE COVER, AND AS THE PLAYABLE PROTAGONIST ...
HUH ...?
"THE PRO-TAGO-NIST"? WHERE ARE THESE MEMORIES COMING FROM ...??
THEN I'M—?
DID YOU SUPPOSE THAT I LOVE YOU, ARROGANT AS YOU ARE?
AILEEN, I'M SICK TO DEATH OF YOUR DELUSIONS.
GYUU (SQUEEZE)

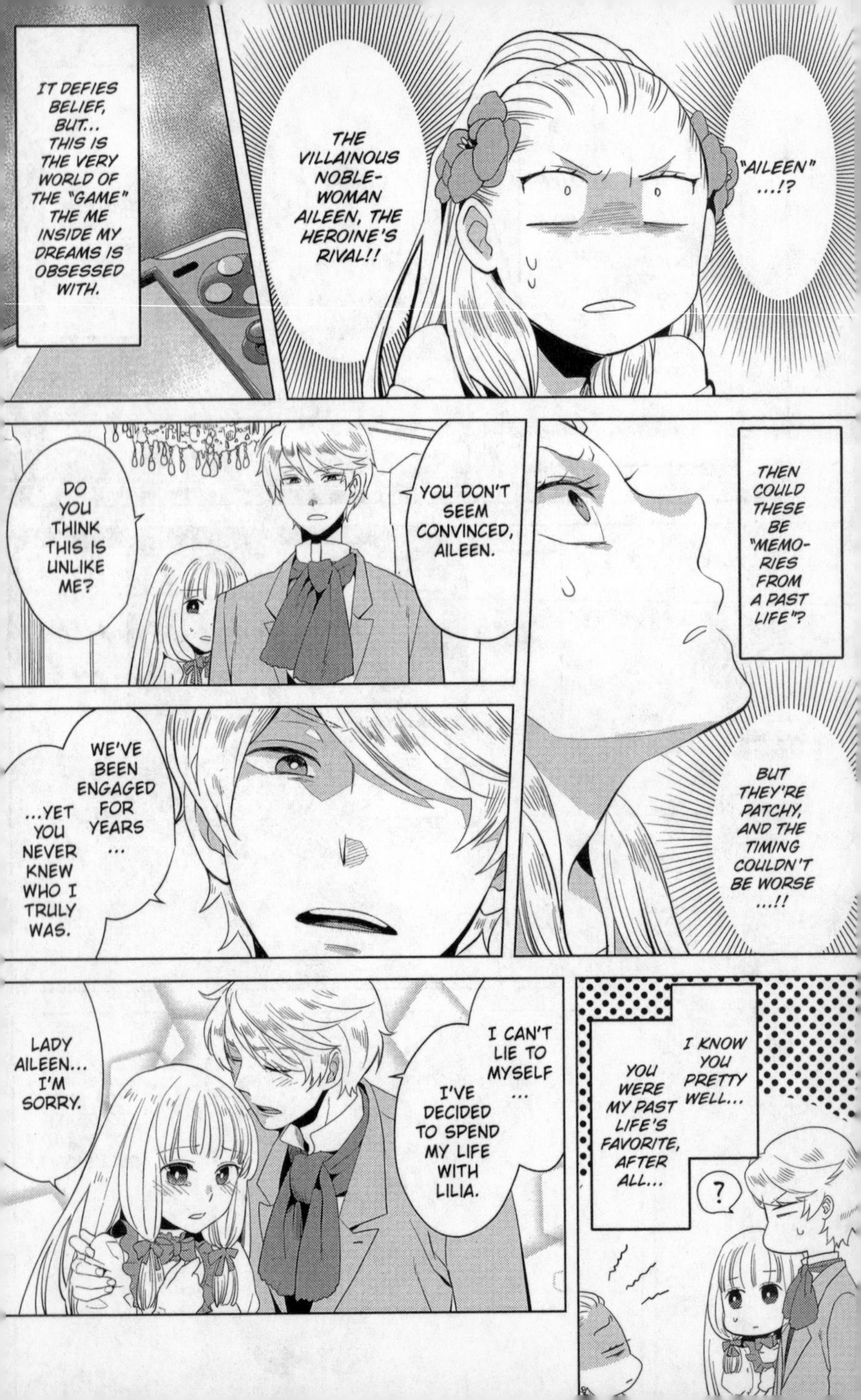
"AILEEN" ...!?
THE VILLAINOUS NOBLE-WOMAN AILEEN, THE HEROINE'S RIVAL!!
IT DEFIES BELIEF, BUT... THIS IS THE VERY WORLD OF THE "GAME" THE ME INSIDE MY DREAMS IS OBSESSED WITH.
THEN COULD THESE BE "MEMO-RIES FROM A PAST LIFE"?
BUT THEY'RE PATCHY, AND THE TIMING COULDN'T BE WORSE ...!!
YOU DON'T SEEM CONVINCED, AILEEN.
DO YOU THINK THIS IS UNLIKE ME?
WE'VE BEEN ENGAGED FOR YEARS ...
...YET YOU NEVER KNEW WHO I TRULY WAS.
I KNOW YOU PRETTY WELL...
YOU WERE MY PAST LIFE'S FAVORITE, AFTER ALL...
?
I CAN'T LIE TO MYSELF ...
I'VE DECIDED TO SPEND MY LIFE WITH LILIA.
LADY AILEEN... I'M SORRY.

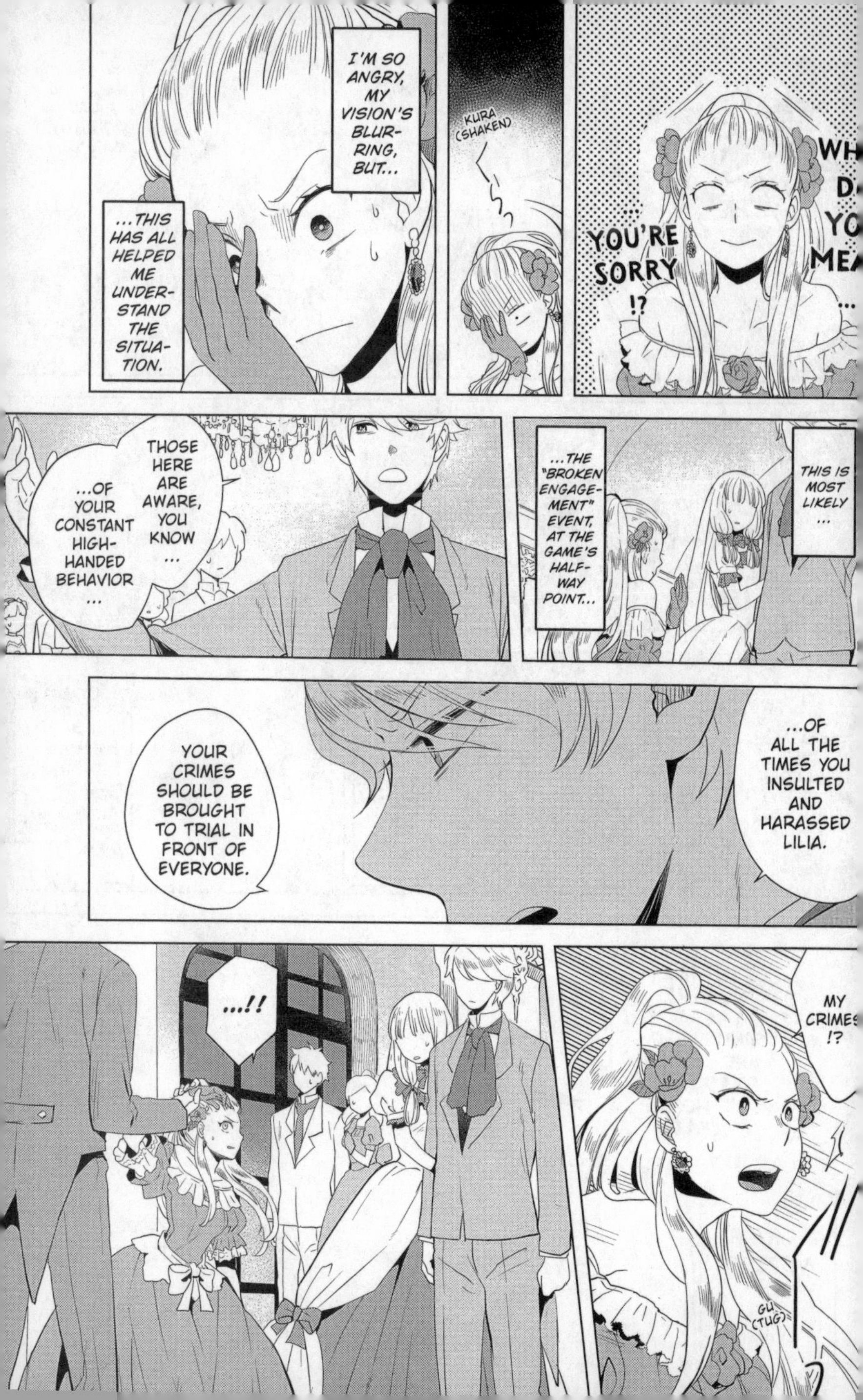

WH D YO MEA ...
...YOU'RE SORRY!?
KURA (SHAKEN)
I'M SO ANGRY, MY VISION'S BLURRING, BUT...
...THIS HAS ALL HELPED ME UNDERSTAND THE SITUATION.
THIS IS MOST LIKELY...
...THE "BROKEN ENGAGEMENT" EVENT, AT THE GAME'S HALFWAY POINT...
THOSE HERE ARE AWARE, YOU KNOW...
...OF YOUR CONSTANT HIGH-HANDED BEHAVIOR...
...OF ALL THE TIMES YOU INSULTED AND HARASSED LILIA.
YOUR CRIMES SHOULD BE BROUGHT TO TRIAL IN FRONT OF EVERYONE.
MY CRIMES !?
GU (TUG)
...!!

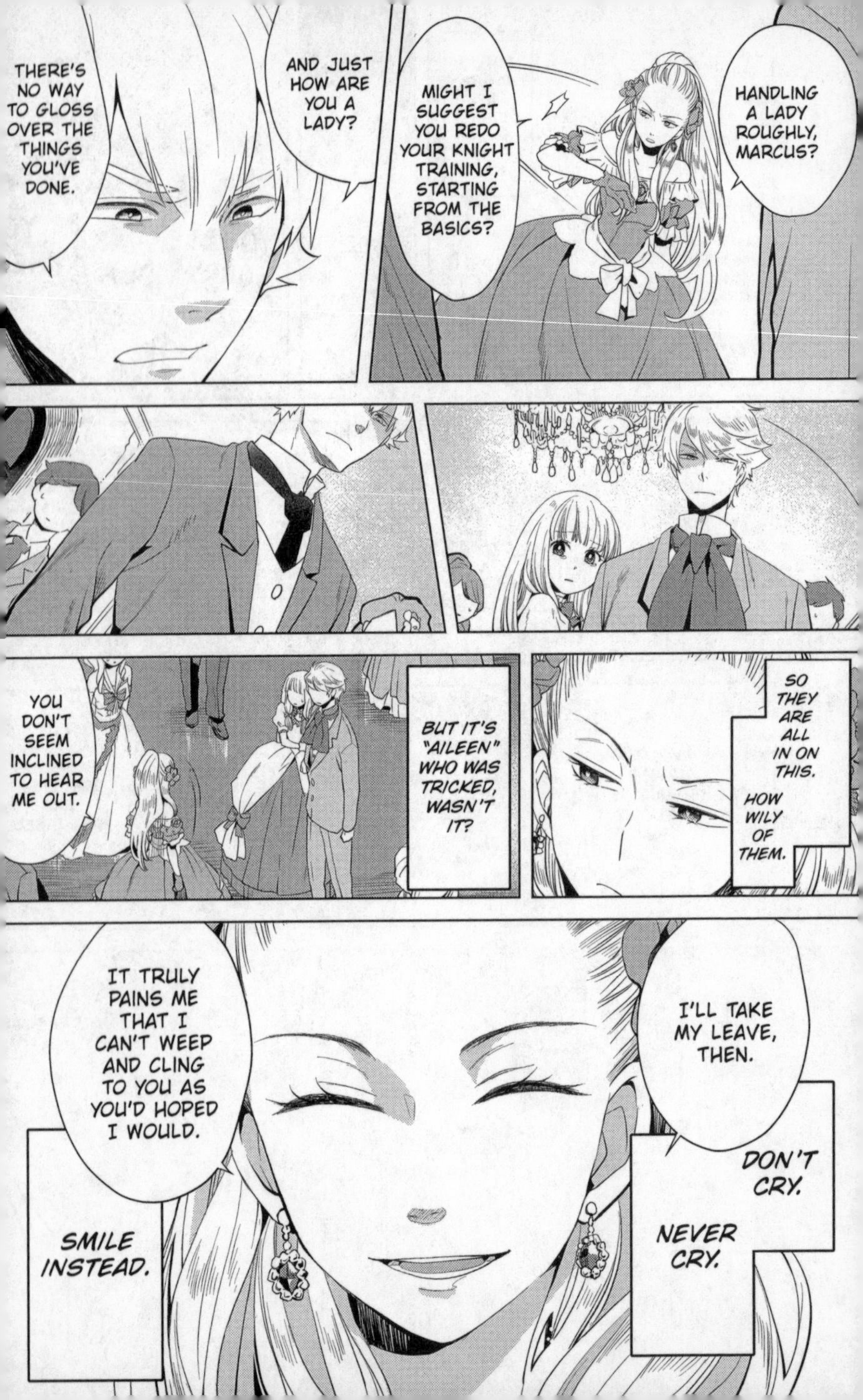
HANDLING A LADY ROUGHLY, MARCUS?
MIGHT I SUGGEST YOU REDO YOUR KNIGHT TRAINING, STARTING FROM THE BASICS?
AND JUST HOW ARE YOU A LADY?
THERE'S NO WAY TO GLOSS OVER THE THINGS YOU'VE DONE.
SO THEY ARE ALL IN ON THIS.
HOW WILY OF THEM.
BUT IT'S "AILEEN" WHO WAS TRICKED, WASN'T IT?
YOU DON'T SEEM INCLINED TO HEAR ME OUT.
I'LL TAKE MY LEAVE, THEN.
DON'T CRY.
NEVER CRY.
IT TRULY PAINS ME THAT I CAN'T WEEP AND CLING TO YOU AS YOU'D HOPED I WOULD.
SMILE INSTEAD.

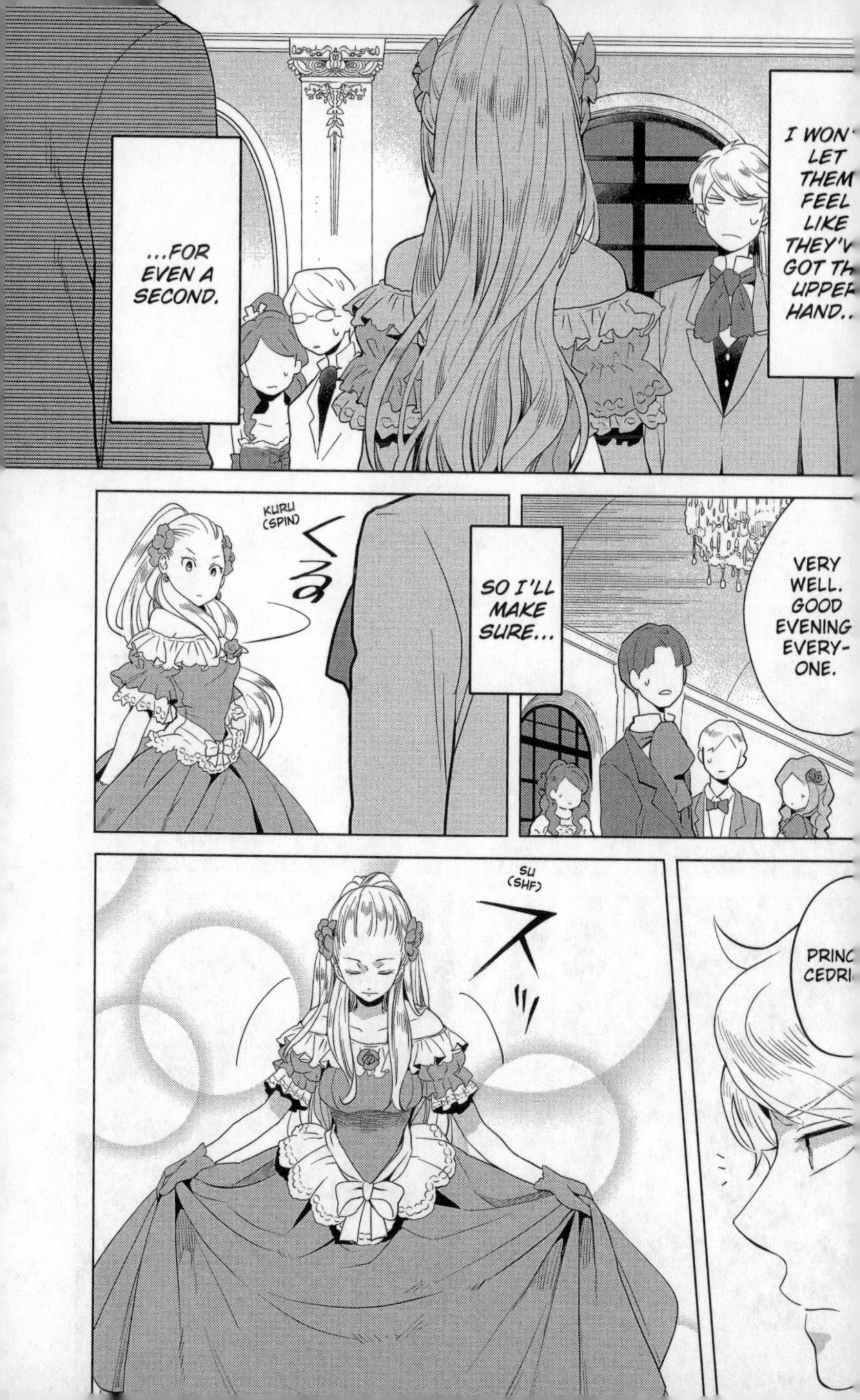
I WON' LET THEM FEEL LIKE THEY'V GOT TH UPPEF HAND..
...FOR EVEN A SECOND.
VERY WELL. GOOD EVENING EVERY-ONE.
SO I'LL MAKE SURE...
KURU (SPIN)
くる
PRINC CEDRI
SU (SHF)
ス

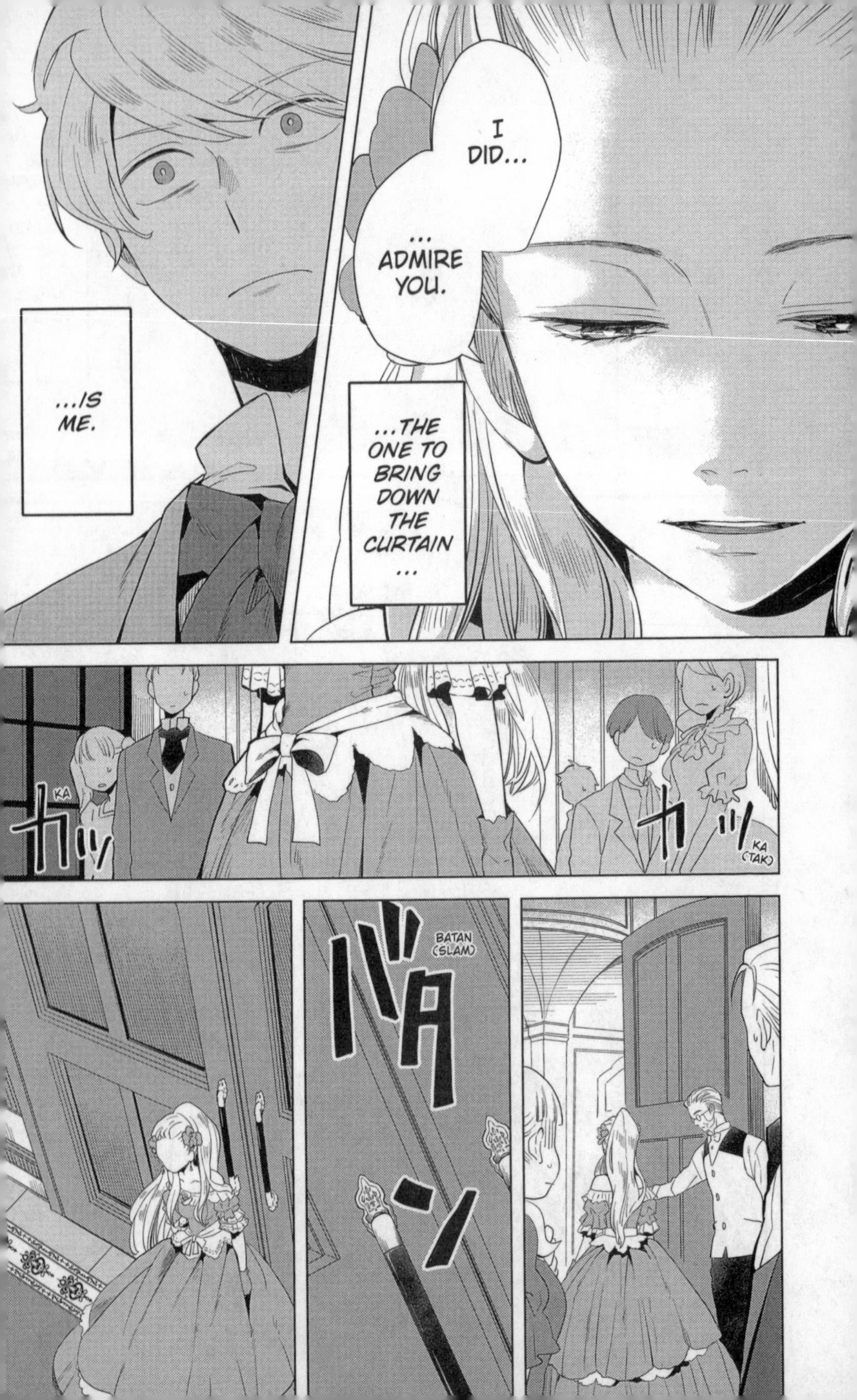
I DID...
...ADMIRE YOU.
...THE ONE TO BRING DOWN THE CURTAIN...
...IS ME.
カッ
KA (TAK)
カッ
KA
バタン
BATAN (SLAM)

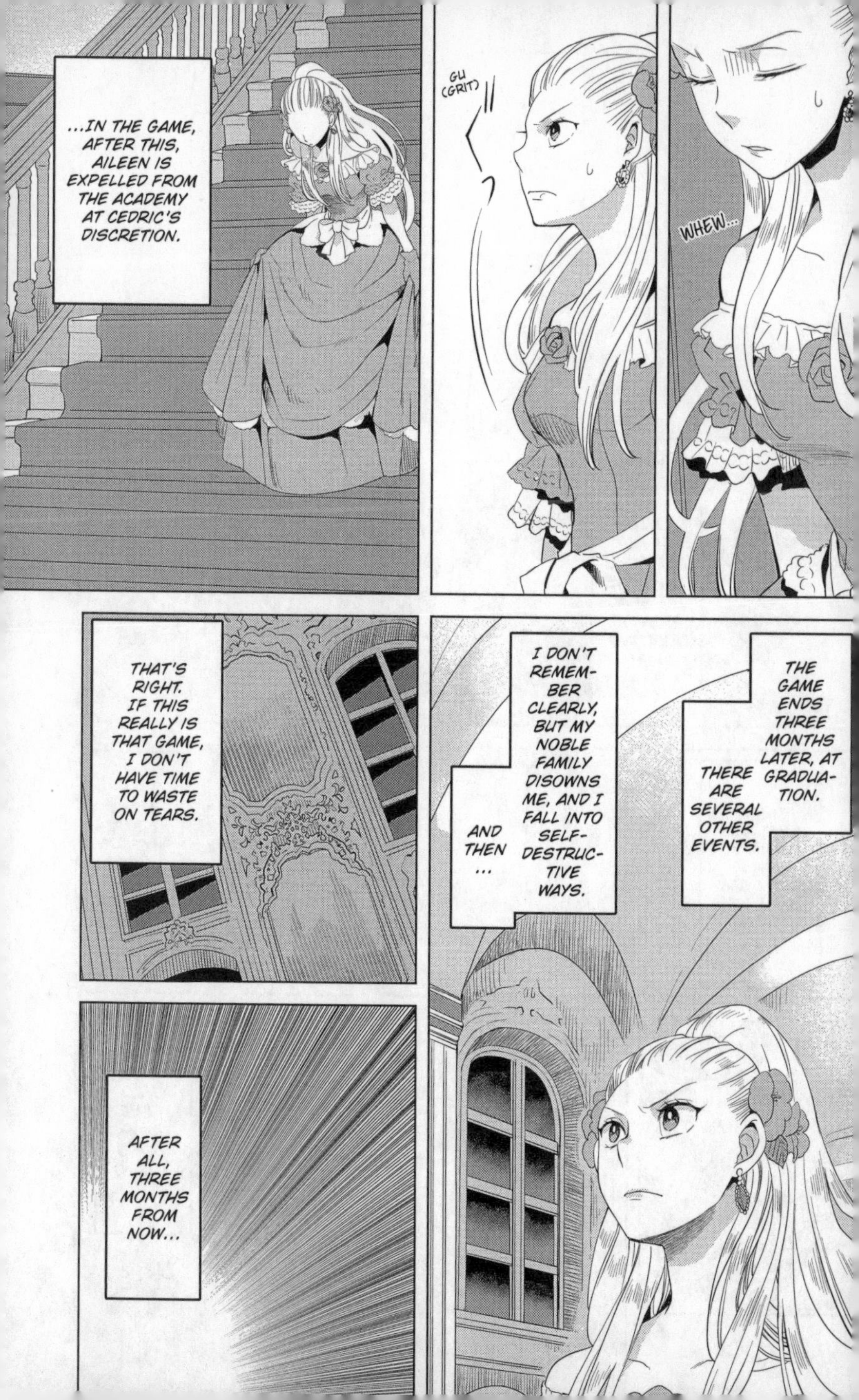
WHEW...
GU (GRIT)
...IN THE GAME, AFTER THIS, AILEEN IS EXPELLED FROM THE ACADEMY AT CEDRIC'S DISCRETION.
THE GAME ENDS THREE MONTHS LATER, AT GRADUATION.
THERE ARE SEVERAL OTHER EVENTS.
I DON'T REMEMBER CLEARLY, BUT MY NOBLE FAMILY DISOWNS ME, AND I FALL INTO SELF-DESTRUCTIVE WAYS.
AND THEN...
THAT'S RIGHT. IF THIS REALLY IS THAT GAME, I DON'T HAVE TIME TO WASTE ON TEARS.
AFTER ALL, THREE MONTHS FROM NOW...

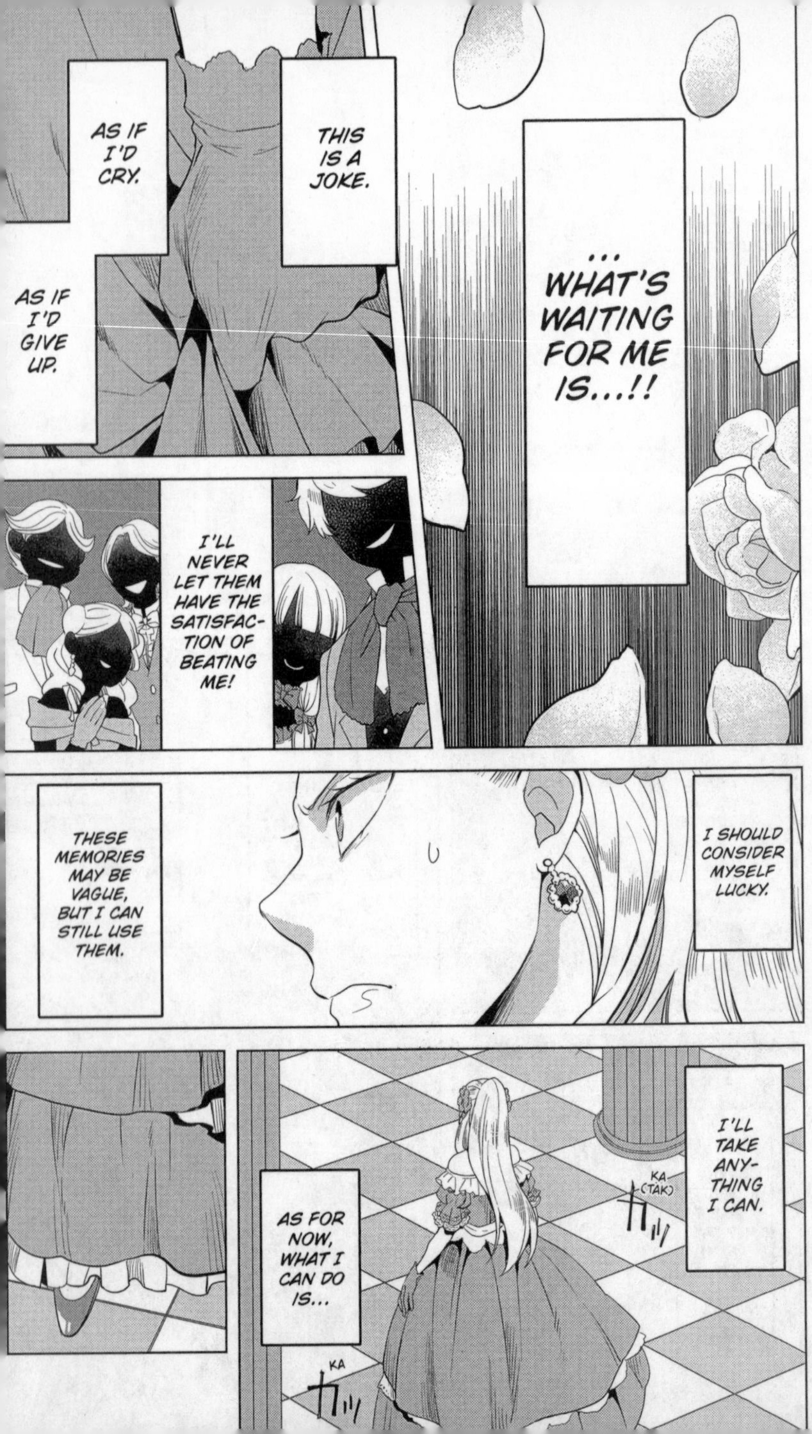

... WHAT'S WAITING FOR ME IS...!!
THIS IS A JOKE.
AS IF I'D CRY.
AS IF I'D GIVE UP.
I'LL NEVER LET THEM HAVE THE SATISFACTION OF BEATING ME!
I SHOULD CONSIDER MYSELF LUCKY.
THESE MEMORIES MAY BE VAGUE, BUT I CAN STILL USE THEM.
I'LL TAKE ANYTHING I CAN.
KA (TAK)
AS FOR NOW, WHAT I CAN DO IS...
KA

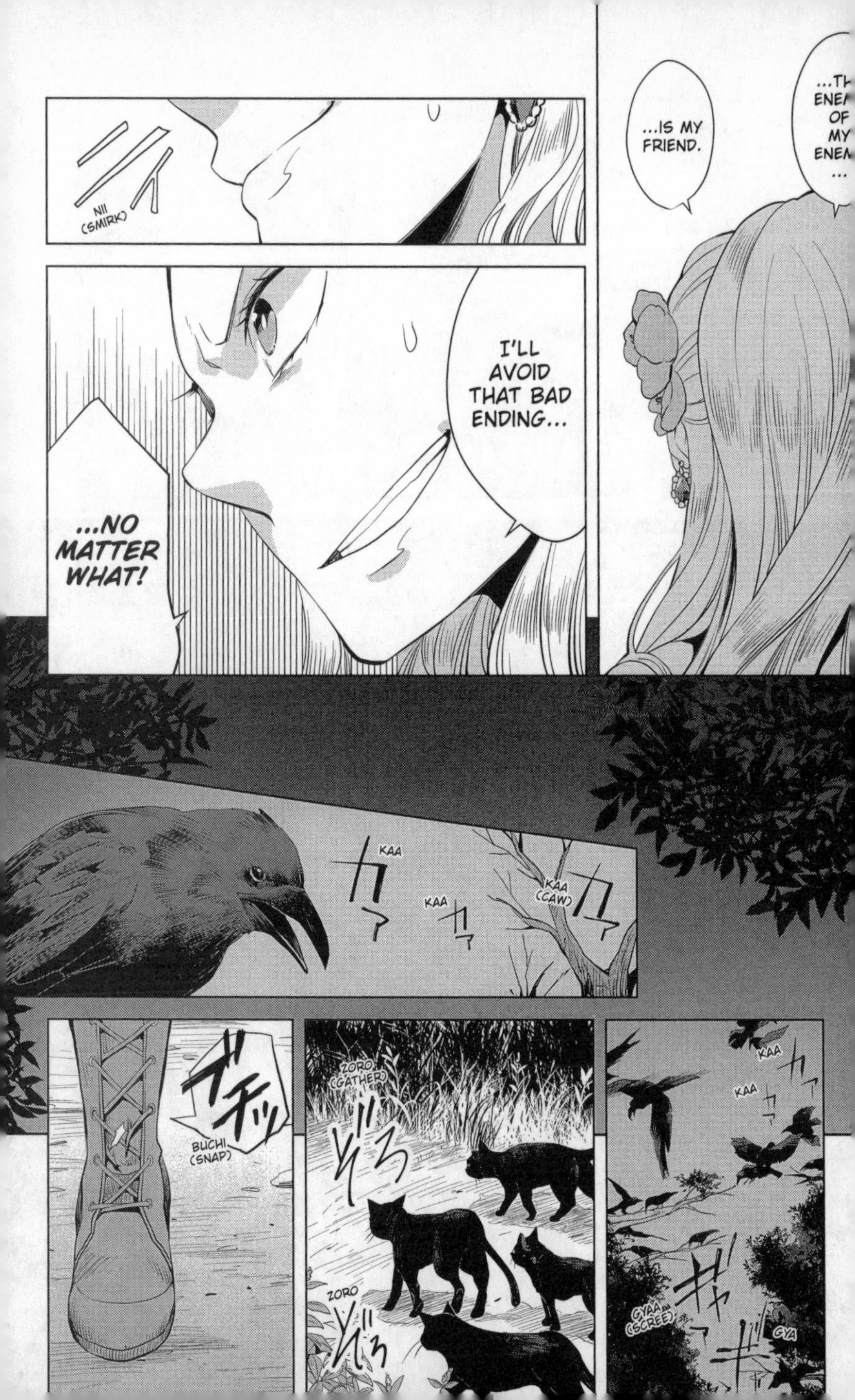
...TH ENEM OF MY ENEM...
...IS MY FRIEND.
NII (SMIRK)
I'LL AVOID THAT BAD ENDING...
...NO MATTER WHAT!
KAA
KAA
KAA (CAW)
KAA
KAA
GYAA (SCREE)
GYA
ZORO (GATHER)
ZORO
BUCHI (SNAP)

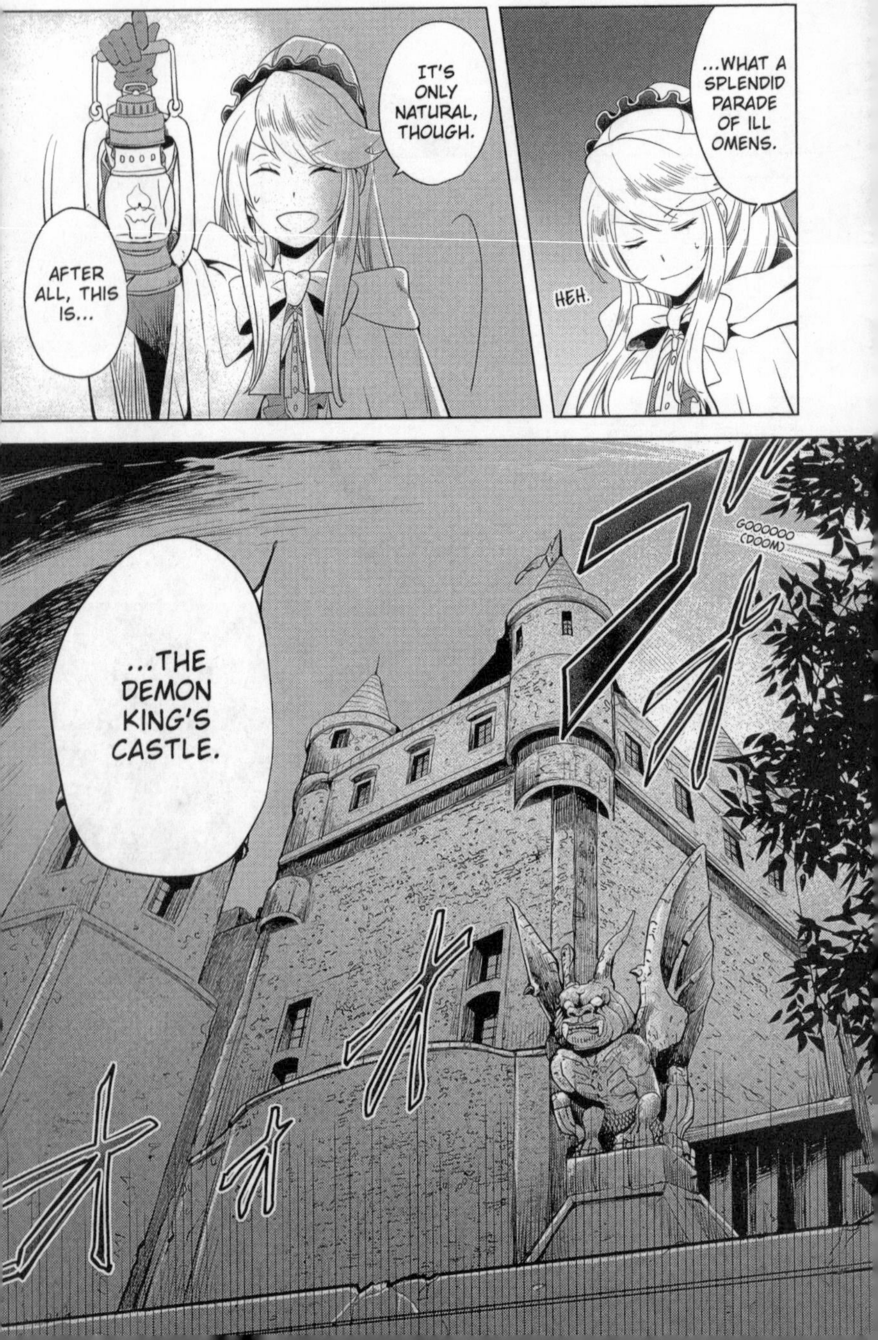
...WHAT A SPLENDID PARADE OF ILL OMENS.
HEH.
IT'S ONLY NATURAL, THOUGH.
AFTER ALL, THIS IS...
GOOOOOO (DOOM)
...THE DEMON KING'S CASTLE.

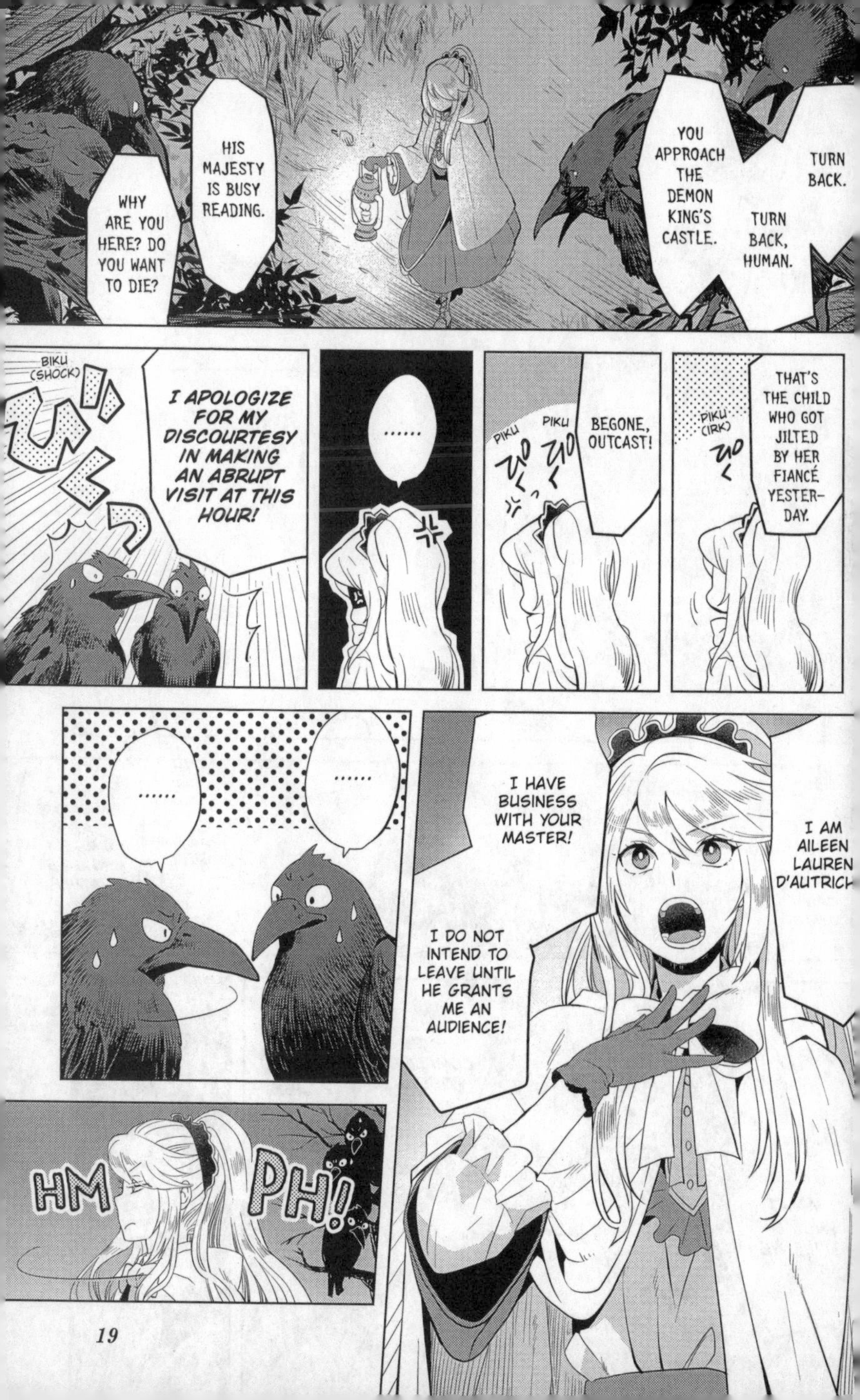

TURN BACK.
TURN BACK, HUMAN.
YOU APPROACH THE DEMON KING'S CASTLE.
HIS MAJESTY IS BUSY READING.
WHY ARE YOU HERE? DO YOU WANT TO DIE?
THAT'S THE CHILD WHO GOT JILTED BY HER FIANCÉ YESTER-DAY.
PIKU (IRK)
BEGONE, OUTCAST!
PIKU
PIKU
......
I APOLOGIZE FOR MY DISCOURTESY IN MAKING AN ABRUPT VISIT AT THIS HOUR!
BIKU (SHOCK)
I AM AILEEN LAUREN D'AUTRICH
I HAVE BUSINESS WITH YOUR MASTER!
I DO NOT INTEND TO LEAVE UNTIL HE GRANTS ME AN AUDIENCE!
......
......
HMPH!

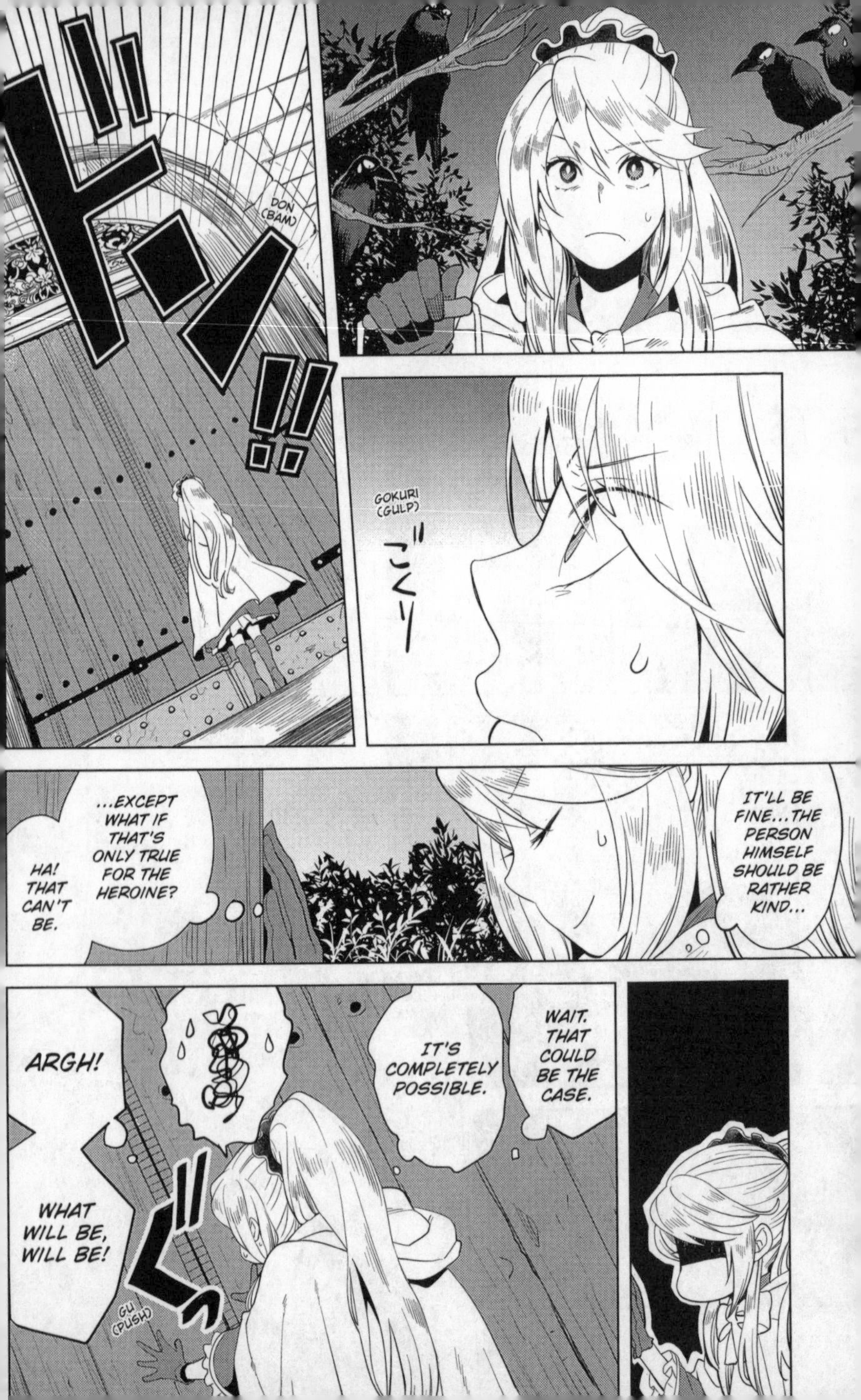
GOKURI (GULP)
DON (BAM)
IT'LL BE FINE...THE PERSON HIMSELF SHOULD BE RATHER KIND...
...EXCEPT WHAT IF THAT'S ONLY TRUE FOR THE HEROINE?
HA! THAT CAN'T BE.
WAIT. THAT COULD BE THE CASE.
IT'S COMPLETELY POSSIBLE.
ARGH!
WHAT WILL BE, WILL BE!
GU (PUSH)

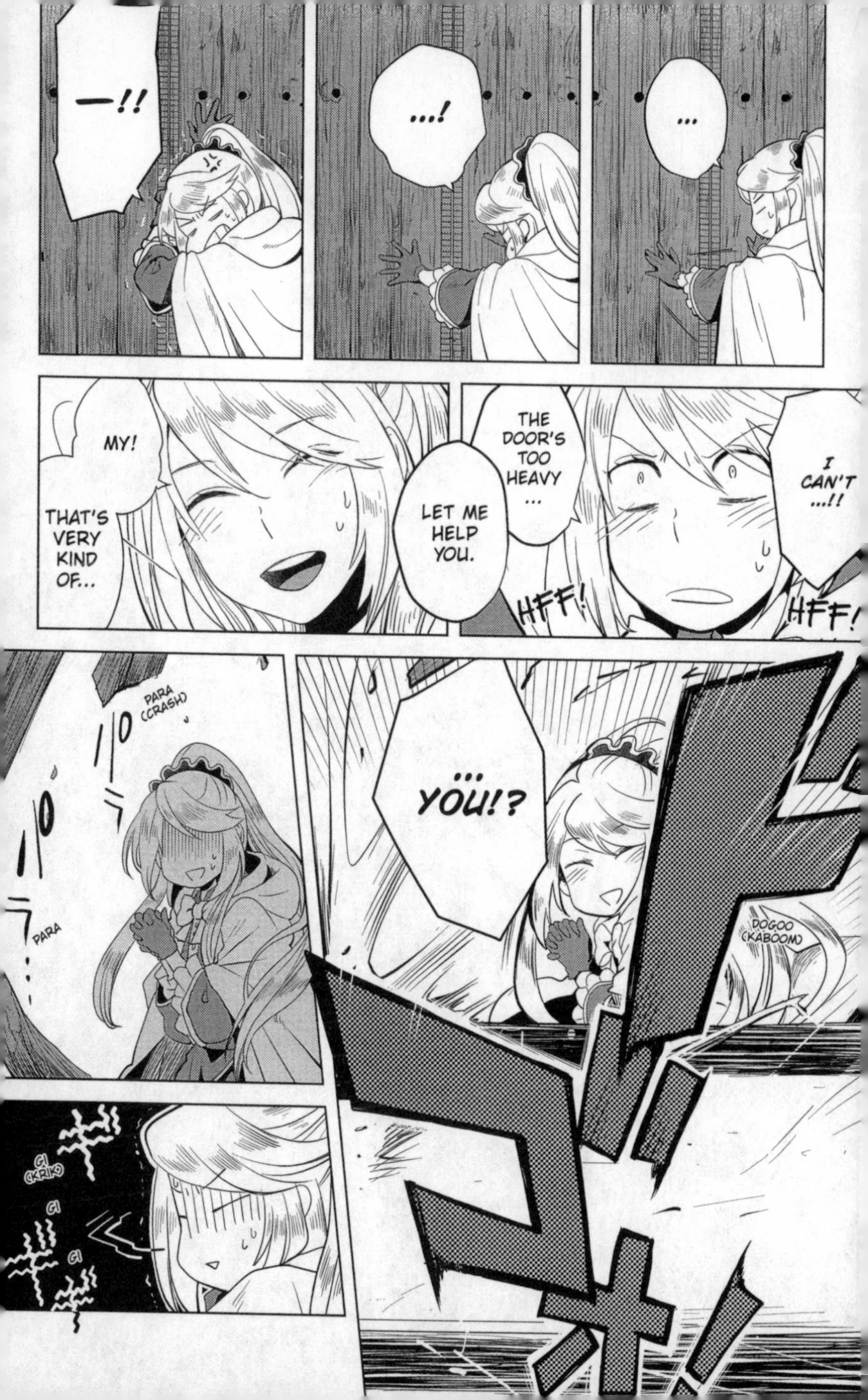
...
...!
—!!
I CAN'T ...!!
THE DOOR'S TOO HEAVY ...
HFF!
HFF!
LET ME HELP YOU.
MY!
THAT'S VERY KIND OF...
... YOU!?
DOGOO (KABOOM)
PARA (CRASH)
PARA
GI (KRIK)
GI
GI

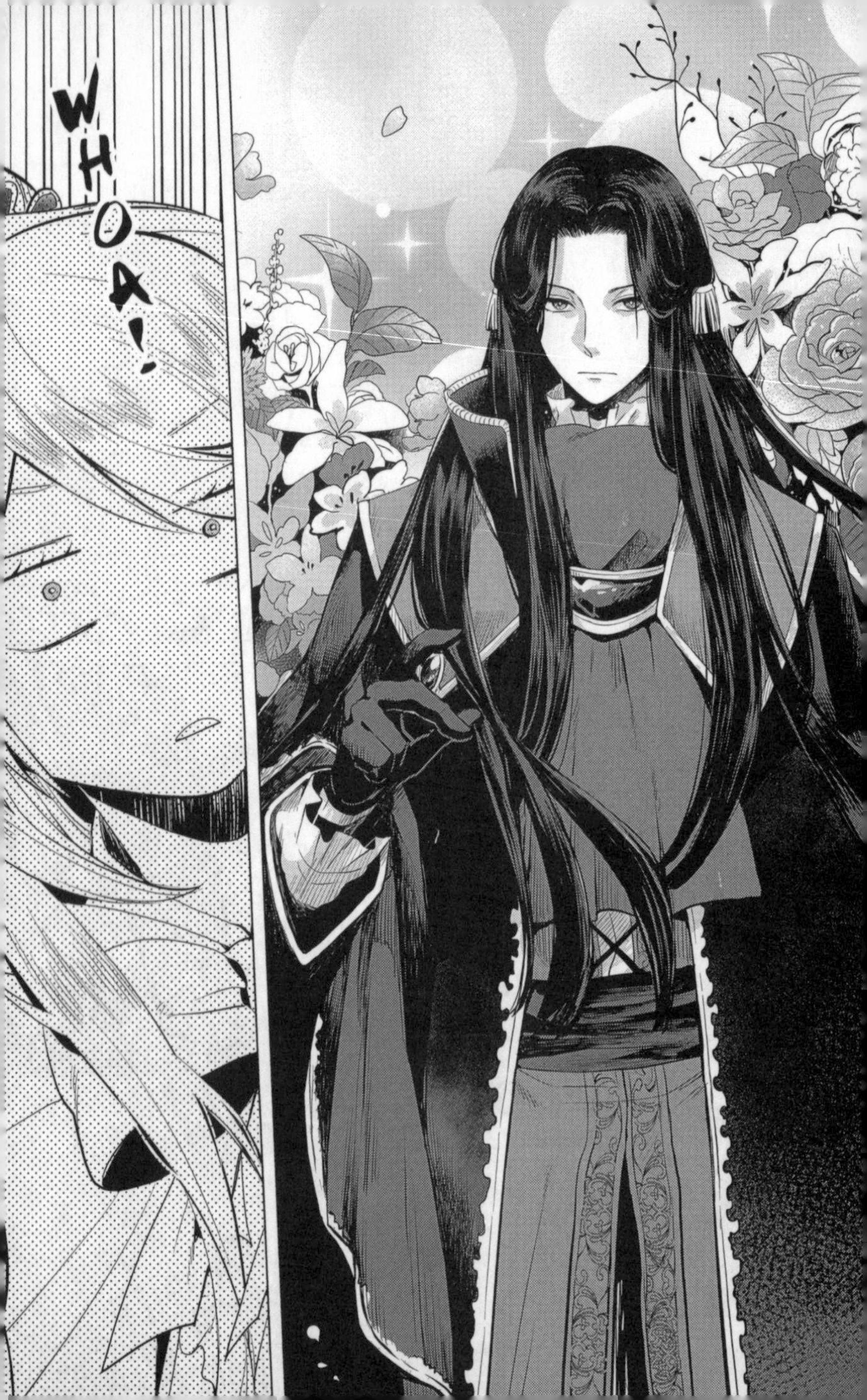
WHOA!

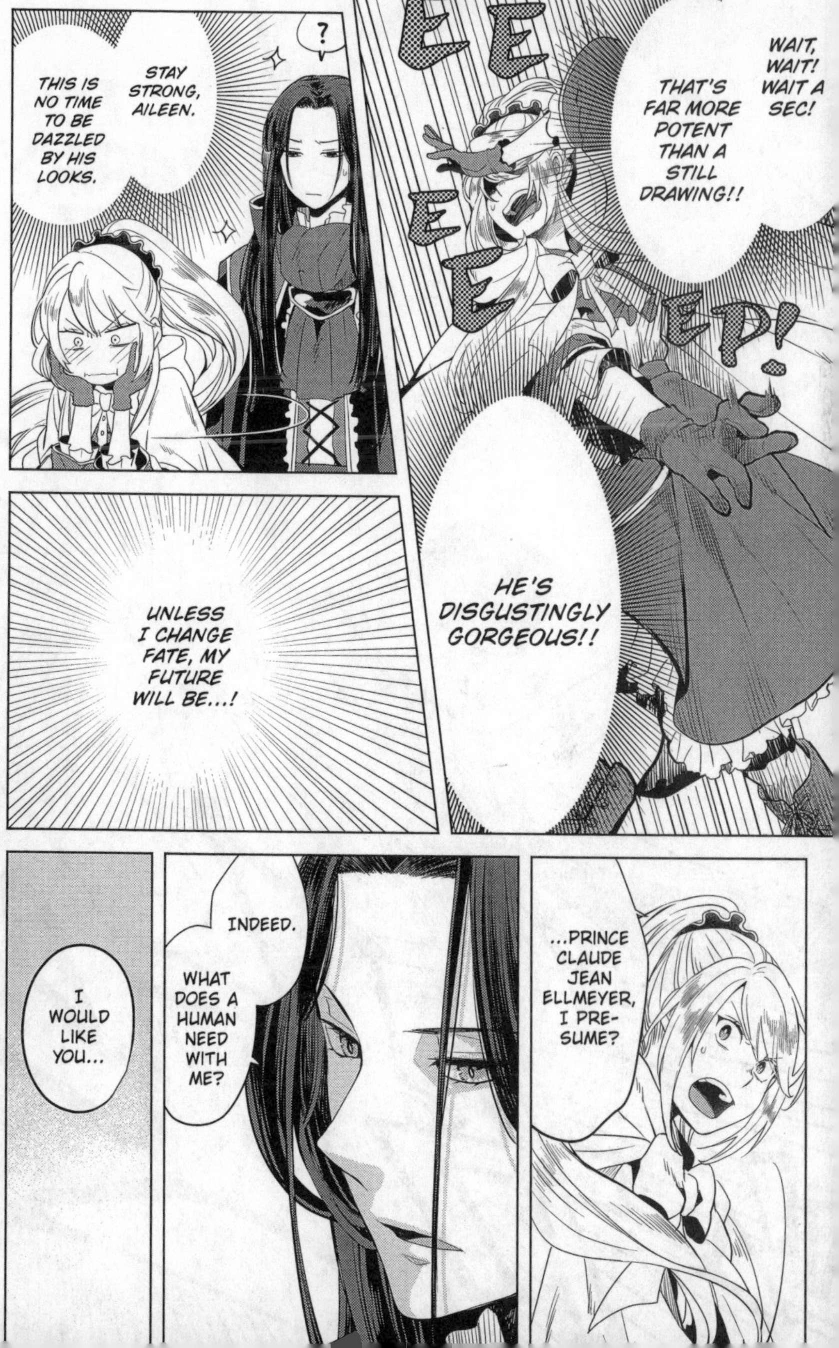
WAIT, WAIT! WAIT A SEC!
THAT'S FAR MORE POTENT THAN A STILL DRAWING!!
EEEEEP!
HE'S DISGUSTINGLY GORGEOUS!!
?
STAY STRONG, AILEEN.
THIS IS NO TIME TO BE DAZZLED BY HIS LOOKS.
UNLESS I CHANGE FATE, MY FUTURE WILL BE...!
...PRINCE CLAUDE JEAN ELLMEYER, I PRE-SUME?
INDEED.
WHAT DOES A HUMAN NEED WITH ME?
I WOULD LIKE YOU...

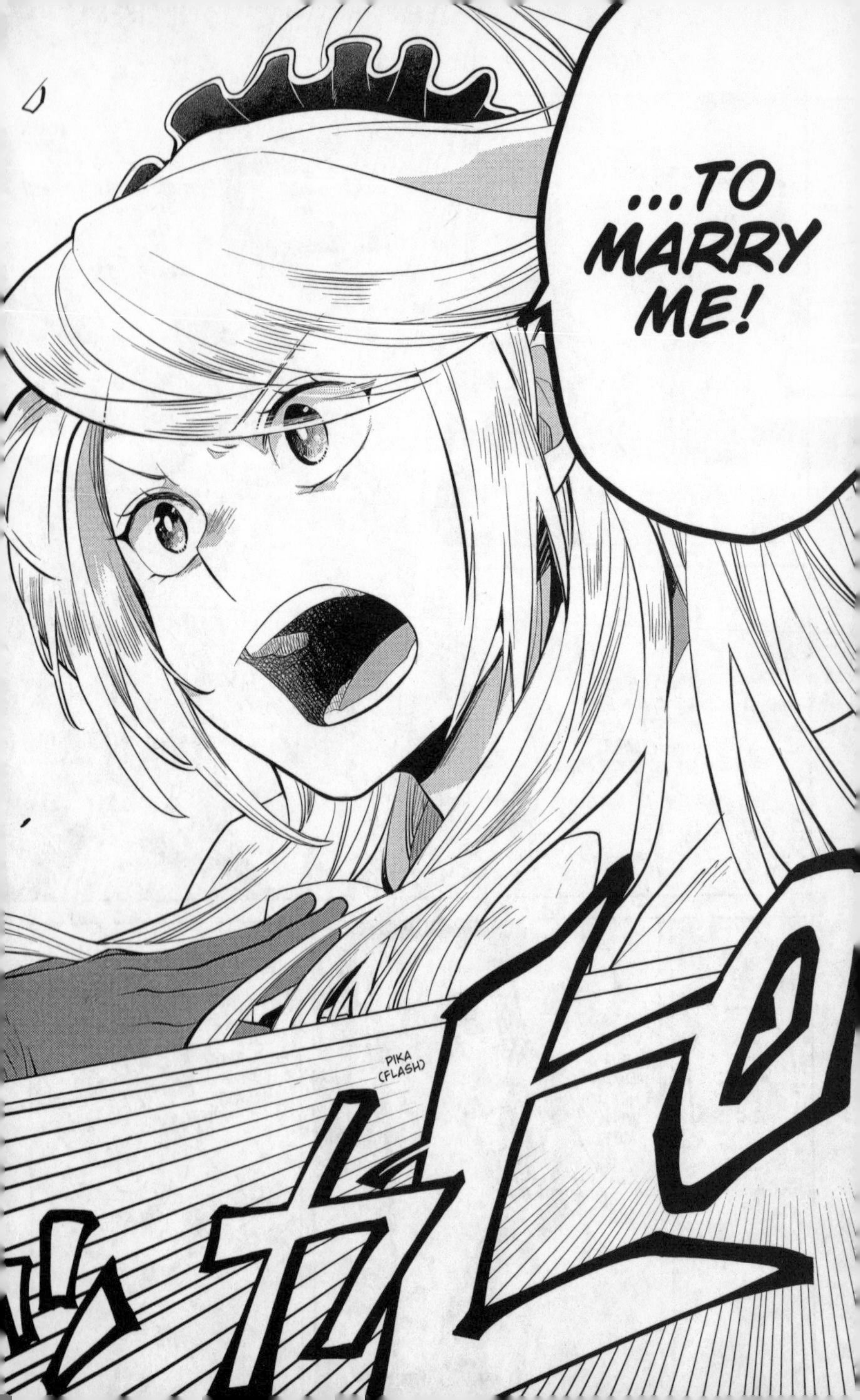
...TO MARRY ME!
PIKA (FLASH)

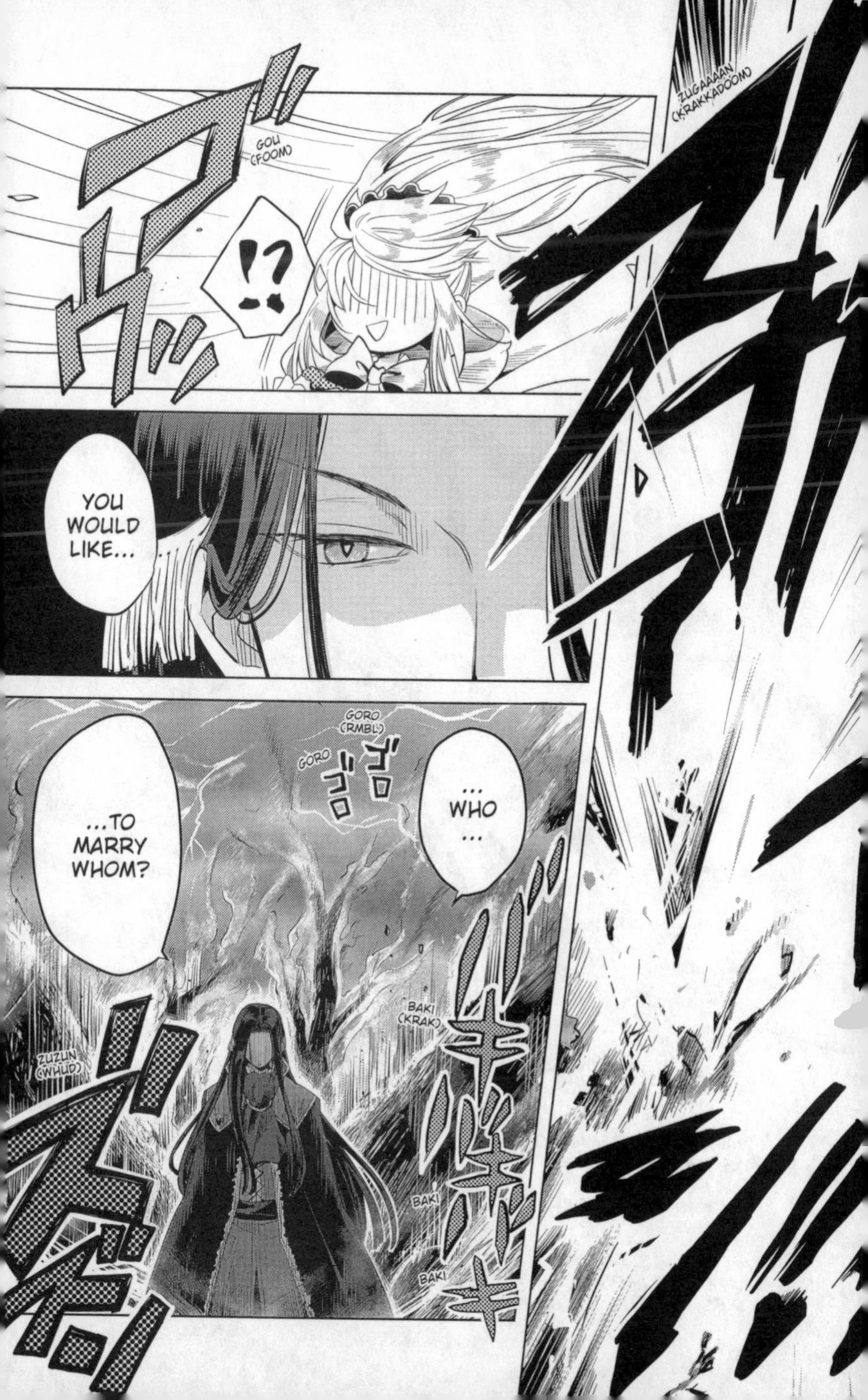
ZUGAAAAN (KRAKKADOOM)
GOU (FOOM)
!?
YOU WOULD LIKE...
GORO (RMBL)
GORO
... WHO ...
...TO MARRY WHOM?
BAKI (KRAK)
ZUZUN (WHUD)
BAKI
BAKI

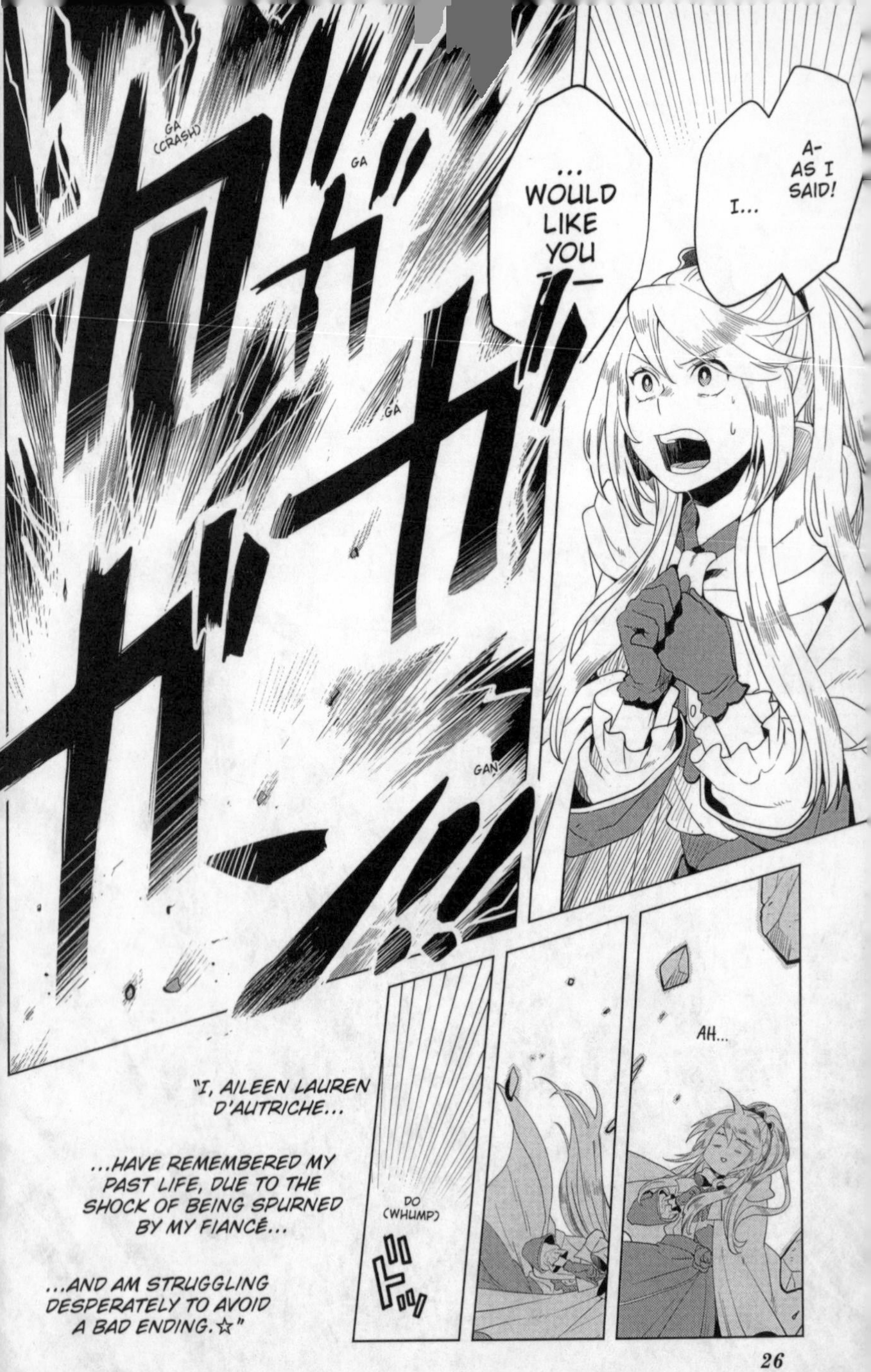
A- AS I SAID!
I...
...WOULD LIKE YOU TO—
GA (CRASH)
GA
GA
GAN
AH...
DO (WHUMP)
"I, AILEEN LAUREN D'AUTRICHE...
...HAVE REMEMBERED MY PAST LIFE, DUE TO THE SHOCK OF BEING SPURNED BY MY FIANCÉ...
...AND AM STRUGGLING DESPERATELY TO AVOID A BAD ENDING.☆"

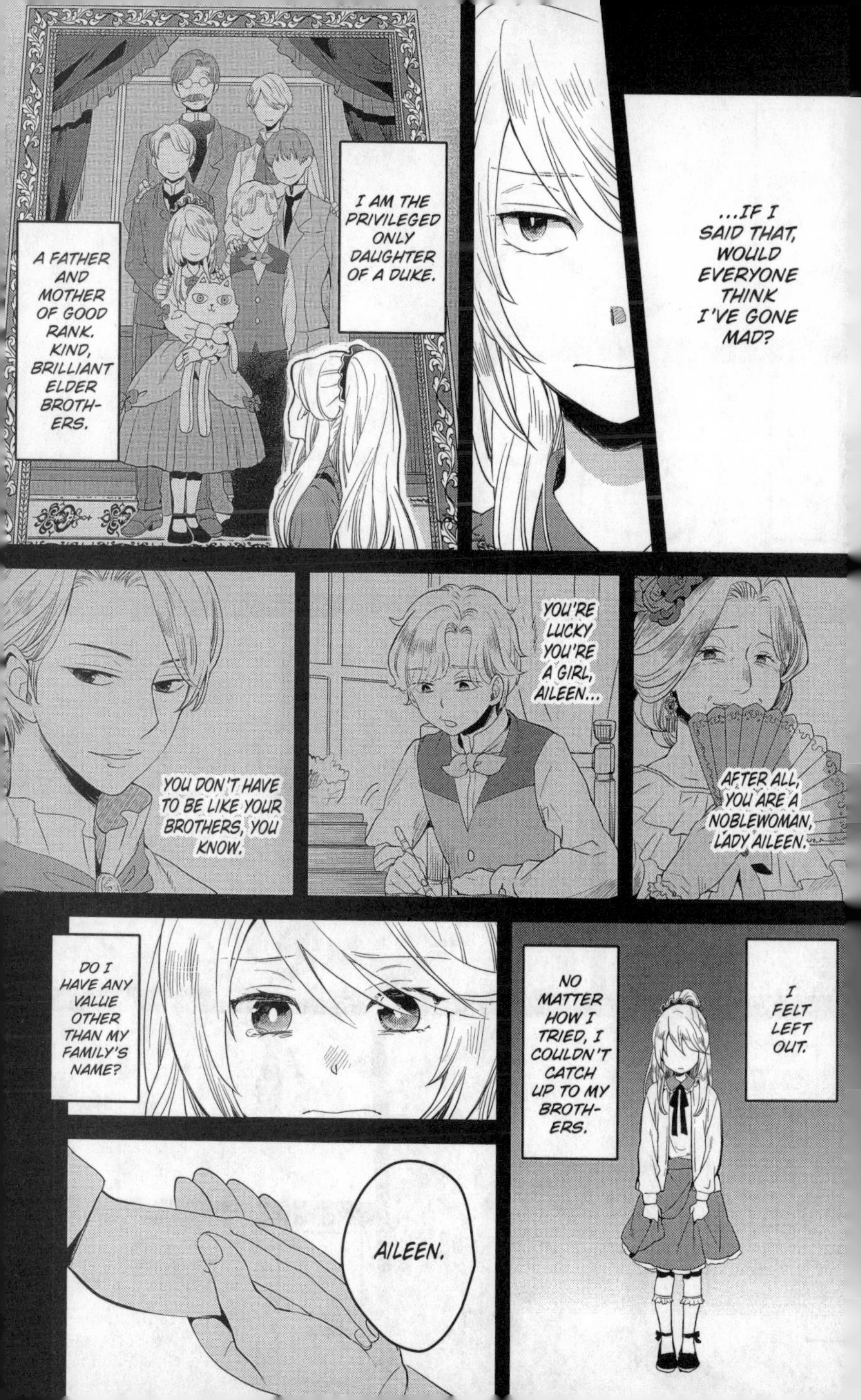
...IF I SAID THAT, WOULD EVERYONE THINK I'VE GONE MAD?
I AM THE PRIVILEGED ONLY DAUGHTER OF A DUKE.
A FATHER AND MOTHER OF GOOD RANK. KIND, BRILLIANT ELDER BROTH-ERS.
AFTER ALL, YOU ARE A NOBLEWOMAN, LADY AILEEN.
YOU'RE LUCKY YOU'RE A GIRL, AILEEN...
YOU DON'T HAVE TO BE LIKE YOUR BROTHERS, YOU KNOW.
I FELT LEFT OUT.
NO MATTER HOW I TRIED, I COULDN'T CATCH UP TO MY BROTH-ERS.
DO I HAVE ANY VALUE OTHER THAN MY FAMILY'S NAME?
AILEEN.

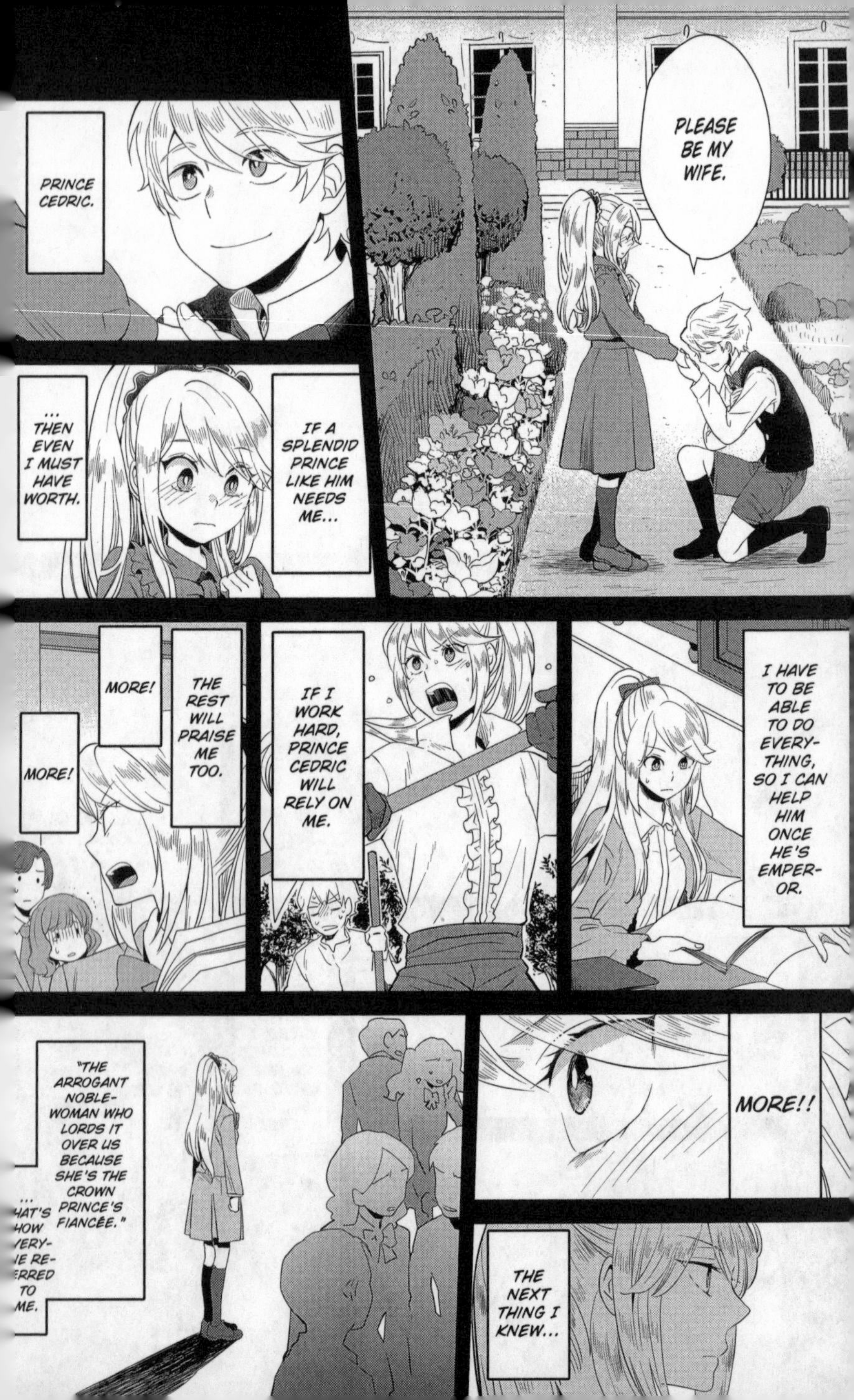
PLEASE BE MY WIFE.
PRINCE CEDRIC.
IF A SPLENDID PRINCE LIKE HIM NEEDS ME...
...THEN EVEN I MUST HAVE WORTH.
I HAVE TO BE ABLE TO DO EVERY-THING, SO I CAN HELP HIM ONCE HE'S EMPER-OR.
IF I WORK HARD, PRINCE CEDRIC WILL RELY ON ME.
THE REST WILL PRAISE ME TOO.
MORE!
MORE!
MORE!!
THE NEXT THING I KNEW...
"THE ARROGANT NOBLE-WOMAN WHO LORDS IT OVER US BECAUSE SHE'S THE CROWN PRINCE'S FIANCÉE."
...HAT'S HOW VERY-NE RE-ERRED TO ME.

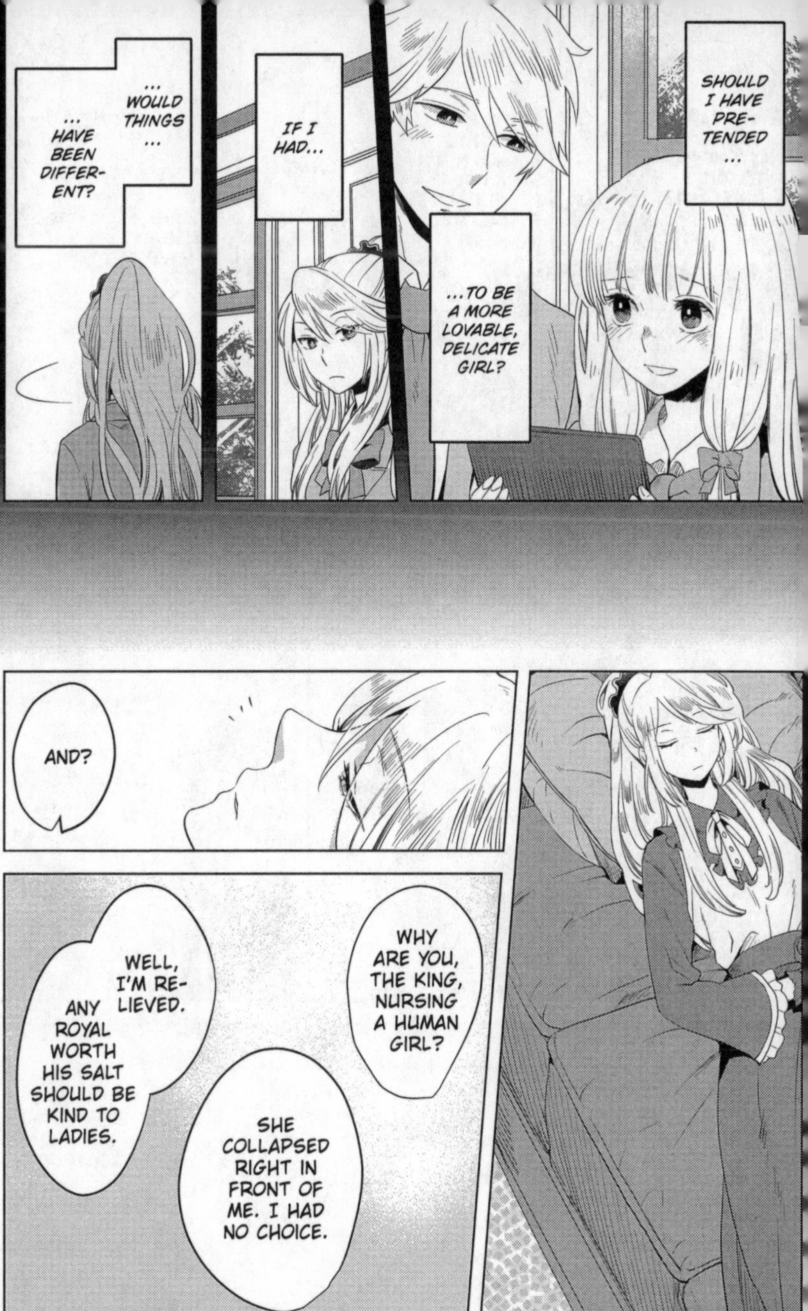
SHOULD I HAVE PRE-TENDED...
...TO BE A MORE LOVABLE, DELICATE GIRL?
IF I HAD...
...WOULD THINGS...
...HAVE BEEN DIFFERENT?
AND?
WHY ARE YOU, THE KING, NURSING A HUMAN GIRL?
SHE COLLAPSED RIGHT IN FRONT OF ME. I HAD NO CHOICE.
WELL, I'M RE-LIEVED.
ANY ROYAL WORTH HIS SALT SHOULD BE KIND TO LADIES.

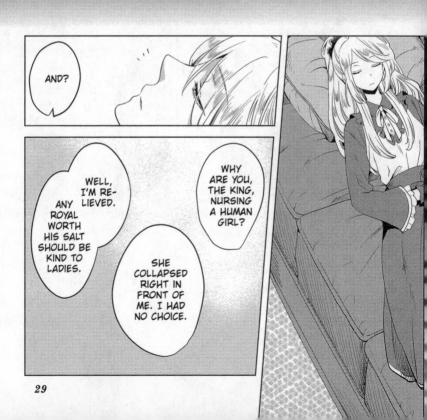

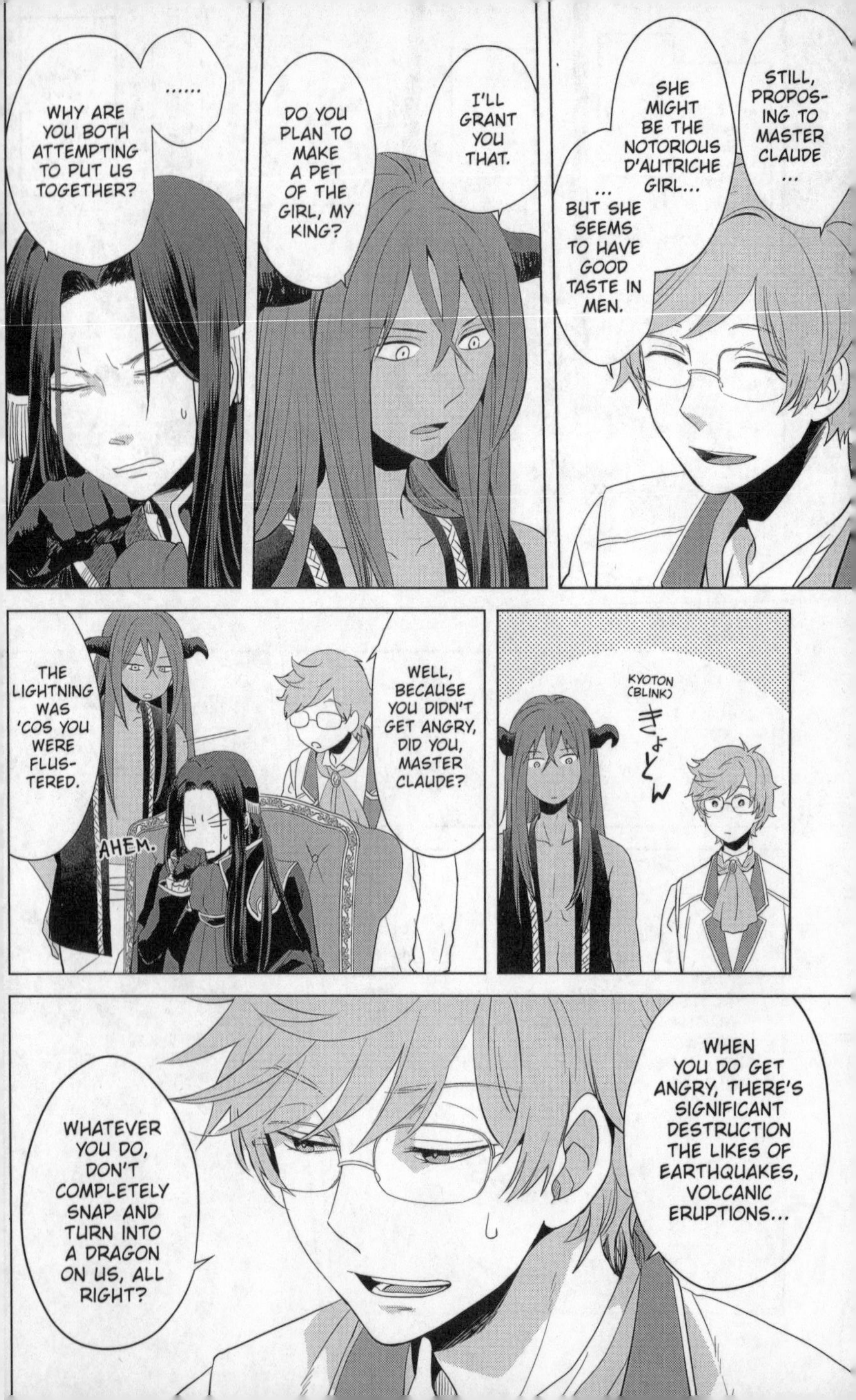
STILL, PROPOSING TO MASTER CLAUDE...
SHE MIGHT BE THE NOTORIOUS D'AUTRICHE GIRL...
...BUT SHE SEEMS TO HAVE GOOD TASTE IN MEN.
I'LL GRANT YOU THAT.
DO YOU PLAN TO MAKE A PET OF THE GIRL, MY KING?
......
WHY ARE YOU BOTH ATTEMPTING TO PUT US TOGETHER?
KYOTON (BLINK)
きょとん
WELL, BECAUSE YOU DIDN'T GET ANGRY, DID YOU, MASTER CLAUDE?
THE LIGHTNING WAS 'COS YOU WERE FLUSTERED.
AHEM.
WHEN YOU DO GET ANGRY, THERE'S SIGNIFICANT DESTRUCTION THE LIKES OF EARTHQUAKES, VOLCANIC ERUPTIONS...
WHATEVER YOU DO, DON'T COMPLETELY SNAP AND TURN INTO A DRAGON ON US, ALL RIGHT?

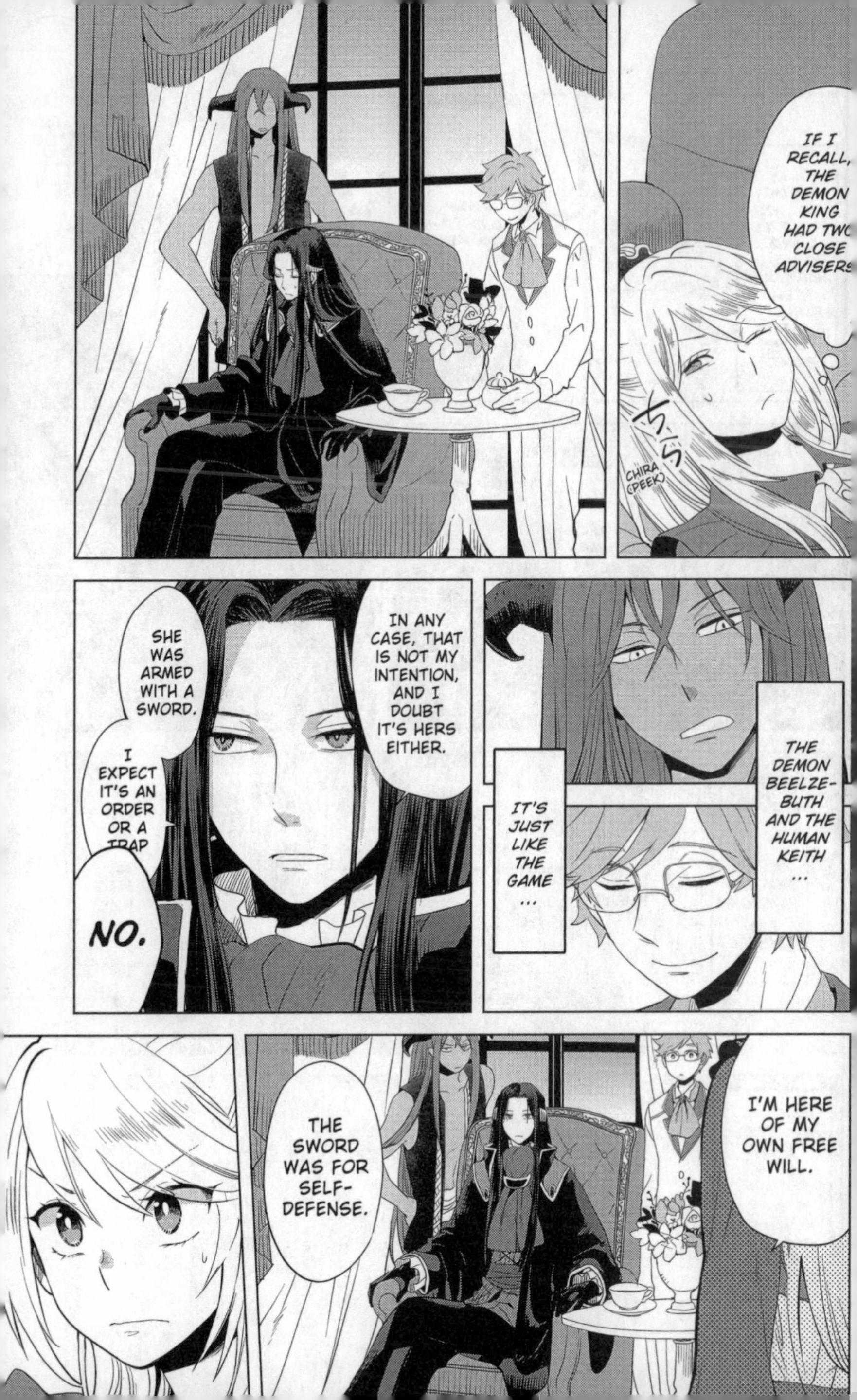
IF I RECALL, THE DEMON KING HAD TWO CLOSE ADVISERS
CHIRA (PEEK)
THE DEMON BEELZE-BUTH AND THE HUMAN KEITH ...
IT'S JUST LIKE THE GAME ...
IN ANY CASE, THAT IS NOT MY INTENTION, AND I DOUBT IT'S HERS EITHER.
SHE WAS ARMED WITH A SWORD.
I EXPECT IT'S AN ORDER OR A TRAP
NO.
I'M HERE OF MY OWN FREE WILL.
THE SWORD WAS FOR SELF-DEFENSE.

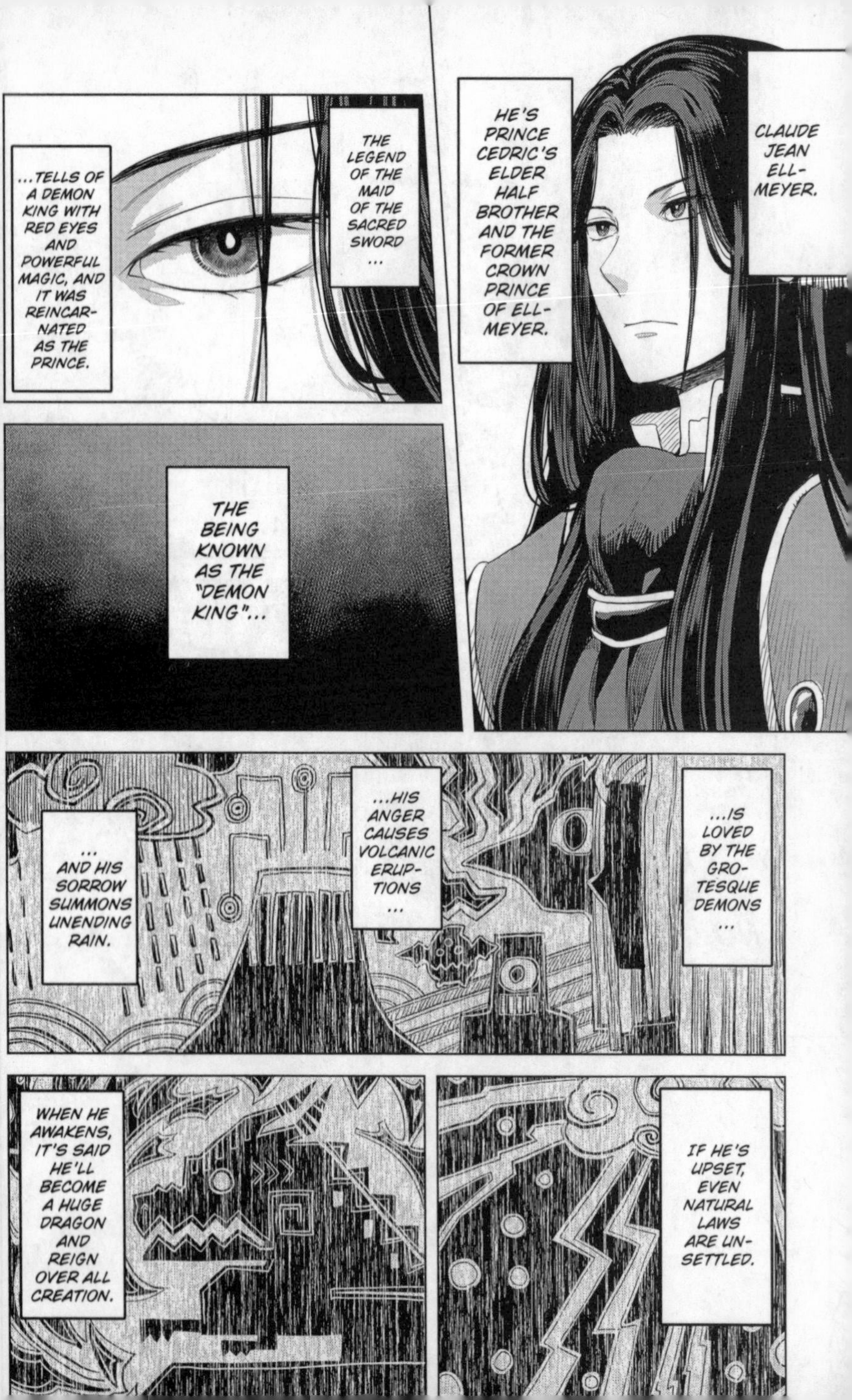
CLAUDE JEAN ELL-MEYER.
HE'S PRINCE CEDRIC'S ELDER HALF BROTHER AND THE FORMER CROWN PRINCE OF ELL-MEYER.
THE LEGEND OF THE MAID OF THE SACRED SWORD...
...TELLS OF A DEMON KING WITH RED EYES AND POWERFUL MAGIC, AND IT WAS REINCARNATED AS THE PRINCE.
THE BEING KNOWN AS THE "DEMON KING"...
...IS LOVED BY THE GROTESQUE DEMONS...
...HIS ANGER CAUSES VOLCANIC ERUPTIONS...
... AND HIS SORROW SUMMONS UNENDING RAIN.
IF HE'S UPSET, EVEN NATURAL LAWS ARE UNSETTLED.
WHEN HE AWAKENS, IT'S SAID HE'LL BECOME A HUGE DRAGON AND REIGN OVER ALL CREATION.

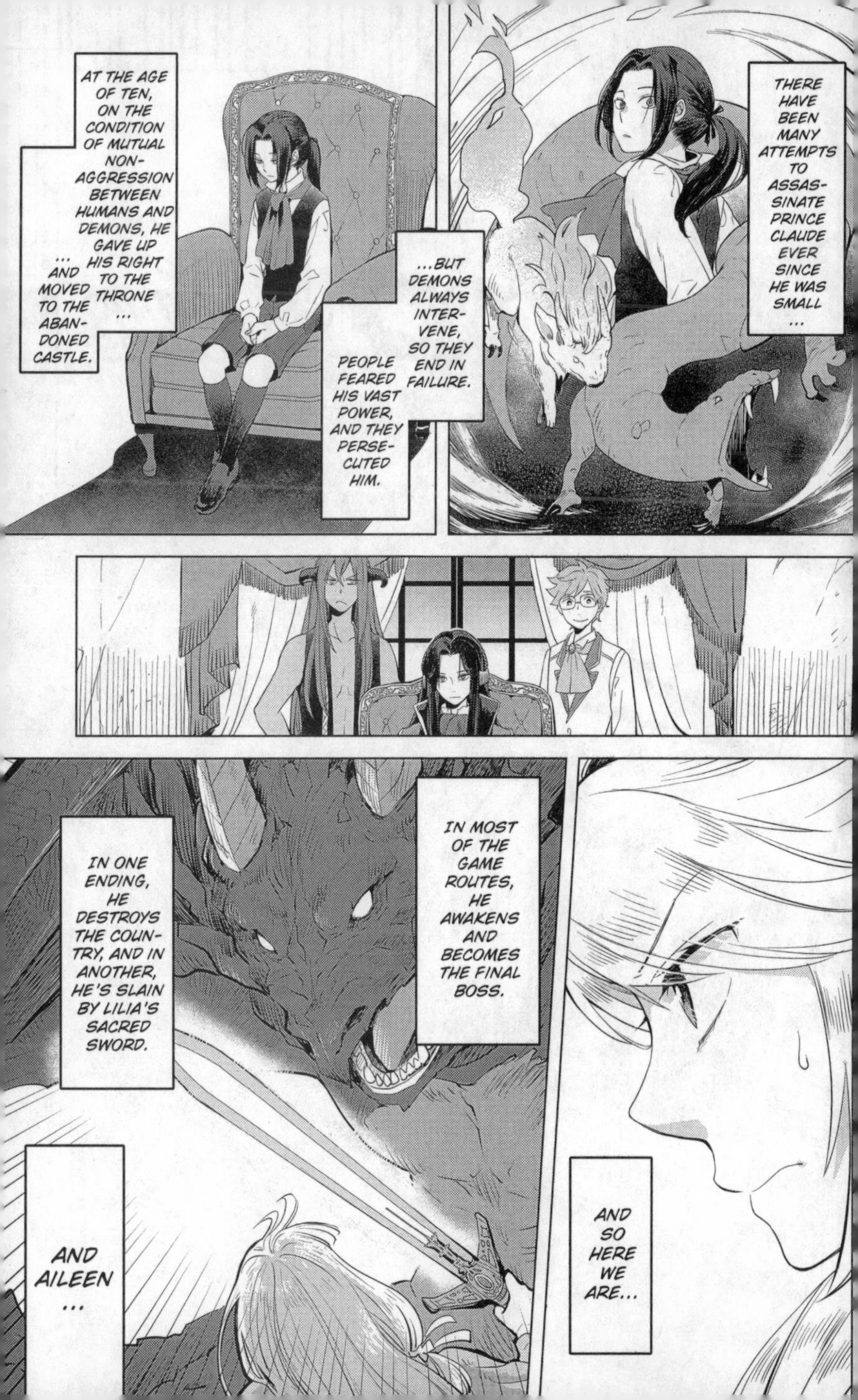

THERE HAVE BEEN MANY ATTEMPTS TO ASSAS-SINATE PRINCE CLAUDE EVER SINCE HE WAS SMALL...
...BUT DEMONS ALWAYS INTER-VENE, SO THEY END IN FAILURE.
PEOPLE FEARED HIS VAST POWER, AND THEY PERSE-CUTED HIM.
AT THE AGE OF TEN, ON THE CONDITION OF MUTUAL NON-AGGRESSION BETWEEN HUMANS AND DEMONS, HE GAVE UP HIS RIGHT TO THE THRONE...
...AND MOVED TO THE ABAN-DONED CASTLE.
AND SO HERE WE ARE...
IN MOST OF THE GAME ROUTES, HE AWAKENS AND BECOMES THE FINAL BOSS.
IN ONE ENDING, HE DESTROYS THE COUN-TRY, AND IN ANOTHER, HE'S SLAIN BY LILIA'S SACRED SWORD.
AND AILEEN...

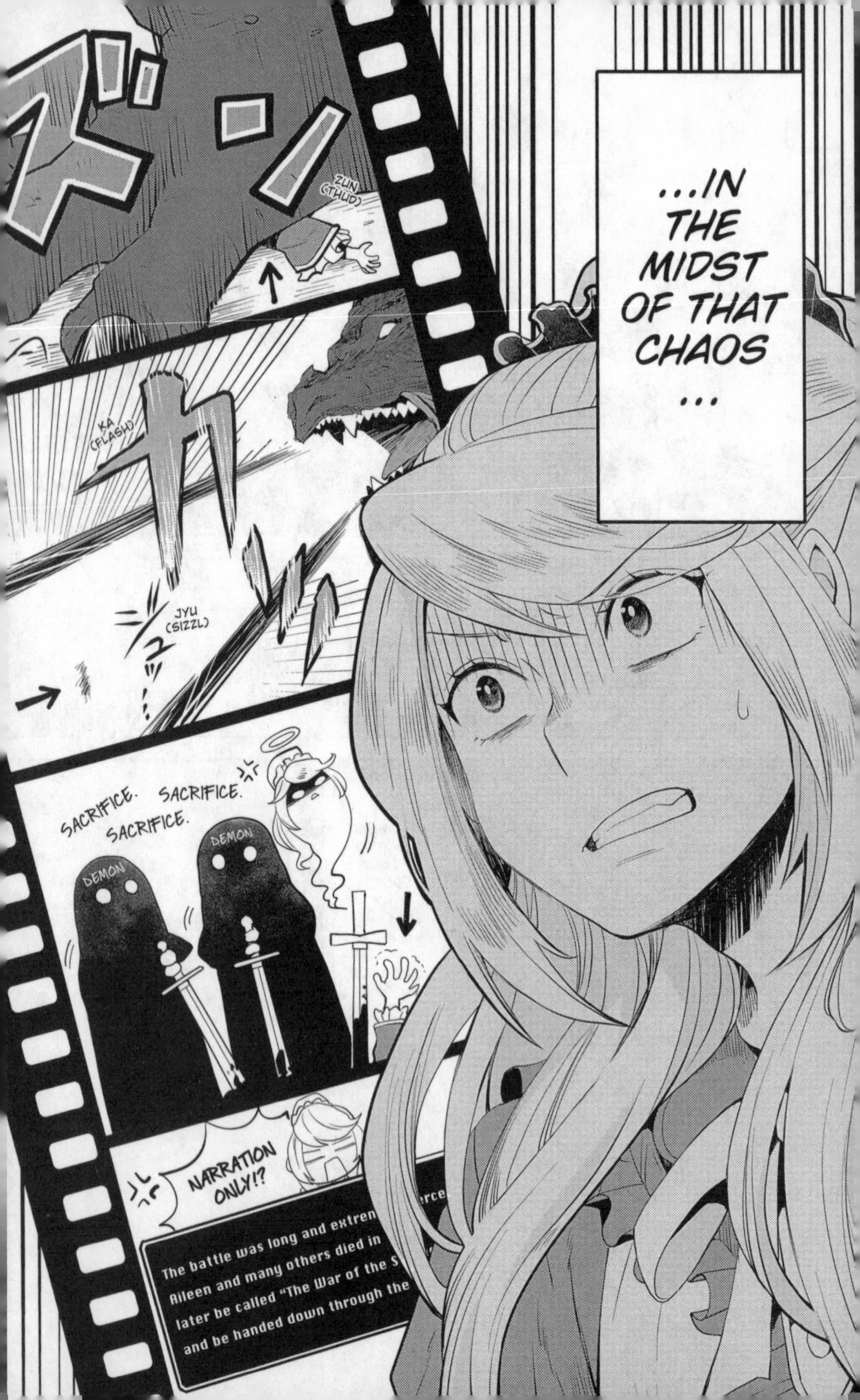
...IN THE MIDST OF THAT CHAOS ...
ZUN (THUD)
KA (FLASH)
JYU (SIZZL)
SACRIFICE. SACRIFICE. SACRIFICE.
DEMON
DEMON
NARRATION ONLY!?
The battle was long and
Aileen and many others died in
later be called "The War of the
and be handed down through the

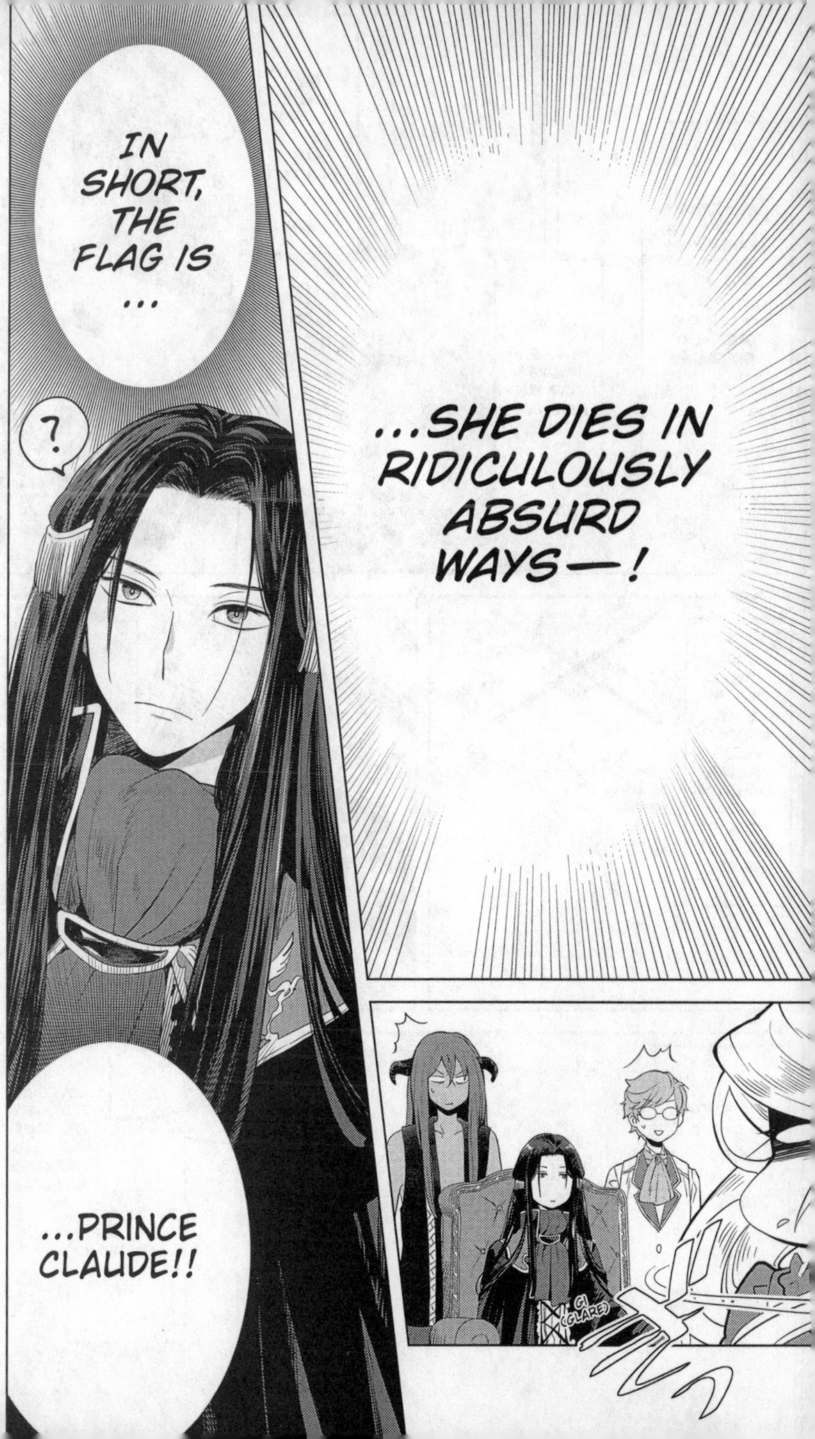
...SHE DIES IN RIDICULOUSLY ABSURD WAYS—!
GI (GLARE)
IN SHORT, THE FLAG IS ...
?
...PRINCE CLAUDE!!

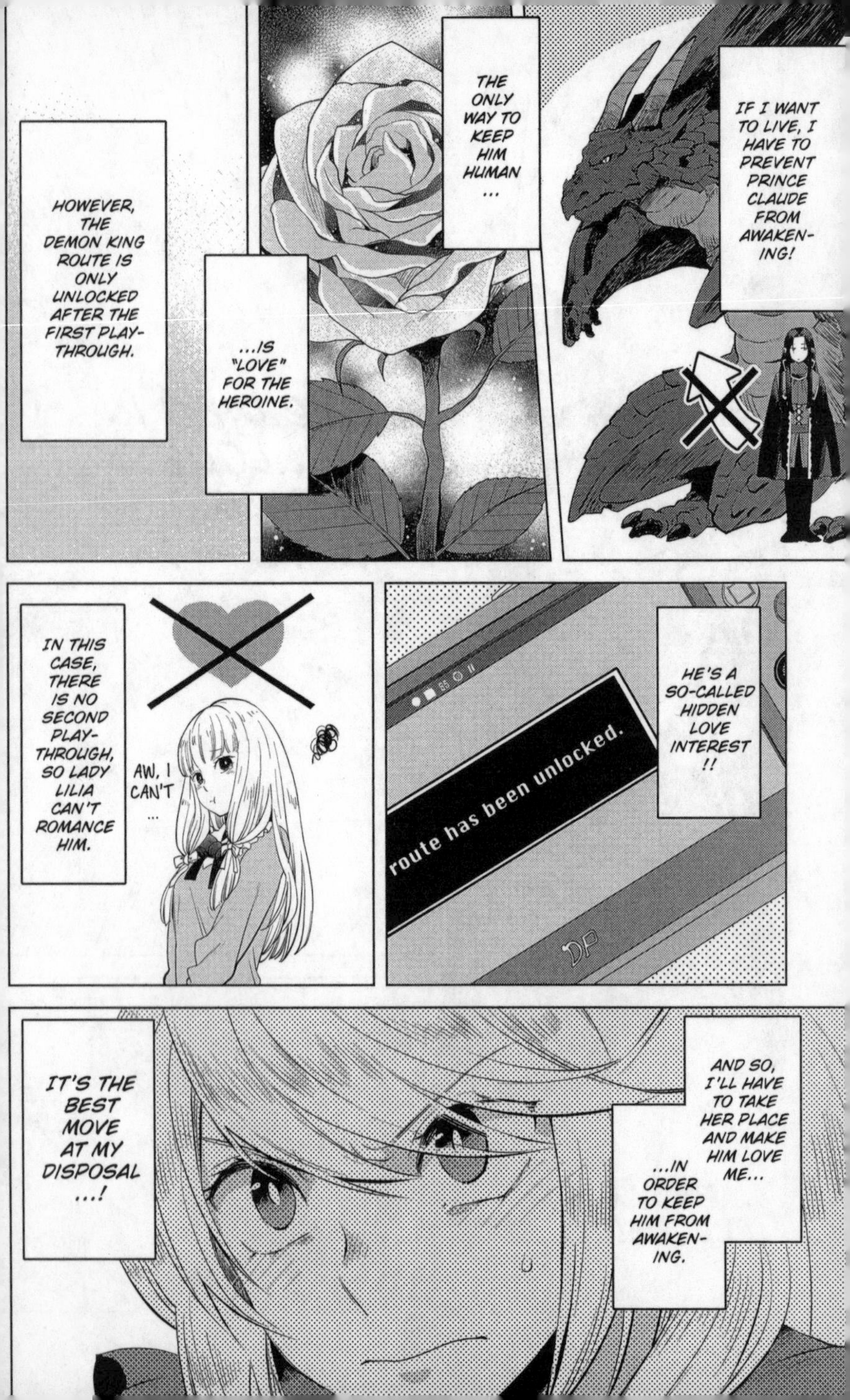
IF I WANT TO LIVE, I HAVE TO PREVENT PRINCE CLAUDE FROM AWAKENING!
THE ONLY WAY TO KEEP HIM HUMAN...
...IS "LOVE" FOR THE HEROINE.
HOWEVER, THE DEMON KING ROUTE IS ONLY UNLOCKED AFTER THE FIRST PLAYTHROUGH.
HE'S A SO-CALLED HIDDEN LOVE INTEREST!!
route has been unlocked.
IN THIS CASE, THERE IS NO SECOND PLAYTHROUGH, SO LADY LILIA CAN'T ROMANCE HIM.
AW, I CAN'T...
AND SO, I'LL HAVE TO TAKE HER PLACE AND MAKE HIM LOVE ME...
...IN ORDER TO KEEP HIM FROM AWAKENING.
IT'S THE BEST MOVE AT MY DISPOSAL...!

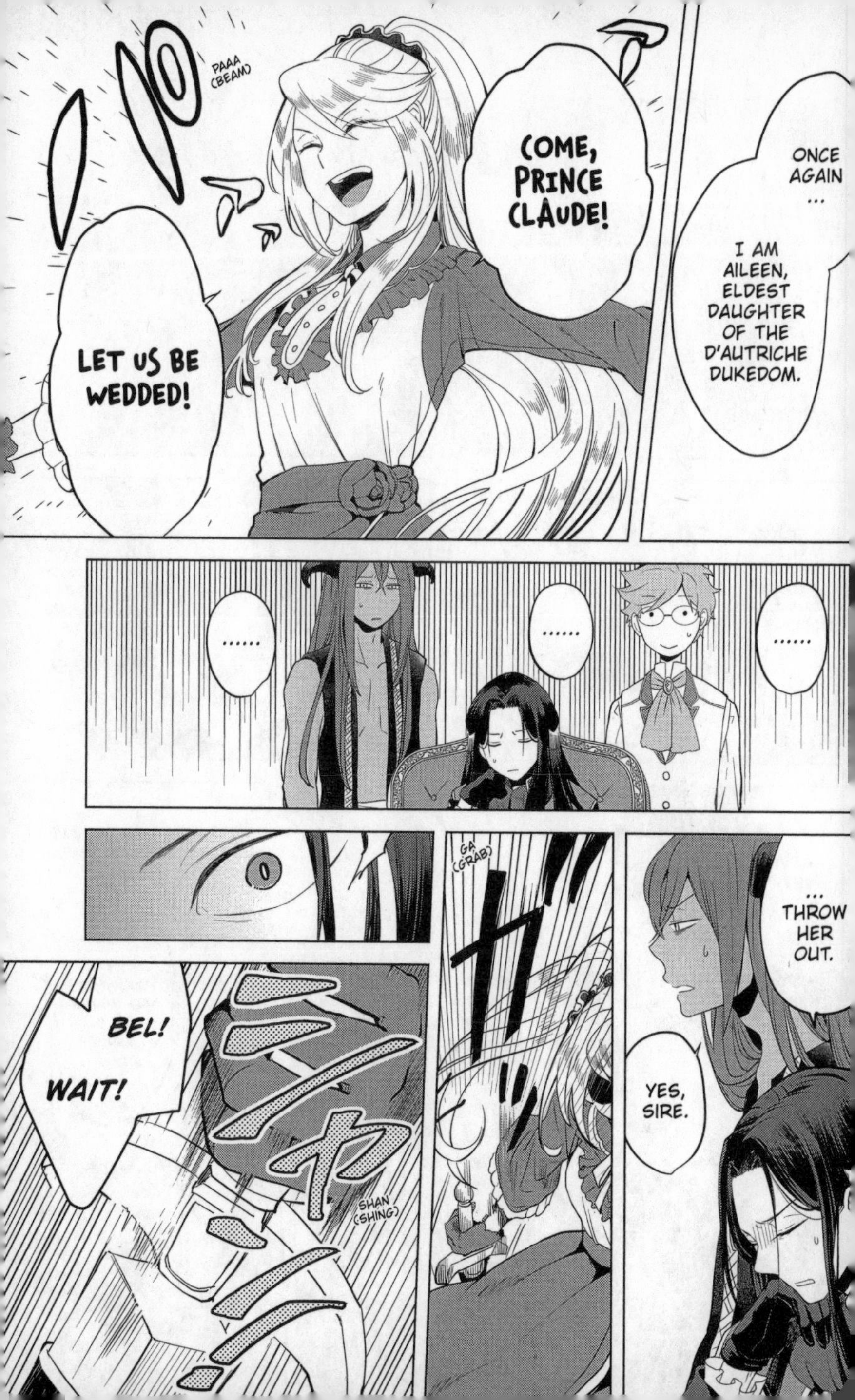
ONCE AGAIN...
I AM AILEEN, ELDEST DAUGHTER OF THE D'AUTRICHE DUKEDOM.
COME, PRINCE CLAUDE!
PAAA (BEAM)
LET US BE WEDDED!
......
......
......
... THROW HER OUT.
YES, SIRE.
GA (GRAB)
SHAN (SHING)
BEL!
WAIT!

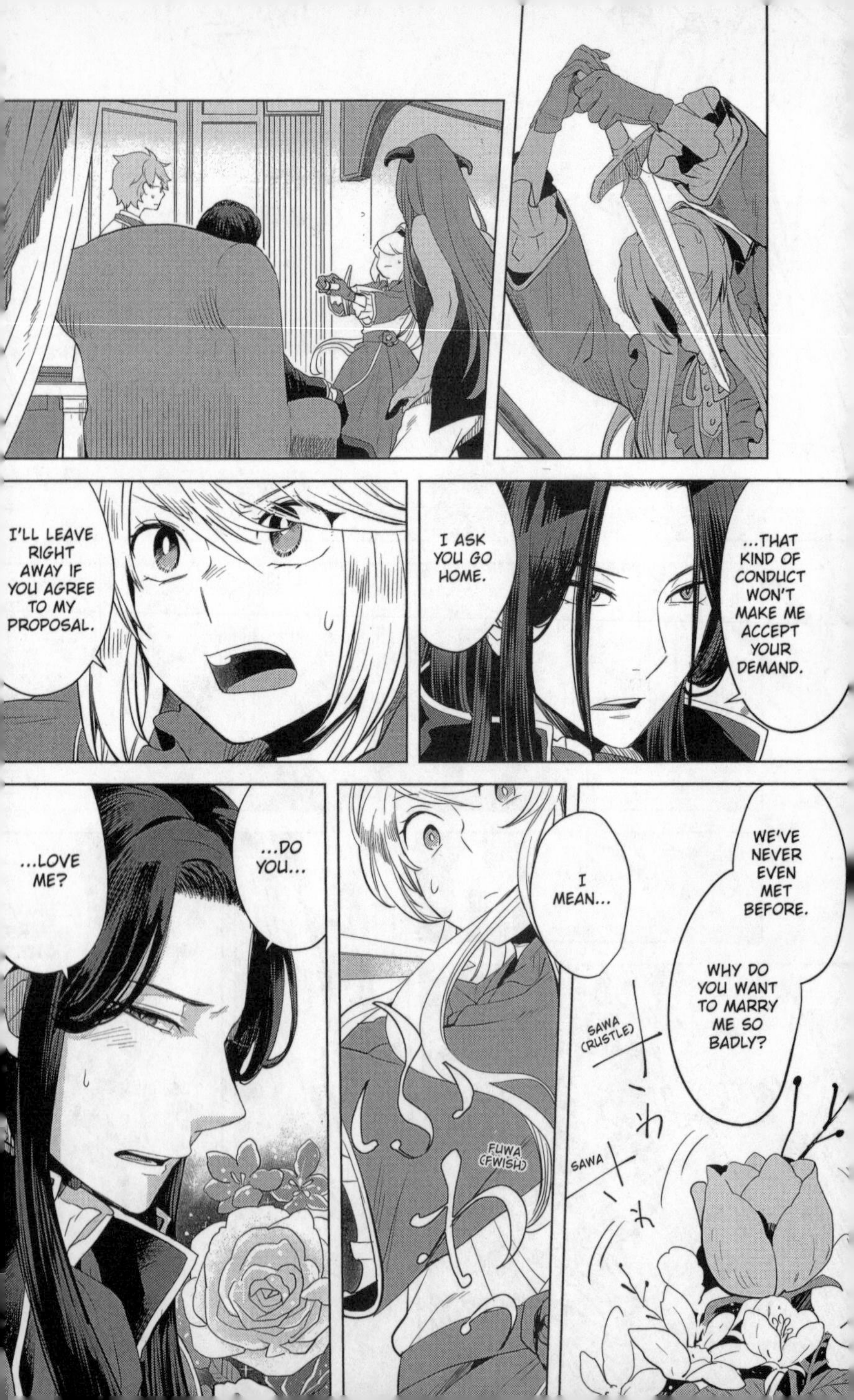
...THAT KIND OF CONDUCT WON'T MAKE ME ACCEPT YOUR DEMAND.
I ASK YOU GO HOME.
I'LL LEAVE RIGHT AWAY IF YOU AGREE TO MY PROPOSAL.
WE'VE NEVER EVEN MET BEFORE.
WHY DO YOU WANT TO MARRY ME SO BADLY?
SAWA (RUSTLE)
SAWA
I MEAN...
FUWA (FWISH)
...DO YOU...
...LOVE ME?

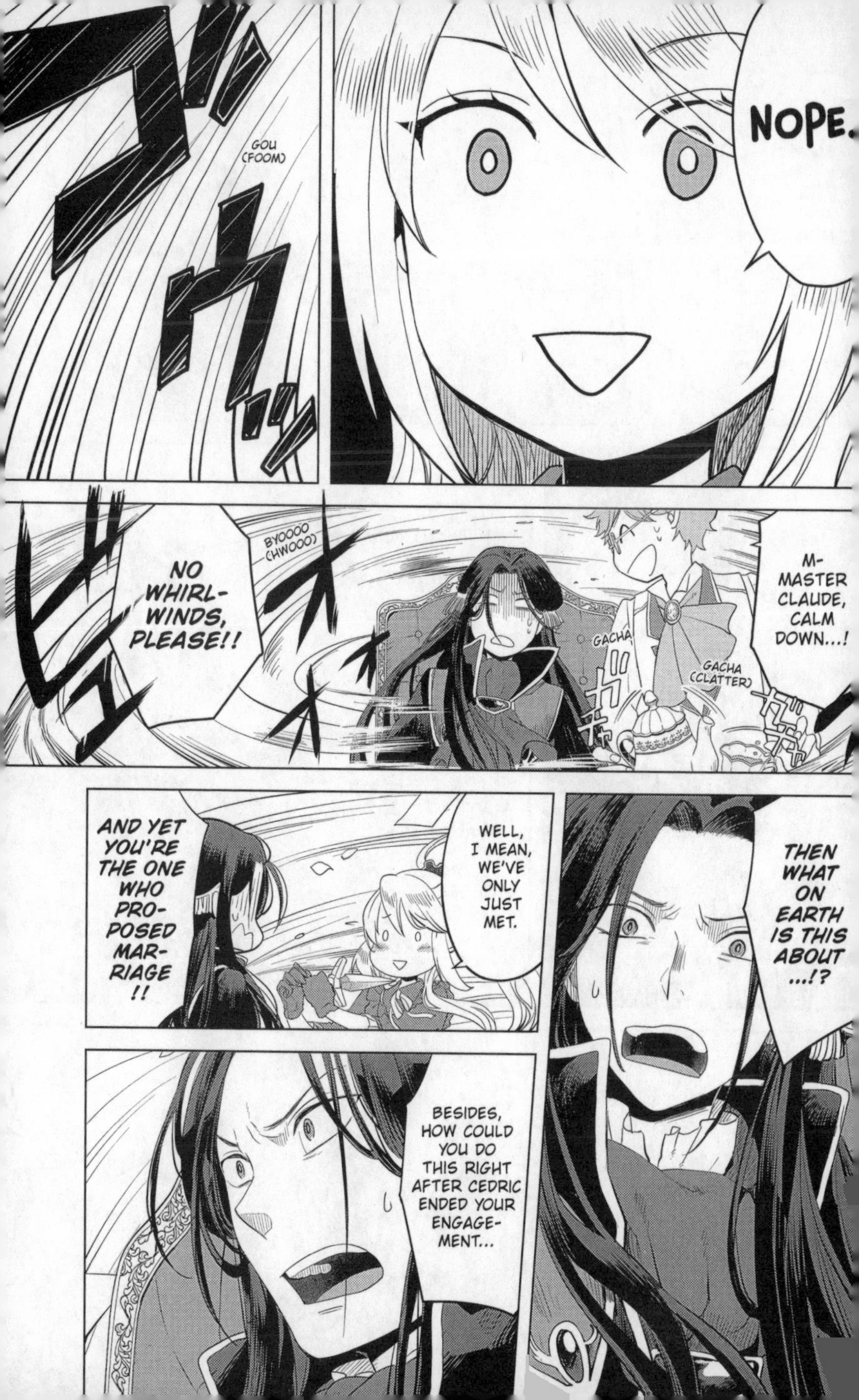
NOPE.
GOU (FOOM)
M-MASTER CLAUDE, CALM DOWN...!
GACHA (CLATTER)
GACHA
BYOOOO (HWOOO)
NO WHIRLWINDS, PLEASE!!
THEN WHAT ON EARTH IS THIS ABOUT...!?
WELL, I MEAN, WE'VE ONLY JUST MET.
AND YET YOU'RE THE ONE WHO PROPOSED MARRIAGE!!
BESIDES, HOW COULD YOU DO THIS RIGHT AFTER CEDRIC ENDED YOUR ENGAGEMENT...

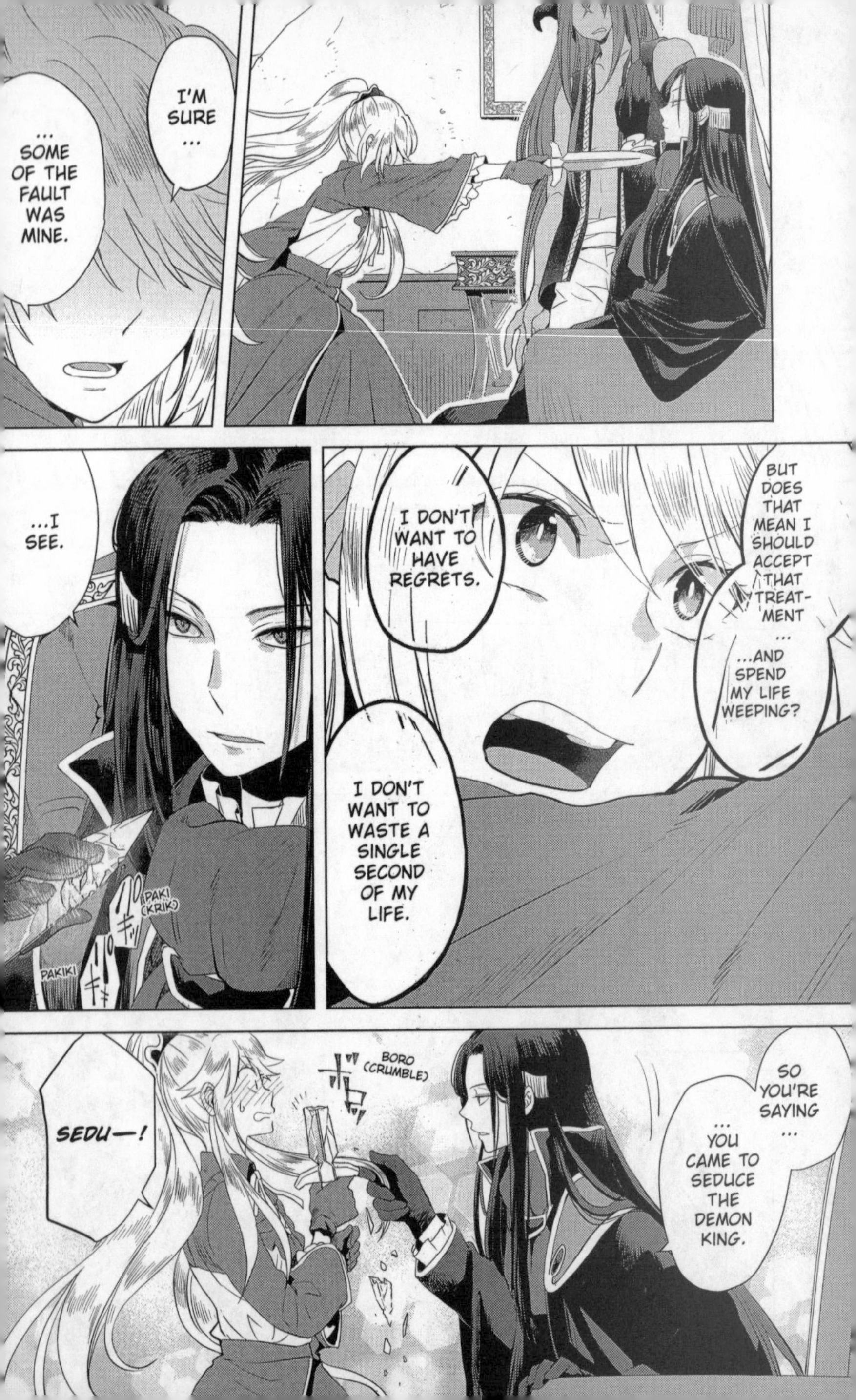
I'M SURE ...
... SOME OF THE FAULT WAS MINE.
BUT DOES THAT MEAN I SHOULD ACCEPT THAT TREATMENT ... ...AND SPEND MY LIFE WEEPING?
I DON'T WANT TO HAVE REGRETS.
I DON'T WANT TO WASTE A SINGLE SECOND OF MY LIFE.
...I SEE.
PAKI (KRIK)
PAKIKI
SO YOU'RE SAYING ... YOU CAME TO SEDUCE THE DEMON KING.
BORO (CRUMBLE)
SEDU—!

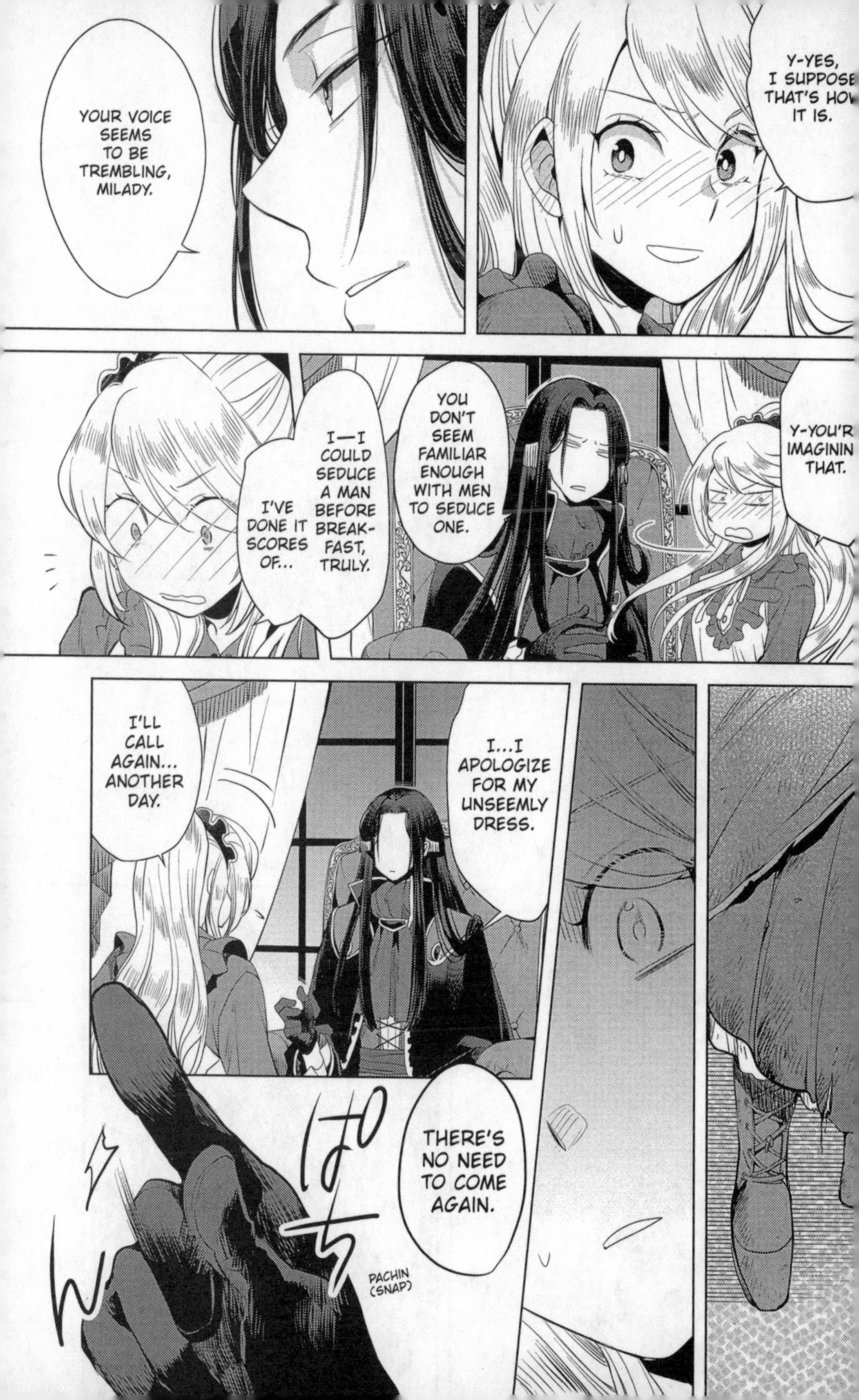
Y-YES, I SUPPOSE THAT'S HOW IT IS.
YOUR VOICE SEEMS TO BE TREMBLING, MILADY.
Y-YOU'R IMAGININ THAT.
YOU DON'T SEEM FAMILIAR ENOUGH WITH MEN TO SEDUCE ONE.
I—I COULD SEDUCE A MAN BEFORE BREAK-FAST, TRULY.
I'VE DONE IT SCORES OF...
I...I APOLOGIZE FOR MY UNSEEMLY DRESS.
I'LL CALL AGAIN... ANOTHER DAY.
THERE'S NO NEED TO COME AGAIN.
PACHIN (SNAP)

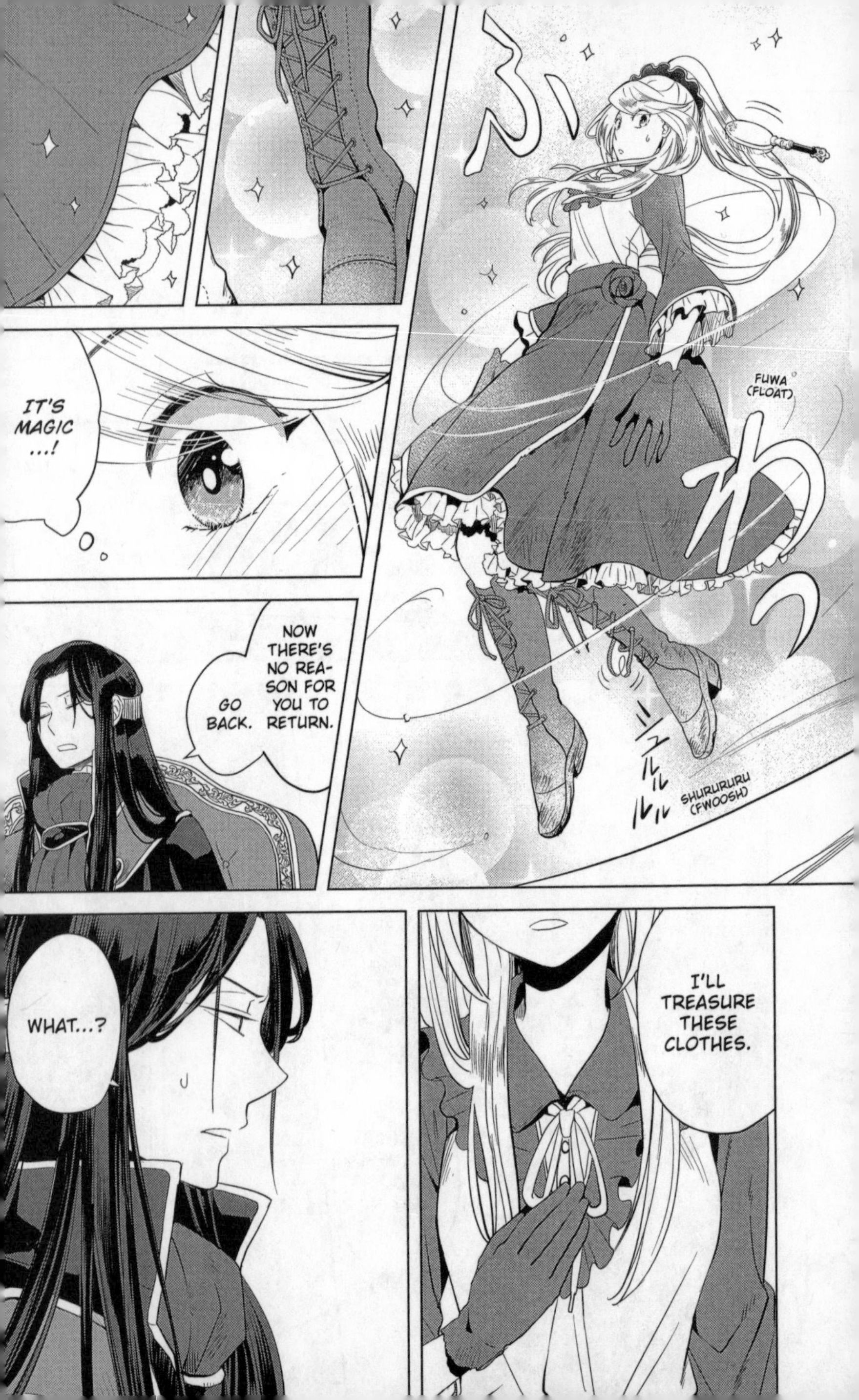
ふわっ
FUWA (FLOAT)
シュルルル
SHURURURU (FWOOSH)
IT'S MAGIC ...!
NOW THERE'S NO REASON FOR YOU TO RETURN.
GO BACK.
I'LL TREASURE THESE CLOTHES.
WHAT...?

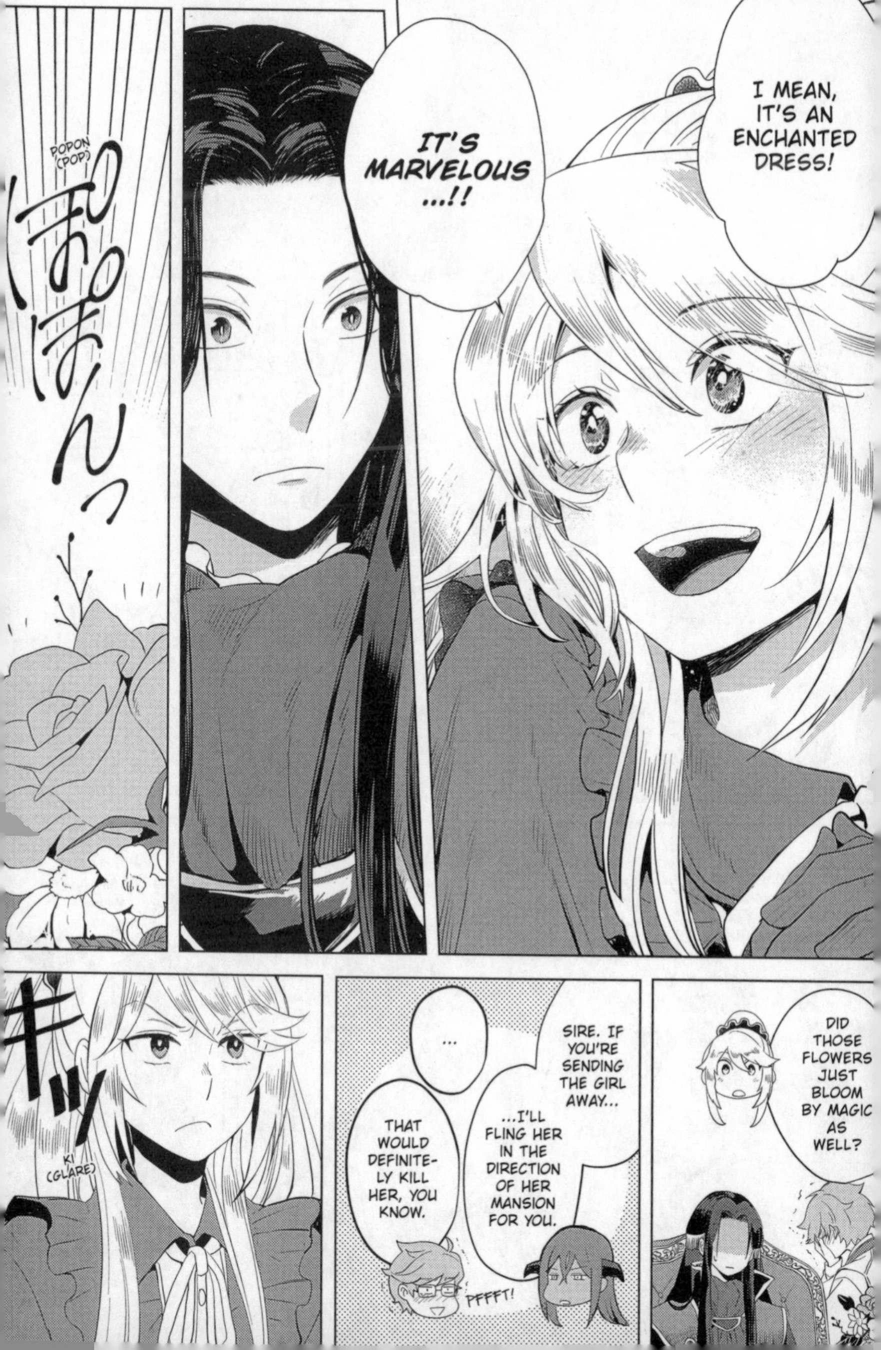
I MEAN, IT'S AN ENCHANTED DRESS!
IT'S MARVELOUS ...!!
ぽぽんっ
POPON (POP)
DID THOSE FLOWERS JUST BLOOM BY MAGIC AS WELL?
SIRE. IF YOU'RE SENDING THE GIRL AWAY...
...I'LL FLING HER IN THE DIRECTION OF HER MANSION FOR YOU.
...
THAT WOULD DEFINITE-LY KILL HER, YOU KNOW.
PFFFT!
キッ
KI (GLARE)

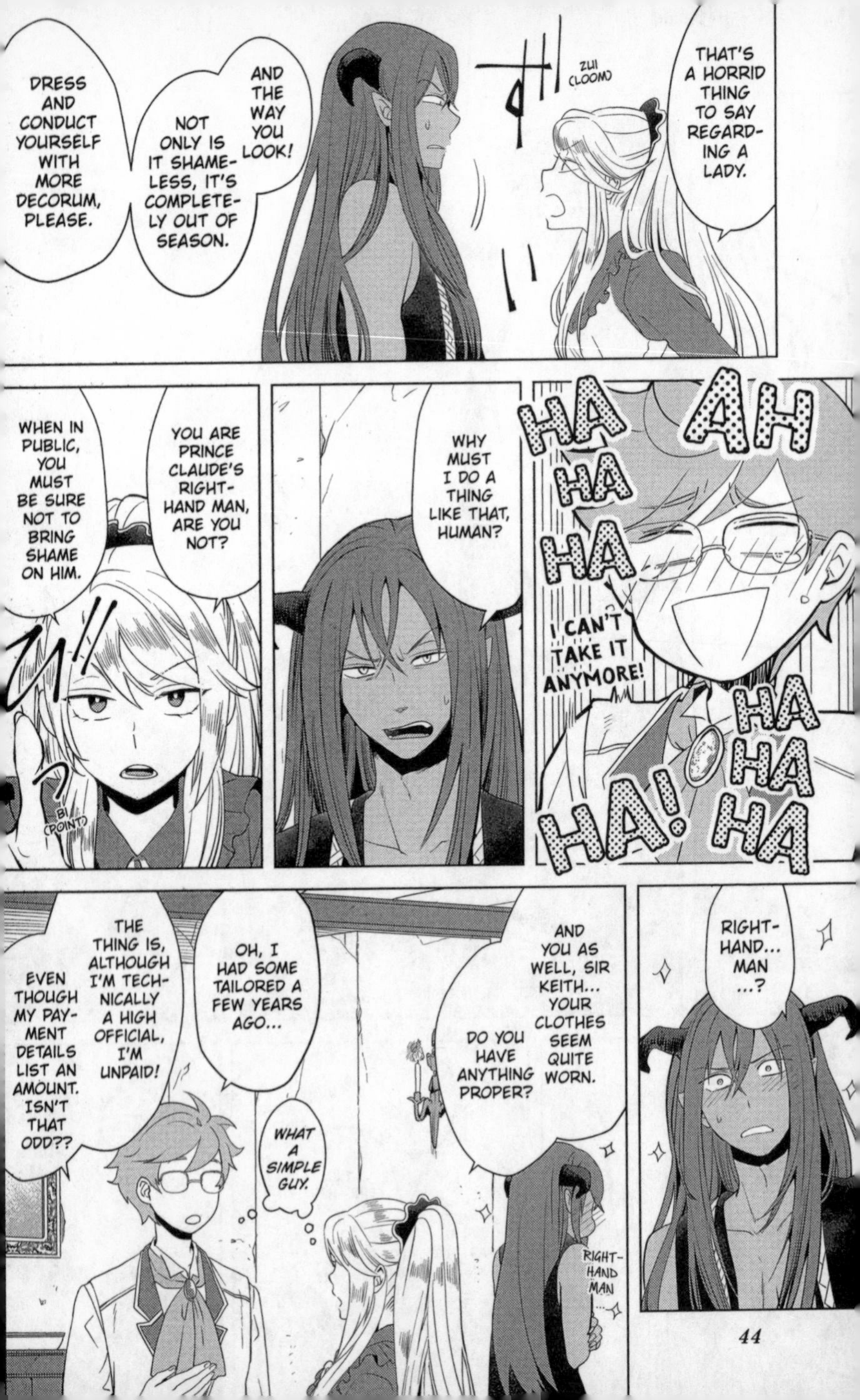
ZUI (LOOM)
THAT'S A HORRID THING TO SAY REGARDING A LADY.
AND THE WAY YOU LOOK!
NOT ONLY IS IT SHAMELESS, IT'S COMPLETELY OUT OF SEASON.
DRESS AND CONDUCT YOURSELF WITH MORE DECORUM, PLEASE.
AH HA HA HA
I CAN'T TAKE IT ANYMORE!
HA HA HA HA HA!
WHY MUST I DO A THING LIKE THAT, HUMAN?
YOU ARE PRINCE CLAUDE'S RIGHT-HAND MAN, ARE YOU NOT?
WHEN IN PUBLIC, YOU MUST BE SURE NOT TO BRING SHAME ON HIM.
BI (POINT)
RIGHT-HAND... MAN ...?
AND YOU AS WELL, SIR KEITH... YOUR CLOTHES SEEM QUITE WORN.
DO YOU HAVE ANYTHING PROPER?
RIGHT-HAND MAN ...
OH, I HAD SOME TAILORED A FEW YEARS AGO...
WHAT A SIMPLE GUY.
THE THING IS, ALTHOUGH I'M TECHNICALLY A HIGH OFFICIAL, I'M UNPAID!
EVEN THOUGH MY PAYMENT DETAILS LIST AN AMOUNT. ISN'T THAT ODD??

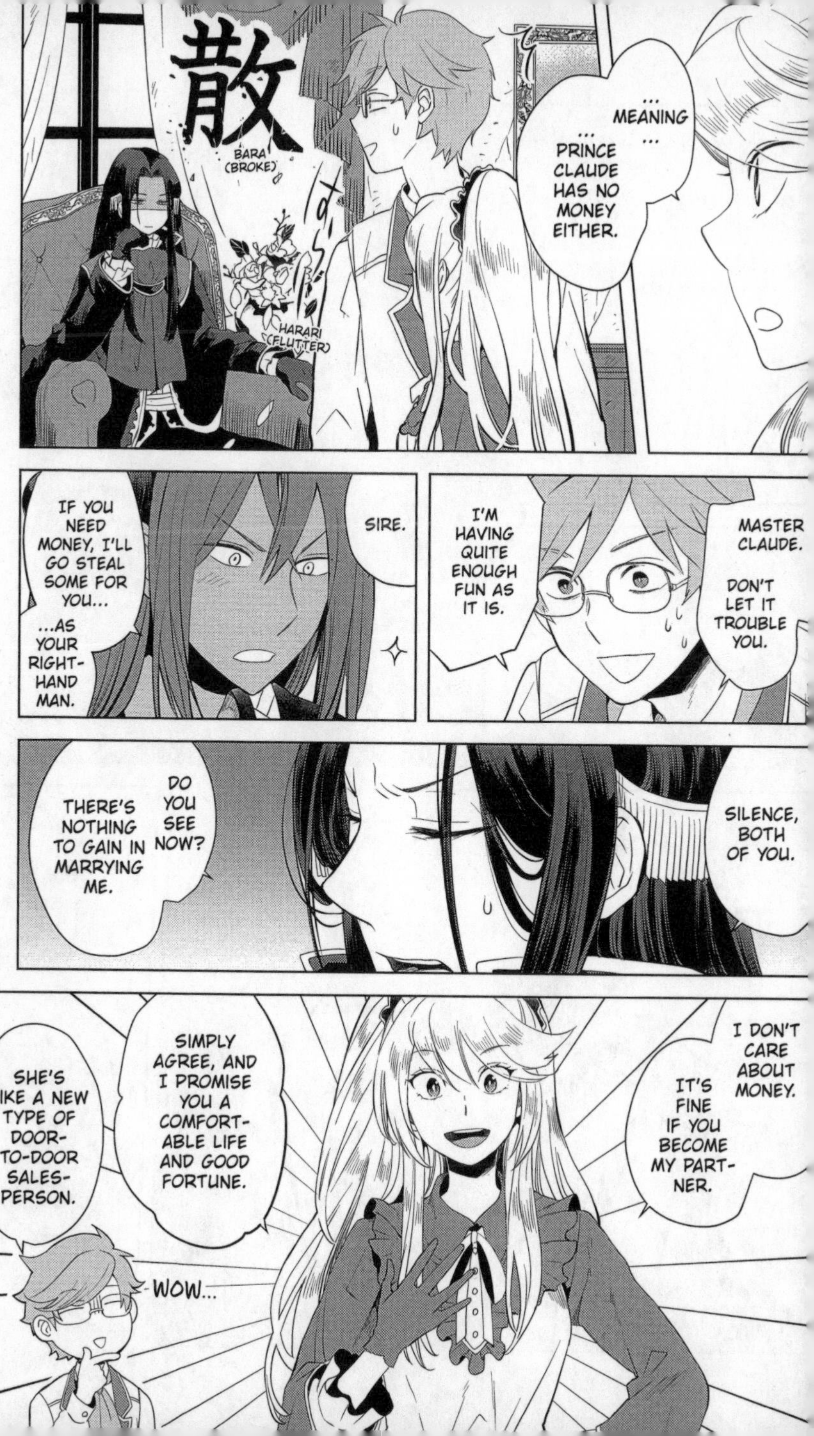
...MEANING... ...PRINCE CLAUDE HAS NO MONEY EITHER.
散
BARA (BROKE)
HARARI (FLUTTER)
MASTER CLAUDE. DON'T LET IT TROUBLE YOU.
I'M HAVING QUITE ENOUGH FUN AS IT IS.
SIRE.
IF YOU NEED MONEY, I'LL GO STEAL SOME FOR YOU... ...AS YOUR RIGHT-HAND MAN.
SILENCE, BOTH OF YOU.
DO YOU SEE NOW?
THERE'S NOTHING TO GAIN IN MARRYING ME.
I DON'T CARE ABOUT MONEY.
IT'S FINE IF YOU BECOME MY PARTNER.
SIMPLY AGREE, AND I PROMISE YOU A COMFORTABLE LIFE AND GOOD FORTUNE.
SHE'S LIKE A NEW TYPE OF DOOR-TO-DOOR SALESPERSON.
WOW...

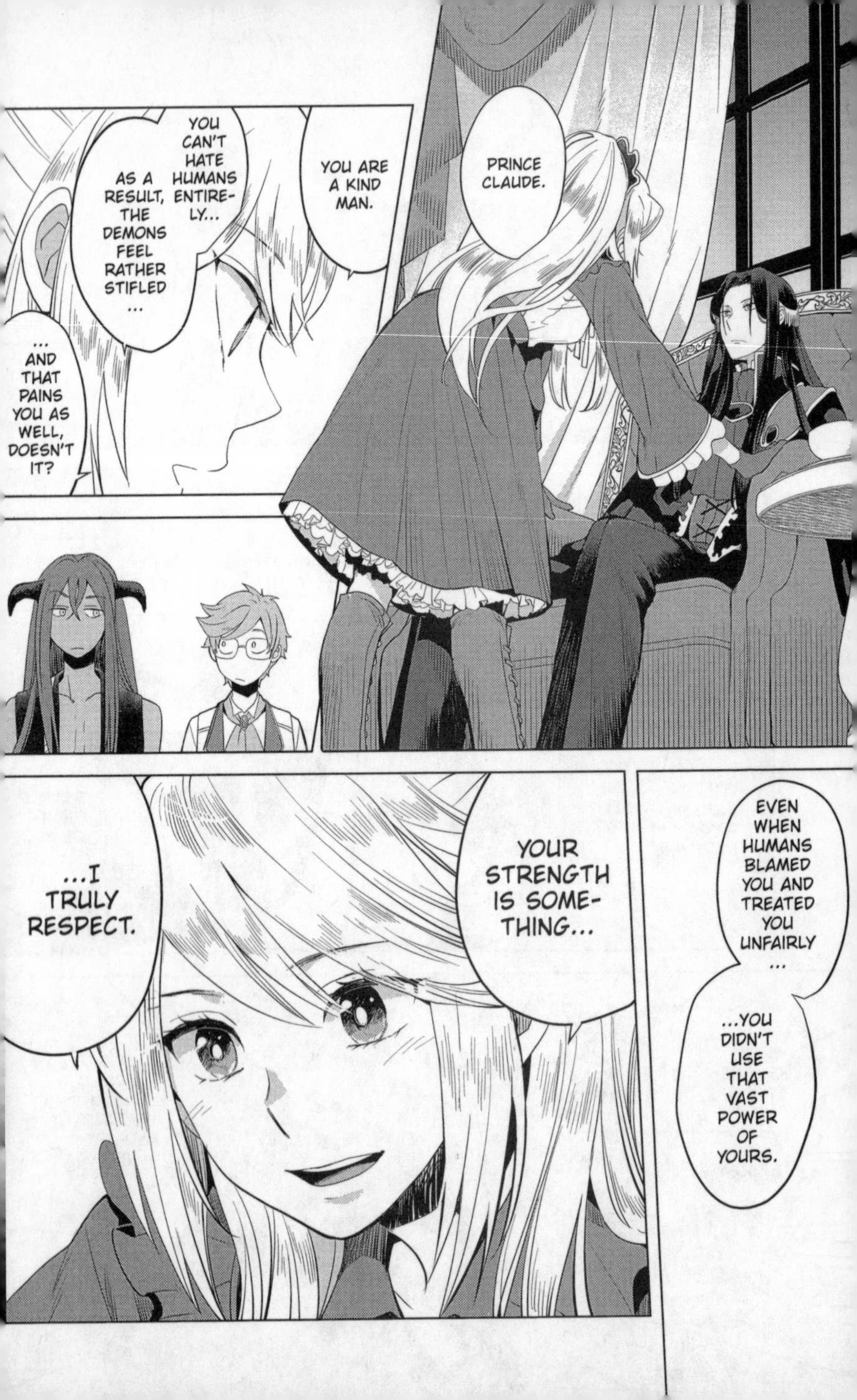
PRINCE CLAUDE.
YOU ARE A KIND MAN.
YOU CAN'T HATE HUMANS ENTIRELY...
AS A RESULT, THE DEMONS FEEL RATHER STIFLED...
...AND THAT PAINS YOU AS WELL, DOESN'T IT?
EVEN WHEN HUMANS BLAMED YOU AND TREATED YOU UNFAIRLY...
...YOU DIDN'T USE THAT VAST POWER OF YOURS.
YOUR STRENGTH IS SOMETHING...
...I TRULY RESPECT.

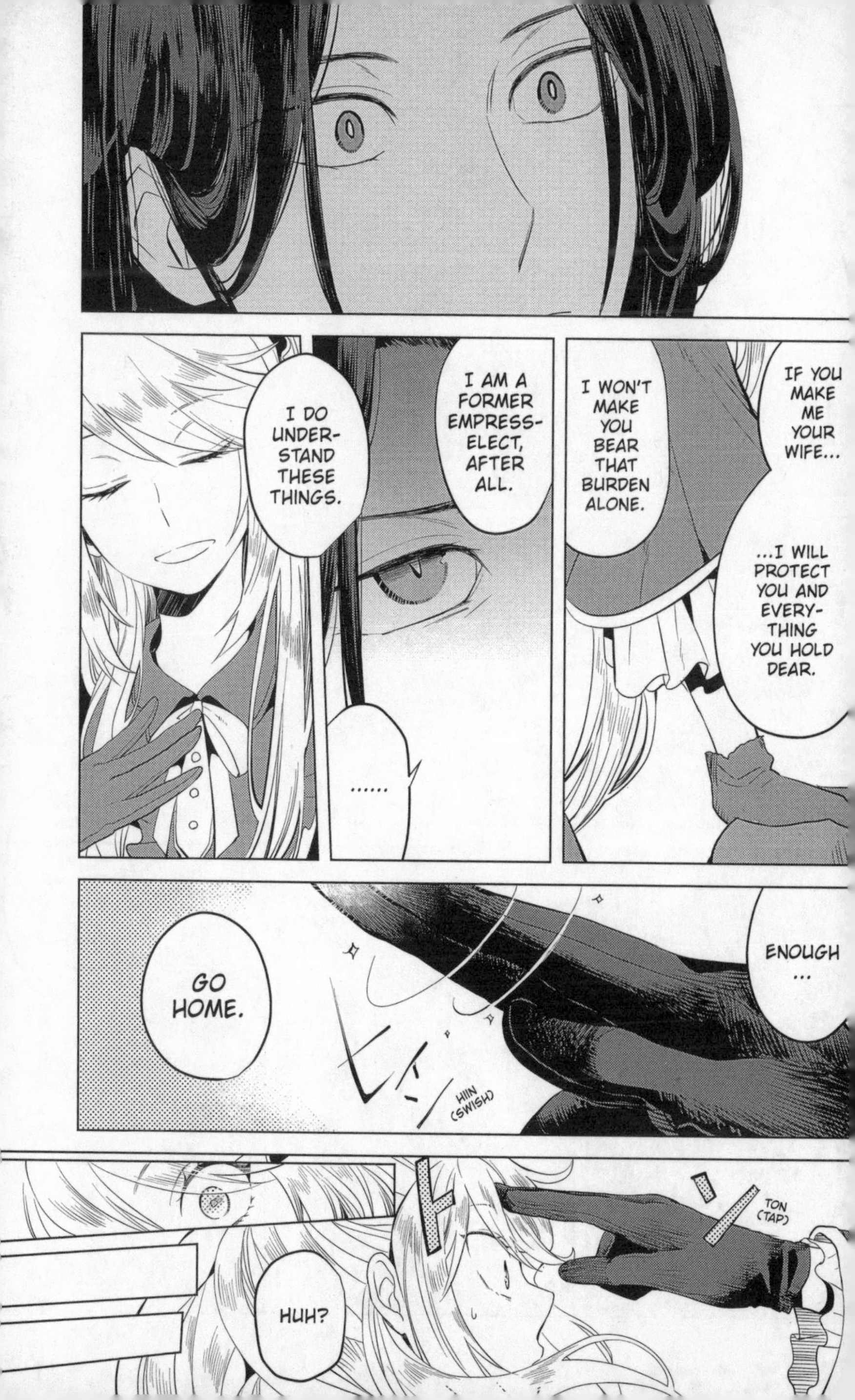
IF YOU MAKE ME YOUR WIFE...
...I WILL PROTECT YOU AND EVERYTHING YOU HOLD DEAR.
I WON'T MAKE YOU BEAR THAT BURDEN ALONE.
I AM A FORMER EMPRESS-ELECT, AFTER ALL.
......
I DO UNDERSTAND THESE THINGS.
ENOUGH ...
HIIN (SWISH)
GO HOME.
TON (TAP)
HUH?

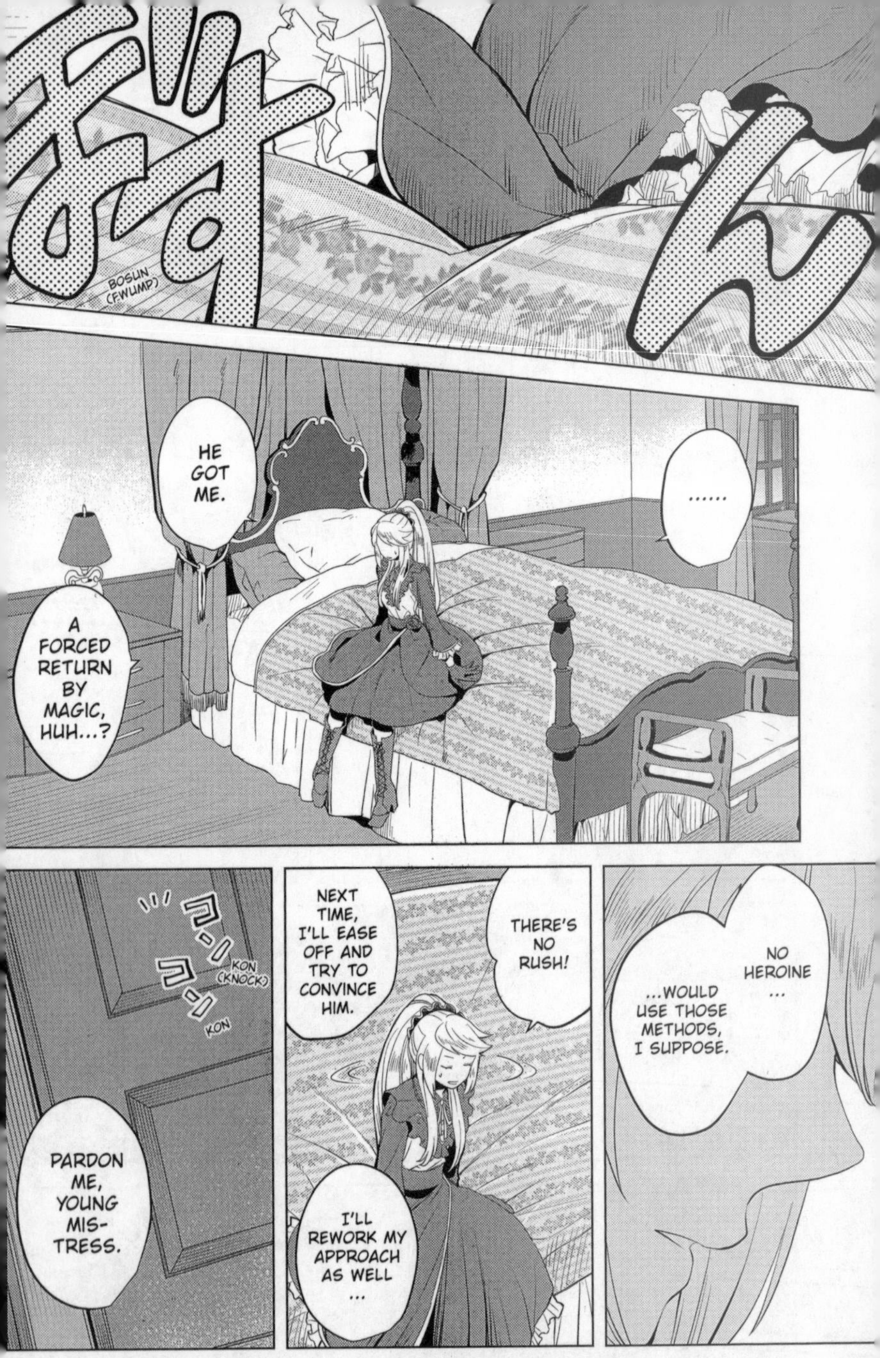
BOSUN (FWUMP)
......
HE GOT ME.
A FORCED RETURN BY MAGIC, HUH...?
NO HEROINE ...
...WOULD USE THOSE METHODS, I SUPPOSE.
THERE'S NO RUSH!
NEXT TIME, I'LL EASE OFF AND TRY TO CONVINCE HIM.
I'LL REWORK MY APPROACH AS WELL ...
KON (KNOCK)
KON
PARDON ME, YOUNG MISTRESS.

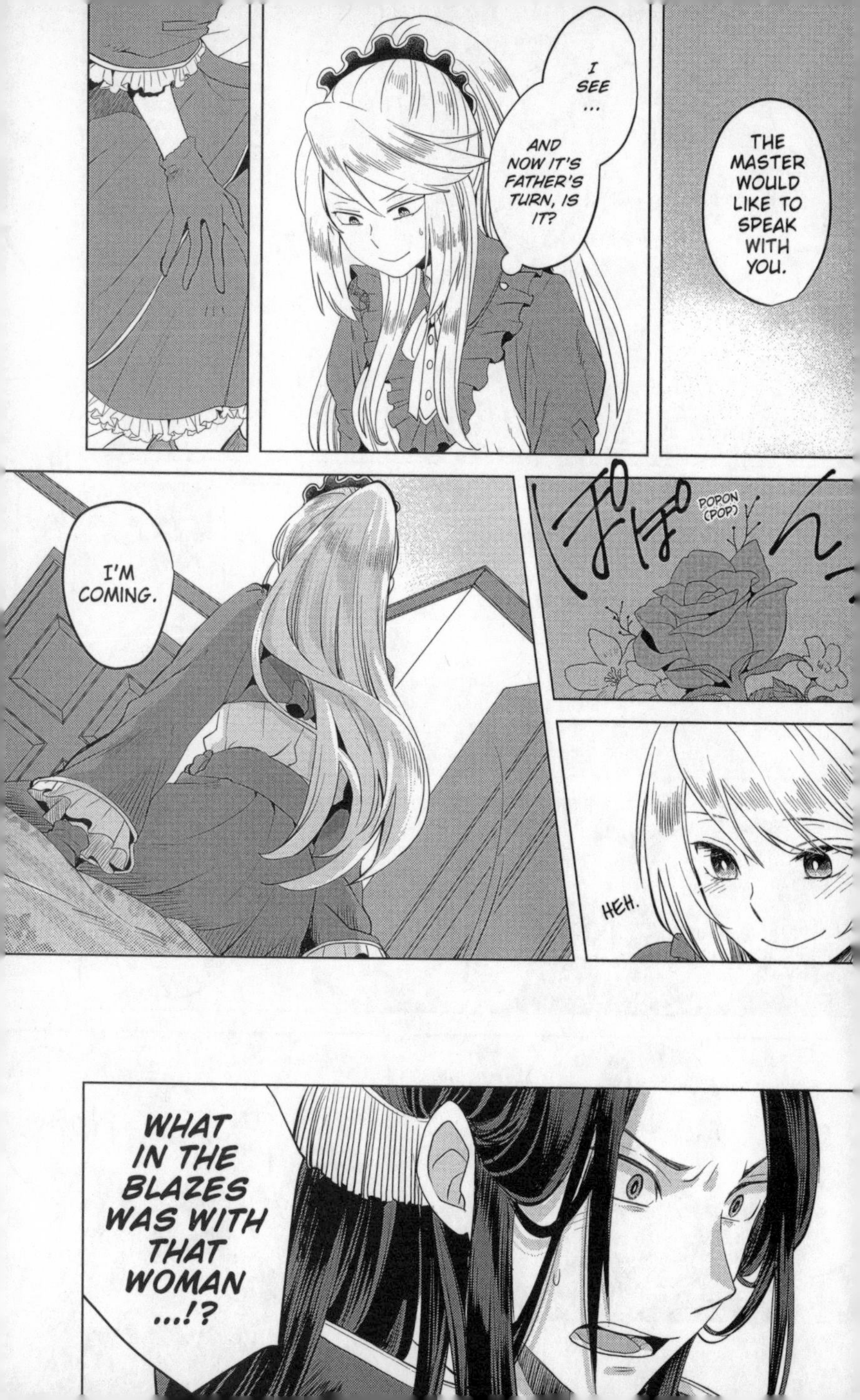
THE MASTER WOULD LIKE TO SPEAK WITH YOU.
I SEE...
AND NOW IT'S FATHER'S TURN, IS IT?
POPON (POP)
HEH.
I'M COMING.
WHAT IN THE BLAZES WAS WITH THAT WOMAN...!?

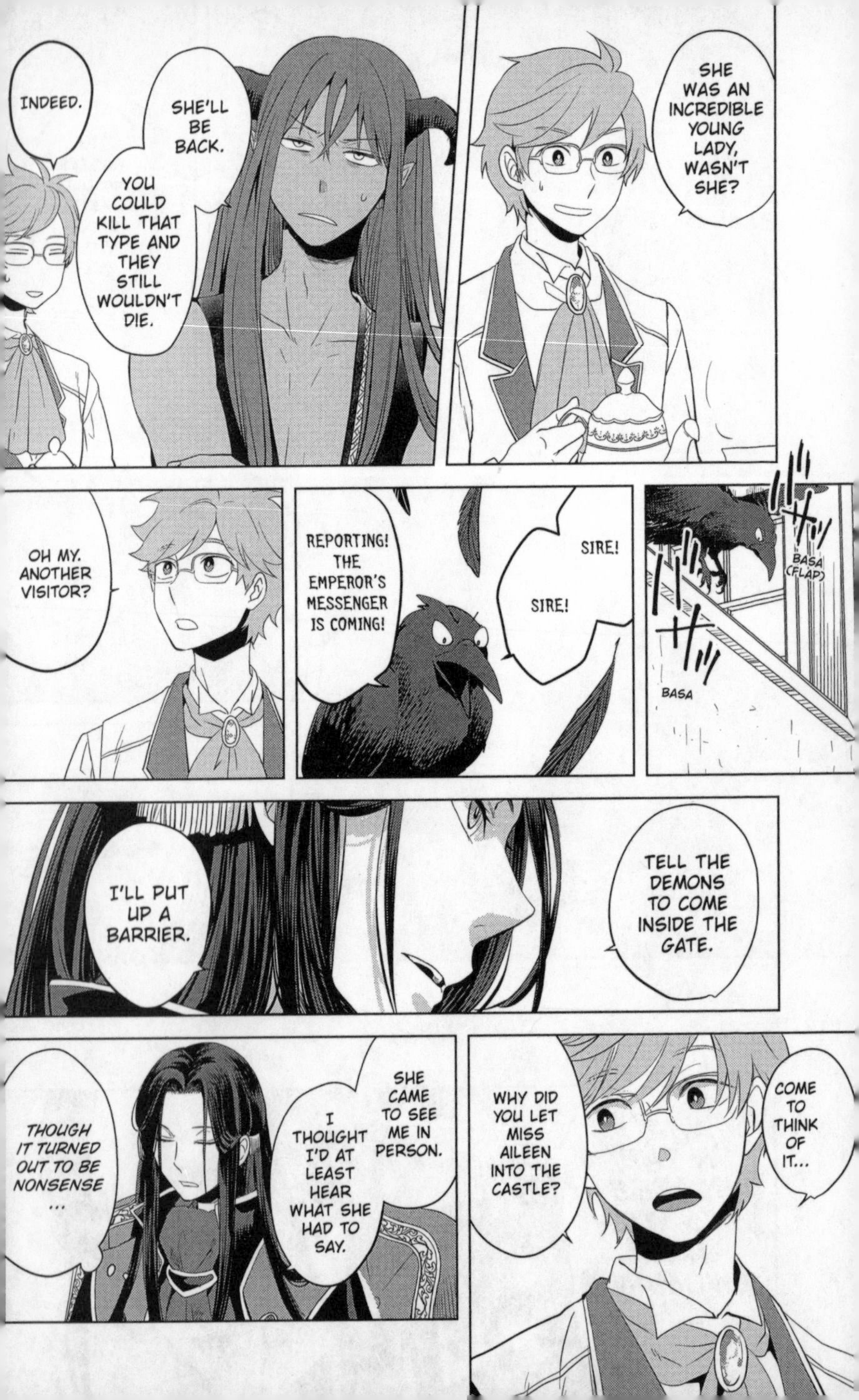
SHE WAS AN INCREDIBLE YOUNG LADY, WASN'T SHE?
SHE'LL BE BACK.
YOU COULD KILL THAT TYPE AND THEY STILL WOULDN'T DIE.
INDEED.
BASA (FLAP)
BASA
SIRE!
SIRE!
REPORTING! THE EMPEROR'S MESSENGER IS COMING!
OH MY. ANOTHER VISITOR?
TELL THE DEMONS TO COME INSIDE THE GATE.
I'LL PUT UP A BARRIER.
COME TO THINK OF IT...
WHY DID YOU LET MISS AILEEN INTO THE CASTLE?
SHE CAME TO SEE ME IN PERSON.
I THOUGHT I'D AT LEAST HEAR WHAT SHE HAD TO SAY.
THOUGH IT TURNED OUT TO BE NONSENSE...

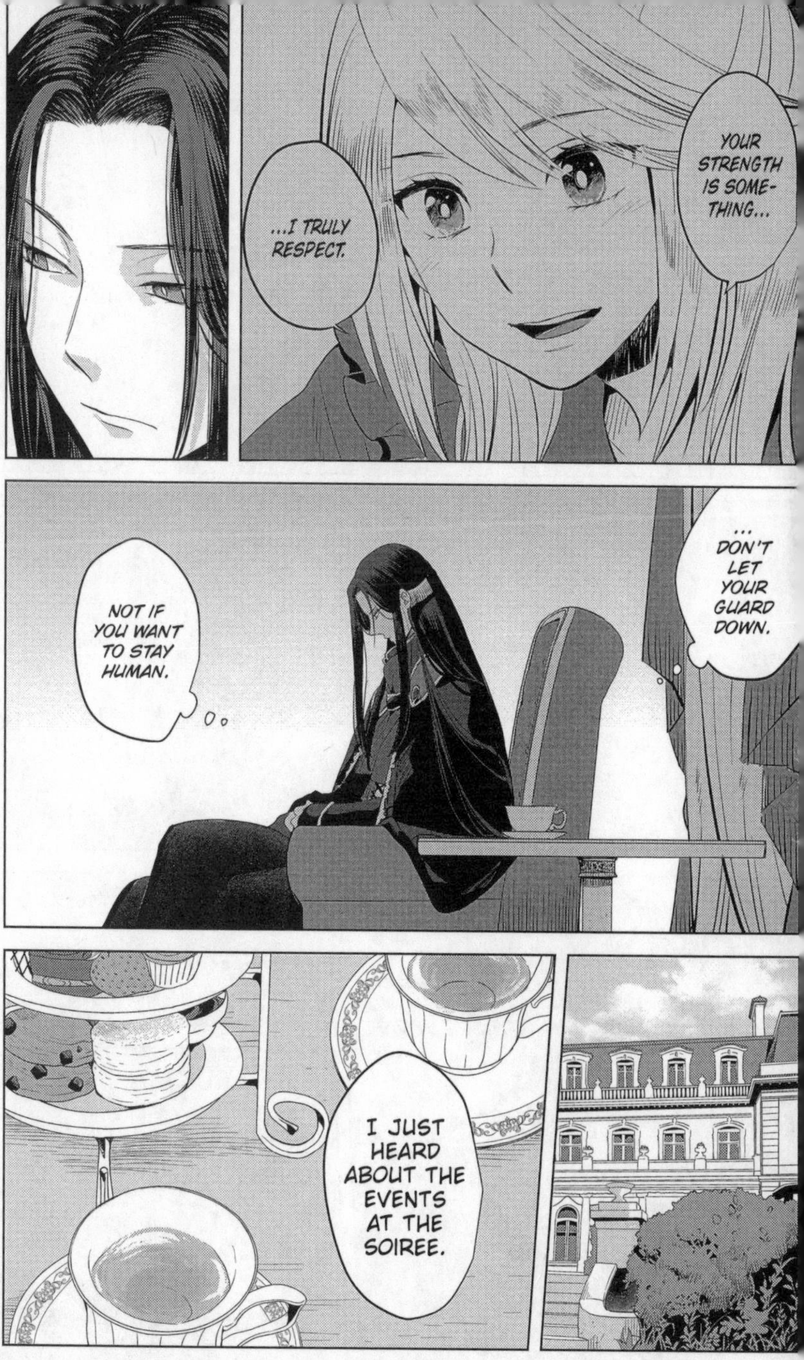
YOUR STRENGTH IS SOMETHING...
...I TRULY RESPECT.
...DON'T LET YOUR GUARD DOWN.
NOT IF YOU WANT TO STAY HUMAN.
I JUST HEARD ABOUT THE EVENTS AT THE SOIREE.

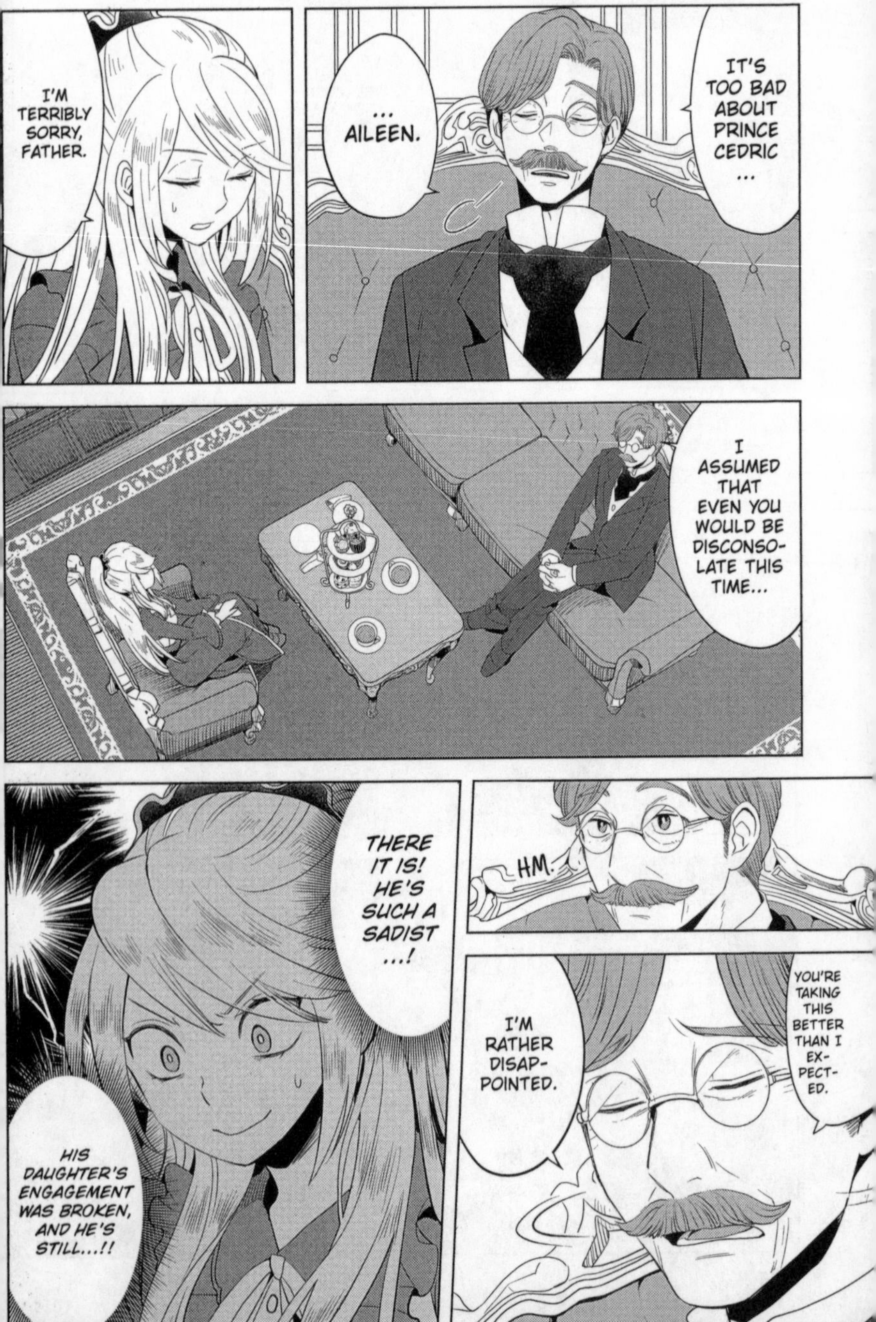
IT'S TOO BAD ABOUT PRINCE CEDRIC ...
... AILEEN.
I'M TERRIBLY SORRY, FATHER.
I ASSUMED THAT EVEN YOU WOULD BE DISCONSOLATE THIS TIME...
HM.
YOU'RE TAKING THIS BETTER THAN I EXPECTED.
I'M RATHER DISAPPOINTED.
THERE IT IS! HE'S SUCH A SADIST ...!
HIS DAUGHTER'S ENGAGEMENT WAS BROKEN, AND HE'S STILL...!!

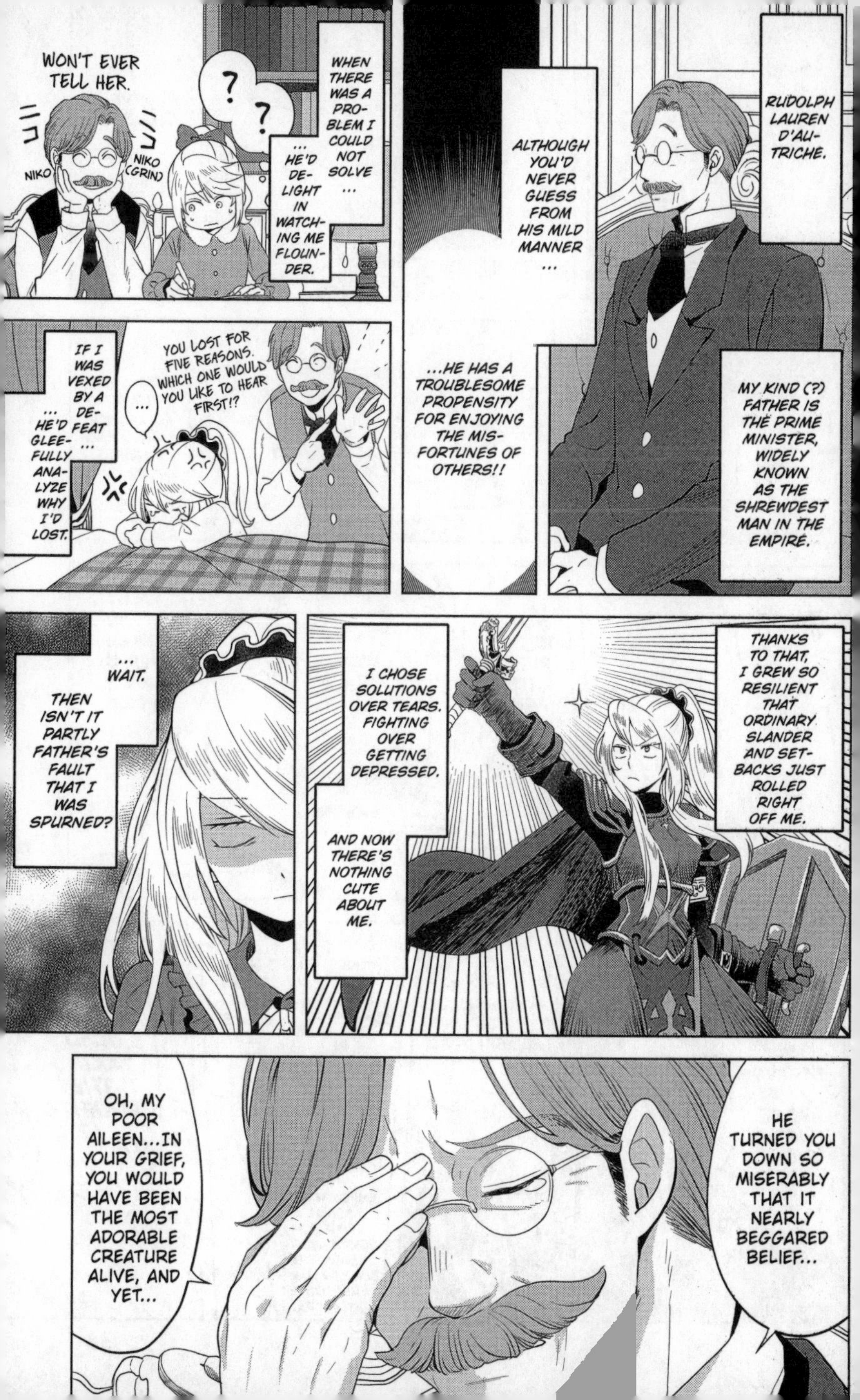
RUDOLPH LAUREN D'AUTRICHE.
MY KIND (?) FATHER IS THE PRIME MINISTER, WIDELY KNOWN AS THE SHREWDEST MAN IN THE EMPIRE.
ALTHOUGH YOU'D NEVER GUESS FROM HIS MILD MANNER...
...HE HAS A TROUBLESOME PROPENSITY FOR ENJOYING THE MISFORTUNES OF OTHERS!!
WHEN THERE WAS A PROBLEM I COULD NOT SOLVE...
...HE'D DELIGHT IN WATCHING ME FLOUNDER.
?
?
WON'T EVER TELL HER.
NIKO (GRIN)
NIKO
YOU LOST FOR FIVE REASONS. WHICH ONE WOULD YOU LIKE TO HEAR FIRST!?
IF I WAS VEXED BY A DEFEAT...
...HE'D GLEEFULLY ANALYZE WHY I'D LOST.
...
THANKS TO THAT, I GREW SO RESILIENT THAT ORDINARY SLANDER AND SETBACKS JUST ROLLED RIGHT OFF ME.
I CHOSE SOLUTIONS OVER TEARS. FIGHTING OVER GETTING DEPRESSED.
AND NOW THERE'S NOTHING CUTE ABOUT ME.
...WAIT.
THEN ISN'T IT PARTLY FATHER'S FAULT THAT I WAS SPURNED?
HE TURNED YOU DOWN SO MISERABLY THAT IT NEARLY BEGGARED BELIEF...
OH, MY POOR AILEEN...IN YOUR GRIEF, YOU WOULD HAVE BEEN THE MOST ADORABLE CREATURE ALIVE, AND YET...

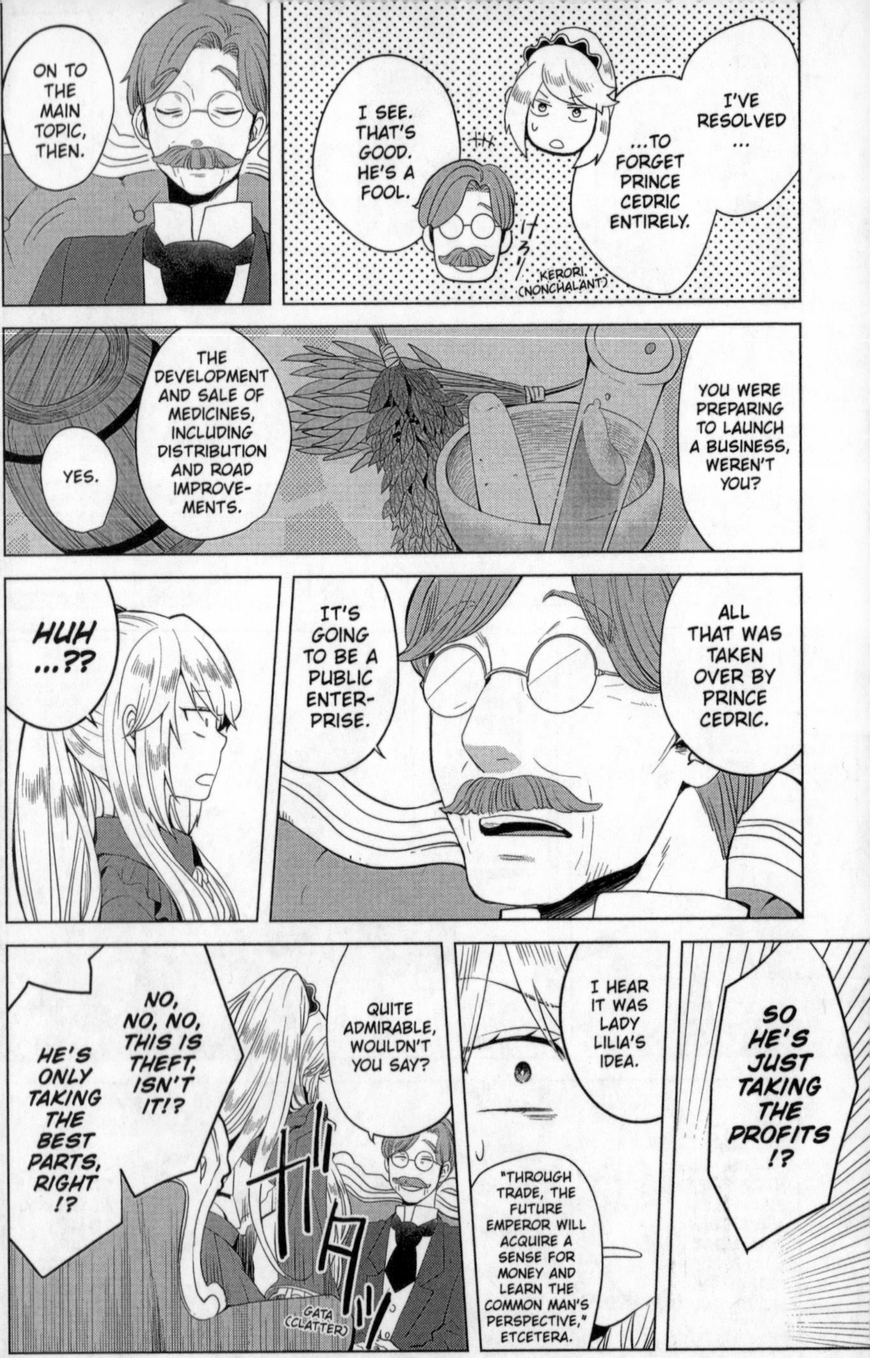
I'VE RESOLVED ...
...TO FORGET PRINCE CEDRIC ENTIRELY.
I SEE. THAT'S GOOD. HE'S A FOOL.
KERORI (NONCHALANT)
ON TO THE MAIN TOPIC, THEN.
YOU WERE PREPARING TO LAUNCH A BUSINESS, WEREN'T YOU?
THE DEVELOPMENT AND SALE OF MEDICINES, INCLUDING DISTRIBUTION AND ROAD IMPROVE-MENTS.
YES.
ALL THAT WAS TAKEN OVER BY PRINCE CEDRIC.
IT'S GOING TO BE A PUBLIC ENTER-PRISE.
HUH ...??
SO HE'S JUST TAKING THE PROFITS !?
I HEAR IT WAS LADY LILIA'S IDEA.
"THROUGH TRADE, THE FUTURE EMPEROR WILL ACQUIRE A SENSE FOR MONEY AND LEARN THE COMMON MAN'S PERSPECTIVE," ETCETERA.
QUITE ADMIRABLE, WOULDN'T YOU SAY?
NO, NO, NO, THIS IS THEFT, ISN'T IT!?
HE'S ONLY TAKING THE BEST PARTS, RIGHT !?
GATA (CLATTER)

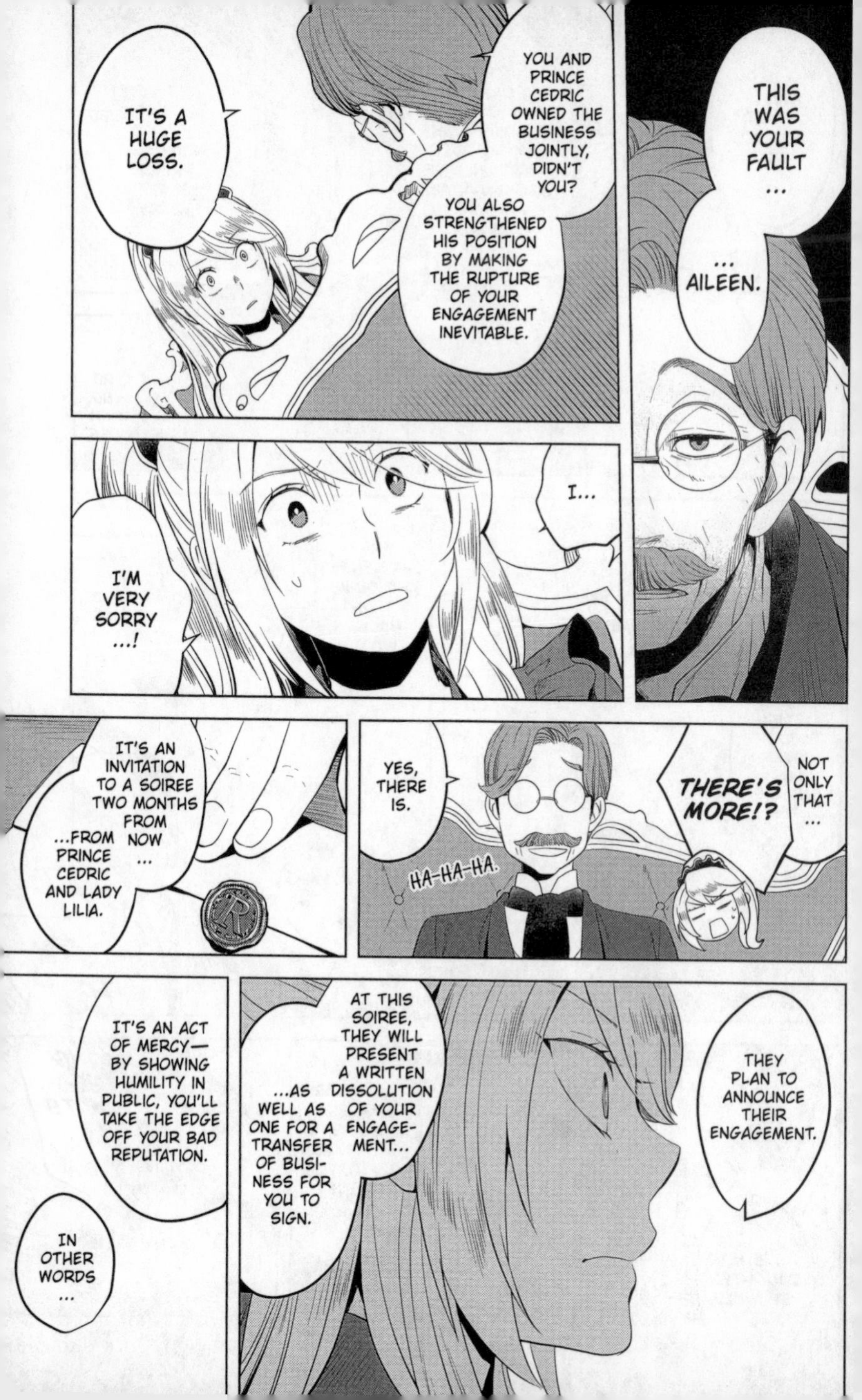
THIS WAS YOUR FAULT...
...AILEEN.
YOU AND PRINCE CEDRIC OWNED THE BUSINESS JOINTLY, DIDN'T YOU?
YOU ALSO STRENGTHENED HIS POSITION BY MAKING THE RUPTURE OF YOUR ENGAGEMENT INEVITABLE.
IT'S A HUGE LOSS.
I...
I'M VERY SORRY...!
NOT ONLY THAT...
THERE'S MORE!?
YES, THERE IS.
HA-HA-HA.
IT'S AN INVITATION TO A SOIREE TWO MONTHS FROM NOW...
...FROM PRINCE CEDRIC AND LADY LILIA.
THEY PLAN TO ANNOUNCE THEIR ENGAGEMENT.
AT THIS SOIREE, THEY WILL PRESENT A WRITTEN DISSOLUTION OF YOUR ENGAGEMENT...
...AS WELL AS ONE FOR A TRANSFER OF BUSINESS FOR YOU TO SIGN.
IT'S AN ACT OF MERCY—BY SHOWING HUMILITY IN PUBLIC, YOU'LL TAKE THE EDGE OFF YOUR BAD REPUTATION.
IN OTHER WORDS...

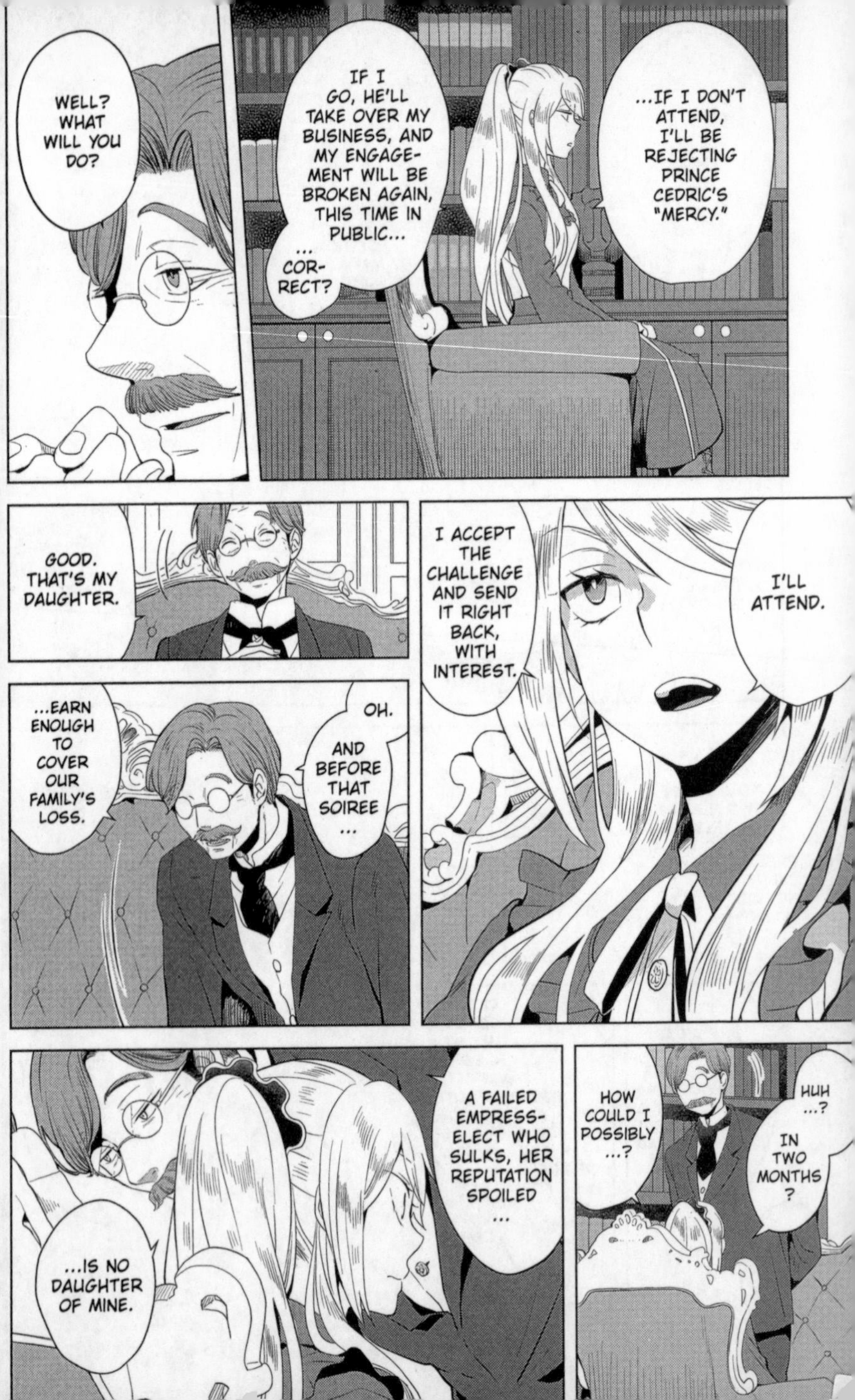
...IF I DON'T ATTEND, I'LL BE REJECTING PRINCE CEDRIC'S "MERCY."
IF I GO, HE'LL TAKE OVER MY BUSINESS, AND MY ENGAGE-MENT WILL BE BROKEN AGAIN, THIS TIME IN PUBLIC...
...CORRECT?
WELL? WHAT WILL YOU DO?
I'LL ATTEND.
I ACCEPT THE CHALLENGE AND SEND IT RIGHT BACK, WITH INTEREST.
GOOD. THAT'S MY DAUGHTER.
OH.
AND BEFORE THAT SOIREE...
...EARN ENOUGH TO COVER OUR FAMILY'S LOSS.
HUH...?
IN TWO MONTHS?
HOW COULD I POSSIBLY...?
A FAILED EMPRESS-ELECT WHO SULKS, HER REPUTATION SPOILED...
...IS NO DAUGHTER OF MINE.

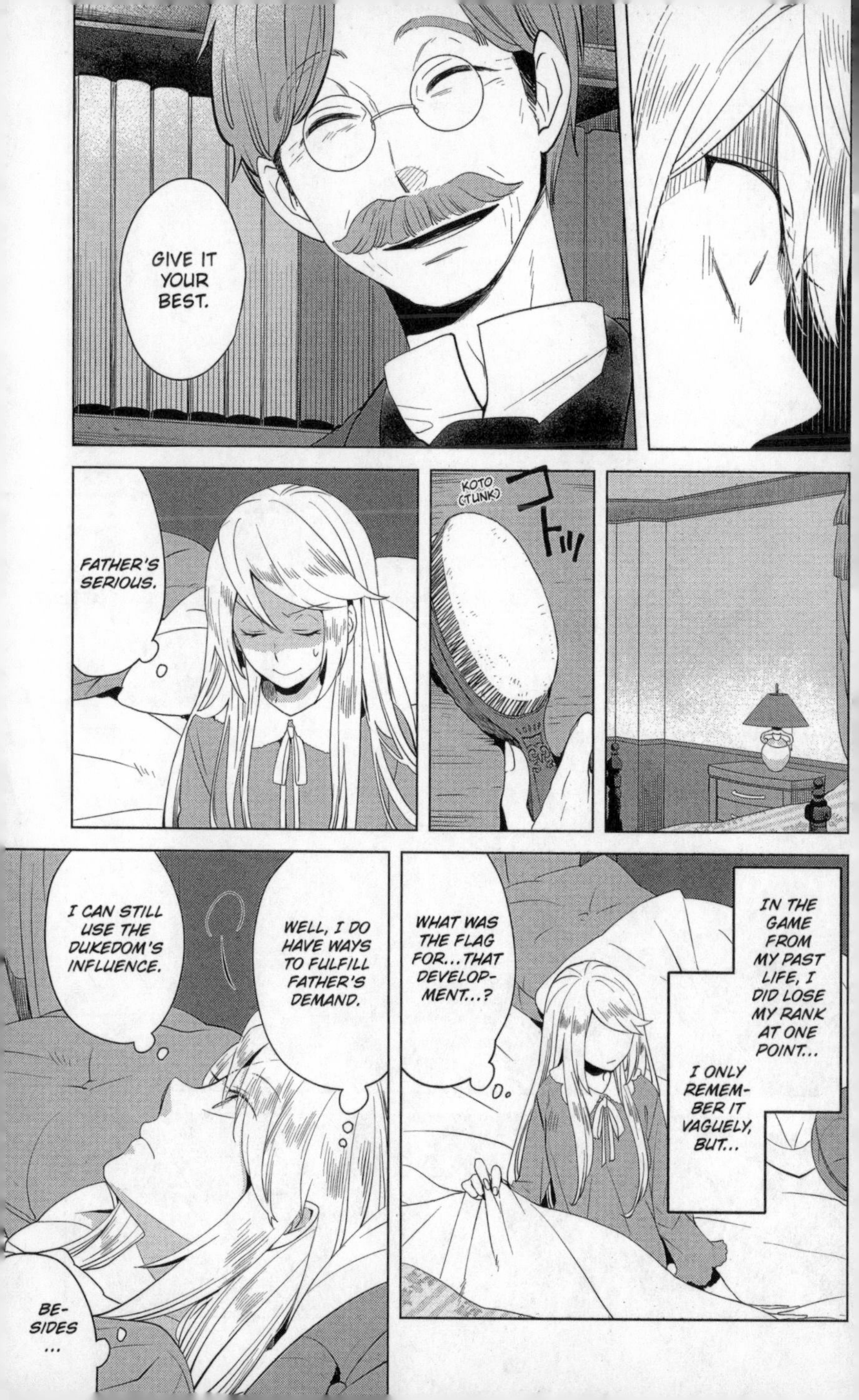
GIVE IT YOUR BEST.
KOTO (TUNK)
FATHER'S SERIOUS.
IN THE GAME FROM MY PAST LIFE, I DID LOSE MY RANK AT ONE POINT...
I ONLY REMEMBER IT VAGUELY, BUT...
WHAT WAS THE FLAG FOR...THAT DEVELOPMENT...?
WELL, I DO HAVE WAYS TO FULFILL FATHER'S DEMAND.
I CAN STILL USE THE DUKEDOM'S INFLUENCE.
BESIDES...

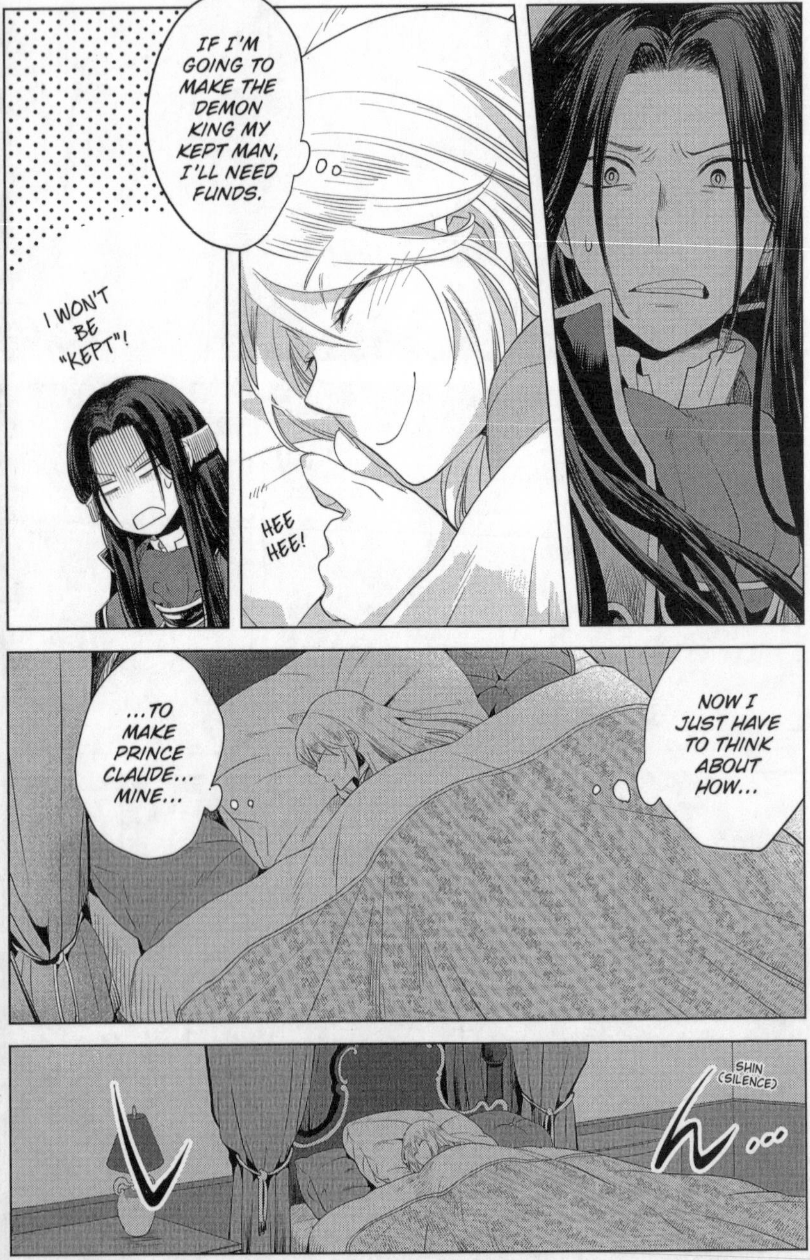
IF I'M GOING TO MAKE THE DEMON KING MY KEPT MAN, I'LL NEED FUNDS.
HEE HEE!
I WON'T BE "KEPT"!
NOW I JUST HAVE TO THINK ABOUT HOW...
...TO MAKE PRINCE CLAUDE... MINE...
SHIN (SILENCE)

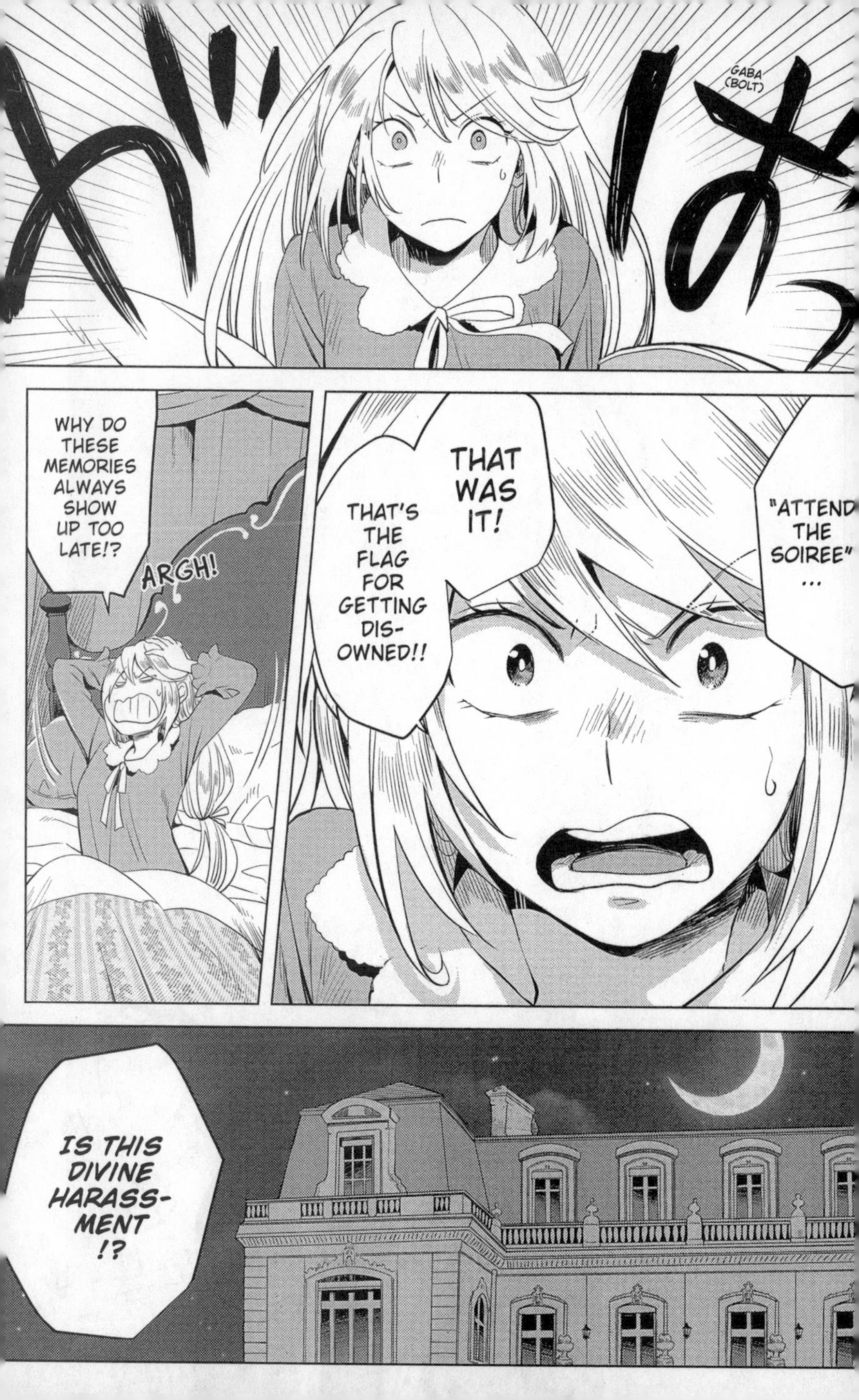
GABA (BOLT)
"ATTEND THE SOIREE"...
THAT WAS IT!
THAT'S THE FLAG FOR GETTING DIS-OWNED!!
WHY DO THESE MEMORIES ALWAYS SHOW UP TOO LATE!?
ARGH!
IS THIS DIVINE HARASS-MENT!?

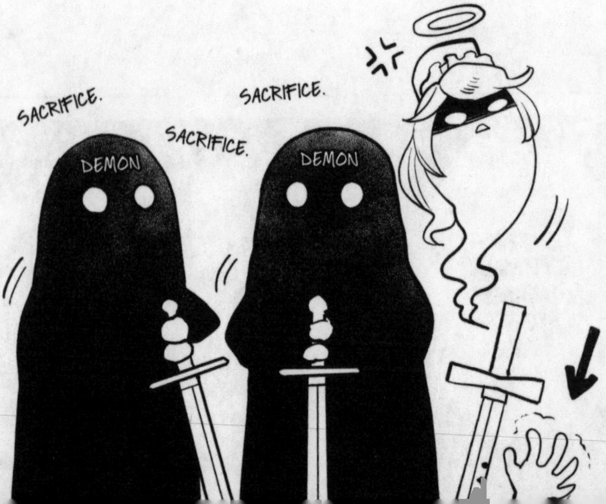
SACRIFICE.
SACRIFICE.
SACRIFICE.
DEMON
DEMON

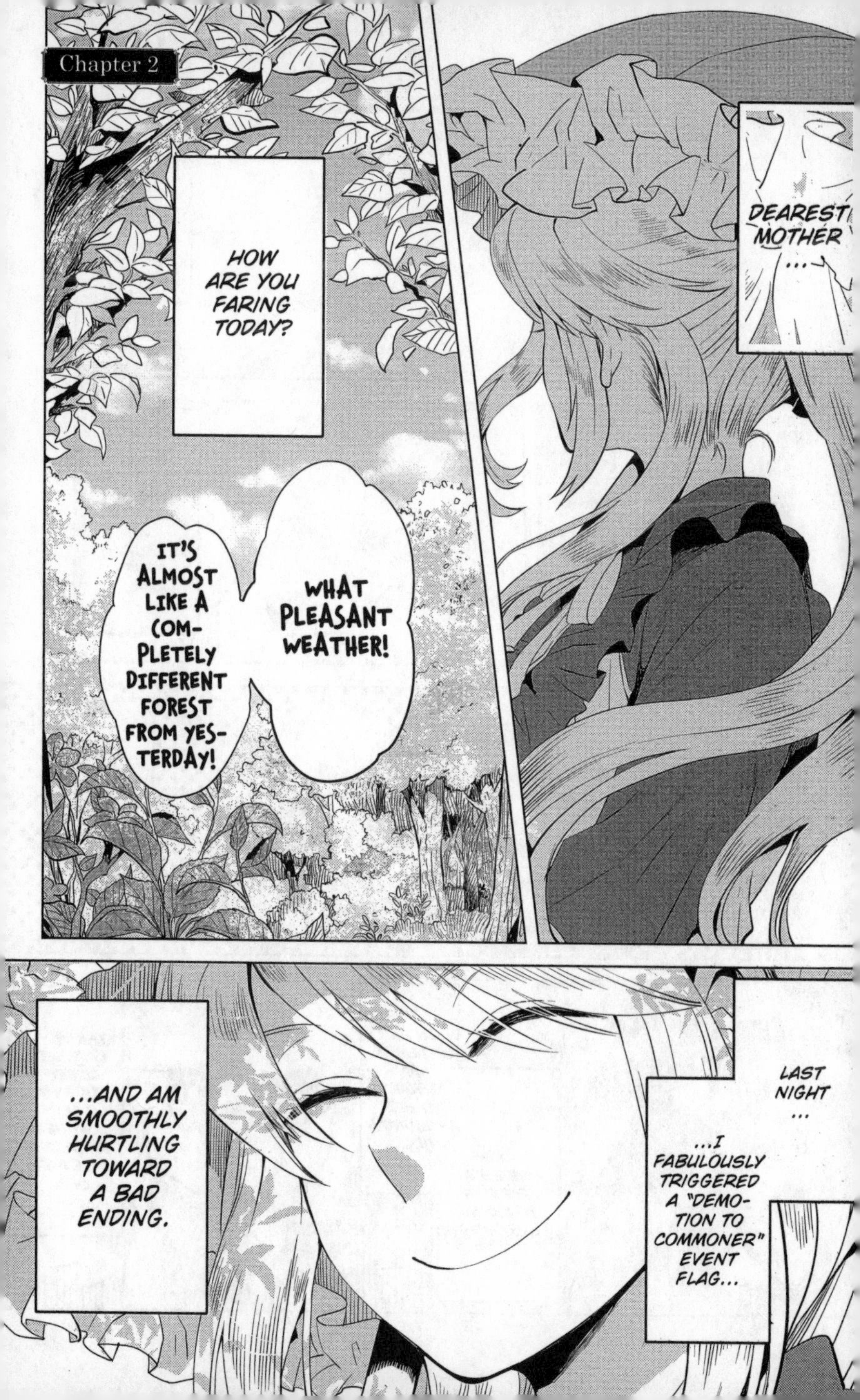
Chapter 2
DEAREST MOTHER ...
HOW ARE YOU FARING TODAY?
WHAT PLEASANT WEATHER!
IT'S ALMOST LIKE A COM-PLETELY DIFFERENT FOREST FROM YES-TERDAY!
LAST NIGHT ...
...I FABULOUSLY TRIGGERED A "DEMO-TION TO COMMONER" EVENT FLAG...
...AND AM SMOOTHLY HURTLING TOWARD A BAD ENDING.

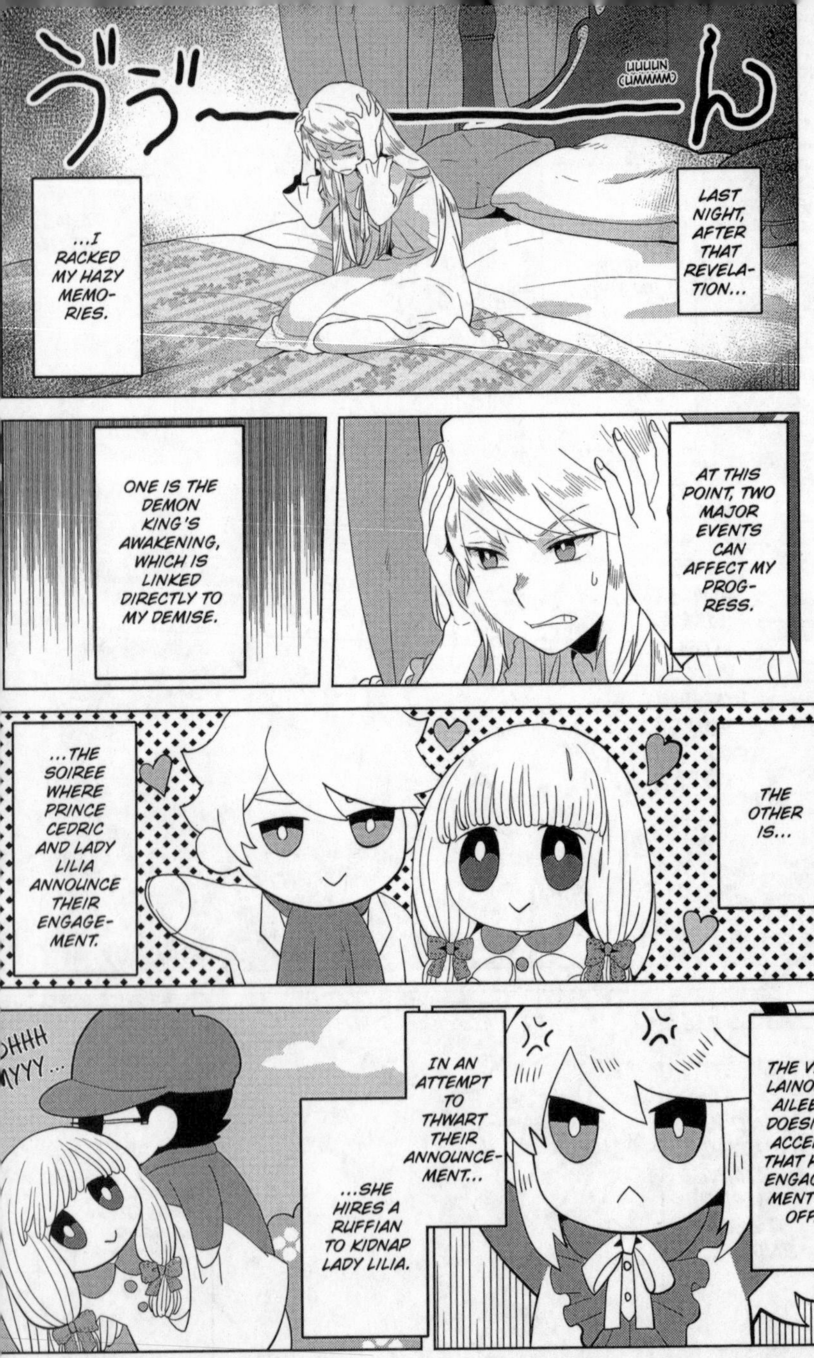
うう゛ーーーん
UUUUN (UMMMMM)
LAST NIGHT, AFTER THAT REVELATION...
...I RACKED MY HAZY MEMORIES.
AT THIS POINT, TWO MAJOR EVENTS CAN AFFECT MY PROGRESS.
ONE IS THE DEMON KING'S AWAKENING, WHICH IS LINKED DIRECTLY TO MY DEMISE.
THE OTHER IS...
...THE SOIREE WHERE PRINCE CEDRIC AND LADY LILIA ANNOUNCE THEIR ENGAGEMENT.
THE VILLAINOUS AILEEN DOESN'T ACCEPT THAT HER ENGAGEMENT IS OFF.
IN AN ATTEMPT TO THWART THEIR ANNOUNCEMENT...
...SHE HIRES A RUFFIAN TO KIDNAP LADY LILIA.
OHHH MYYY...

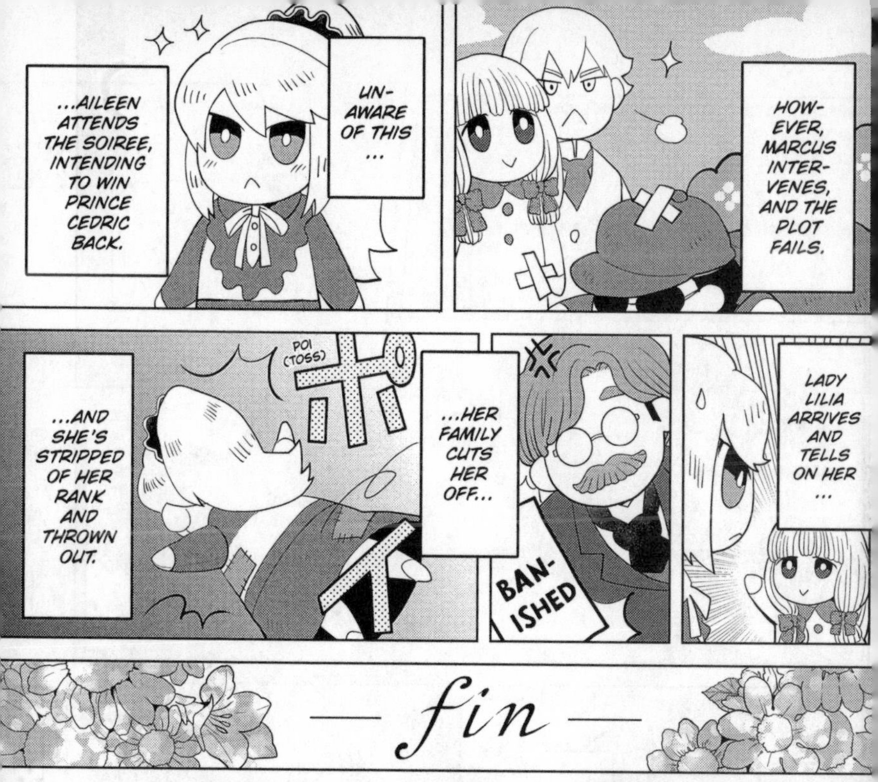
HOW-EVER, MARCUS INTER-VENES, AND THE PLOT FAILS.
UN-AWARE OF THIS ...
...AILEEN ATTENDS THE SOIREE, INTENDING TO WIN PRINCE CEDRIC BACK.
LADY LILIA ARRIVES AND TELLS ON HER ...
...HER FAMILY CUTS HER OFF...
BAN-ISHED
ポイ
POI (TOSS)
...AND SHE'S STRIPPED OF HER RANK AND THROWN OUT.
— fin —
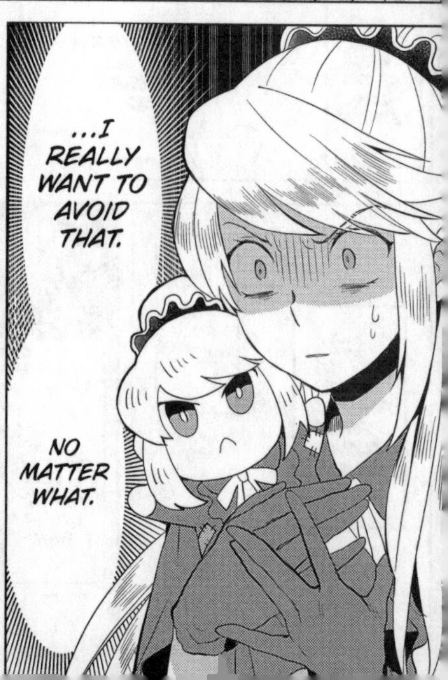
...I REALLY WANT TO AVOID THAT.
NO MATTER WHAT.
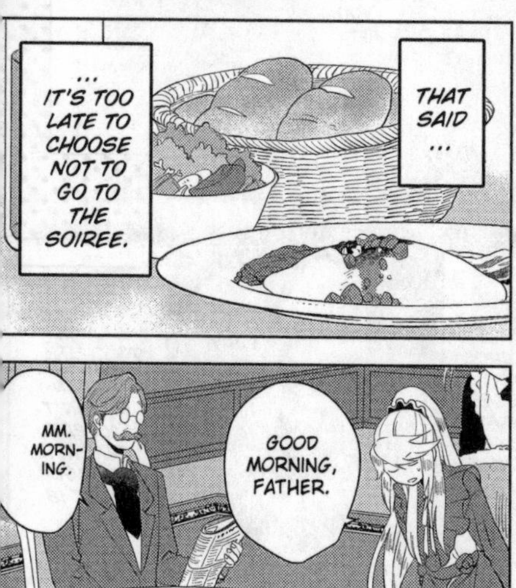
THAT SAID ...
... IT'S TOO LATE TO CHOOSE NOT TO GO TO THE SOIREE.
GOOD MORNING, FATHER.
MM. MORN-ING.

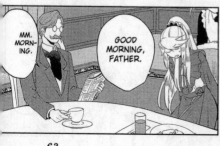

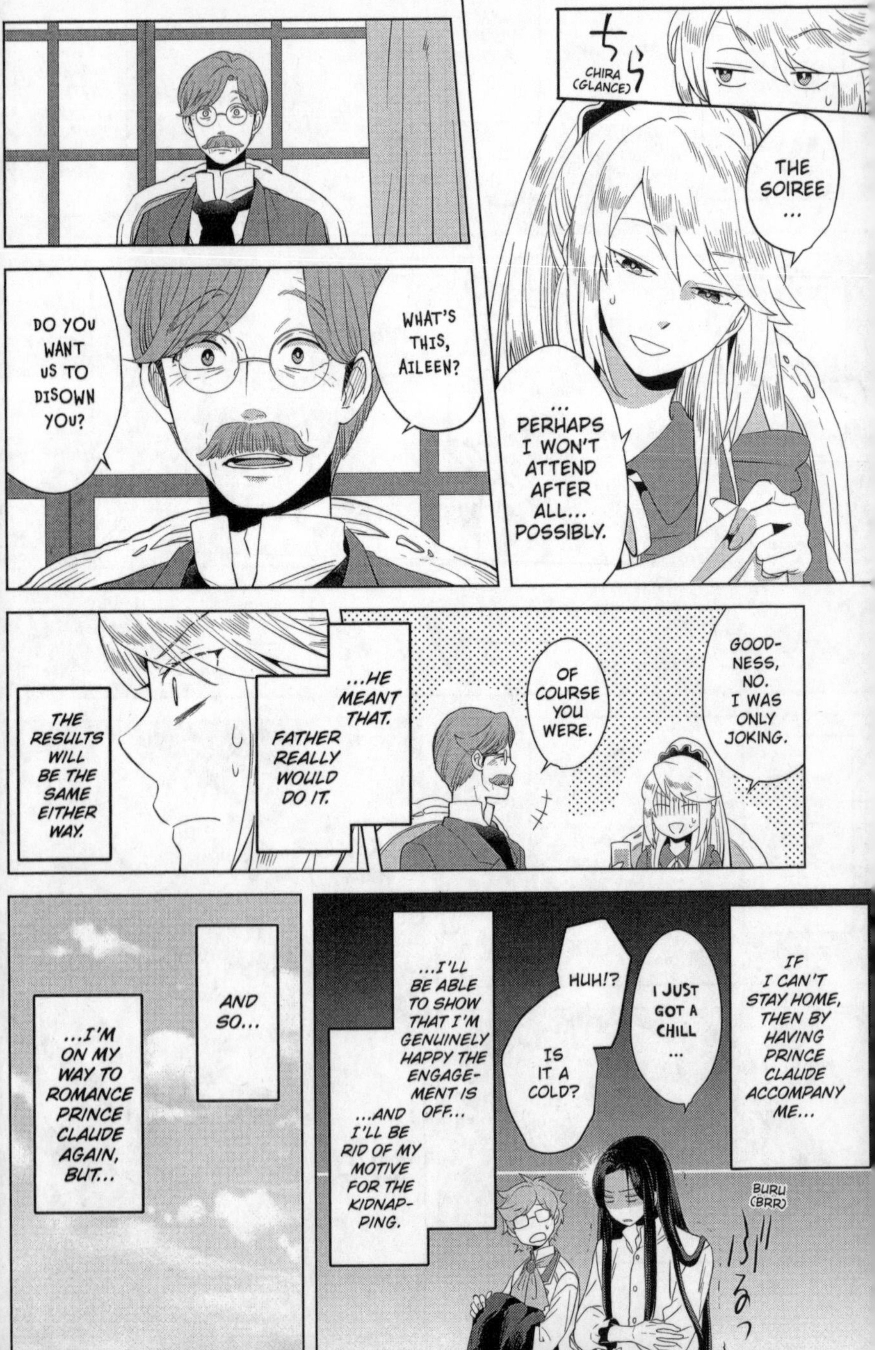
CHIRA (GLANCE)
THE SOIREE...
...PERHAPS I WON'T ATTEND AFTER ALL... POSSIBLY.
WHAT'S THIS, AILEEN?
DO YOU WANT US TO DISOWN YOU?
GOODNESS, NO. I WAS ONLY JOKING.
OF COURSE YOU WERE.
...HE MEANT THAT.
FATHER REALLY WOULD DO IT.
THE RESULTS WILL BE THE SAME EITHER WAY.
IF I CAN'T STAY HOME, THEN BY HAVING PRINCE CLAUDE ACCOMPANY ME...
I JUST GOT A CHILL...
HUH!?
IS IT A COLD?
BURU (BRR)
...I'LL BE ABLE TO SHOW THAT I'M GENUINELY HAPPY THE ENGAGEMENT IS OFF...
...AND I'LL BE RID OF MY MOTIVE FOR THE KIDNAPPING.
AND SO...
...I'M ON MY WAY TO ROMANCE PRINCE CLAUDE AGAIN, BUT...

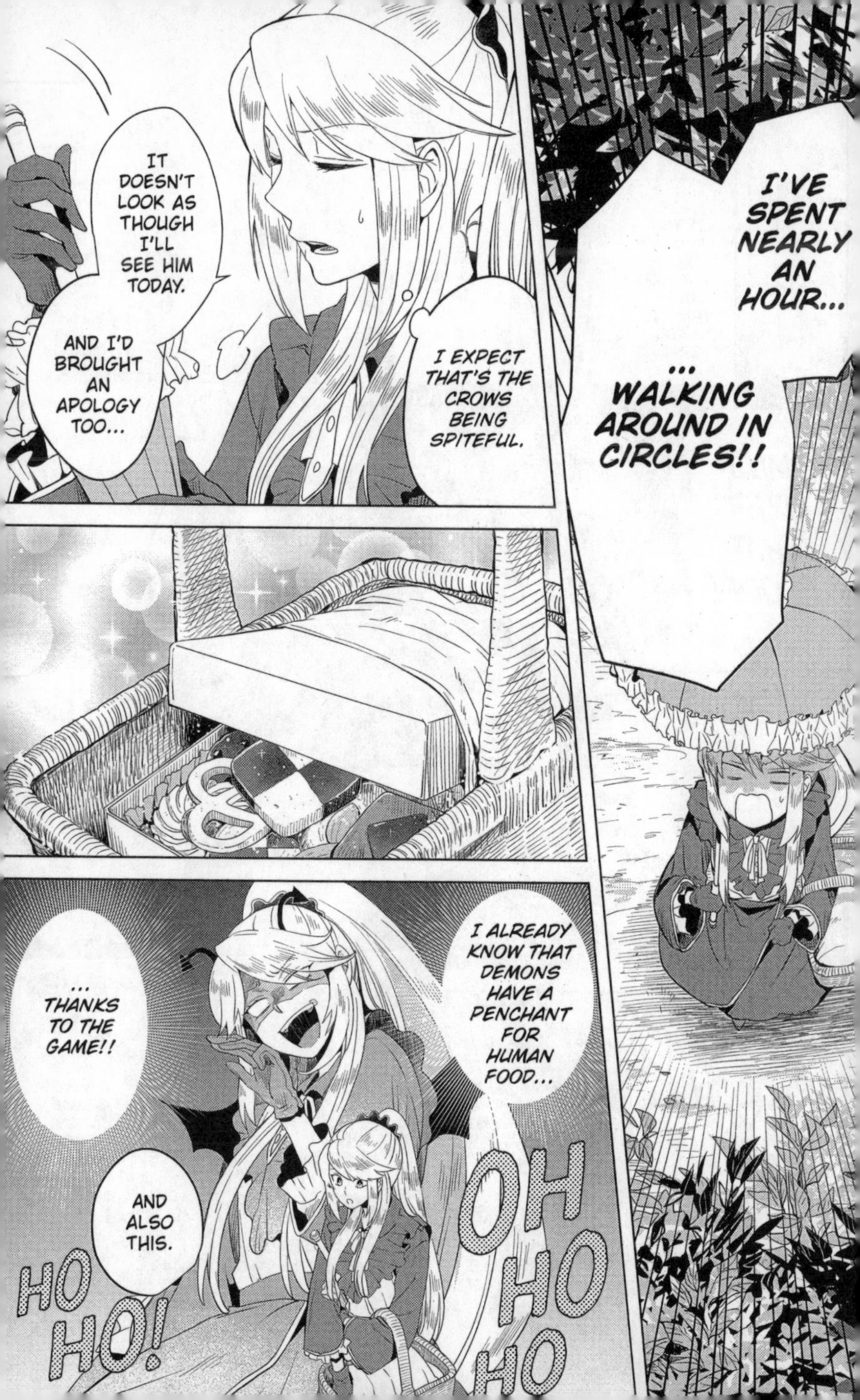
I'VE SPENT NEARLY AN HOUR...
... WALKING AROUND IN CIRCLES!!
I EXPECT THAT'S THE CROWS BEING SPITEFUL.
IT DOESN'T LOOK AS THOUGH I'LL SEE HIM TODAY.
AND I'D BROUGHT AN APOLOGY TOO...
I ALREADY KNOW THAT DEMONS HAVE A PENCHANT FOR HUMAN FOOD...
... THANKS TO THE GAME!!
OH HO HO HO HO
AND ALSO THIS.
HO HO!

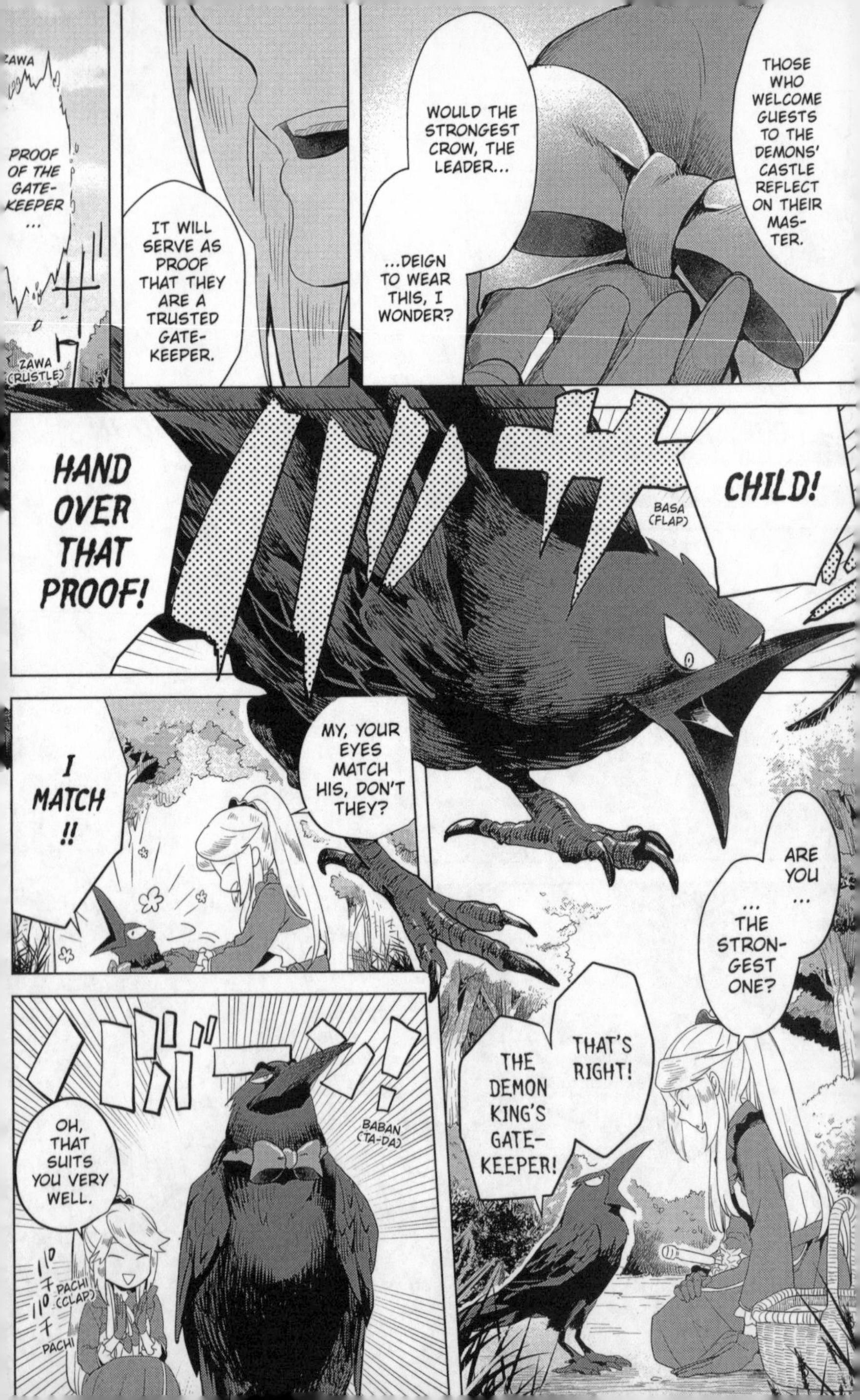
THOSE WHO WELCOME GUESTS TO THE DEMONS' CASTLE REFLECT ON THEIR MASTER.
WOULD THE STRONGEST CROW, THE LEADER...
...DEIGN TO WEAR THIS, I WONDER?
IT WILL SERVE AS PROOF THAT THEY ARE A TRUSTED GATE-KEEPER.
ZAWA
PROOF OF THE GATE-KEEPER...
ZAWA (RUSTLE)
CHILD!
BASA (FLAP)
HAND OVER THAT PROOF!
ARE YOU... THE STRONGEST ONE?
THAT'S RIGHT!
THE DEMON KING'S GATE-KEEPER!
MY, YOUR EYES MATCH HIS, DON'T THEY?
I MATCH!!
BABAN (TA-DA)
OH, THAT SUITS YOU VERY WELL.
PACHI (CLAP)
PACHI

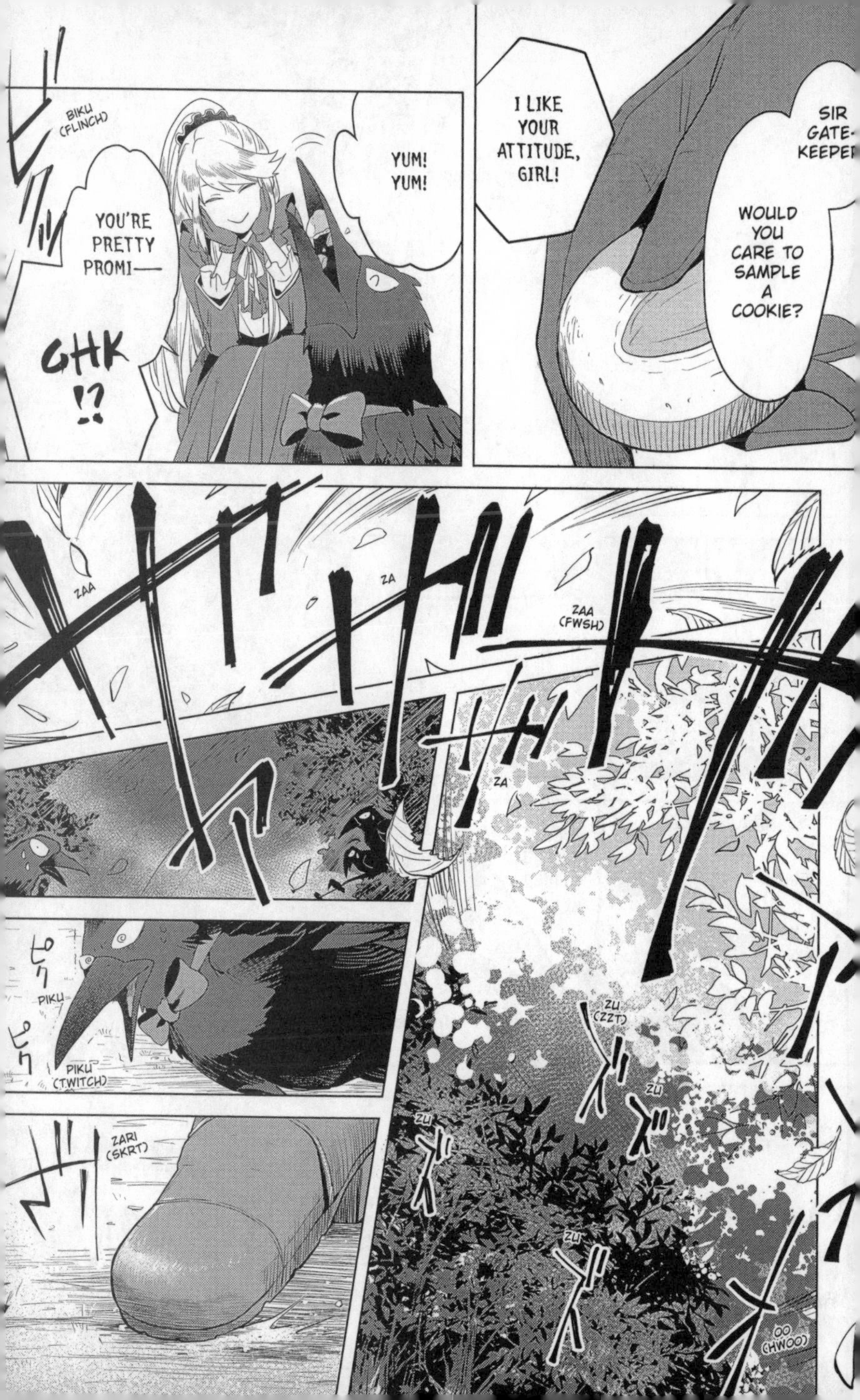
SIR GATE-KEEPER
WOULD YOU CARE TO SAMPLE A COOKIE?
I LIKE YOUR ATTITUDE, GIRL!
YUM! YUM!
BIKU (FLINCH)
YOU'RE PRETTY PROMI—
GHK !?
ZAA (FWSH)
ZA
ZAA
ZA
ZU (ZZT)
ZU
ZU
ZU
OO (HWOO)
PIKU
PIKU (TWITCH)
ZARI (SKRT)

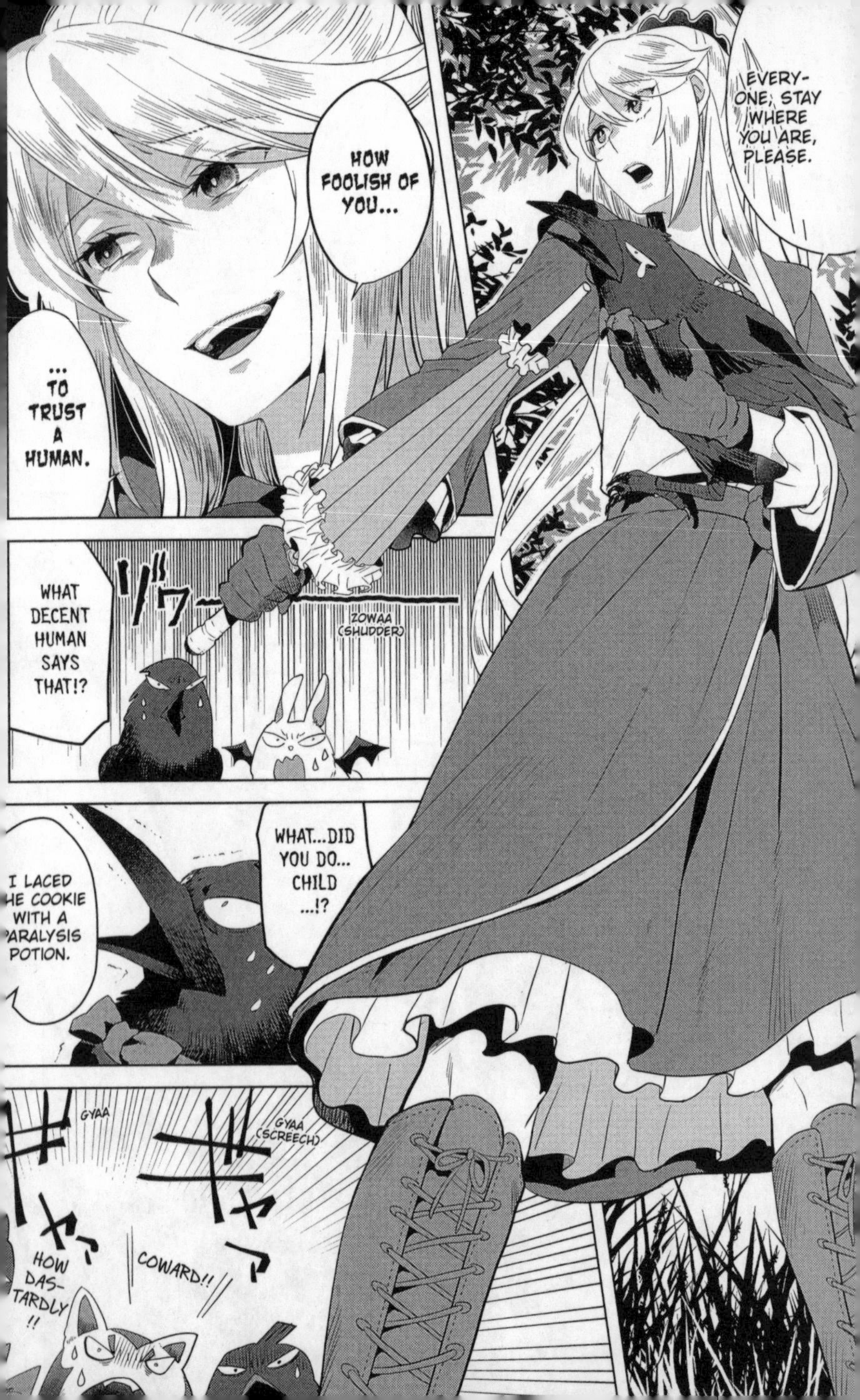
EVERY-ONE, STAY WHERE YOU ARE, PLEASE.
HOW FOOLISH OF YOU...
...TO TRUST A HUMAN.
ZOWAA (SHUDDER)
WHAT DECENT HUMAN SAYS THAT!?
WHAT...DID YOU DO... CHILD ...!?
I LACED HE COOKIE WITH A ARALYSIS POTION.
GYAA (SCREECH)
GYAA
COWARD!!
HOW DAS-TARDLY!!

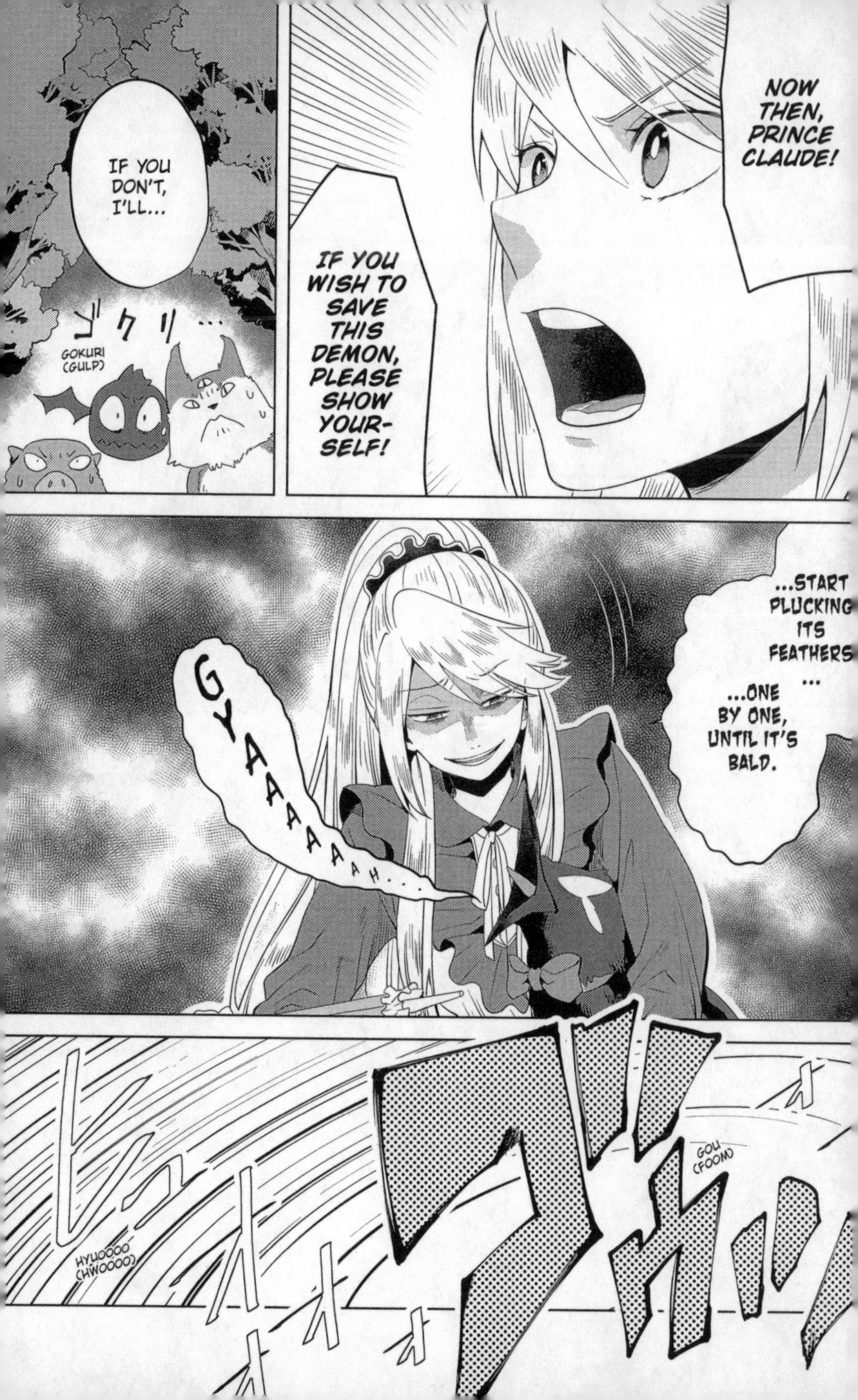
NOW THEN, PRINCE CLAUDE!
IF YOU WISH TO SAVE THIS DEMON, PLEASE SHOW YOURSELF!
IF YOU DON'T, I'LL...
ゴクリ…
GOKURI (GULP)
...START PLUCKING ITS FEATHERS...
...ONE BY ONE, UNTIL IT'S BALD.
GYAAAAAAH...
GOU (FOOM)
HYUOOOO (HWOOOO)

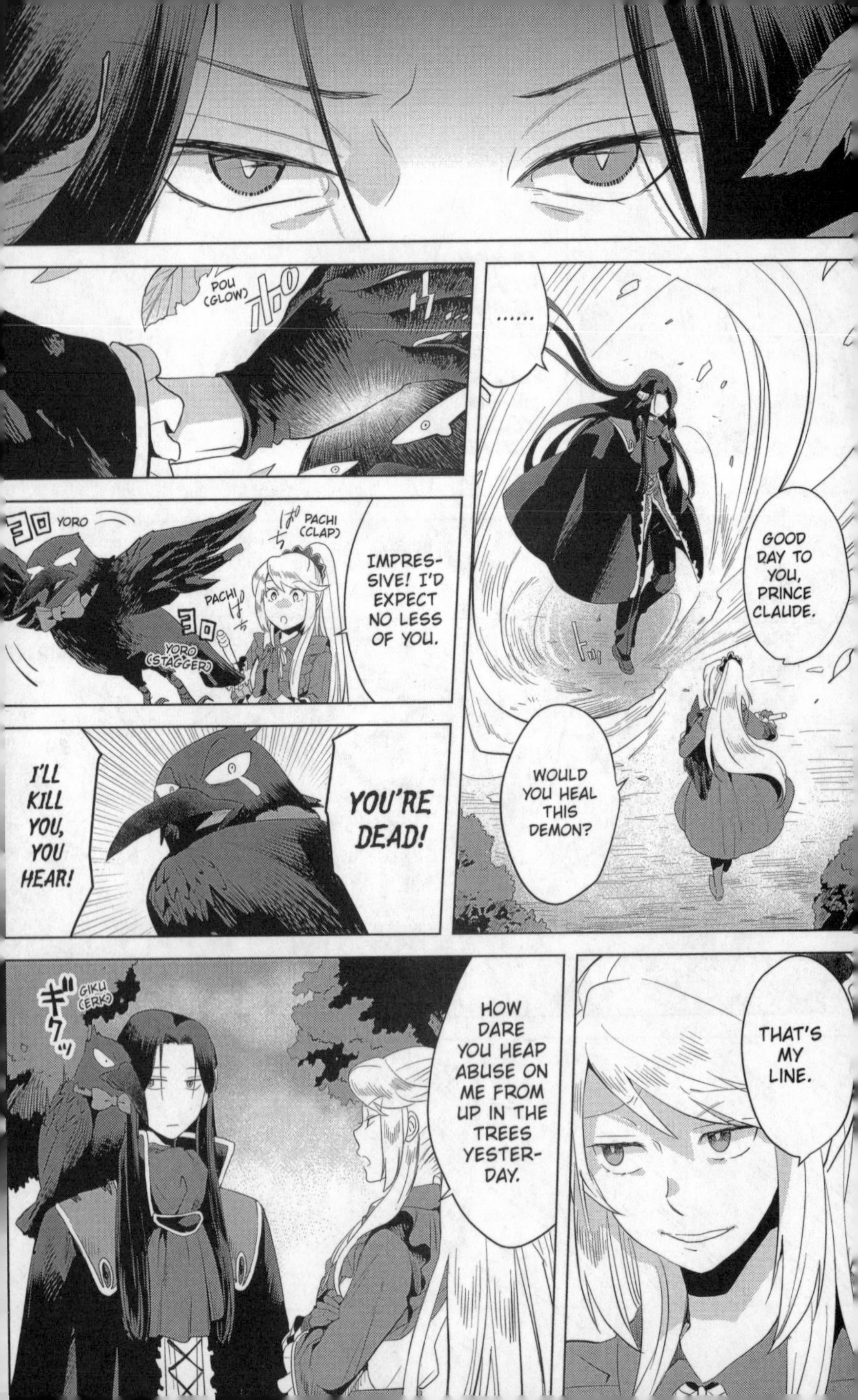

......
GOOD DAY TO YOU, PRINCE CLAUDE.
WOULD YOU HEAL THIS DEMON?
POU (GLOW)
PACHI (CLAP)
IMPRESSIVE! I'D EXPECT NO LESS OF YOU.
PACHI
YORO
YORO (STAGGER)
YOU'RE DEAD!
I'LL KILL YOU, YOU HEAR!
THAT'S MY LINE.
HOW DARE YOU HEAP ABUSE ON ME FROM UP IN THE TREES YESTERDAY.
GIKU (ERK)

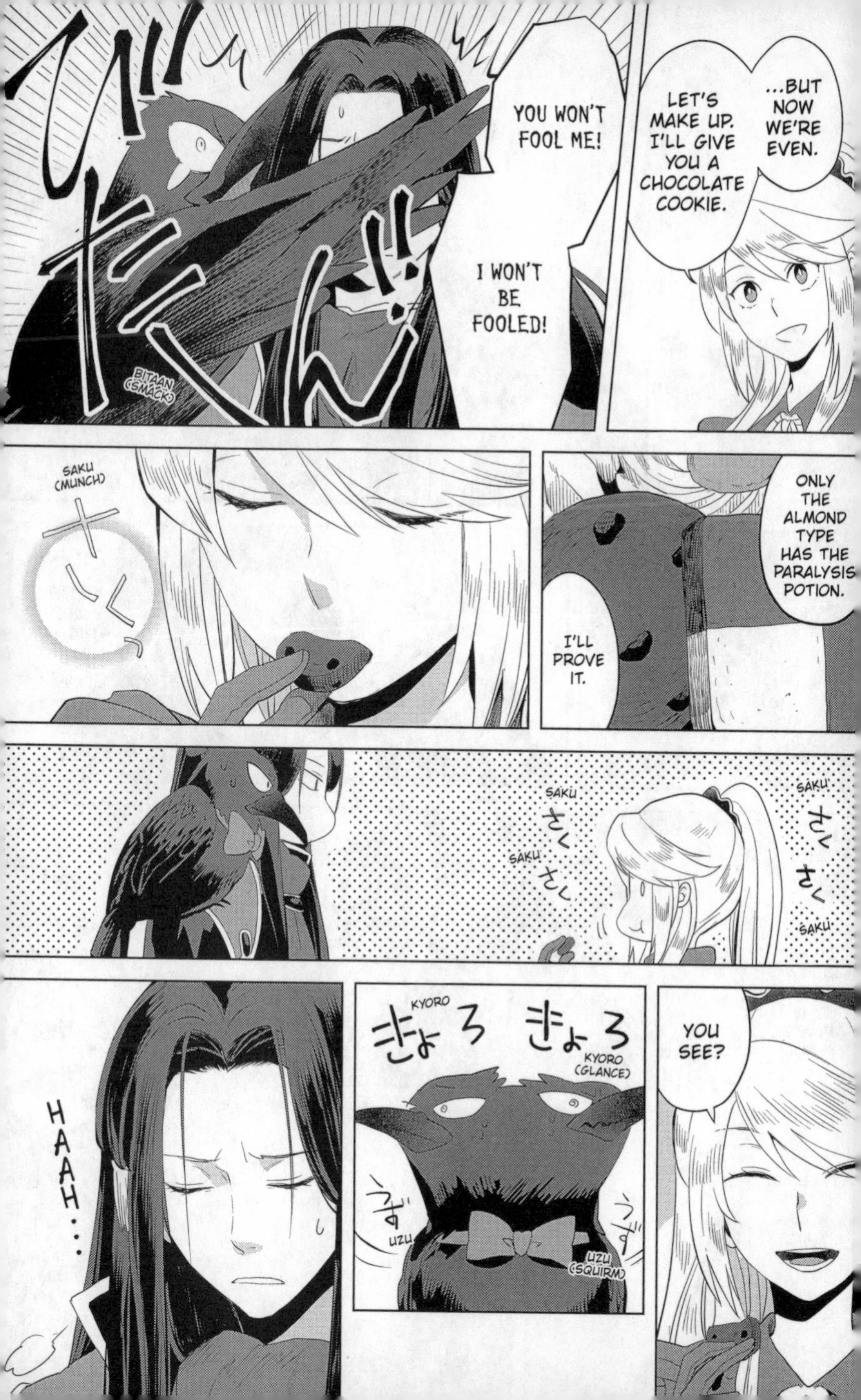
...BUT NOW WE'RE EVEN.
LET'S MAKE UP. I'LL GIVE YOU A CHOCOLATE COOKIE.
YOU WON'T FOOL ME!
I WON'T BE FOOLED!
BITAAN (SMACK)
ONLY THE ALMOND TYPE HAS THE PARALYSIS POTION.
I'LL PROVE IT.
SAKU (MUNCH)
SAKU
SAKU
SAKU
SAKU
YOU SEE?
KYORO
KYORO (GLANCE)
UZU
UZU (SQUIRM)
HAAH...

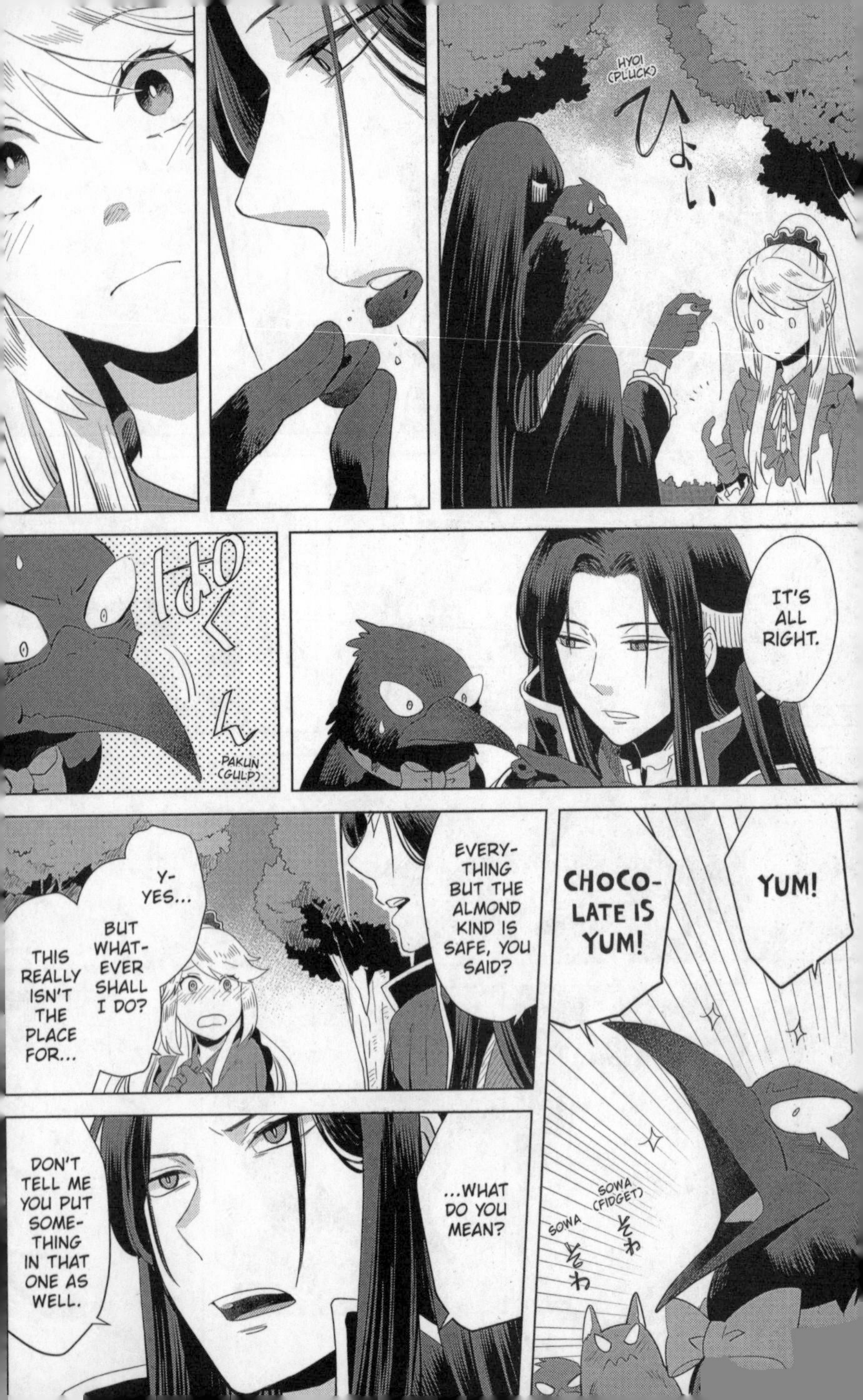
HYOI (PLUCK)
IT'S ALL RIGHT.
PAKUN (GULP)
YUM!
CHOCO-LATE IS YUM!
SOWA (FIDGET)
SOWA
EVERY-THING BUT THE ALMOND KIND IS SAFE, YOU SAID?
Y-YES...
BUT WHAT-EVER SHALL I DO?
THIS REALLY ISN'T THE PLACE FOR...
...WHAT DO YOU MEAN?
DON'T TELL ME YOU PUT SOME-THING IN THAT ONE AS WELL.

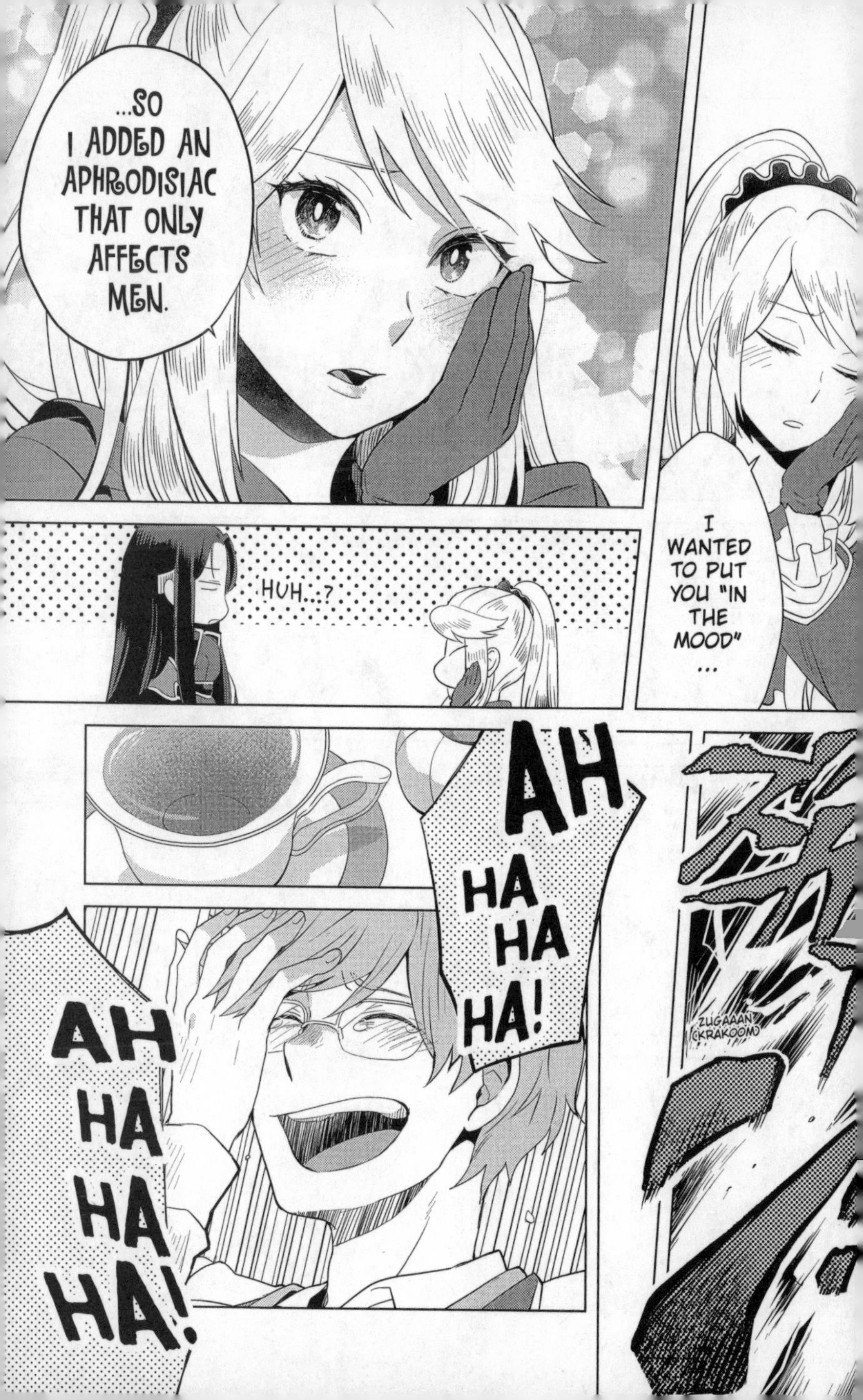
I WANTED TO PUT YOU "IN THE MOOD"...
...SO I ADDED AN APHRODISIAC THAT ONLY AFFECTS MEN.
HUH...?
ZUGAAAN (KRAKOOM)
AH HA HA HA!
AH HA HA HA HA!

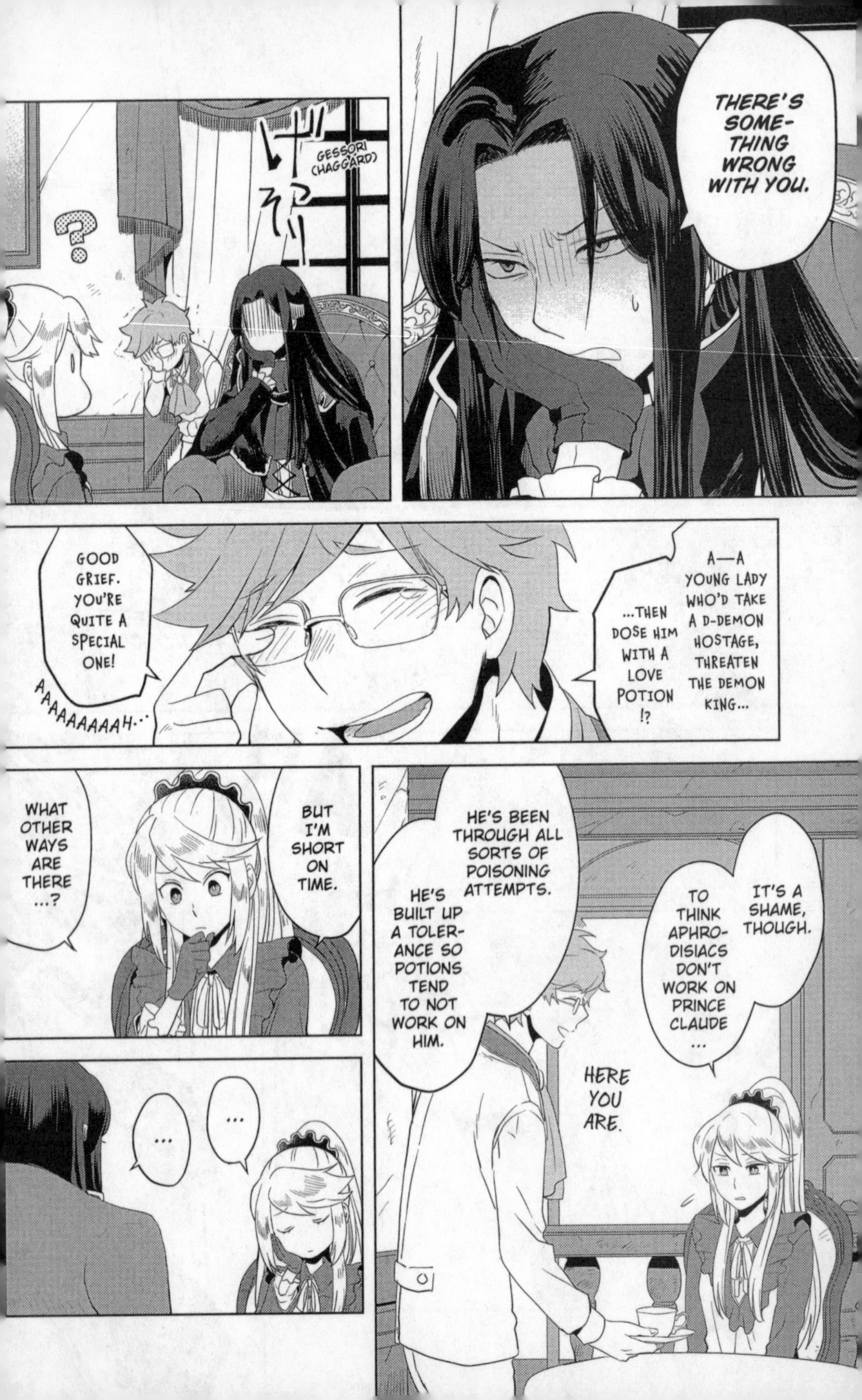
THERE'S SOME-THING WRONG WITH YOU.
GESSORI (HAGGARD)
?
A—A YOUNG LADY WHO'D TAKE A D-DEMON HOSTAGE, THREATEN THE DEMON KING...
...THEN DOSE HIM WITH A LOVE POTION!?
GOOD GRIEF. YOU'RE QUITE A SPECIAL ONE!
AAAAAAAAAH...
IT'S A SHAME, THOUGH.
TO THINK APHRO-DISIACS DON'T WORK ON PRINCE CLAUDE...
HERE YOU ARE.
HE'S BEEN THROUGH ALL SORTS OF POISONING ATTEMPTS.
HE'S BUILT UP A TOLER-ANCE SO POTIONS TEND TO NOT WORK ON HIM.
BUT I'M SHORT ON TIME.
WHAT OTHER WAYS ARE THERE...?
...
...

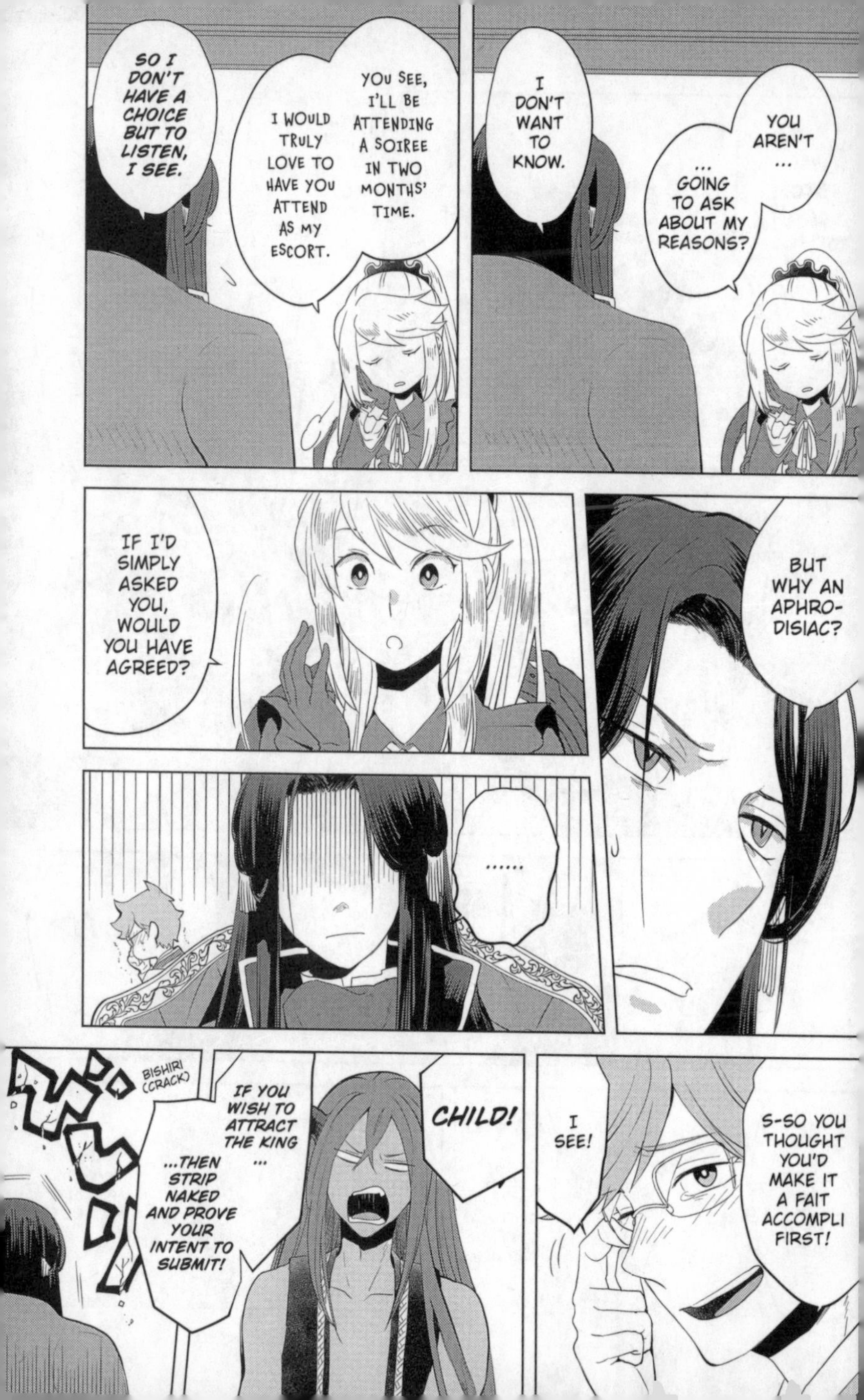
YOU AREN'T ...
... GOING TO ASK ABOUT MY REASONS?
I DON'T WANT TO KNOW.
YOU SEE, I'LL BE ATTENDING A SOIREE IN TWO MONTHS' TIME.
I WOULD TRULY LOVE TO HAVE YOU ATTEND AS MY ESCORT.
SO I DON'T HAVE A CHOICE BUT TO LISTEN, I SEE.
BUT WHY AN APHRO-DISIAC?
IF I'D SIMPLY ASKED YOU, WOULD YOU HAVE AGREED?
......
S-SO YOU THOUGHT YOU'D MAKE IT A FAIT ACCOMPLI FIRST!
I SEE!
CHILD!
IF YOU WISH TO ATTRACT THE KING ...
...THEN STRIP NAKED AND PROVE YOUR INTENT TO SUBMIT!
BISHIRI (CRACK)

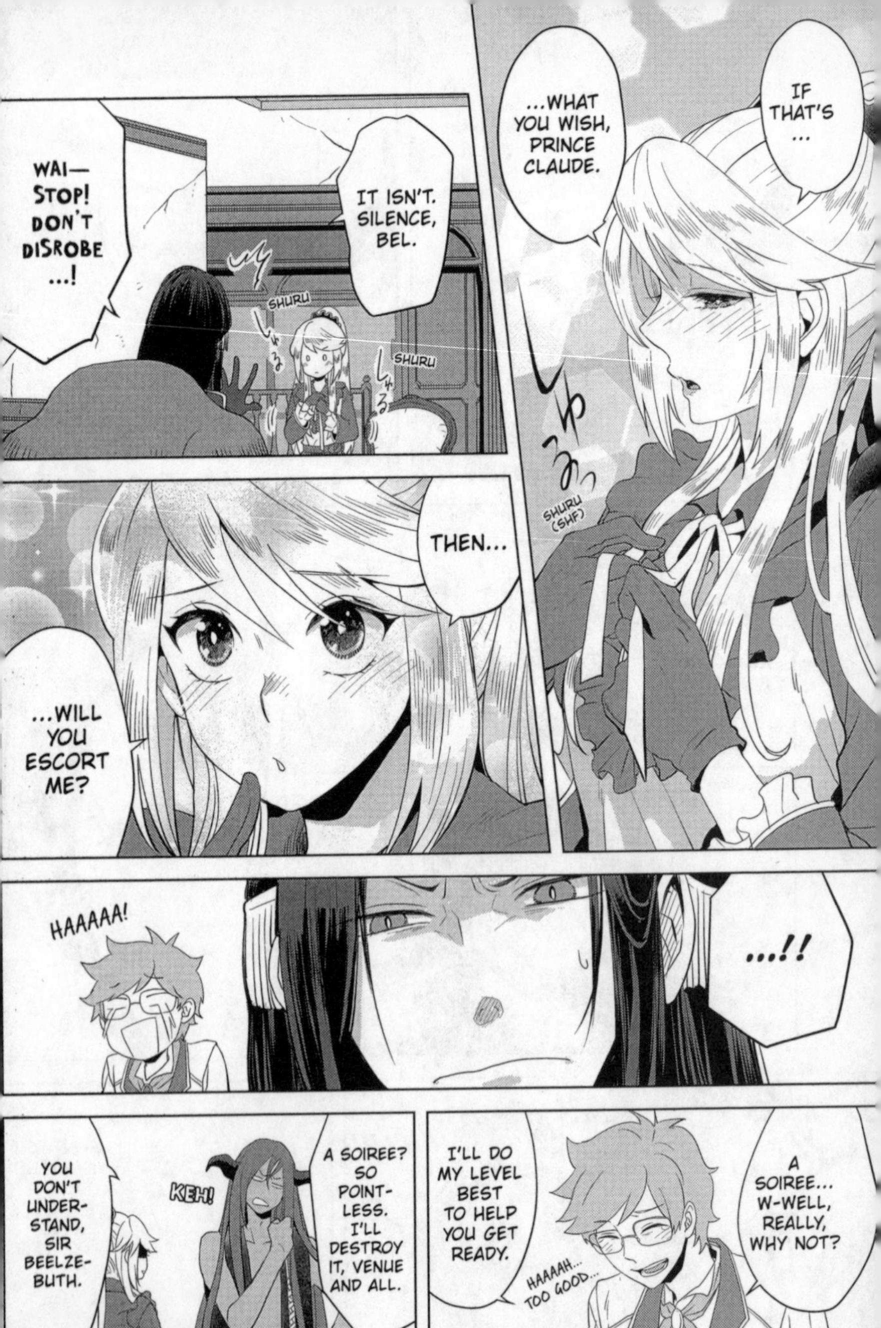
IF THAT'S...
...WHAT YOU WISH, PRINCE CLAUDE.
SHURU (SHF)
IT ISN'T. SILENCE, BEL.
WAI— STOP! DON'T DISROBE ...!
SHURU
SHURU
THEN...
...WILL YOU ESCORT ME?
...!!
HAAAAA!
A SOIREE... W-WELL, REALLY, WHY NOT?
I'LL DO MY LEVEL BEST TO HELP YOU GET READY.
HAAAAH... TOO GOOD...
A SOIREE? SO POINT-LESS. I'LL DESTROY IT, VENUE AND ALL.
KEH!
YOU DON'T UNDER-STAND, SIR BEELZE-BUTH.

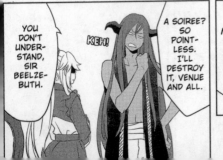

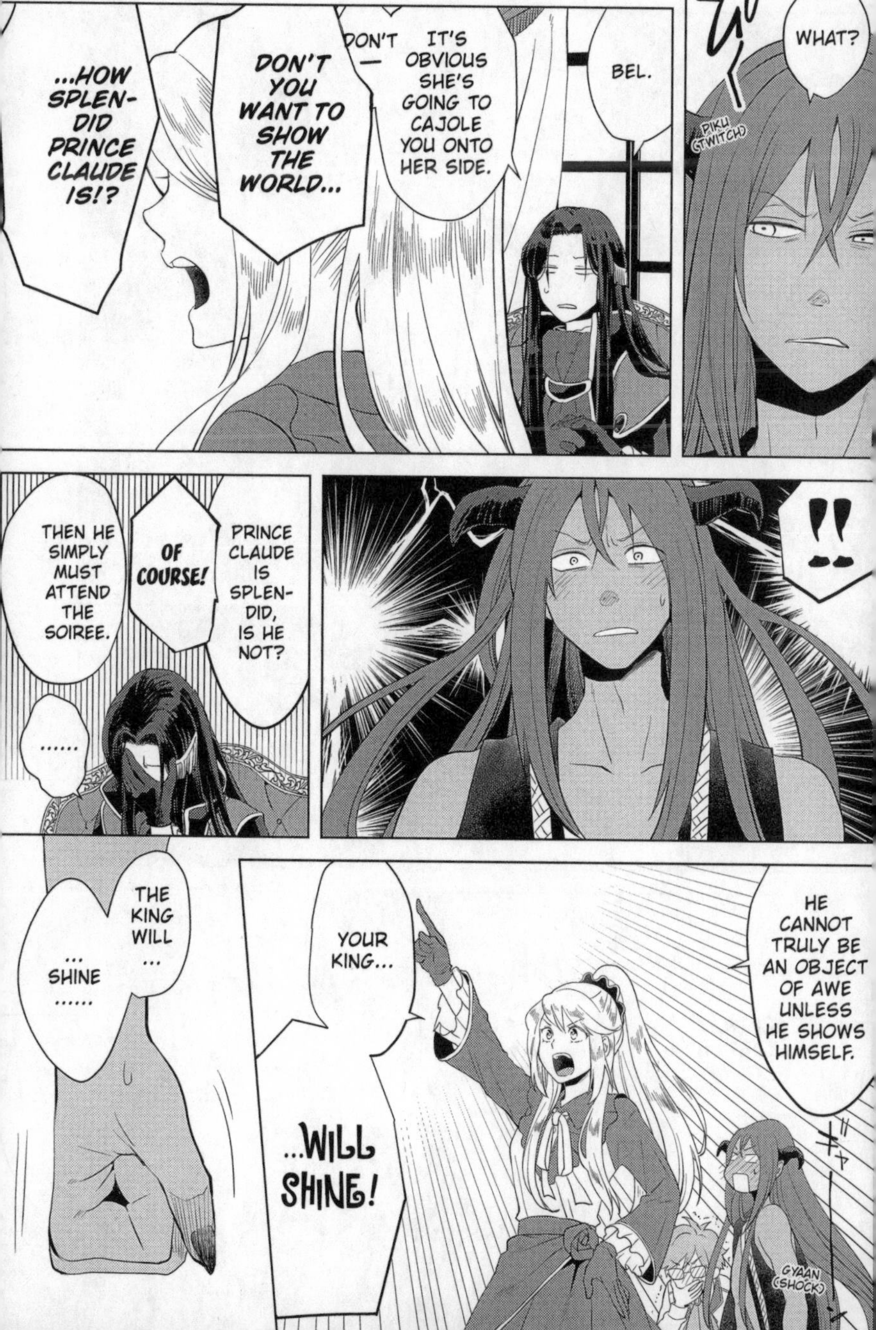
WHAT?
PIKU (TWITCH)
BEL.
DON'T — IT'S OBVIOUS SHE'S GOING TO CAJOLE YOU ONTO HER SIDE.
DON'T YOU WANT TO SHOW THE WORLD...
...HOW SPLENDID PRINCE CLAUDE IS!?
!!
PRINCE CLAUDE IS SPLENDID, IS HE NOT?
OF COURSE!
THEN HE SIMPLY MUST ATTEND THE SOIREE.
......
HE CANNOT TRULY BE AN OBJECT OF AWE UNLESS HE SHOWS HIMSELF.
YOUR KING...
...WILL SHINE!
GYAAN (SHOCK)
THE KING WILL ...
... SHINE ......

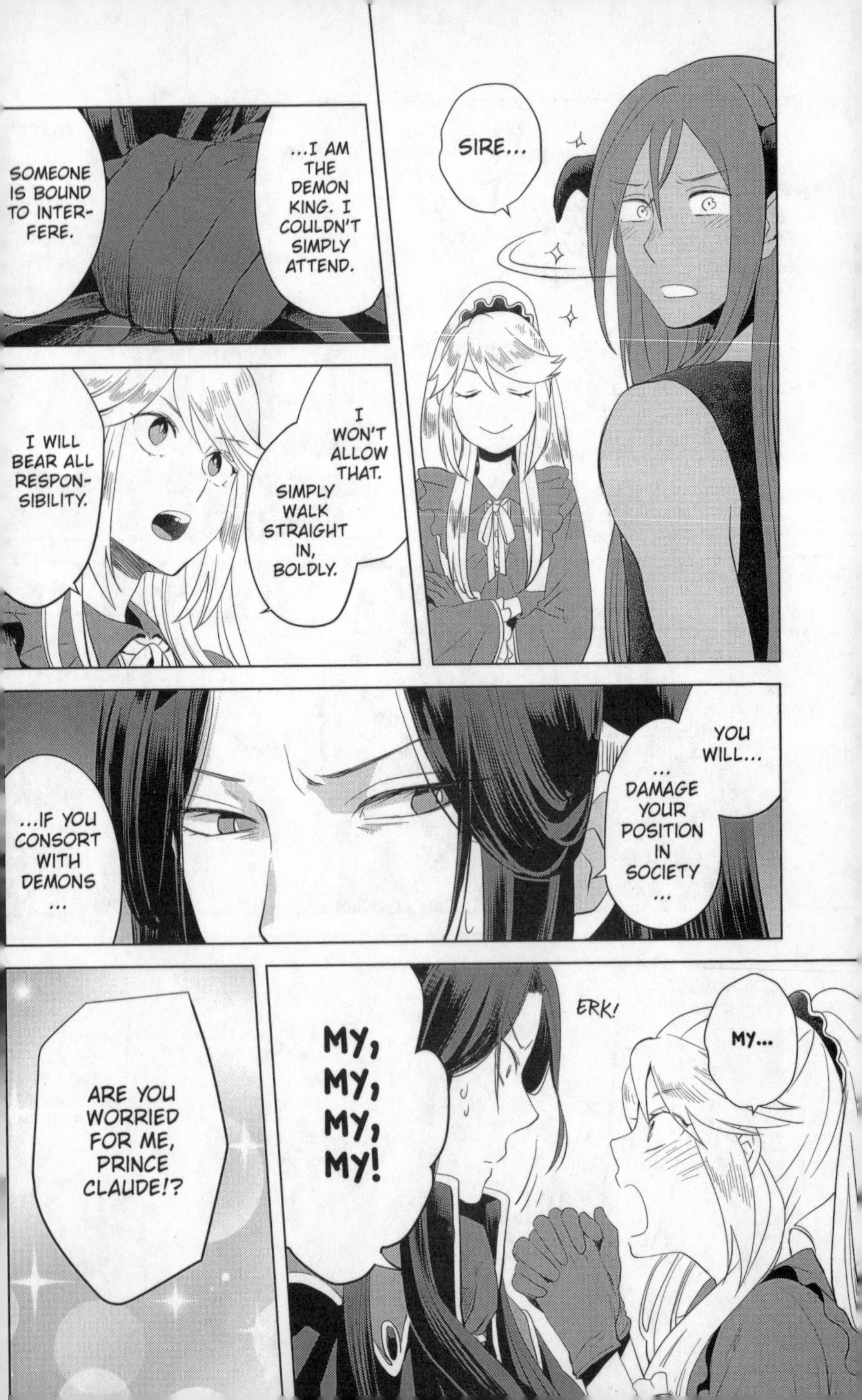
SIRE...
...I AM THE DEMON KING. I COULDN'T SIMPLY ATTEND.
SOMEONE IS BOUND TO INTERFERE.
I WON'T ALLOW THAT.
SIMPLY WALK STRAIGHT IN, BOLDLY.
I WILL BEAR ALL RESPONSIBILITY.
YOU WILL... ...DAMAGE YOUR POSITION IN SOCIETY...
...IF YOU CONSORT WITH DEMONS...
MY...
ERK!
MY, MY, MY, MY!
ARE YOU WORRIED FOR ME, PRINCE CLAUDE!?

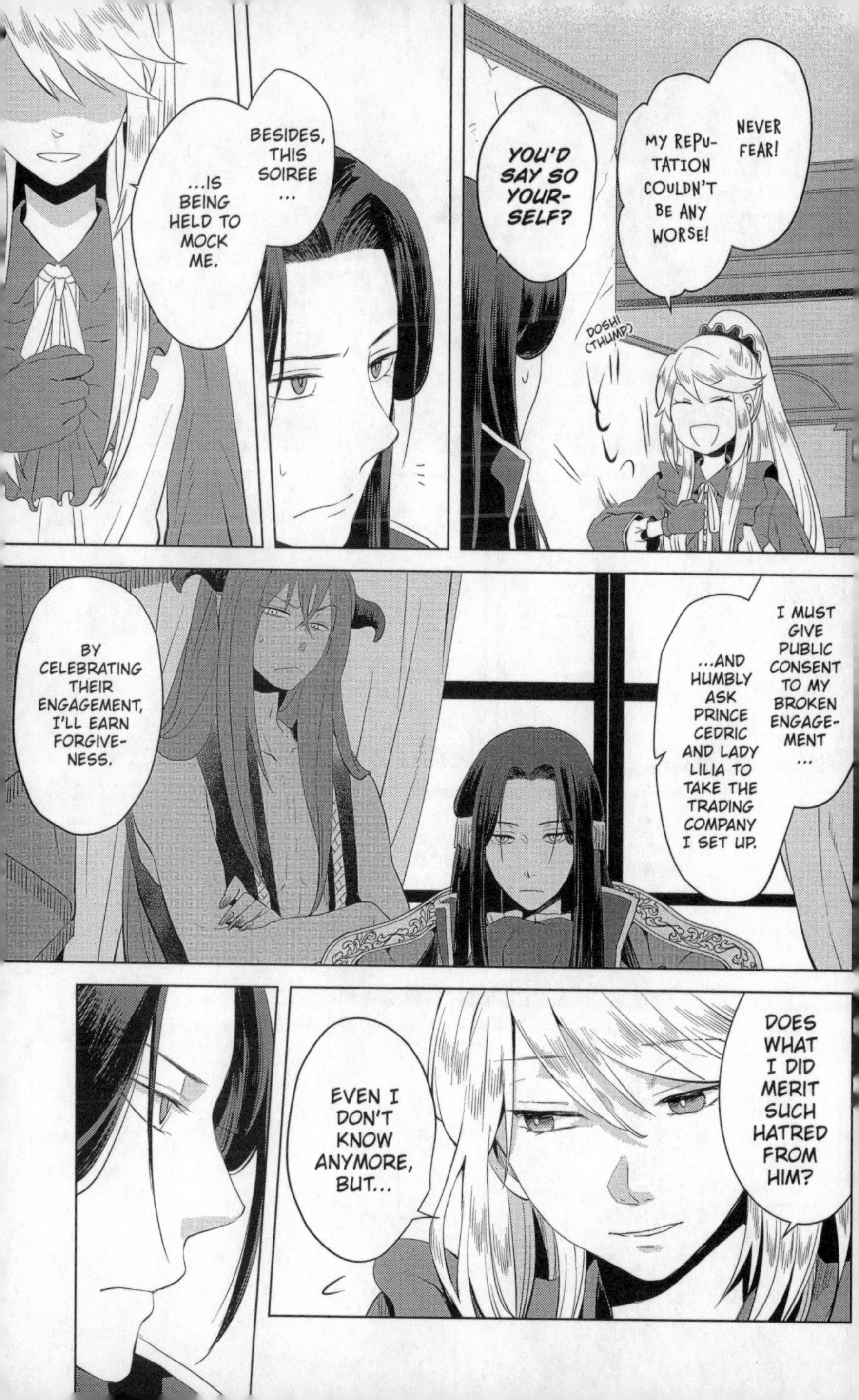
NEVER FEAR!
MY REPU-TATION COULDN'T BE ANY WORSE!
YOU'D SAY SO YOUR-SELF?
DOSHI (THUMP)
BESIDES, THIS SOIREE ...
...IS BEING HELD TO MOCK ME.
I MUST GIVE PUBLIC CONSENT TO MY BROKEN ENGAGE-MENT ...
...AND HUMBLY ASK PRINCE CEDRIC AND LADY LILIA TO TAKE THE TRADING COMPANY I SET UP.
BY CELEBRATING THEIR ENGAGEMENT, I'LL EARN FORGIVE-NESS.
DOES WHAT I DID MERIT SUCH HATRED FROM HIM?
EVEN I DON'T KNOW ANYMORE, BUT...

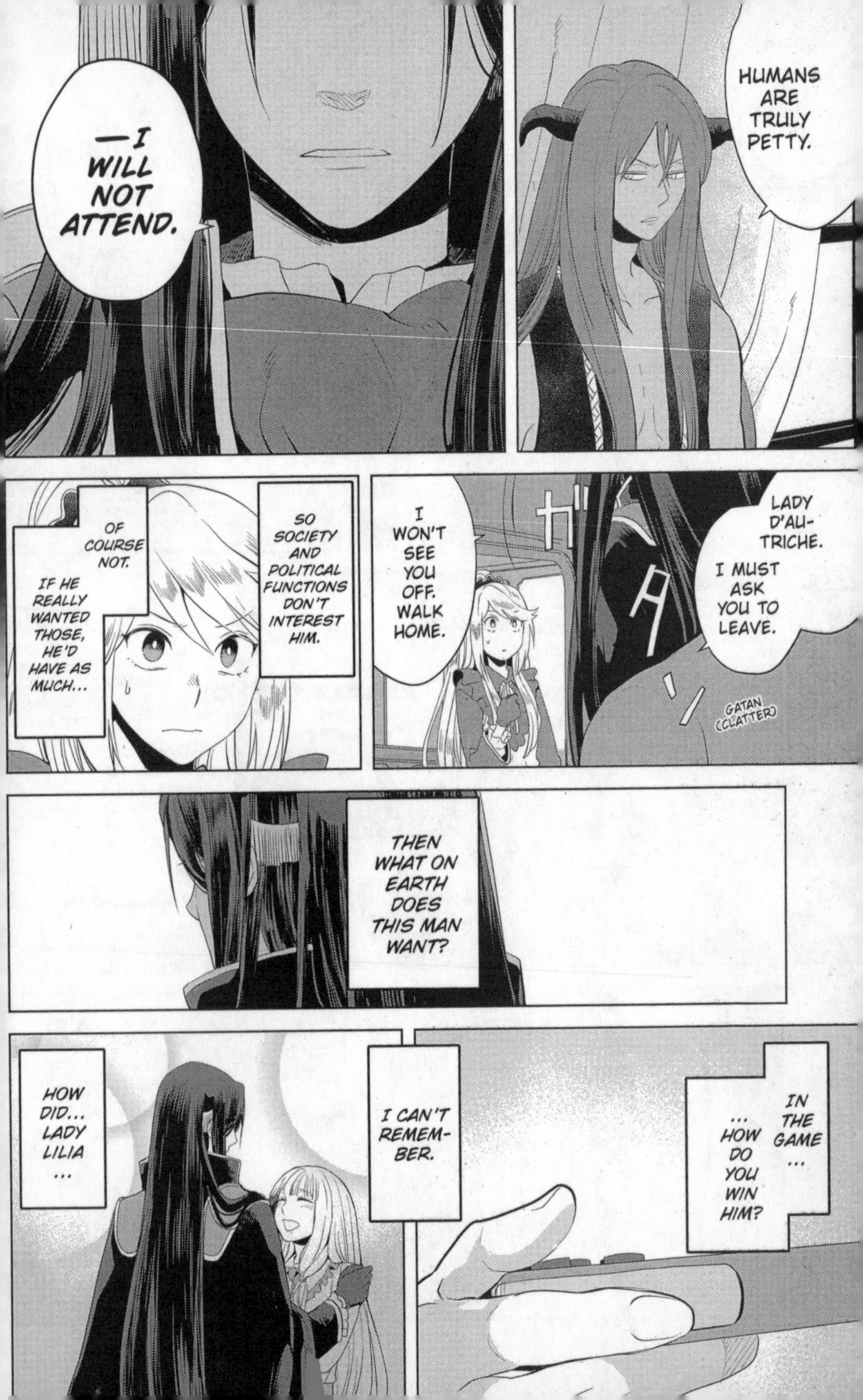
HUMANS ARE TRULY PETTY.
—I WILL NOT ATTEND.
LADY D'AUTRICHE. I MUST ASK YOU TO LEAVE.
GATAN (CLATTER)
I WON'T SEE YOU OFF. WALK HOME.
SO SOCIETY AND POLITICAL FUNCTIONS DON'T INTEREST HIM.
OF COURSE NOT.
IF HE REALLY WANTED THOSE, HE'D HAVE AS MUCH...
THEN WHAT ON EARTH DOES THIS MAN WANT?
IN THE GAME...
...HOW DO YOU WIN HIM?
I CAN'T REMEMBER.
HOW DID... LADY LILIA...

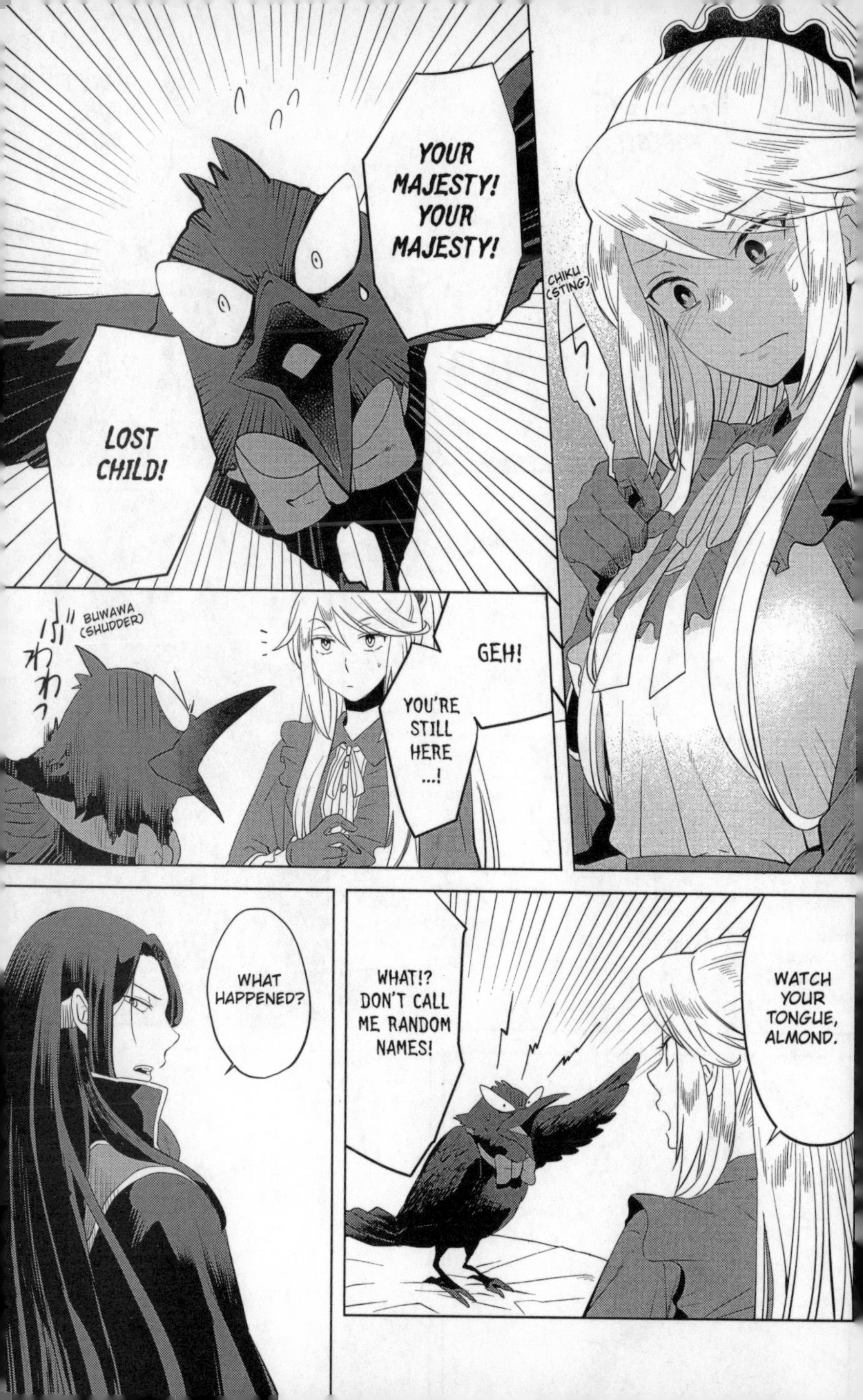
CHIKU (STING)
YOUR MAJESTY! YOUR MAJESTY!
LOST CHILD!
GEH!
YOU'RE STILL HERE ...!
BUWAWA (SHUDDER)
WATCH YOUR TONGUE, ALMOND.
WHAT!? DON'T CALL ME RANDOM NAMES!
WHAT HAPPENED?

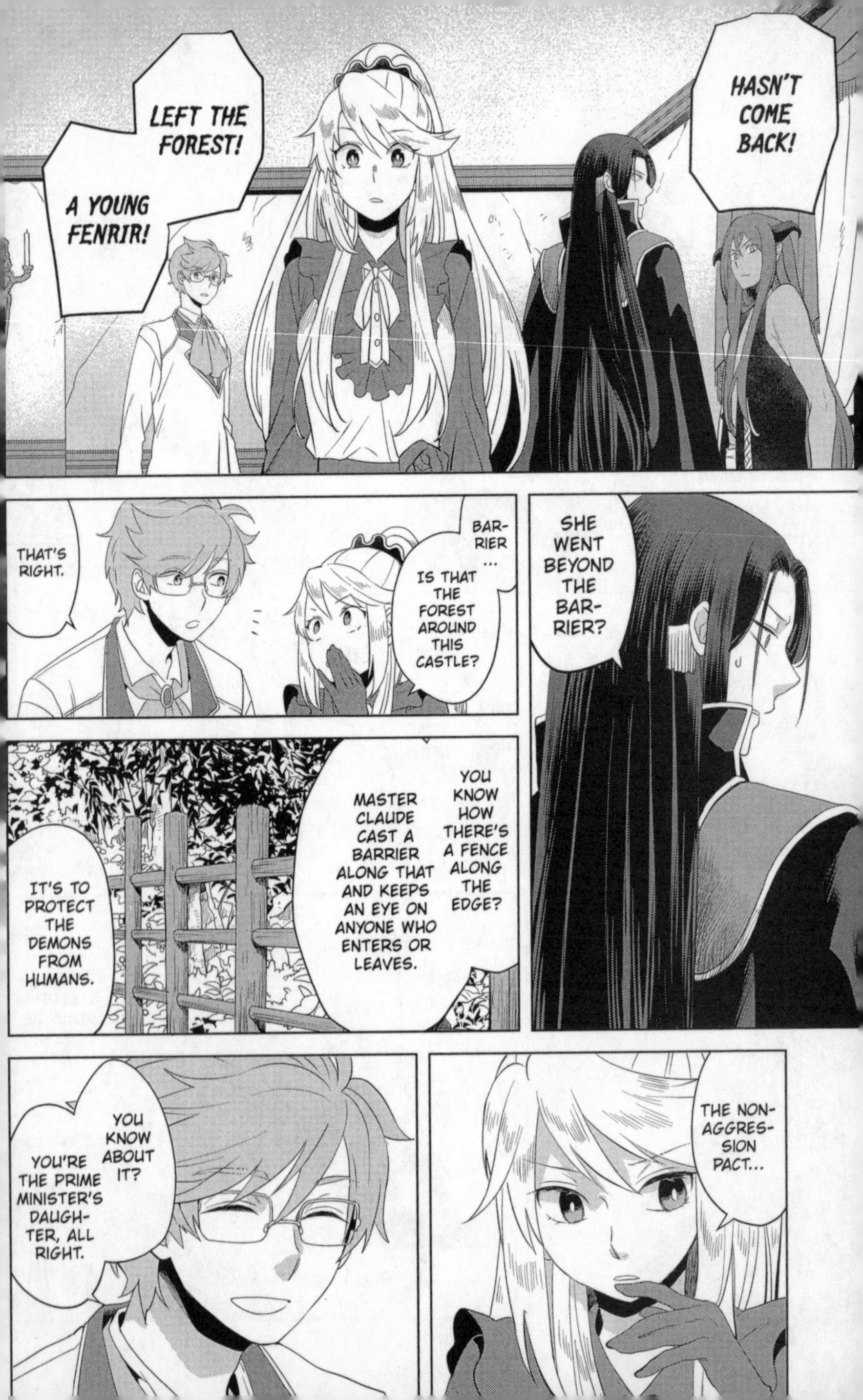
HASN'T COME BACK!
LEFT THE FOREST!
A YOUNG FENRIR!
SHE WENT BEYOND THE BARRIER?
BARRIER... IS THAT THE FOREST AROUND THIS CASTLE?
THAT'S RIGHT.
YOU KNOW HOW THERE'S A FENCE ALONG THE EDGE?
MASTER CLAUDE CAST A BARRIER ALONG THAT AND KEEPS AN EYE ON ANYONE WHO ENTERS OR LEAVES.
IT'S TO PROTECT THE DEMONS FROM HUMANS.
THE NON-AGGRESSION PACT...
YOU KNOW ABOUT IT?
YOU'RE THE PRIME MINISTER'S DAUGHTER, ALL RIGHT.

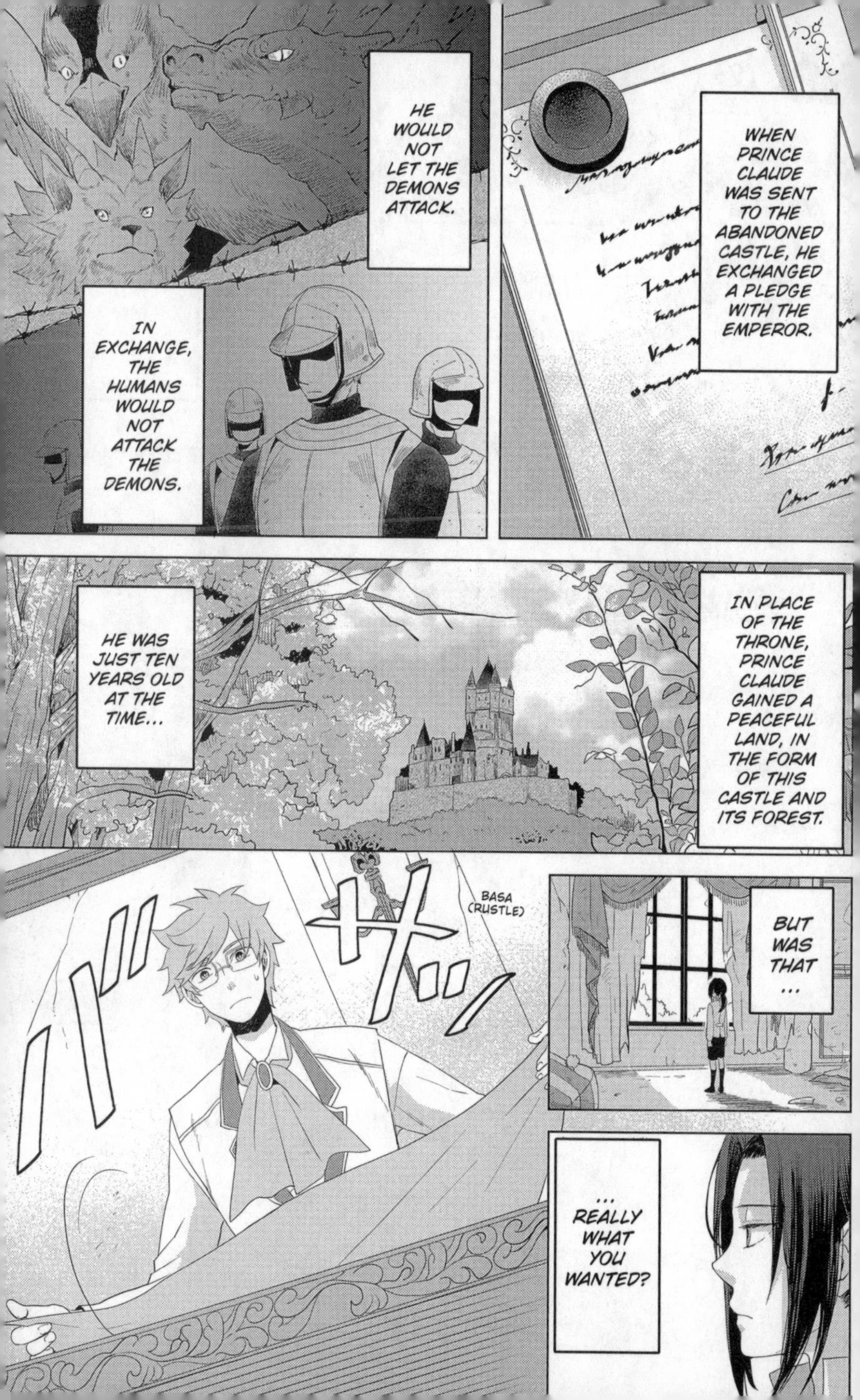
WHEN PRINCE CLAUDE WAS SENT TO THE ABANDONED CASTLE, HE EXCHANGED A PLEDGE WITH THE EMPEROR.
HE WOULD NOT LET THE DEMONS ATTACK.
IN EXCHANGE, THE HUMANS WOULD NOT ATTACK THE DEMONS.
IN PLACE OF THE THRONE, PRINCE CLAUDE GAINED A PEACEFUL LAND, IN THE FORM OF THIS CASTLE AND ITS FOREST.
HE WAS JUST TEN YEARS OLD AT THE TIME...
BUT WAS THAT ...
... REALLY WHAT YOU WANTED?
BASA (RUSTLE)

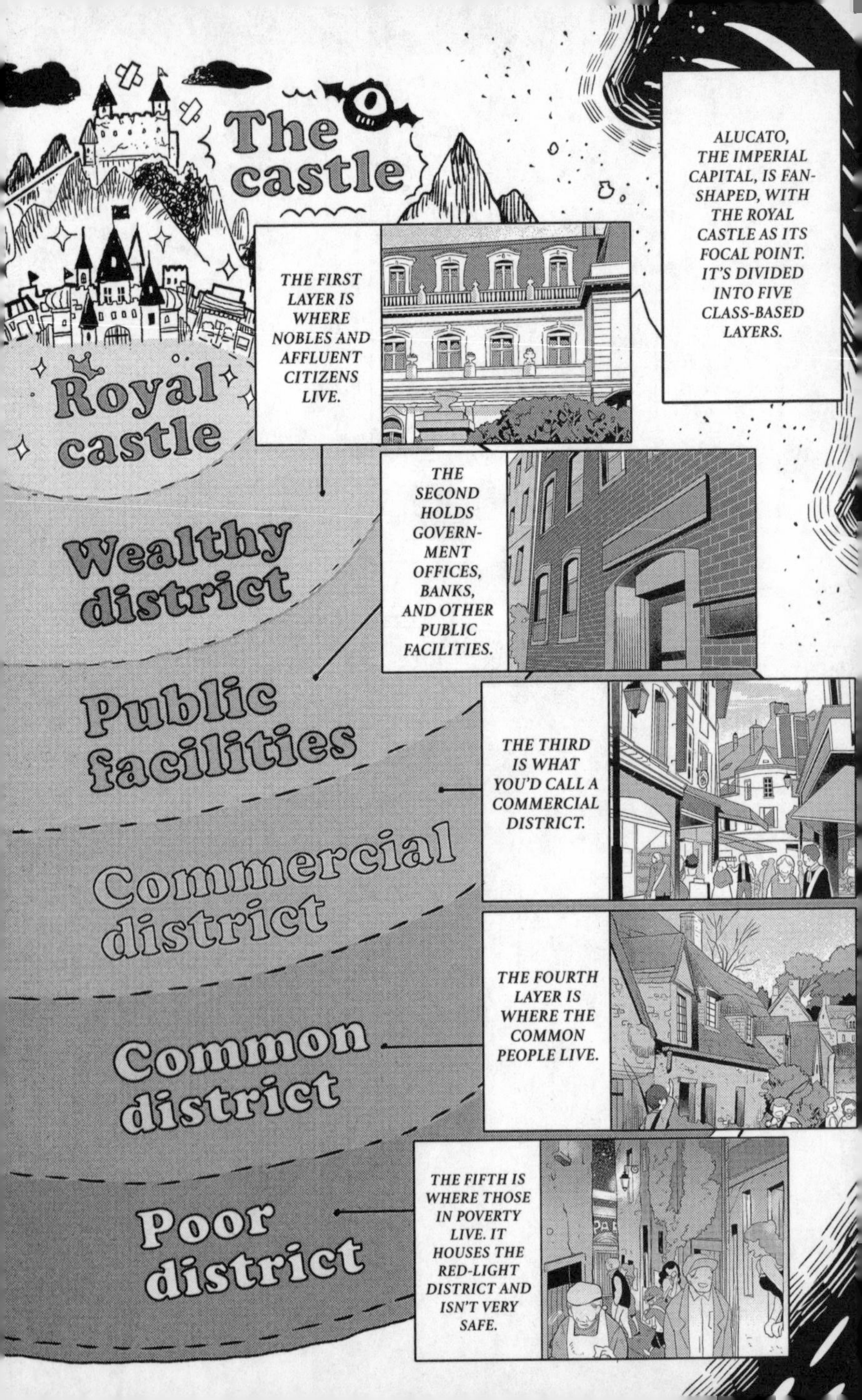
ALUCATO, THE IMPERIAL CAPITAL, IS FAN-SHAPED, WITH THE ROYAL CASTLE AS ITS FOCAL POINT. IT'S DIVIDED INTO FIVE CLASS-BASED LAYERS.
The castle
Royal castle
THE FIRST LAYER IS WHERE NOBLES AND AFFLUENT CITIZENS LIVE.
Wealthy district
THE SECOND HOLDS GOVERN-MENT OFFICES, BANKS, AND OTHER PUBLIC FACILITIES.
Public facilities
THE THIRD IS WHAT YOU'D CALL A COMMERCIAL DISTRICT.
Commercial district
THE FOURTH LAYER IS WHERE THE COMMON PEOPLE LIVE.
Common district
THE FIFTH IS WHERE THOSE IN POVERTY LIVE. IT HOUSES THE RED-LIGHT DISTRICT AND ISN'T VERY SAFE.
Poor district

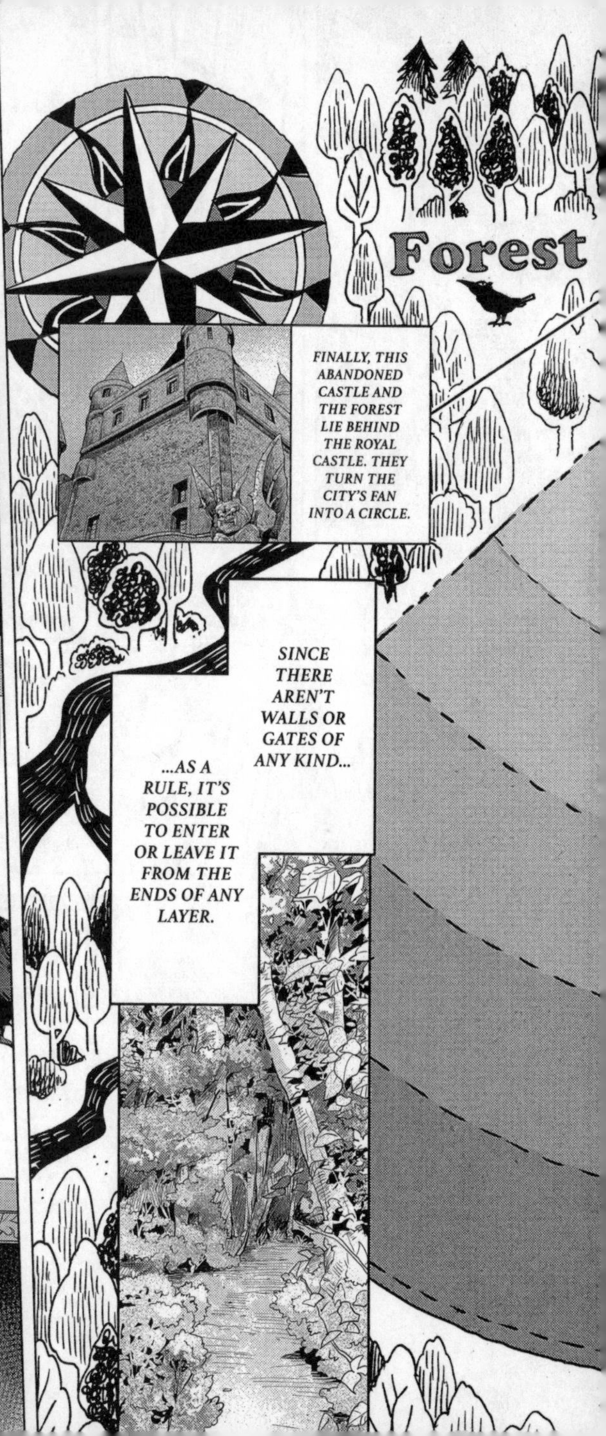
Forest
FINALLY, THIS ABANDONED CASTLE AND THE FOREST LIE BEHIND THE ROYAL CASTLE. THEY TURN THE CITY'S FAN INTO A CIRCLE.
SINCE THERE AREN'T WALLS OR GATES OF ANY KIND...
...AS A RULE, IT'S POSSIBLE TO ENTER OR LEAVE IT FROM THE ENDS OF ANY LAYER.
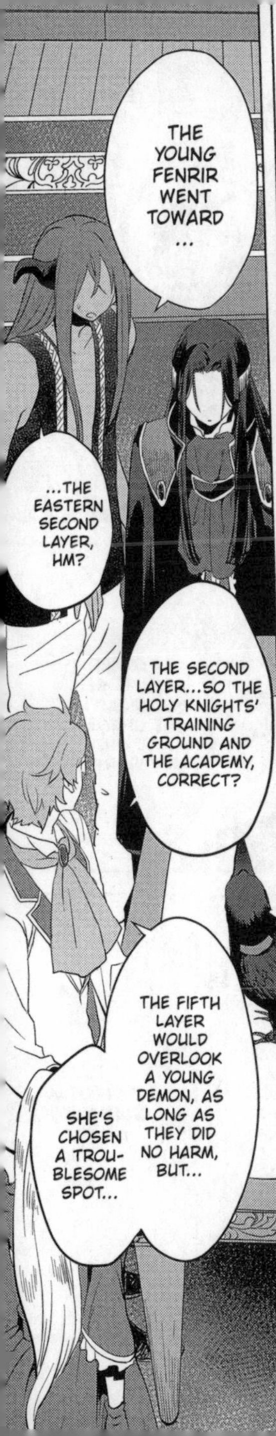
THE YOUNG FENRIR WENT TOWARD ...
...THE EASTERN SECOND LAYER, HM?
THE SECOND LAYER...SO THE HOLY KNIGHTS' TRAINING GROUND AND THE ACADEMY, CORRECT?
THE FIFTH LAYER WOULD OVERLOOK A YOUNG DEMON, AS LONG AS THEY DID NO HARM, BUT...
SHE'S CHOSEN A TROU-BLESOME SPOT...

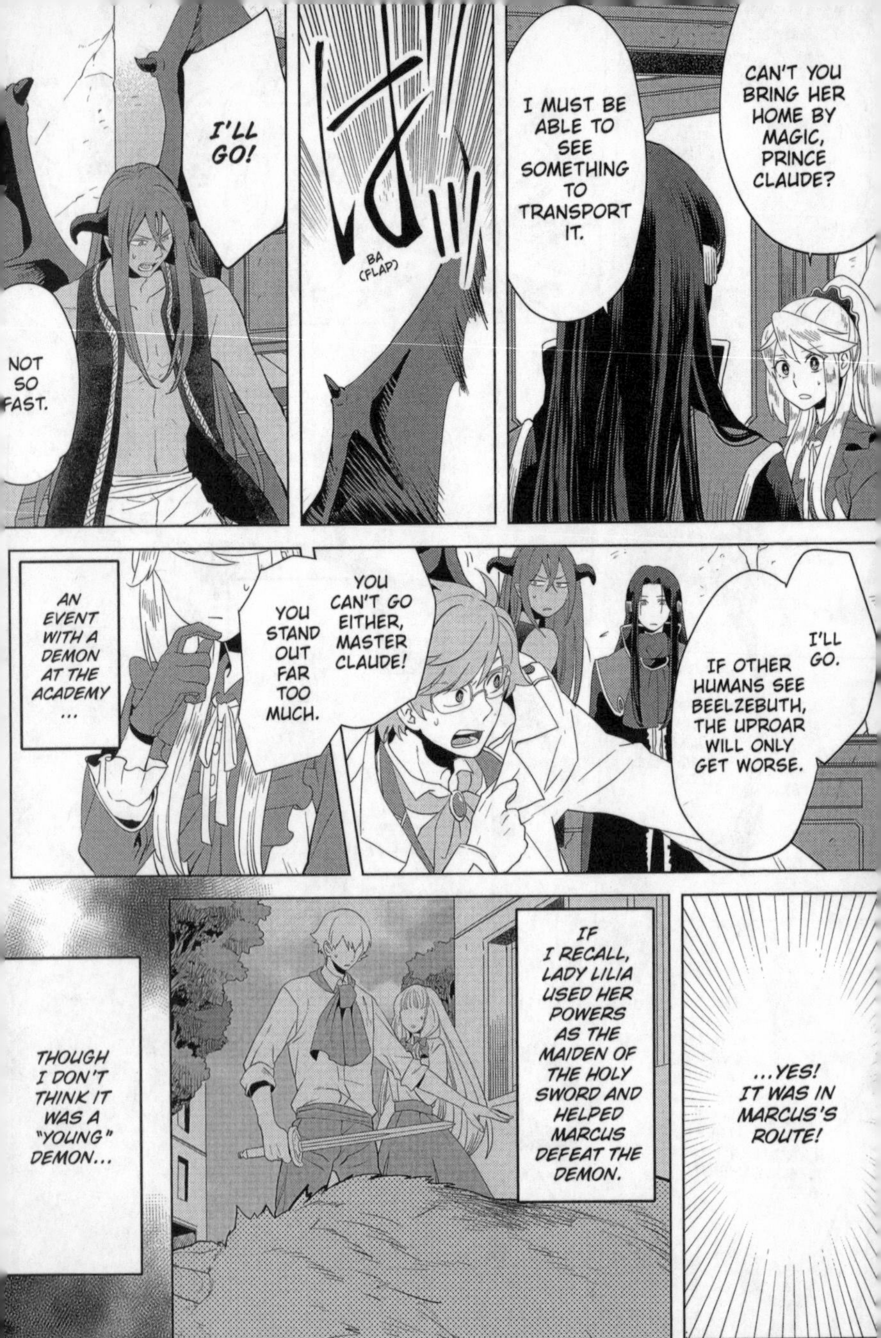
CAN'T YOU BRING HER HOME BY MAGIC, PRINCE CLAUDE?
I MUST BE ABLE TO SEE SOMETHING TO TRANSPORT IT.
BA (FLAP)
I'LL GO!
NOT SO FAST.
I'LL GO.
IF OTHER HUMANS SEE BEELZEBUTH, THE UPROAR WILL ONLY GET WORSE.
YOU CAN'T GO EITHER, MASTER CLAUDE!
YOU STAND OUT FAR TOO MUCH.
AN EVENT WITH A DEMON AT THE ACADEMY...
...YES! IT WAS IN MARCUS'S ROUTE!
IF I RECALL, LADY LILIA USED HER POWERS AS THE MAIDEN OF THE HOLY SWORD AND HELPED MARCUS DEFEAT THE DEMON.
THOUGH I DON'T THINK IT WAS A "YOUNG" DEMON...

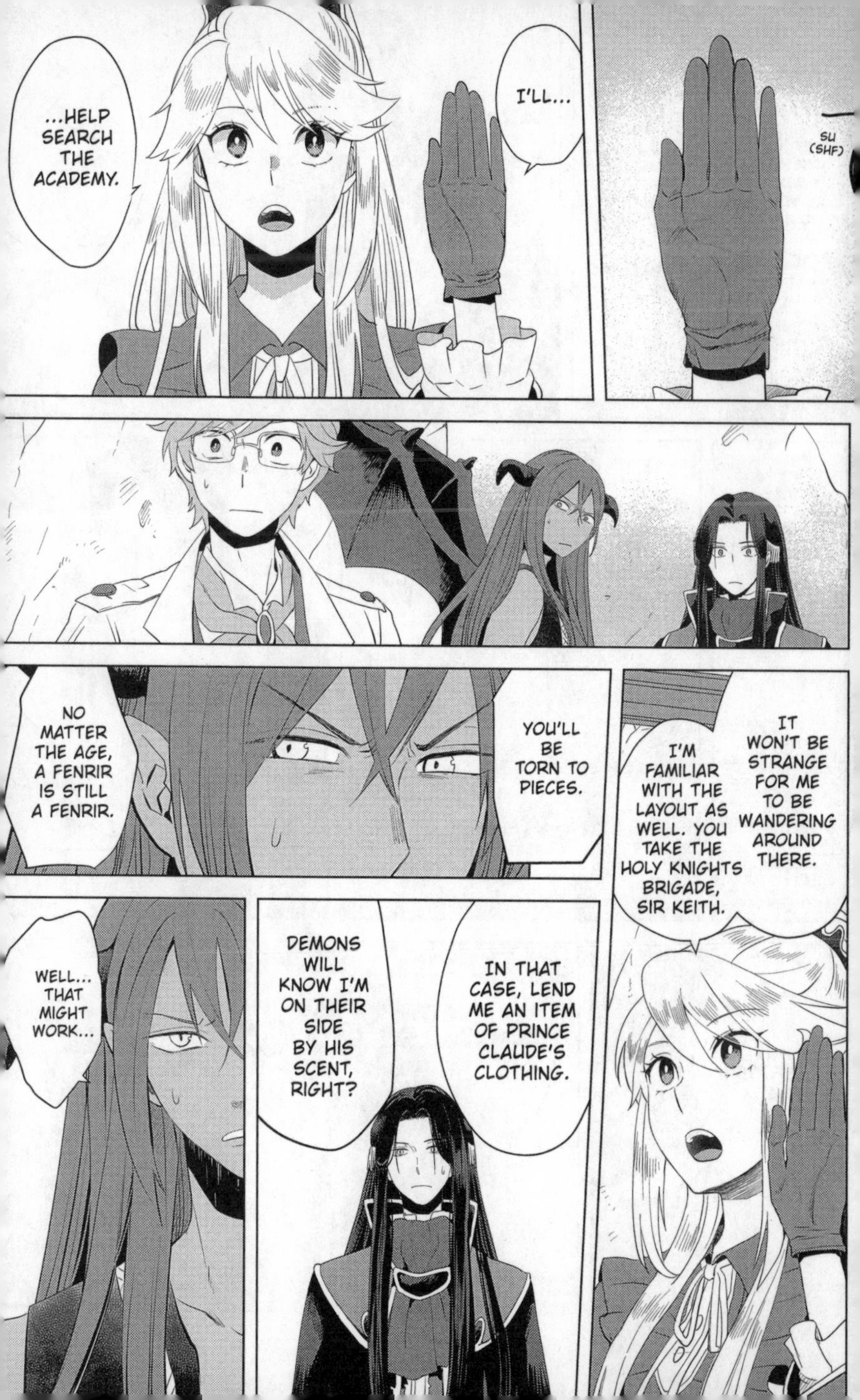
SU (SHF)
I'LL...
...HELP SEARCH THE ACADEMY.
IT WON'T BE STRANGE FOR ME TO BE WANDERING AROUND THERE.
I'M FAMILIAR WITH THE LAYOUT AS WELL. YOU TAKE THE HOLY KNIGHTS BRIGADE, SIR KEITH.
YOU'LL BE TORN TO PIECES.
NO MATTER THE AGE, A FENRIR IS STILL A FENRIR.
IN THAT CASE, LEND ME AN ITEM OF PRINCE CLAUDE'S CLOTHING.
DEMONS WILL KNOW I'M ON THEIR SIDE BY HIS SCENT, RIGHT?
WELL... THAT MIGHT WORK...

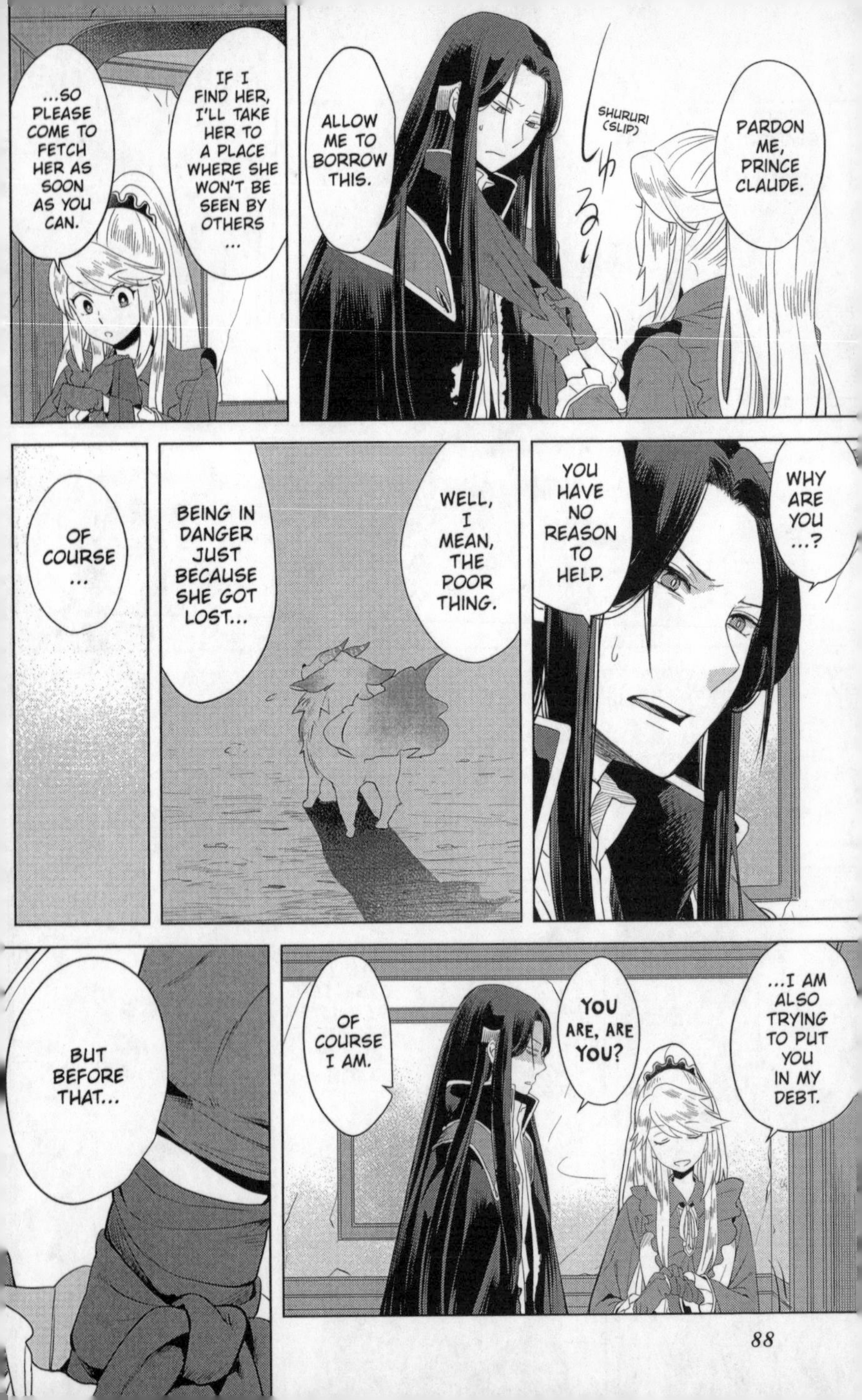
PARDON ME, PRINCE CLAUDE.
SHURURI (SLIP)
ALLOW ME TO BORROW THIS.
IF I FIND HER, I'LL TAKE HER TO A PLACE WHERE SHE WON'T BE SEEN BY OTHERS...
...SO PLEASE COME TO FETCH HER AS SOON AS YOU CAN.
WHY ARE YOU ...?
YOU HAVE NO REASON TO HELP.
WELL, I MEAN, THE POOR THING.
BEING IN DANGER JUST BECAUSE SHE GOT LOST...
OF COURSE ...
...I AM ALSO TRYING TO PUT YOU IN MY DEBT.
YOU ARE, ARE YOU?
OF COURSE I AM.
BUT BEFORE THAT...

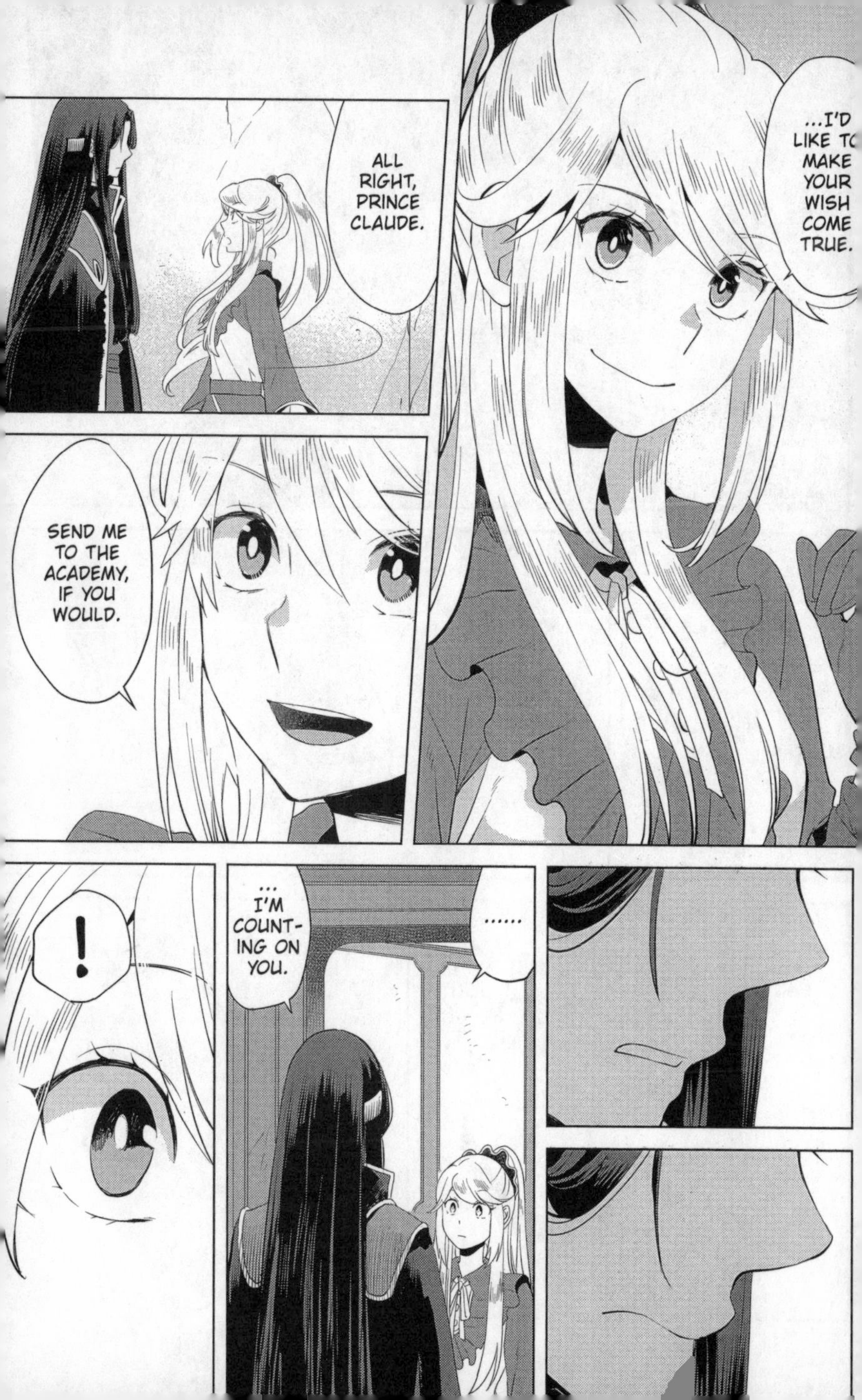
...I'D LIKE TO MAKE YOUR WISH COME TRUE.
ALL RIGHT, PRINCE CLAUDE.
SEND ME TO THE ACADEMY, IF YOU WOULD.
......
... I'M COUNTING ON YOU.
!

POU
(GLOW)

TO
(TMP)

"I'M
COUNT-
ING ON
YOU"
...

... HE
SAID.

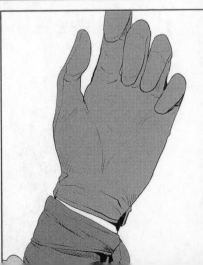

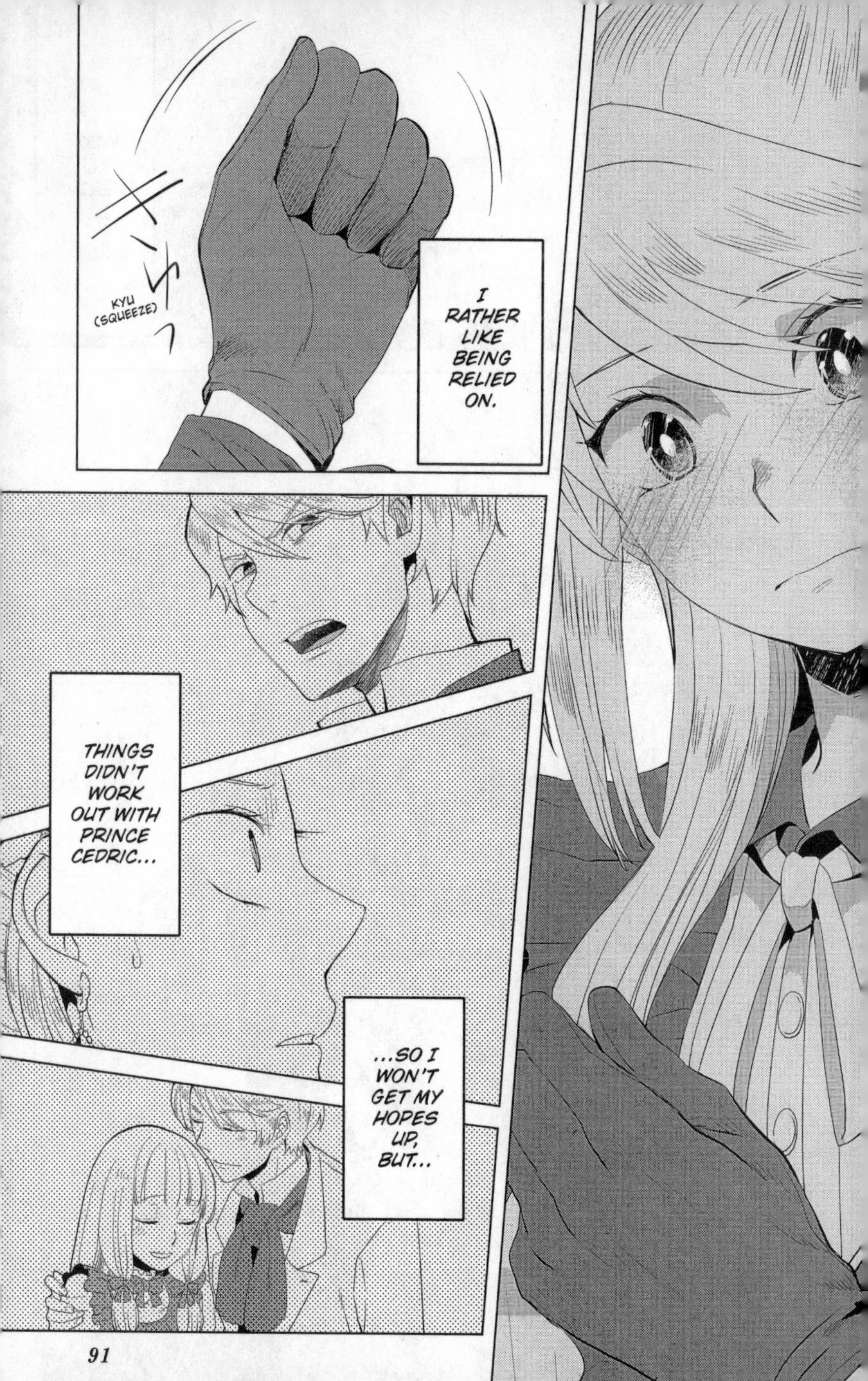
I RATHER LIKE BEING RELIED ON.
KYU (SQUEEZE)
THINGS DIDN'T WORK OUT WITH PRINCE CEDRIC...
...SO I WON'T GET MY HOPES UP, BUT...

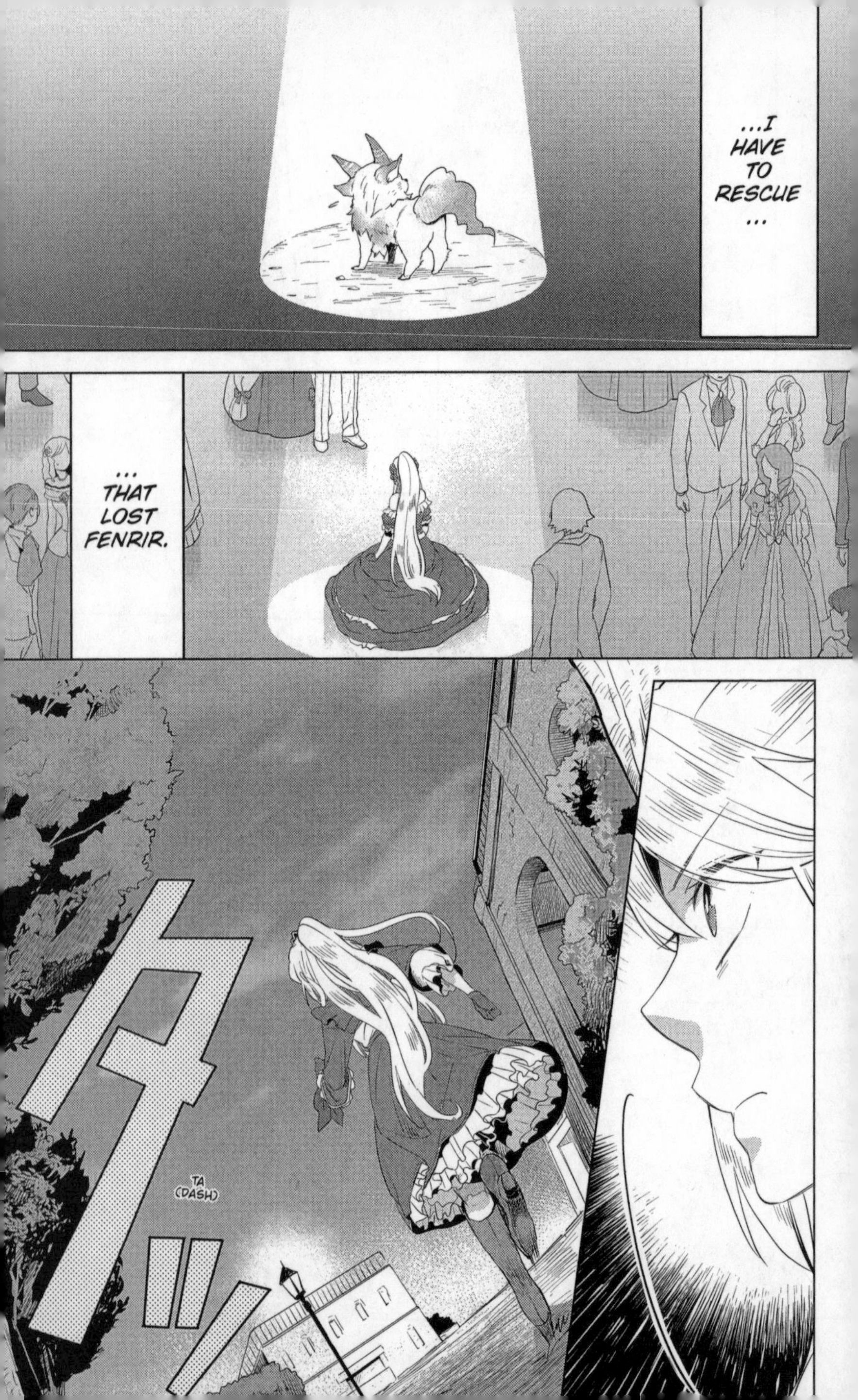
...I HAVE TO RESCUE ...
... THAT LOST FENRIR.
TA (DASH)

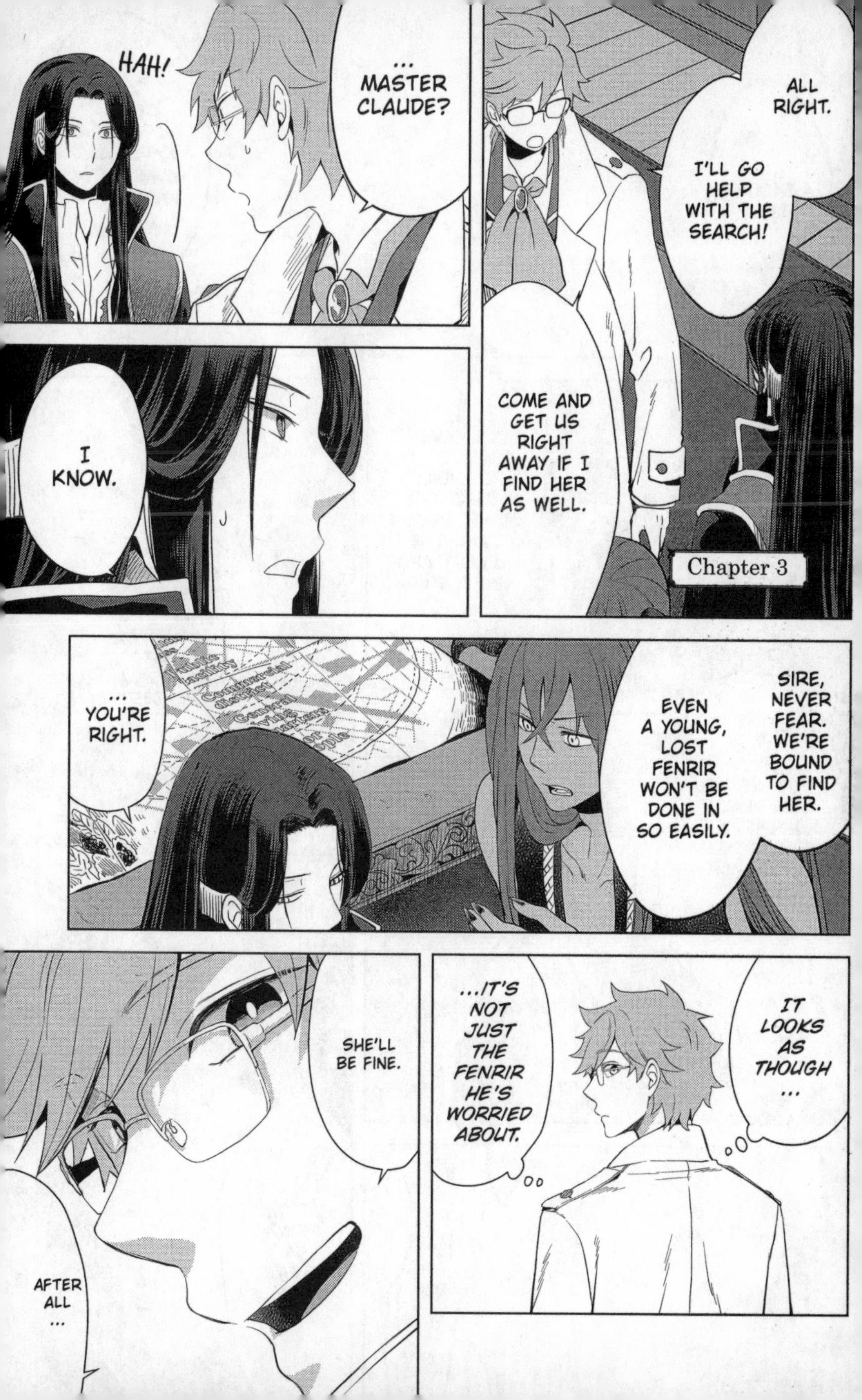
ALL RIGHT.
I'LL GO HELP WITH THE SEARCH!
COME AND GET US RIGHT AWAY IF I FIND HER AS WELL.
Chapter 3
... MASTER CLAUDE?
HAH!
I KNOW.
SIRE, NEVER FEAR. WE'RE BOUND TO FIND HER.
EVEN A YOUNG, LOST FENRIR WON'T BE DONE IN SO EASILY.
... YOU'RE RIGHT.
IT LOOKS AS THOUGH ...
...IT'S NOT JUST THE FENRIR HE'S WORRIED ABOUT.
SHE'LL BE FINE.
AFTER ALL ...

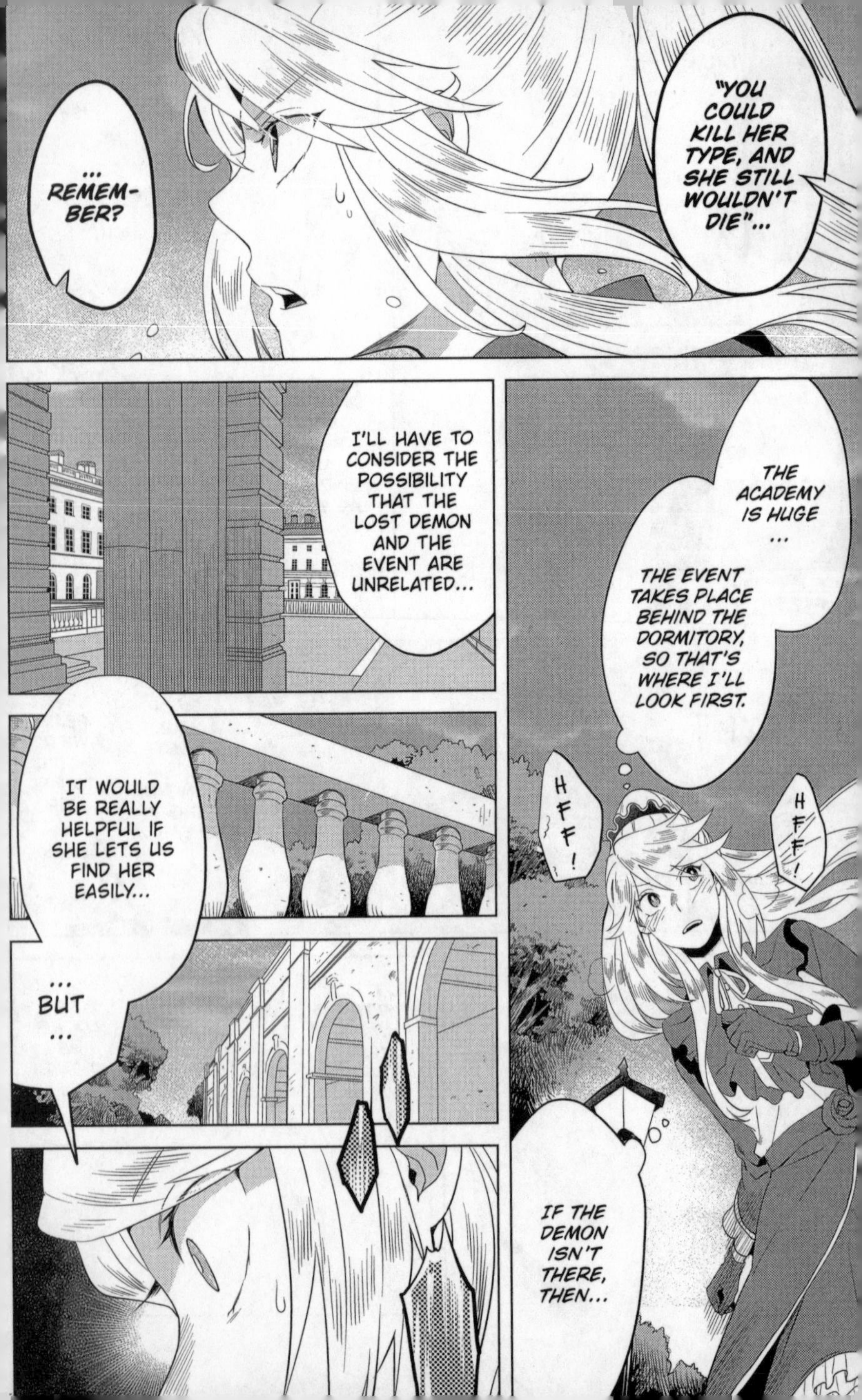

"YOU COULD KILL HER TYPE, AND SHE STILL WOULDN'T DIE"...
... REMEMBER?
THE ACADEMY IS HUGE ...
THE EVENT TAKES PLACE BEHIND THE DORMITORY, SO THAT'S WHERE I'LL LOOK FIRST.
HFF!
HFF!
IF THE DEMON ISN'T THERE, THEN...
I'LL HAVE TO CONSIDER THE POSSIBILITY THAT THE LOST DEMON AND THE EVENT ARE UNRELATED...
IT WOULD BE REALLY HELPFUL IF SHE LETS US FIND HER EASILY...
... BUT ...

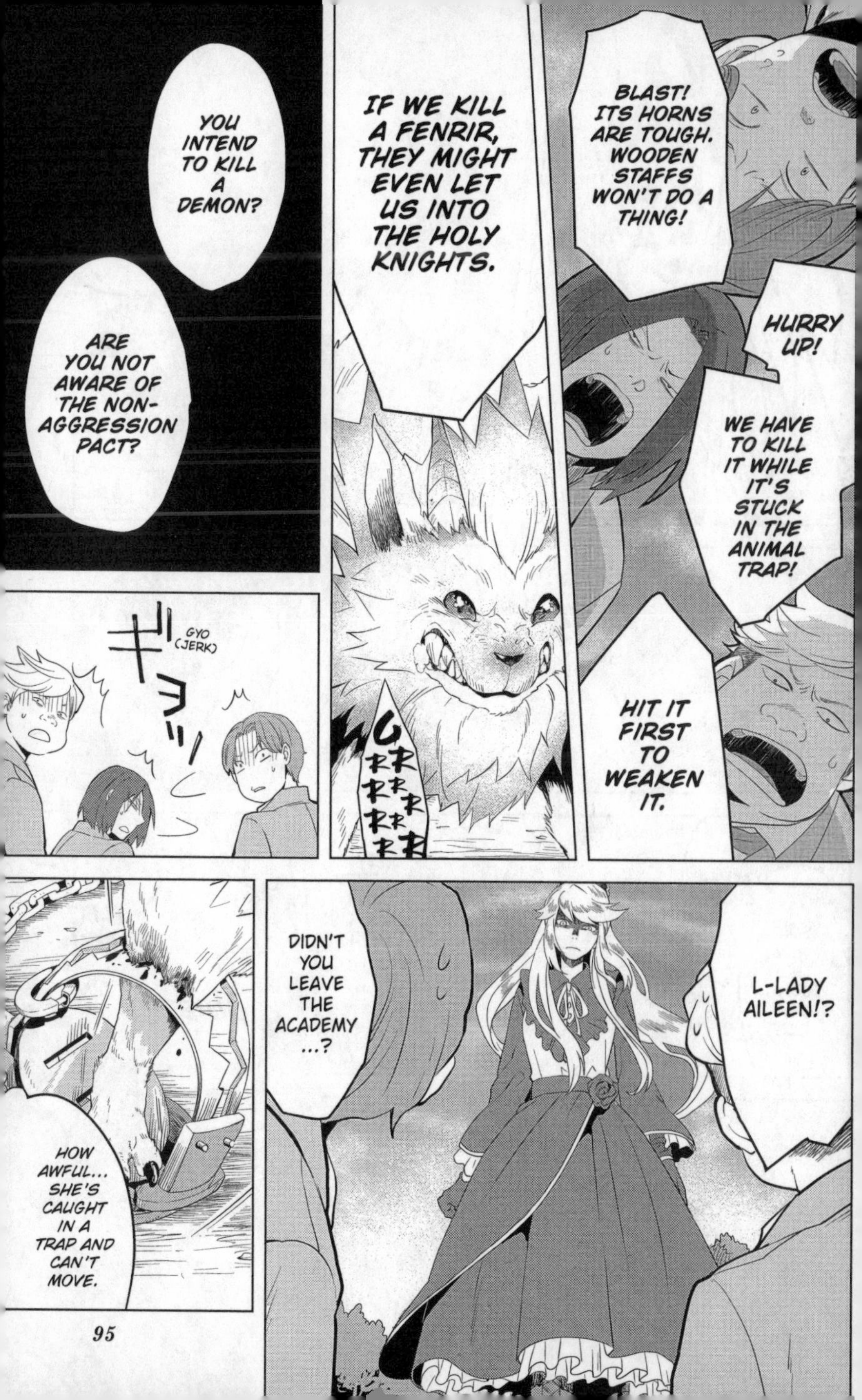
BLAST! ITS HORNS ARE TOUGH. WOODEN STAFFS WON'T DO A THING!
HURRY UP!
WE HAVE TO KILL IT WHILE IT'S STUCK IN THE ANIMAL TRAP!
HIT IT FIRST TO WEAKEN IT.
IF WE KILL A FENRIR, THEY MIGHT EVEN LET US INTO THE HOLY KNIGHTS.
GRRRRRRRRRR
YOU INTEND TO KILL A DEMON?
ARE YOU NOT AWARE OF THE NON-AGGRESSION PACT?
GYO (JERK)
L-LADY AILEEN!?
DIDN'T YOU LEAVE THE ACADEMY ...?
HOW AWFUL... SHE'S CAUGHT IN A TRAP AND CAN'T MOVE.

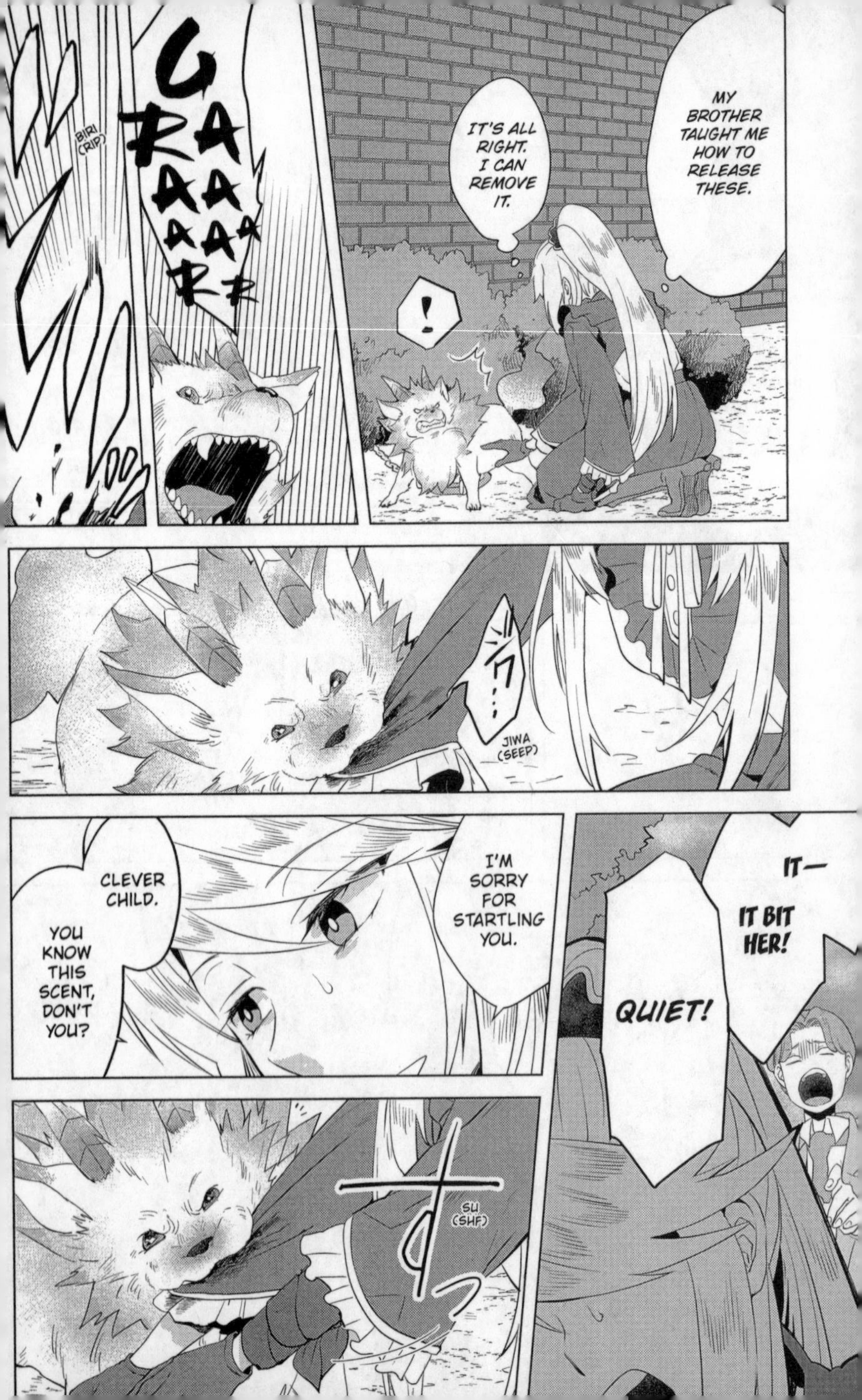

MY BROTHER TAUGHT ME HOW TO RELEASE THESE.
IT'S ALL RIGHT. I CAN REMOVE IT.
!
GRAAAAAARR
BIRI (RIP)
ジワ…
JIWA (SEEP)
IT— IT BIT HER!
QUIET!
I'M SORRY FOR STARTLING YOU.
CLEVER CHILD.
YOU KNOW THIS SCENT, DON'T YOU?
SU (SHF)

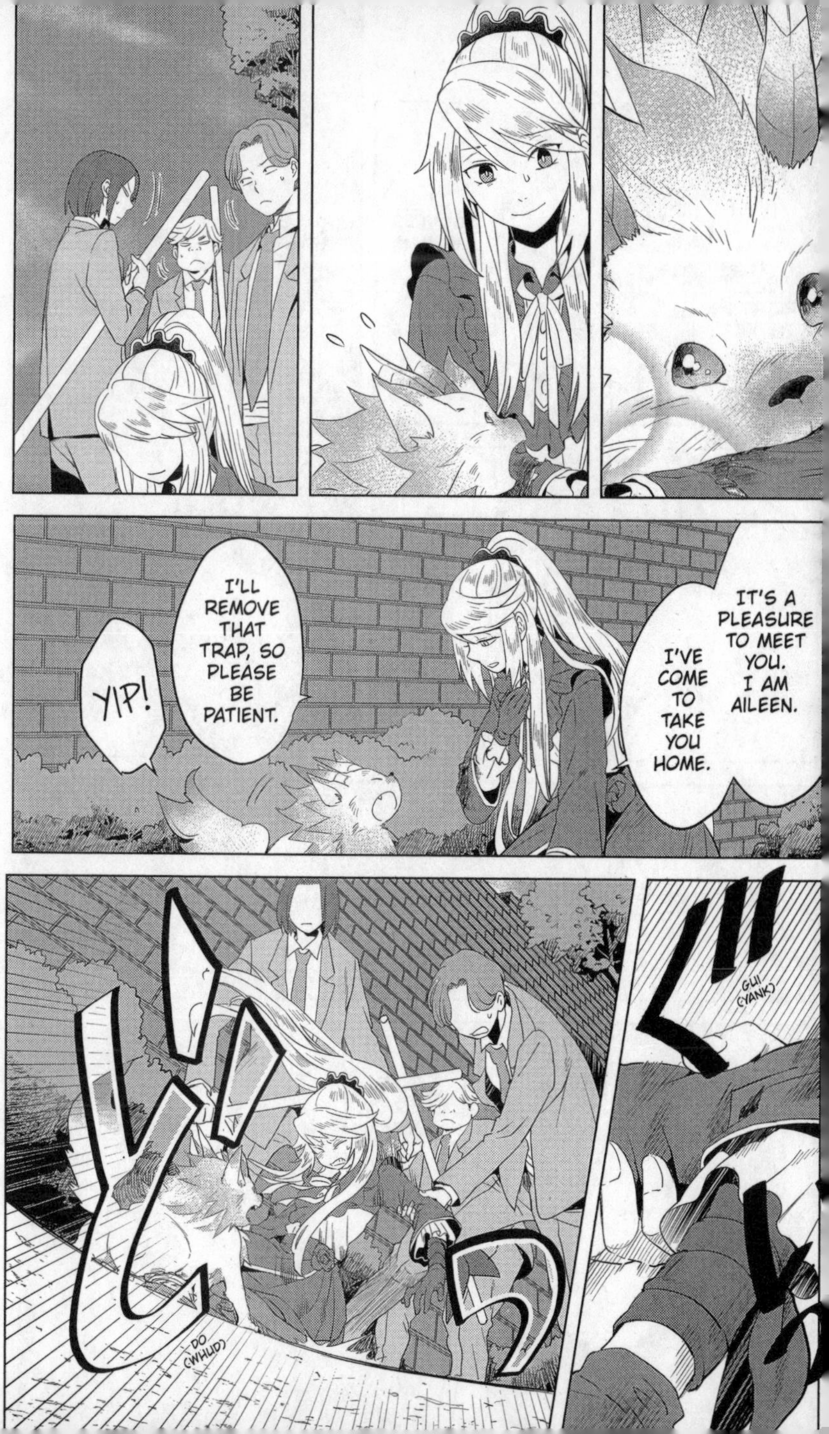
IT'S A PLEASURE TO MEET YOU. I AM AILEEN.
I'VE COME TO TAKE YOU HOME.
I'LL REMOVE THAT TRAP, SO PLEASE BE PATIENT.
YIP!
GUI (YANK)
DO (WHUD)

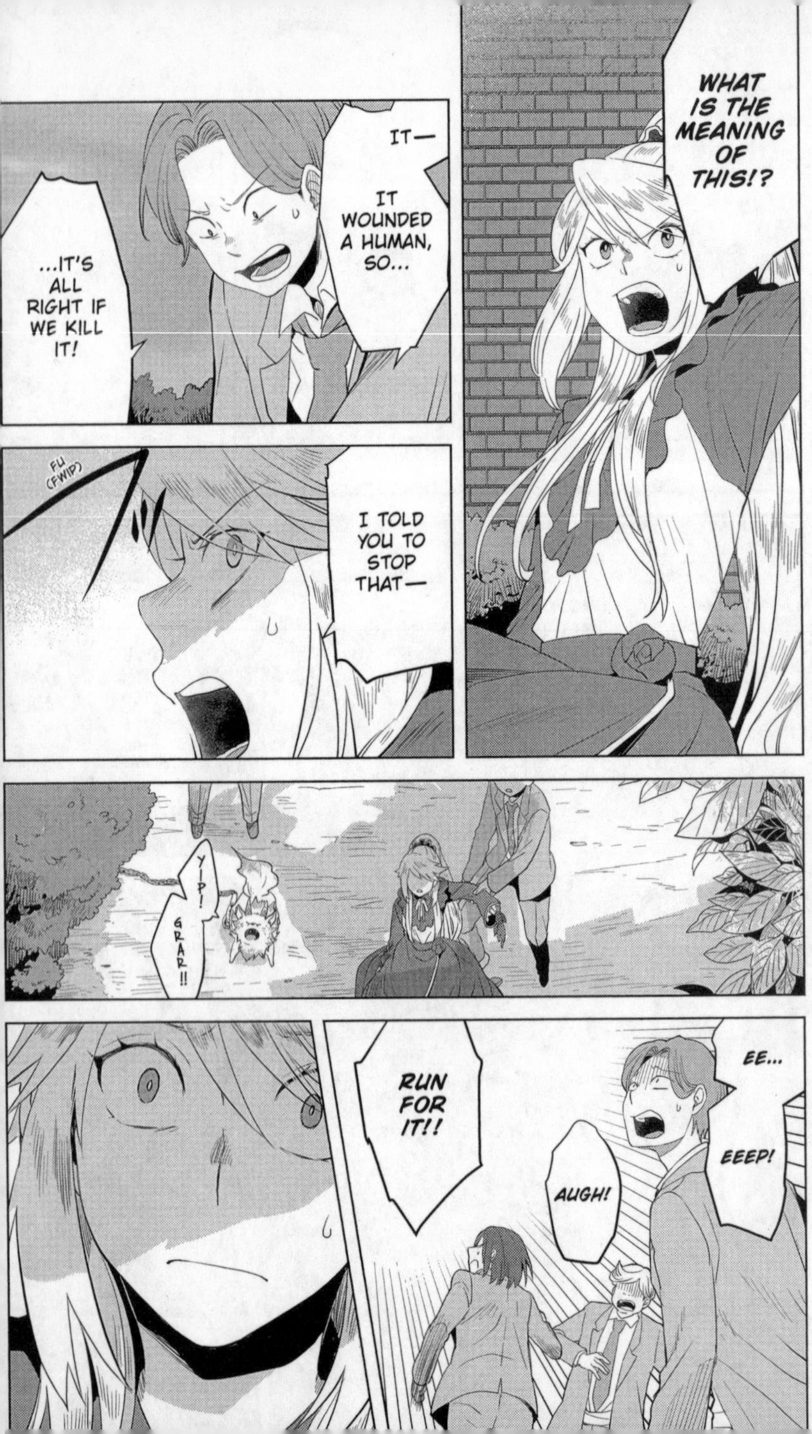
WHAT IS THE MEANING OF THIS!?
IT—
IT WOUNDED A HUMAN, SO...
...IT'S ALL RIGHT IF WE KILL IT!
I TOLD YOU TO STOP THAT—
FU (FWIP)
YIP!
GRAR!!
EE...
EEEP!
AUGH!
RUN FOR IT!!

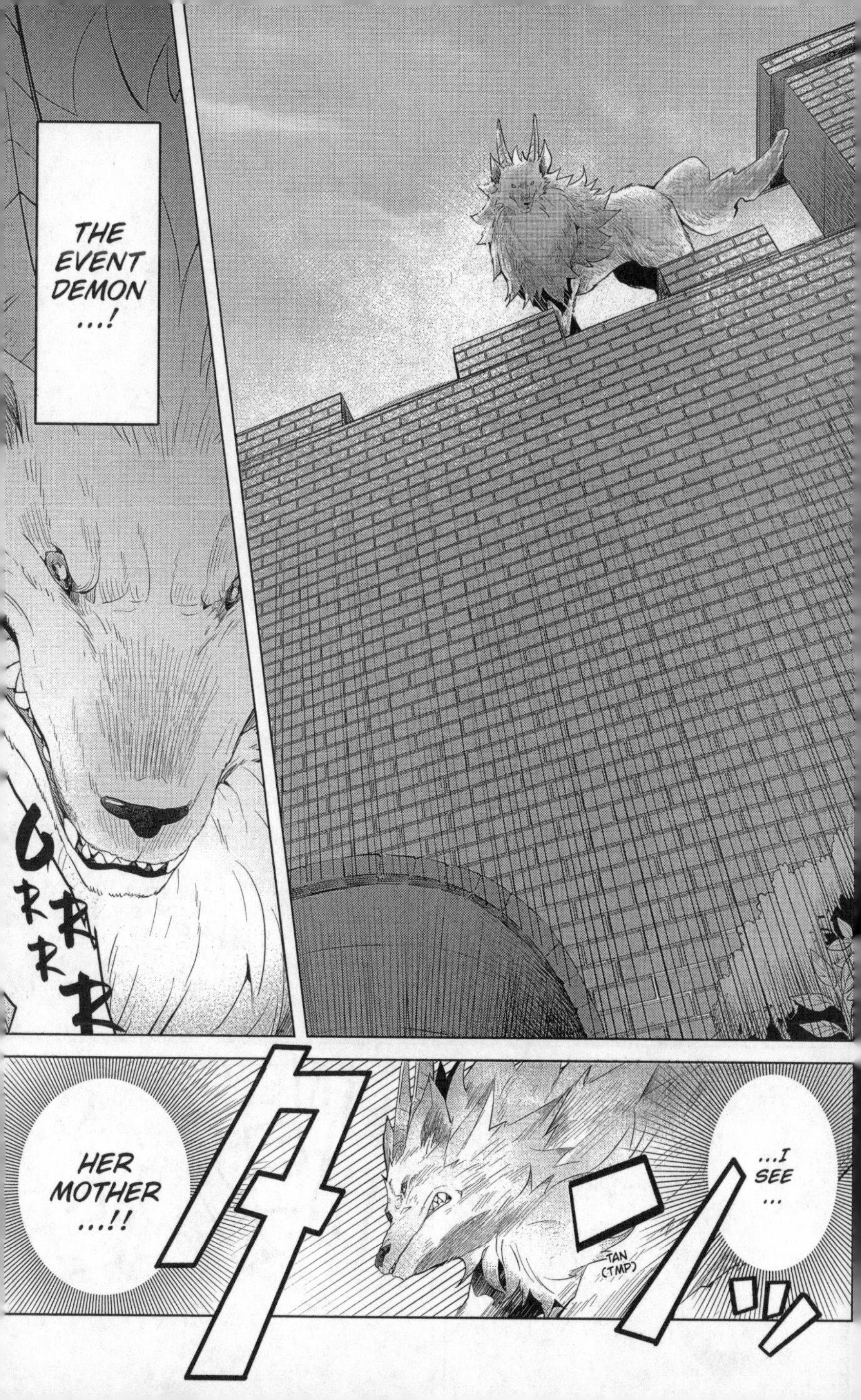
THE EVENT DEMON ...!
GRRRRR
...I SEE ...
TAN (TMP)
HER MOTHER ...!!

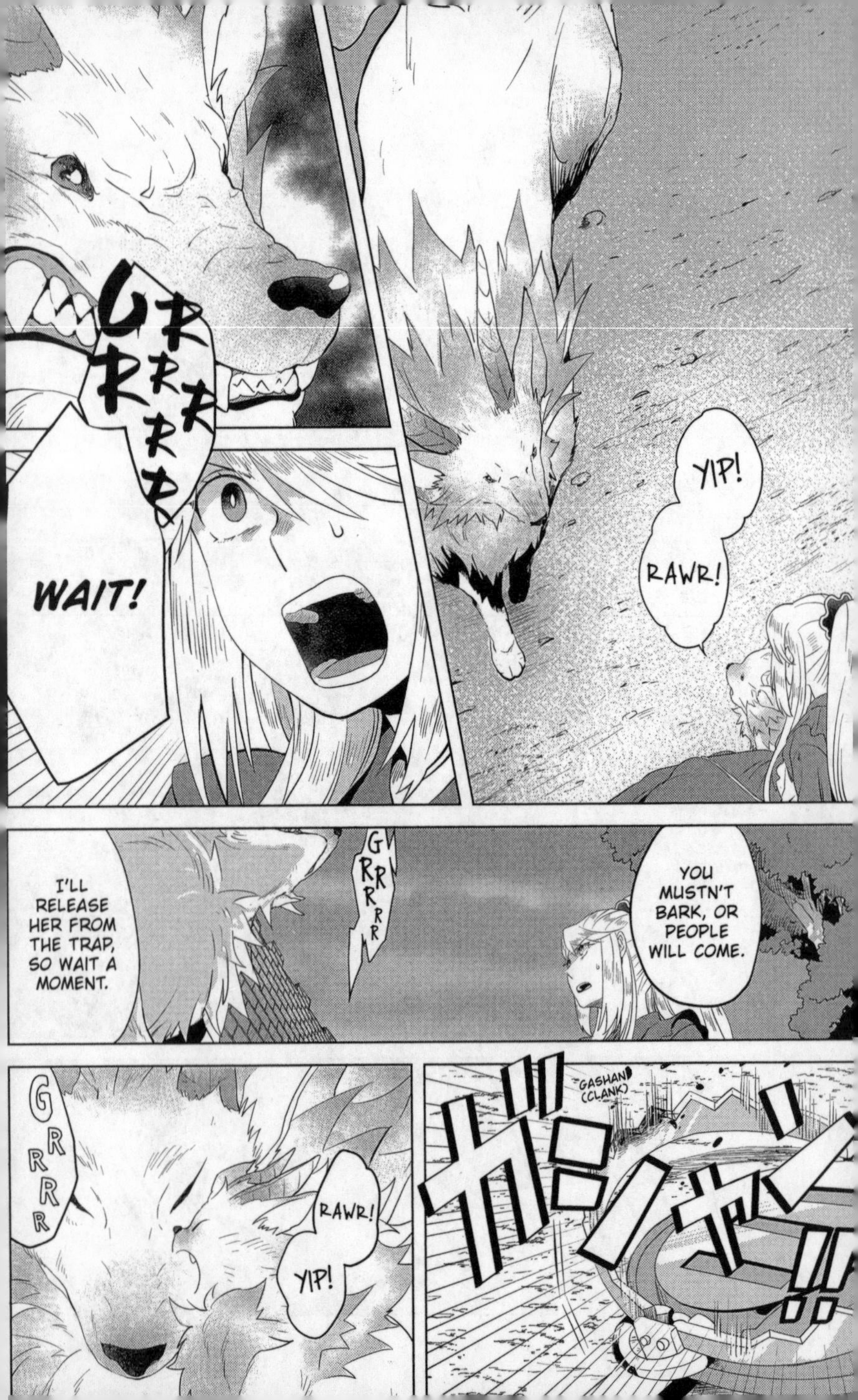
YIP!
RAWR!
GRRRRRRR
WAIT!
YOU MUSTN'T BARK, OR PEOPLE WILL COME.
GRRRRR
I'LL RELEASE HER FROM THE TRAP, SO WAIT A MOMENT.
GASHAN (CLANK)
ガシャーン!!
RAWR!
YIP!
GRRRRR

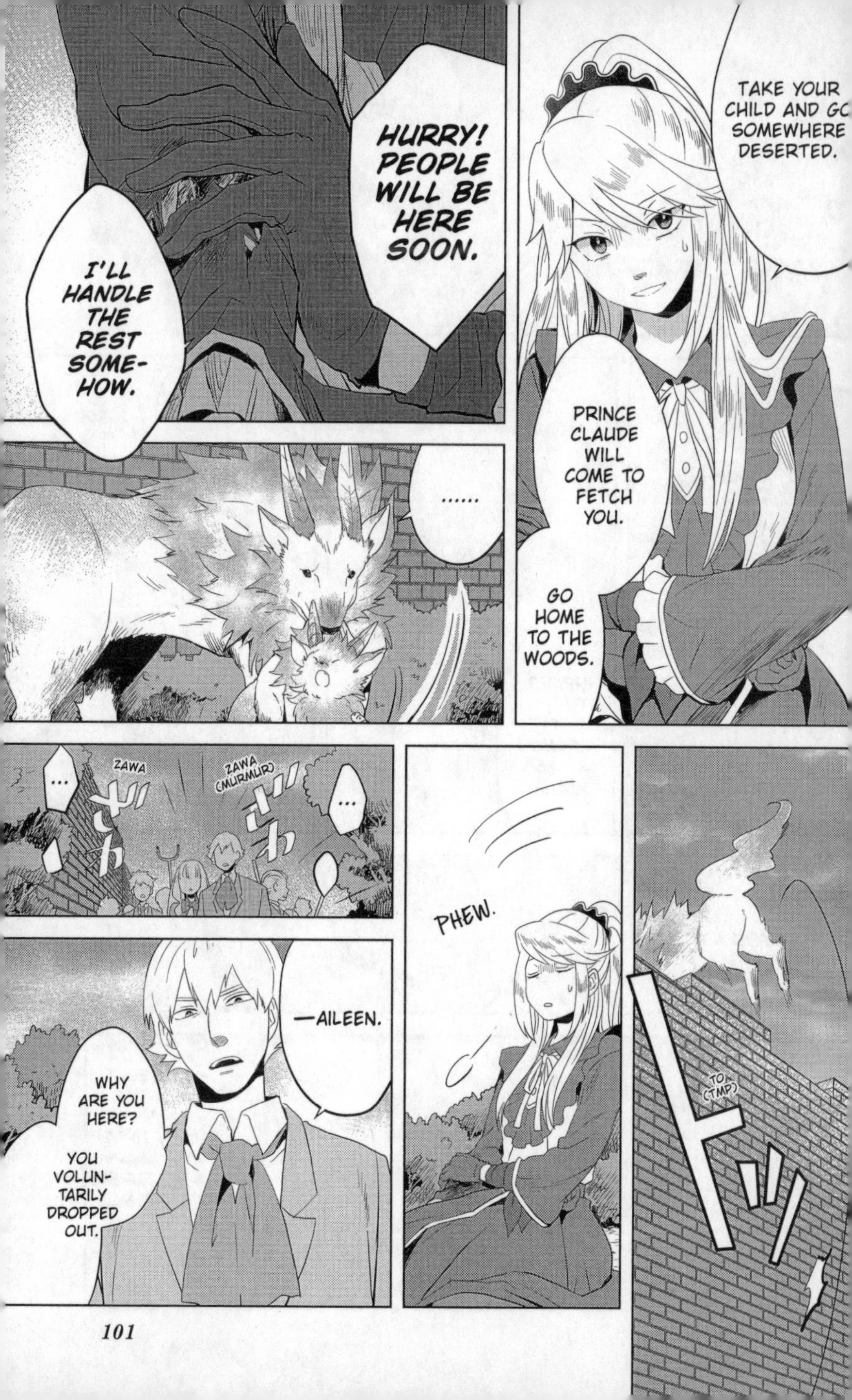
TAKE YOUR CHILD AND GO SOMEWHERE DESERTED.
PRINCE CLAUDE WILL COME TO FETCH YOU.
GO HOME TO THE WOODS.
HURRY! PEOPLE WILL BE HERE SOON.
I'LL HANDLE THE REST SOME-HOW.
......
TO (TMP)
PHEW.
...
ZAWA (MURMUR)
ZAWA
...
—AILEEN.
WHY ARE YOU HERE?
YOU VOLUN-TARILY DROPPED OUT.

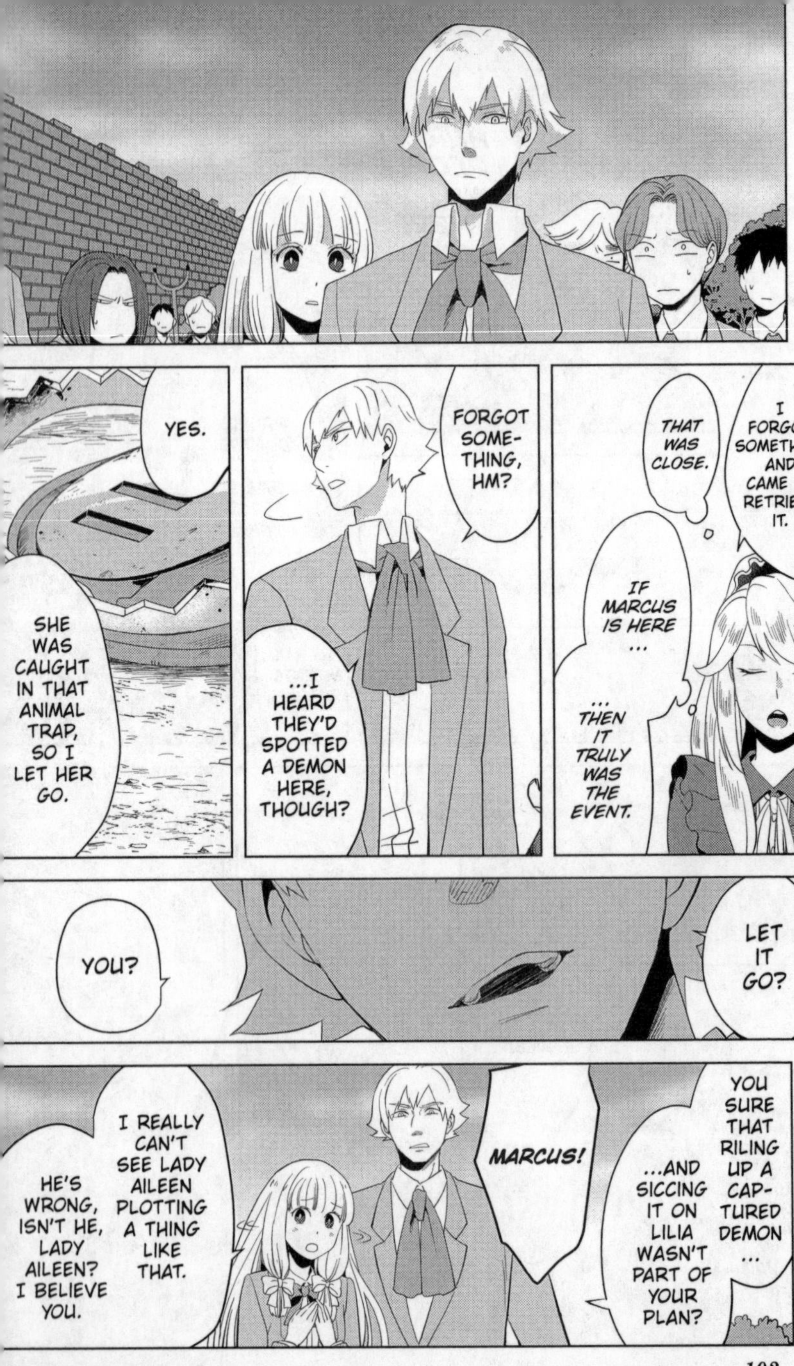
I FORGOT SOMETHING AND CAME TO RETRIEVE IT.
THAT WAS CLOSE.
IF MARCUS IS HERE...
...THEN IT TRULY WAS THE EVENT.
FORGOT SOME-THING, HM?
...I HEARD THEY'D SPOTTED A DEMON HERE, THOUGH?
YES.
SHE WAS CAUGHT IN THAT ANIMAL TRAP, SO I LET HER GO.
LET IT GO?
YOU?
YOU SURE THAT RILING UP A CAP-TURED DEMON...
...AND SICCING IT ON LILIA WASN'T PART OF YOUR PLAN?
MARCUS!
I REALLY CAN'T SEE LADY AILEEN PLOTTING A THING LIKE THAT.
HE'S WRONG, ISN'T HE, LADY AILEEN? I BELIEVE YOU.

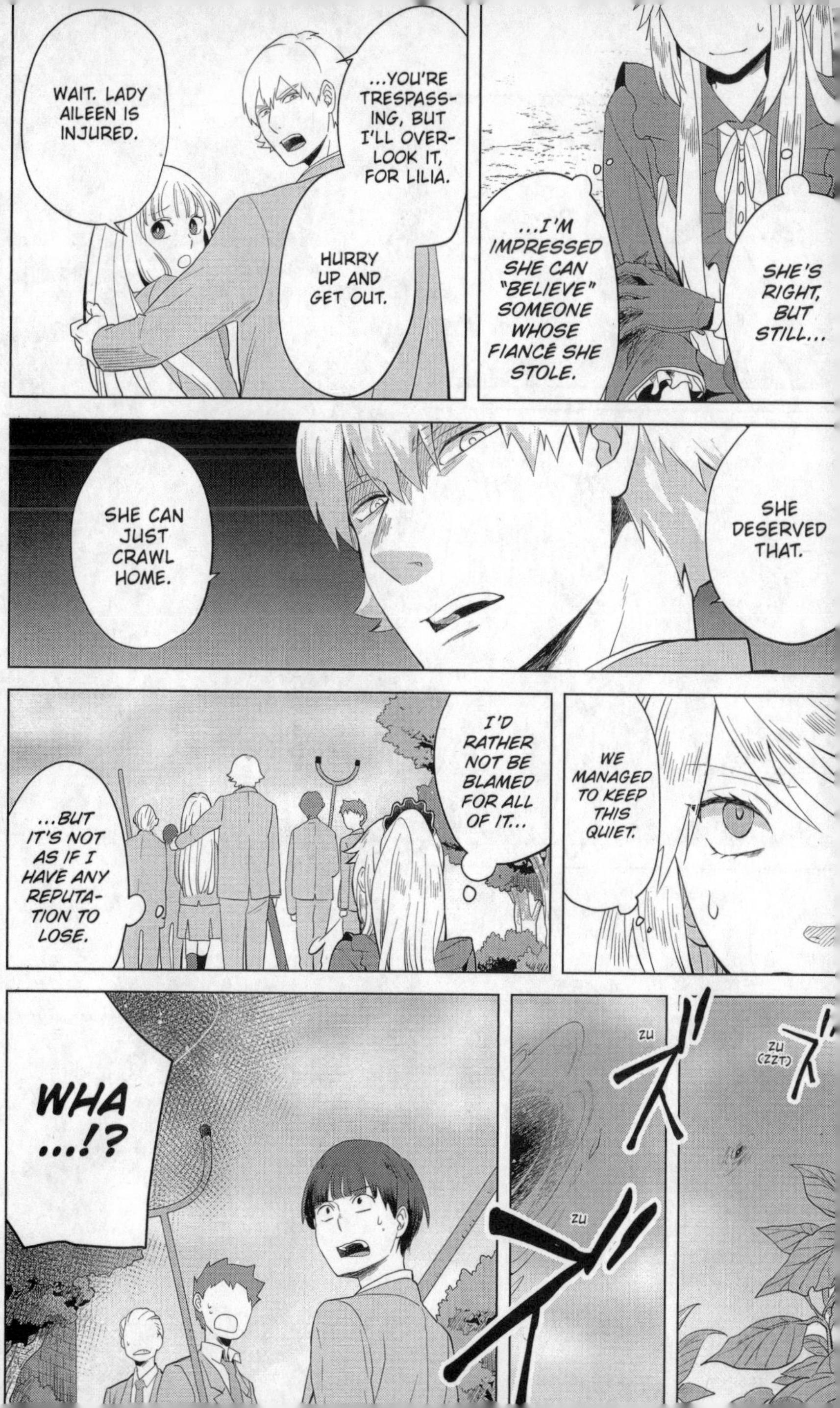
SHE'S RIGHT, BUT STILL...
...I'M IMPRESSED SHE CAN "BELIEVE" SOMEONE WHOSE FIANCÉ SHE STOLE.
...YOU'RE TRESPASSING, BUT I'LL OVERLOOK IT, FOR LILIA.
HURRY UP AND GET OUT.
WAIT. LADY AILEEN IS INJURED.
SHE DESERVED THAT.
SHE CAN JUST CRAWL HOME.
WE MANAGED TO KEEP THIS QUIET.
I'D RATHER NOT BE BLAMED FOR ALL OF IT...
...BUT IT'S NOT AS IF I HAVE ANY REPUTATION TO LOSE.
ZU
ZU (ZZT)
ZU
WHA...!?

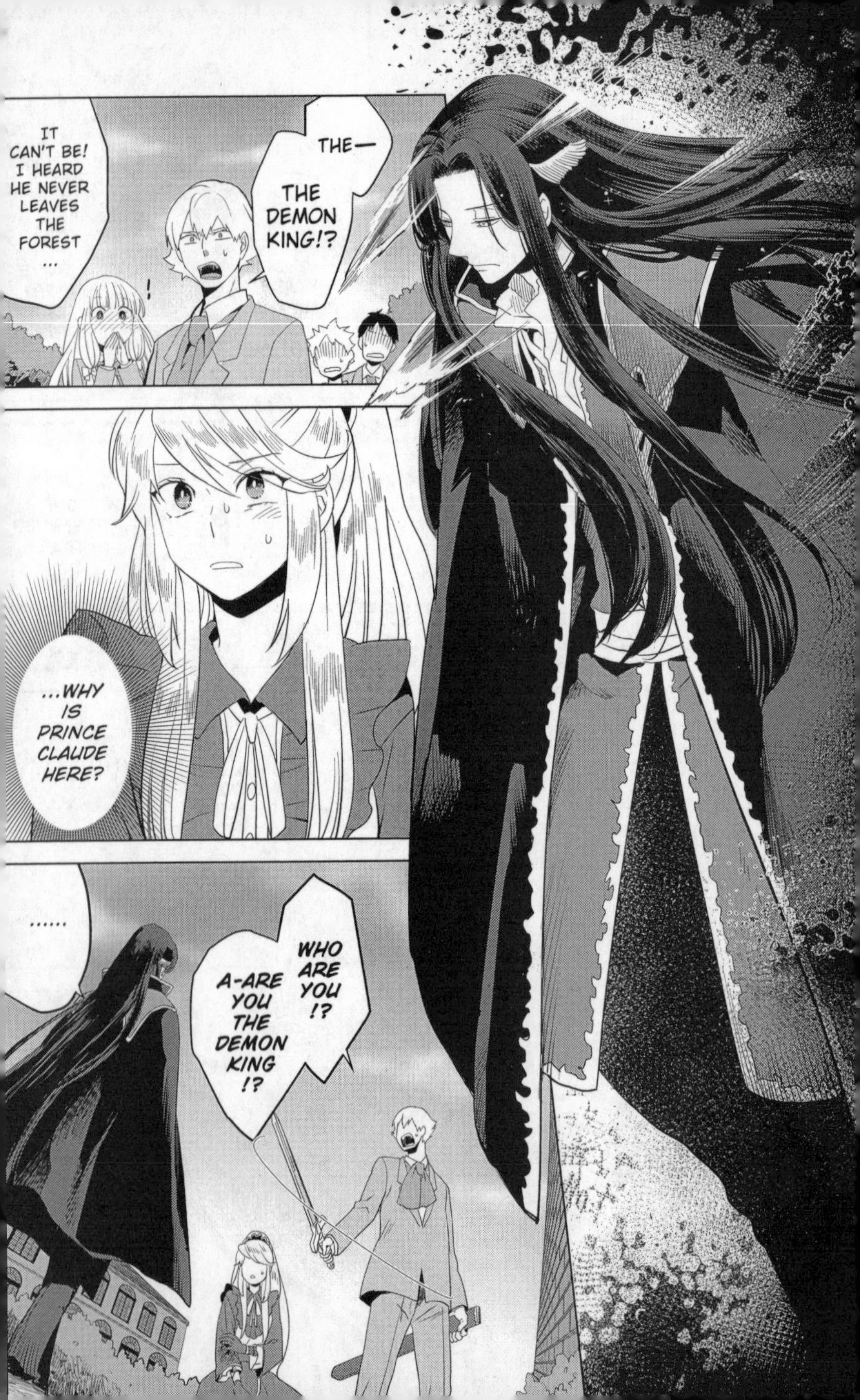
THE—
THE DEMON KING!?
IT CAN'T BE! I HEARD HE NEVER LEAVES THE FOREST ...
!
...WHY IS PRINCE CLAUDE HERE?
WHO ARE YOU!?
A-ARE YOU THE DEMON KING!?
......

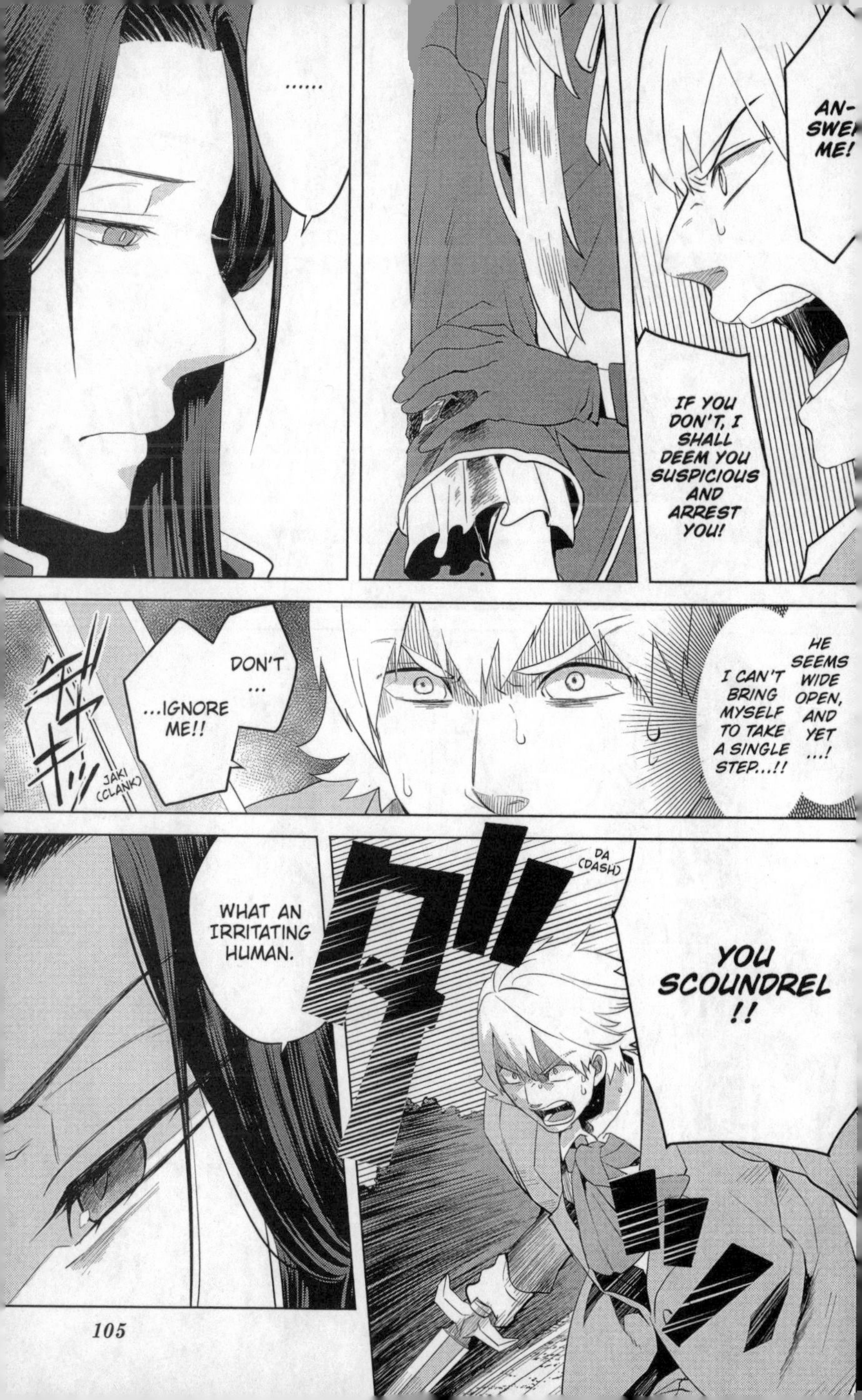
AN- SWE ME!
IF YOU DON'T, I SHALL DEEM YOU SUSPICIOUS AND ARREST YOU!
......
HE SEEMS WIDE OPEN, AND YET ...!
I CAN'T BRING MYSELF TO TAKE A SINGLE STEP...!!
DON'T ...
...IGNORE ME!!
JAKI (CLANK)
DA (DASH)
YOU SCOUNDREL !!
WHAT AN IRRITATING HUMAN.

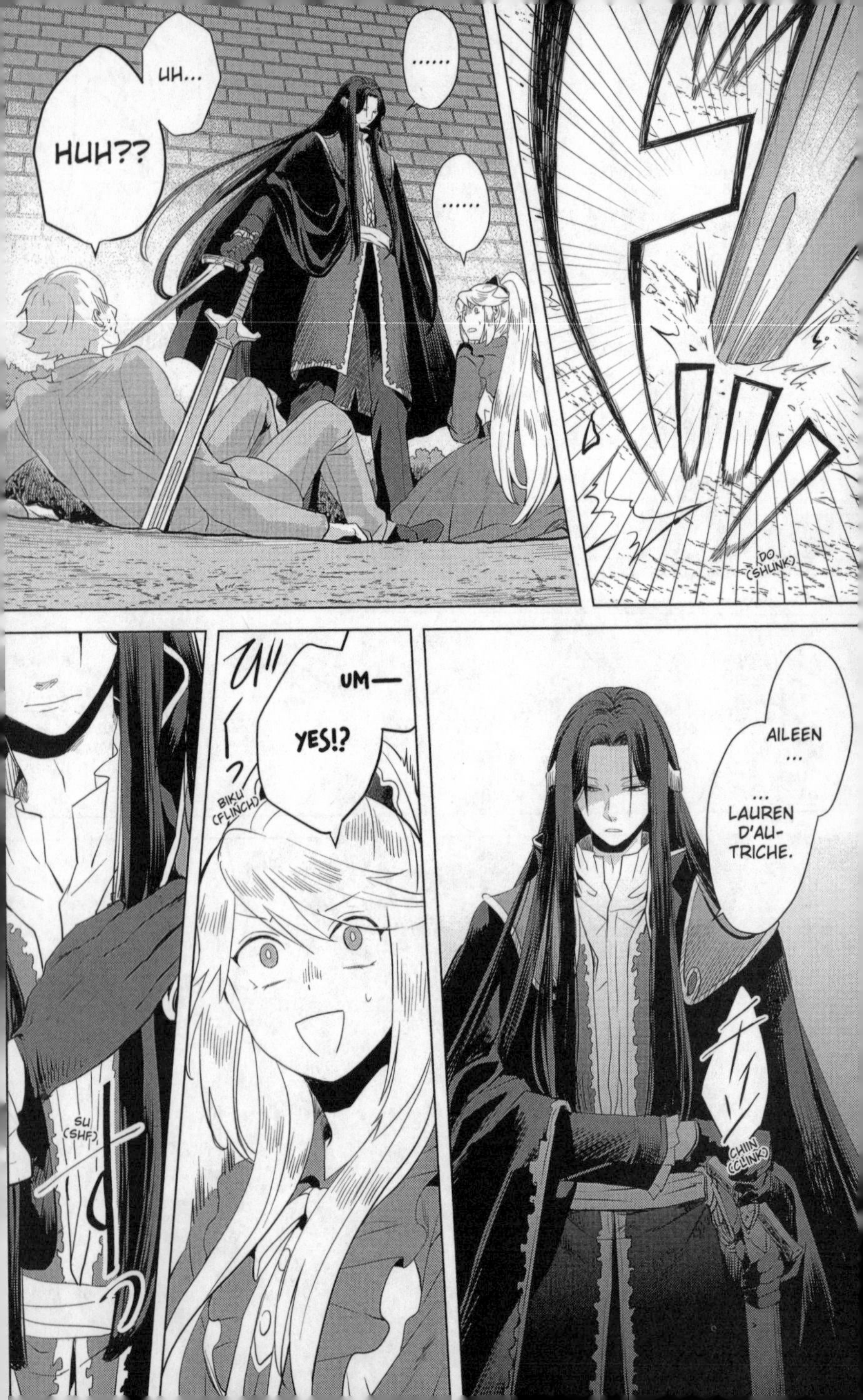
DO (SHUNK)
....
UH...
HUH??
....
AILEEN ... ... LAUREN D'AUTRICHE.
CHIIN (CLINK)
UM— YES!?
BIKU (FLINCH)
SU (SHF)

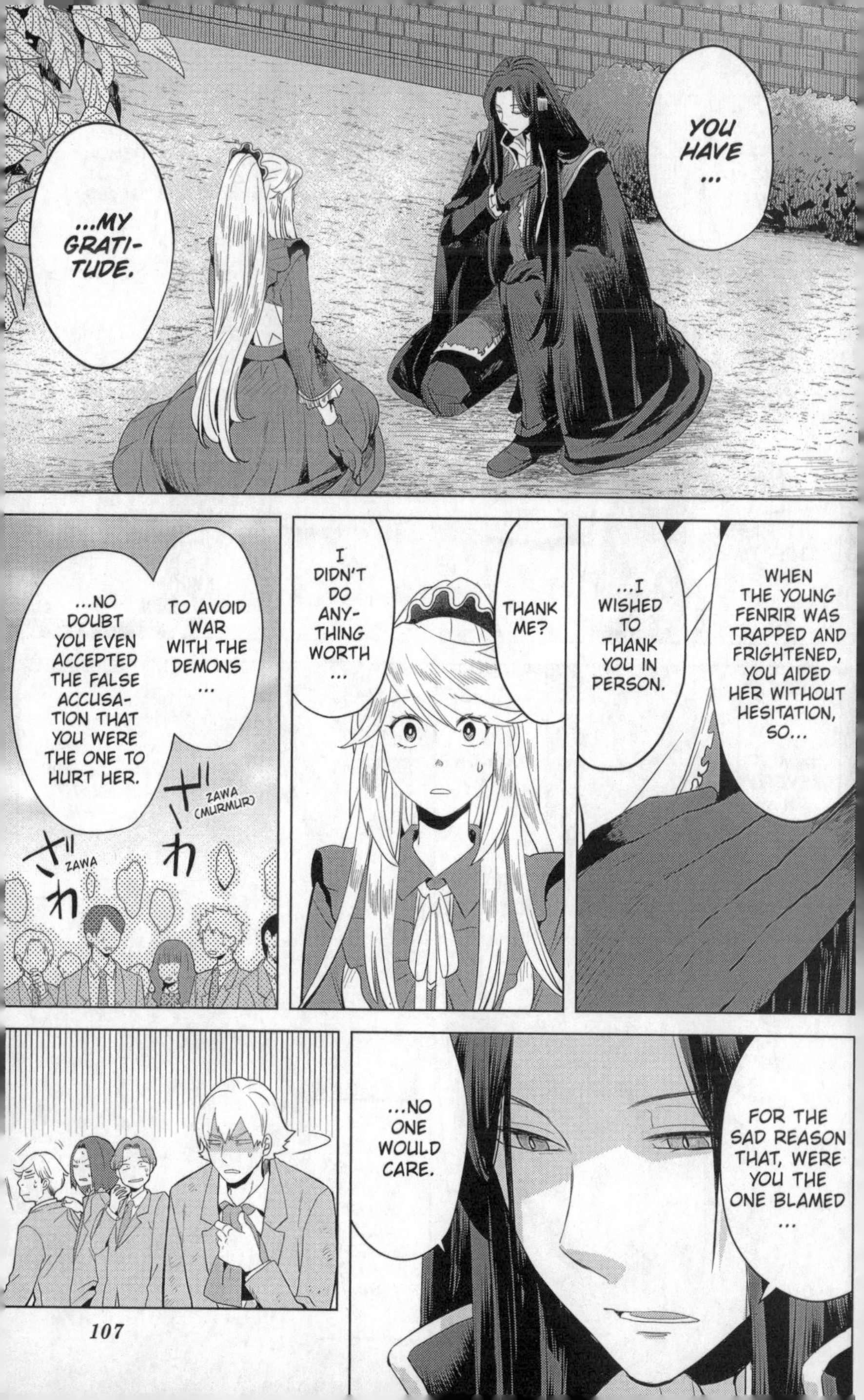
YOU HAVE ...
...MY GRATITUDE.
WHEN THE YOUNG FENRIR WAS TRAPPED AND FRIGHTENED, YOU AIDED HER WITHOUT HESITATION, SO...
...I WISHED TO THANK YOU IN PERSON.
THANK ME?
I DIDN'T DO ANYTHING WORTH ...
TO AVOID WAR WITH THE DEMONS ...
...NO DOUBT YOU EVEN ACCEPTED THE FALSE ACCUSATION THAT YOU WERE THE ONE TO HURT HER.
ざわ ZAWA (MURMUR)
ざわ ZAWA
FOR THE SAD REASON THAT, WERE YOU THE ONE BLAMED ...
...NO ONE WOULD CARE.

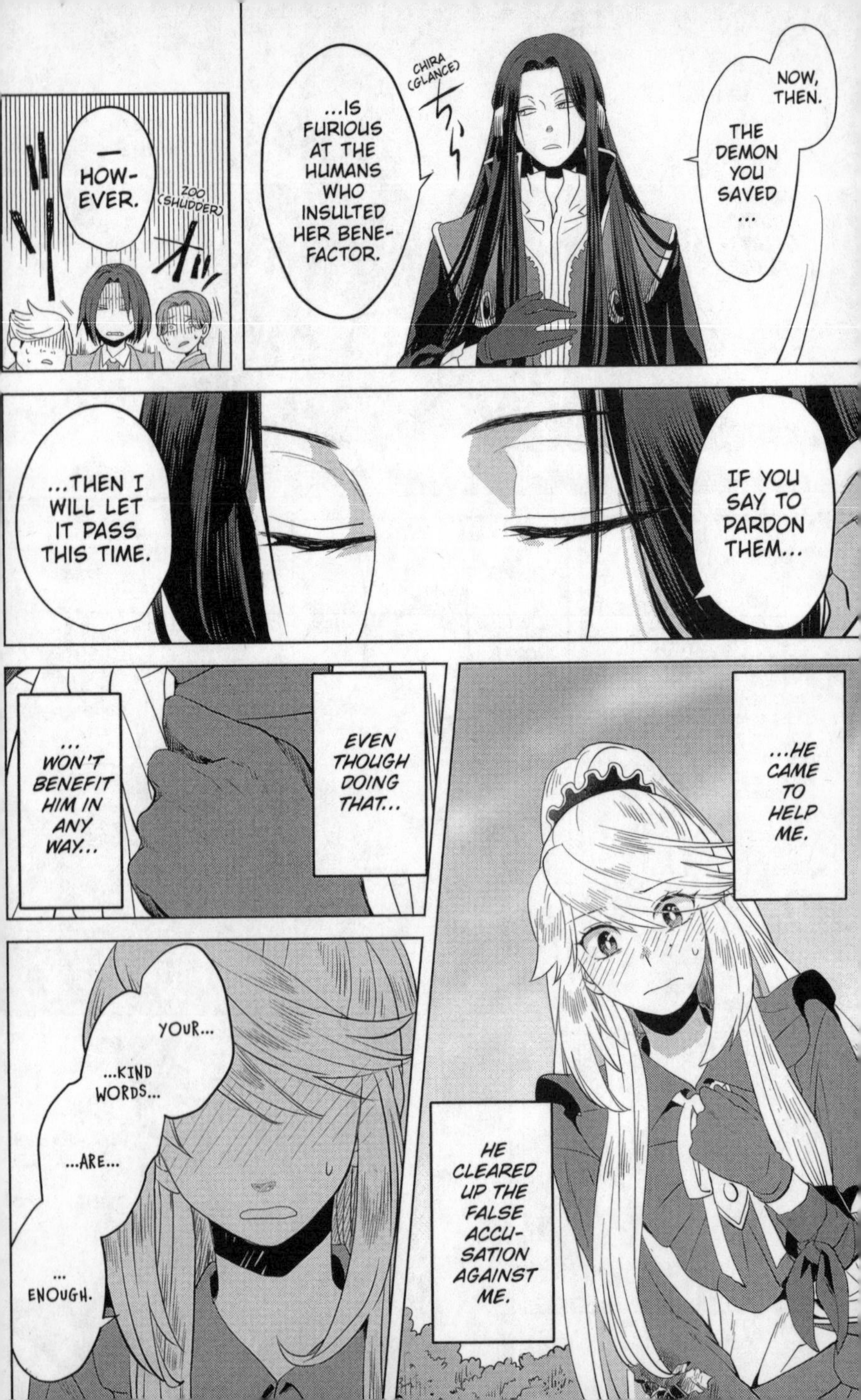
NOW, THEN.
THE DEMON YOU SAVED ...
CHIRA (GLANCE)
...IS FURIOUS AT THE HUMANS WHO INSULTED HER BENE-FACTOR.
ZOO (SHUDDER)
—HOW-EVER.
IF YOU SAY TO PARDON THEM...
...THEN I WILL LET IT PASS THIS TIME.
...HE CAME TO HELP ME.
HE CLEARED UP THE FALSE ACCU-SATION AGAINST ME.
EVEN THOUGH DOING THAT...
...WON'T BENEFIT HIM IN ANY WAY...
YOUR...
...KIND WORDS...
...ARE...
... ENOUGH.

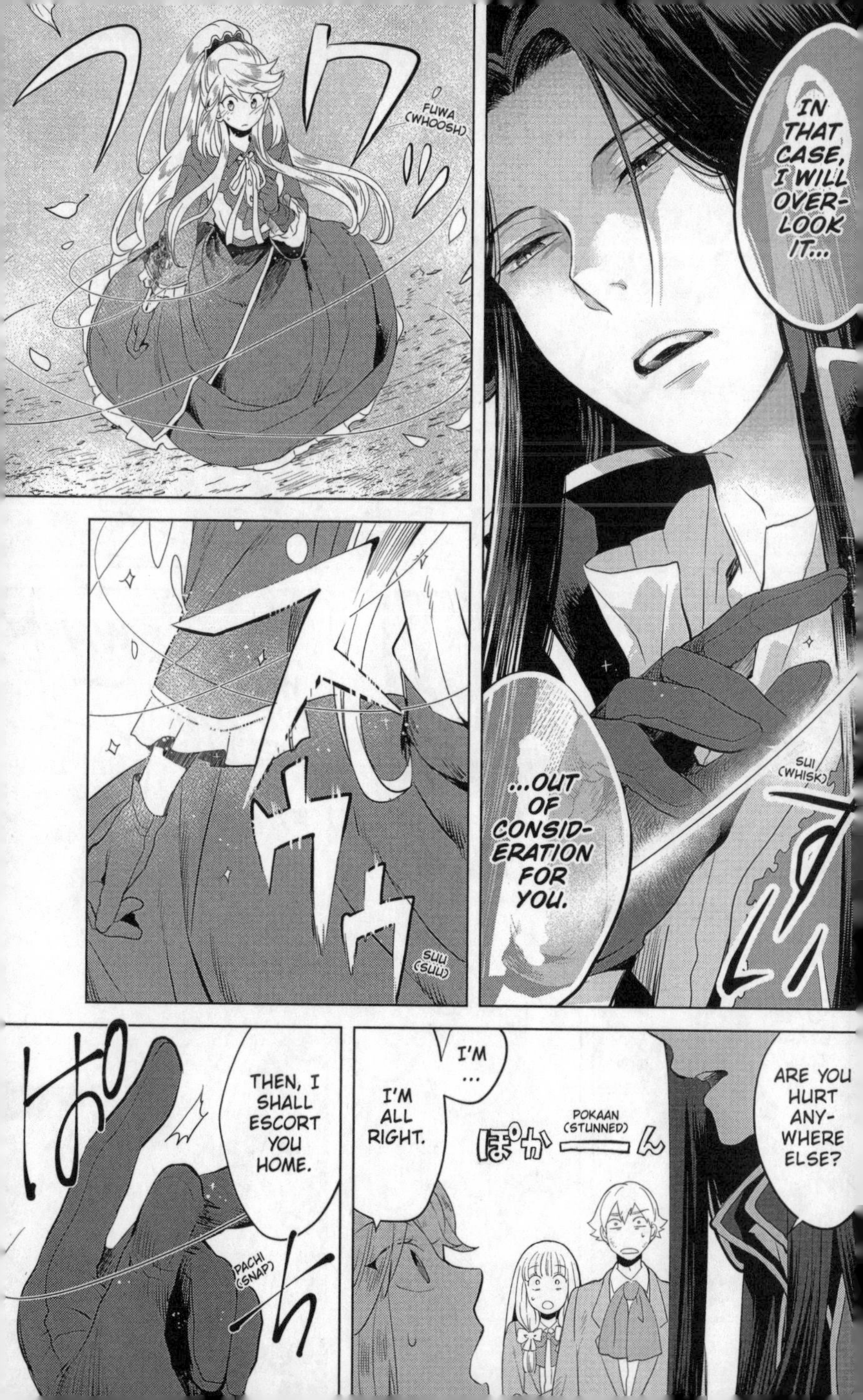
IN THAT CASE, I WILL OVER-LOOK IT...
...OUT OF CONSID-ERATION FOR YOU.
SUI (WHISK)
FUWA (WHOOSH)
SUU (SUU)
ARE YOU HURT ANY-WHERE ELSE?
POKAAN (STUNNED)
ぽか——ん
I'M ...
I'M ALL RIGHT.
THEN, I SHALL ESCORT YOU HOME.
PACHI (SNAP)

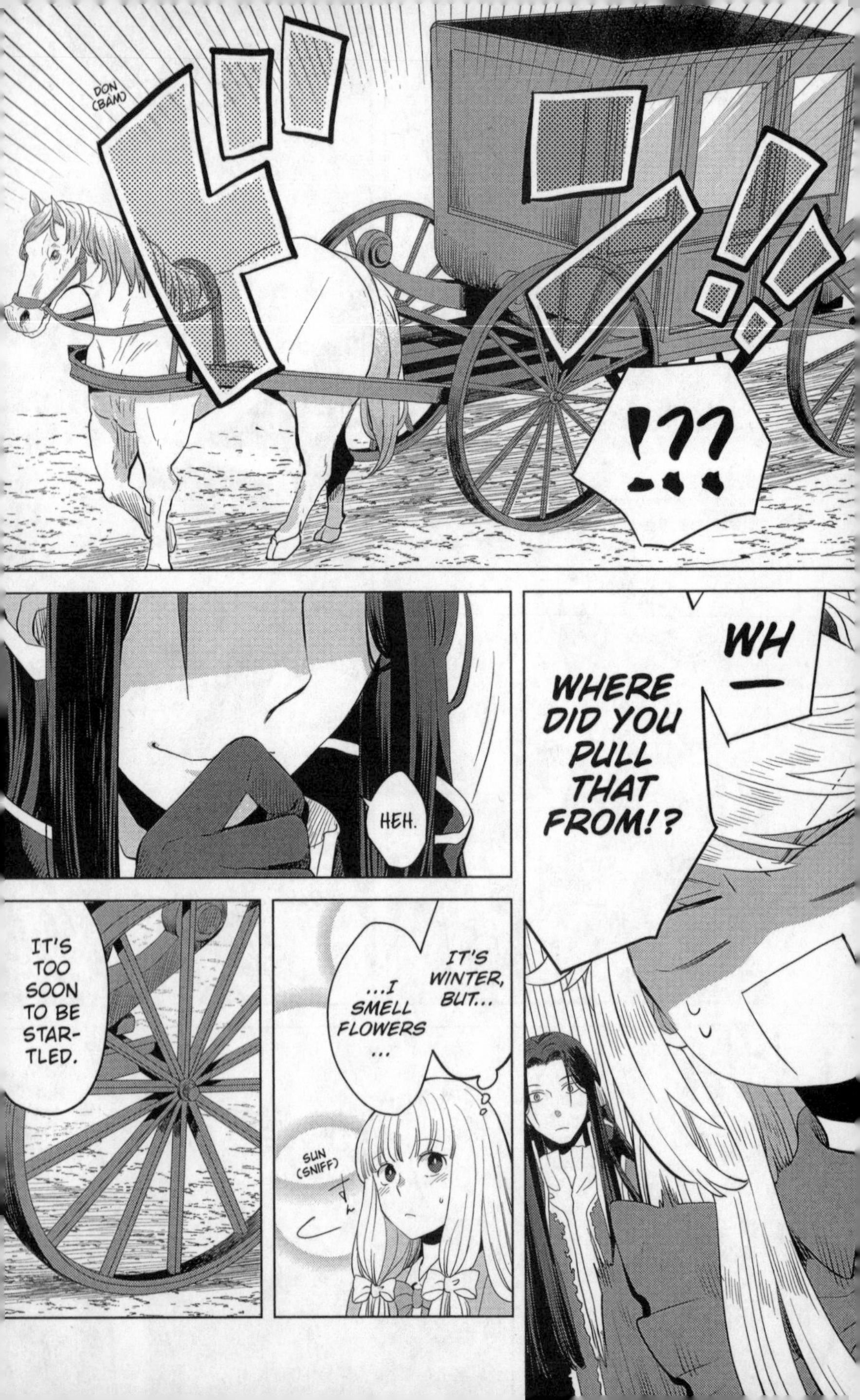
DON (BAM)
!??
WH—
WHERE DID YOU PULL THAT FROM!?
HEH.
IT'S WINTER, BUT...
...I SMELL FLOWERS...
SUN (SNIFF)
IT'S TOO SOON TO BE STAR-TLED.

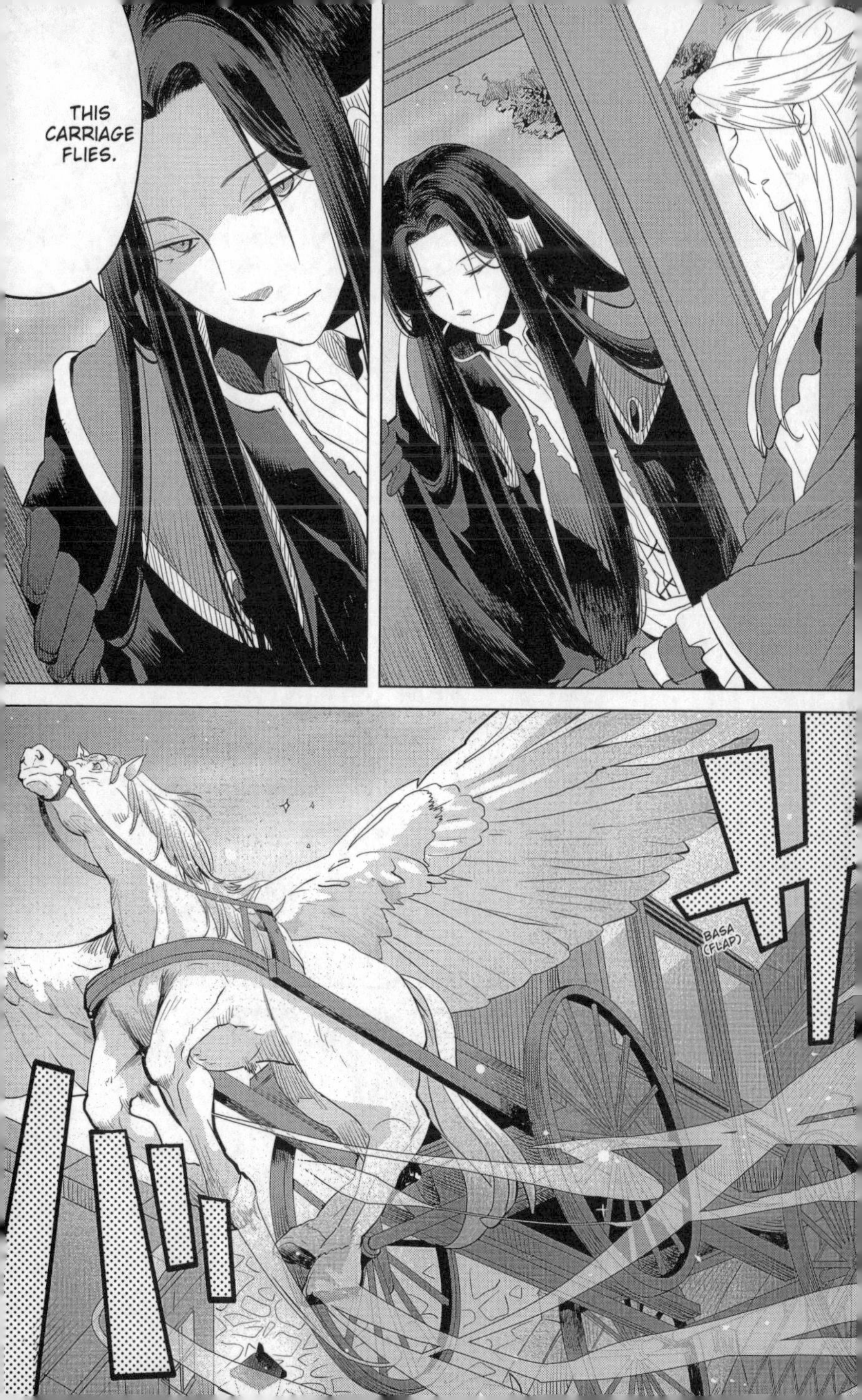
THIS CARRIAGE FLIES.
BASA (FLAP)

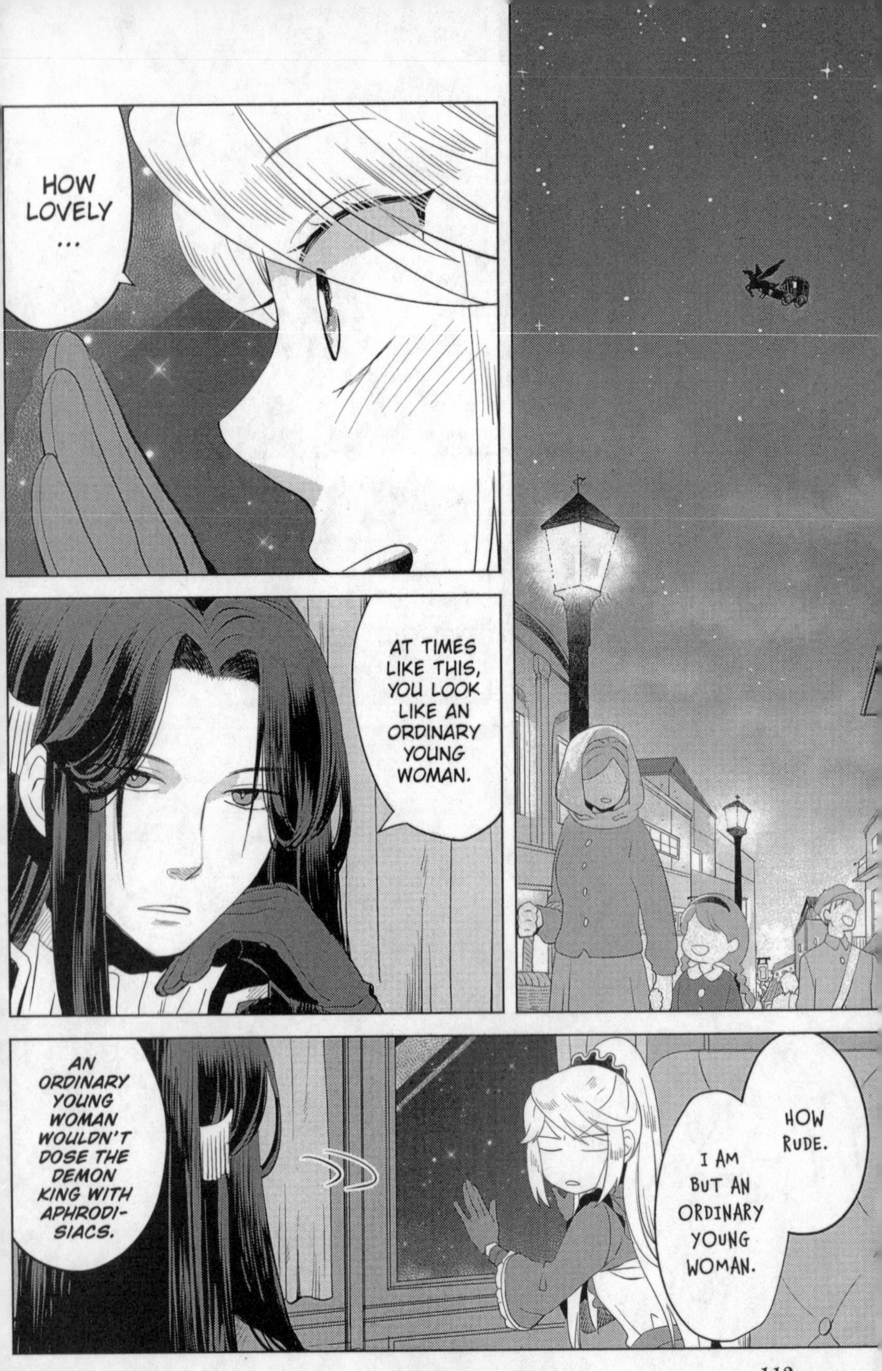
HOW LOVELY ...
AT TIMES LIKE THIS, YOU LOOK LIKE AN ORDINARY YOUNG WOMAN.
HOW RUDE.
I AM BUT AN ORDINARY YOUNG WOMAN.
AN ORDINARY YOUNG WOMAN WOULDN'T DOSE THE DEMON KING WITH APHRODISIACS.

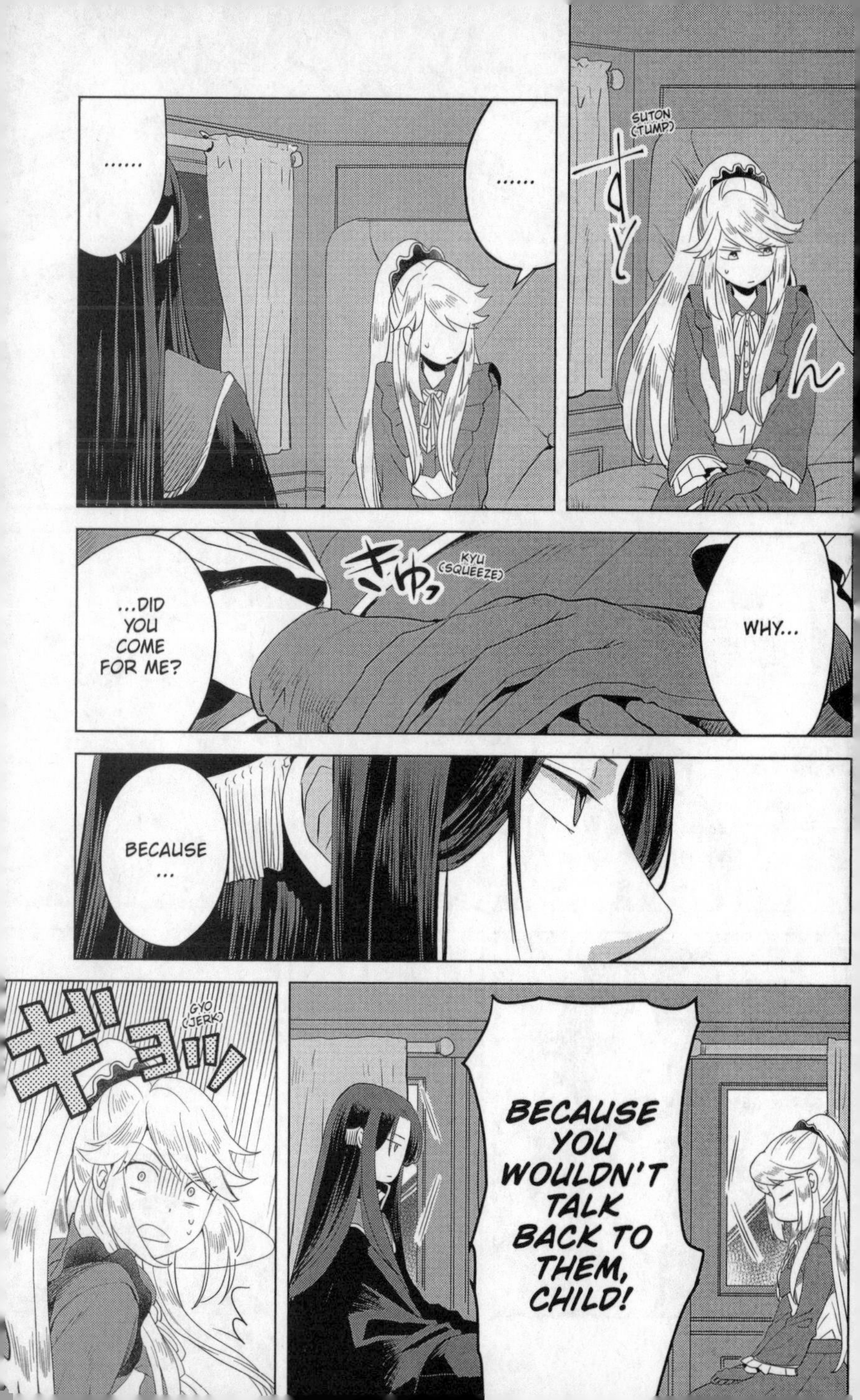

SUTON (TUMP)
......
......
WHY...
KYU (SQUEEZE)
...DID YOU COME FOR ME?
BECAUSE ...
BECAUSE YOU WOULDN'T TALK BACK TO THEM, CHILD!
GYO (JERK)

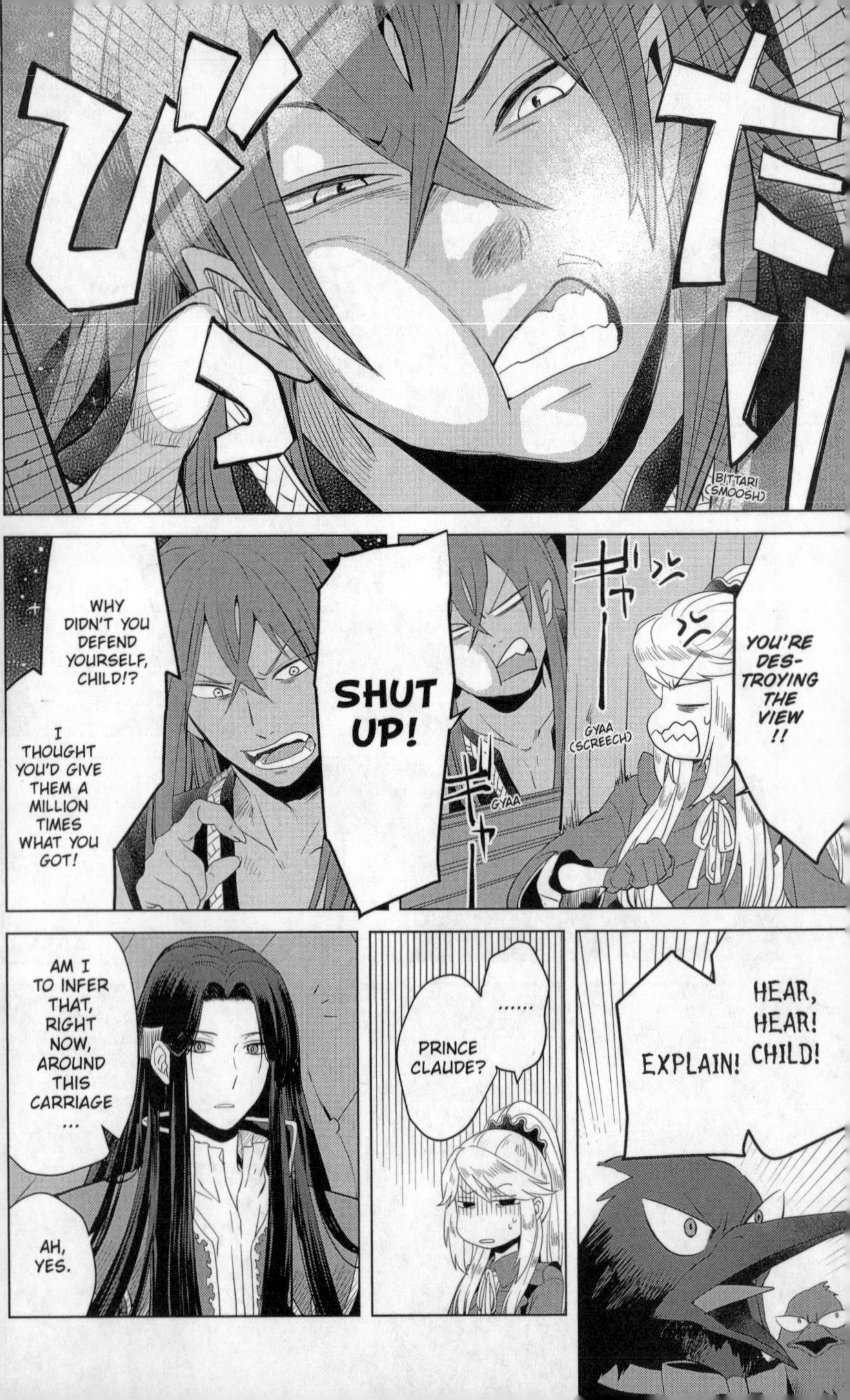
BITTARI (SMOOSH)
YOU'RE DES-TROYING THE VIEW!!
GYAA (SCREECH)
GYAA
SHUT UP!
WHY DIDN'T YOU DEFEND YOURSELF, CHILD!?
I THOUGHT YOU'D GIVE THEM A MILLION TIMES WHAT YOU GOT!
HEAR, HEAR! CHILD!
EXPLAIN!
......
PRINCE CLAUDE?
AM I TO INFER THAT, RIGHT NOW, AROUND THIS CARRIAGE ...
AH, YES.

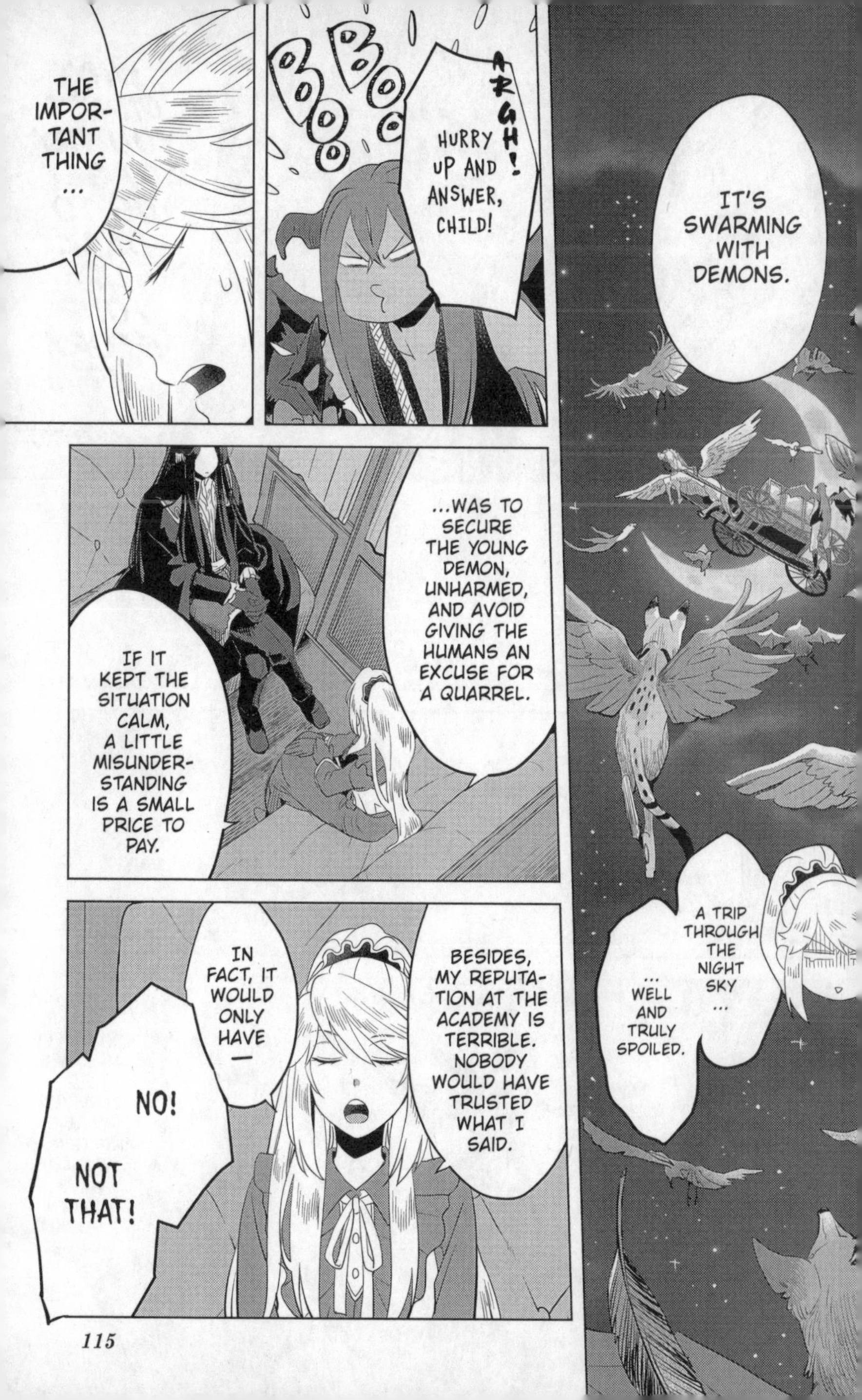
IT'S SWARMING WITH DEMONS.
A TRIP THROUGH THE NIGHT SKY...
...WELL AND TRULY SPOILED.
BOOOOO
BOOOO
ARGH!
HURRY UP AND ANSWER, CHILD!
THE IMPORTANT THING...
...WAS TO SECURE THE YOUNG DEMON, UNHARMED, AND AVOID GIVING THE HUMANS AN EXCUSE FOR A QUARREL.
IF IT KEPT THE SITUATION CALM, A LITTLE MISUNDERSTANDING IS A SMALL PRICE TO PAY.
BESIDES, MY REPUTATION AT THE ACADEMY IS TERRIBLE. NOBODY WOULD HAVE TRUSTED WHAT I SAID.
IN FACT, IT WOULD ONLY HAVE—
NO!
NOT THAT!

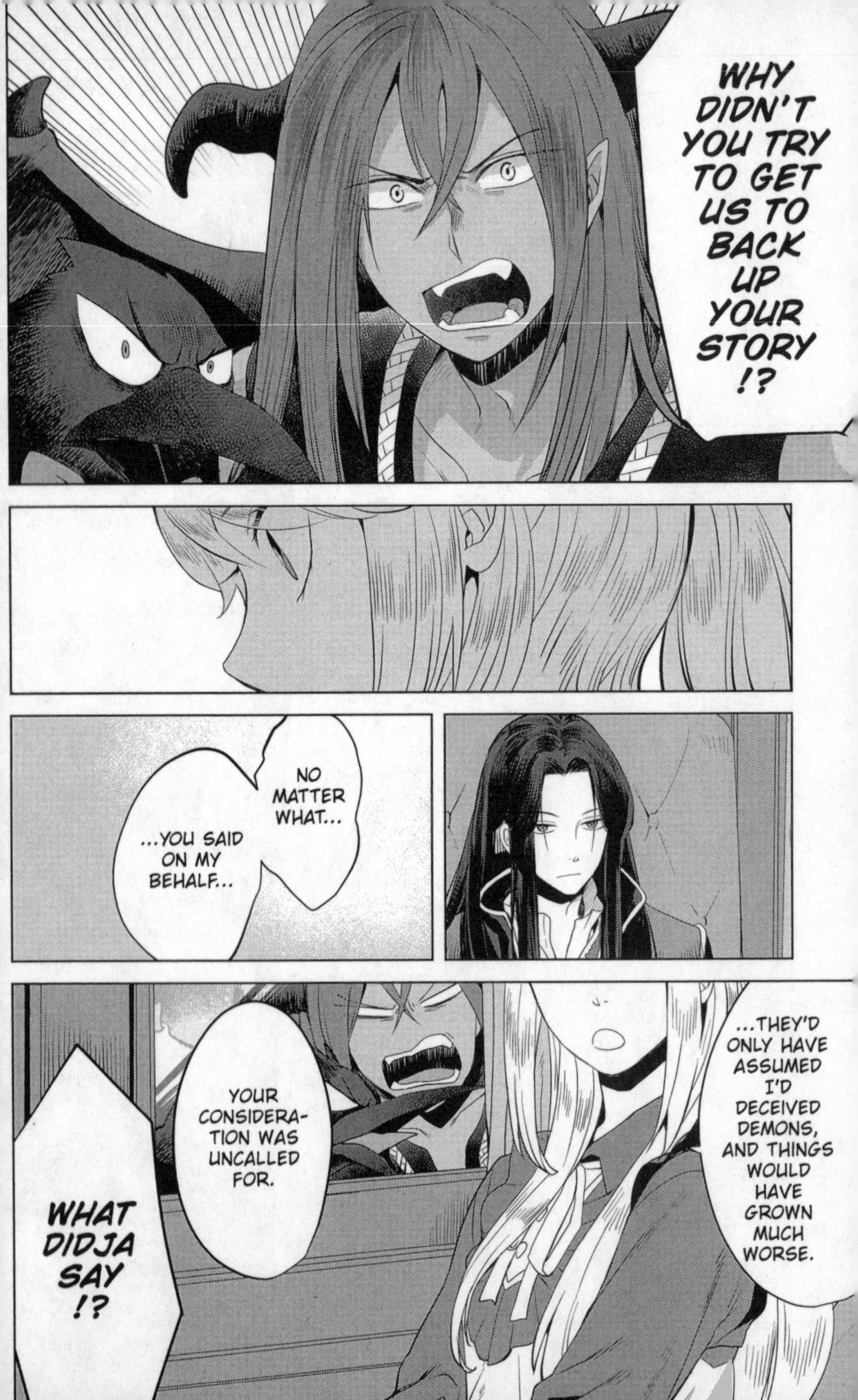
WHY DIDN'T YOU TRY TO GET US TO BACK UP YOUR STORY!?
NO MATTER WHAT...
...YOU SAID ON MY BEHALF...
...THEY'D ONLY HAVE ASSUMED I'D DECEIVED DEMONS, AND THINGS WOULD HAVE GROWN MUCH WORSE.
YOUR CONSIDERA-TION WAS UNCALLED FOR.
WHAT DIDJA SAY!?

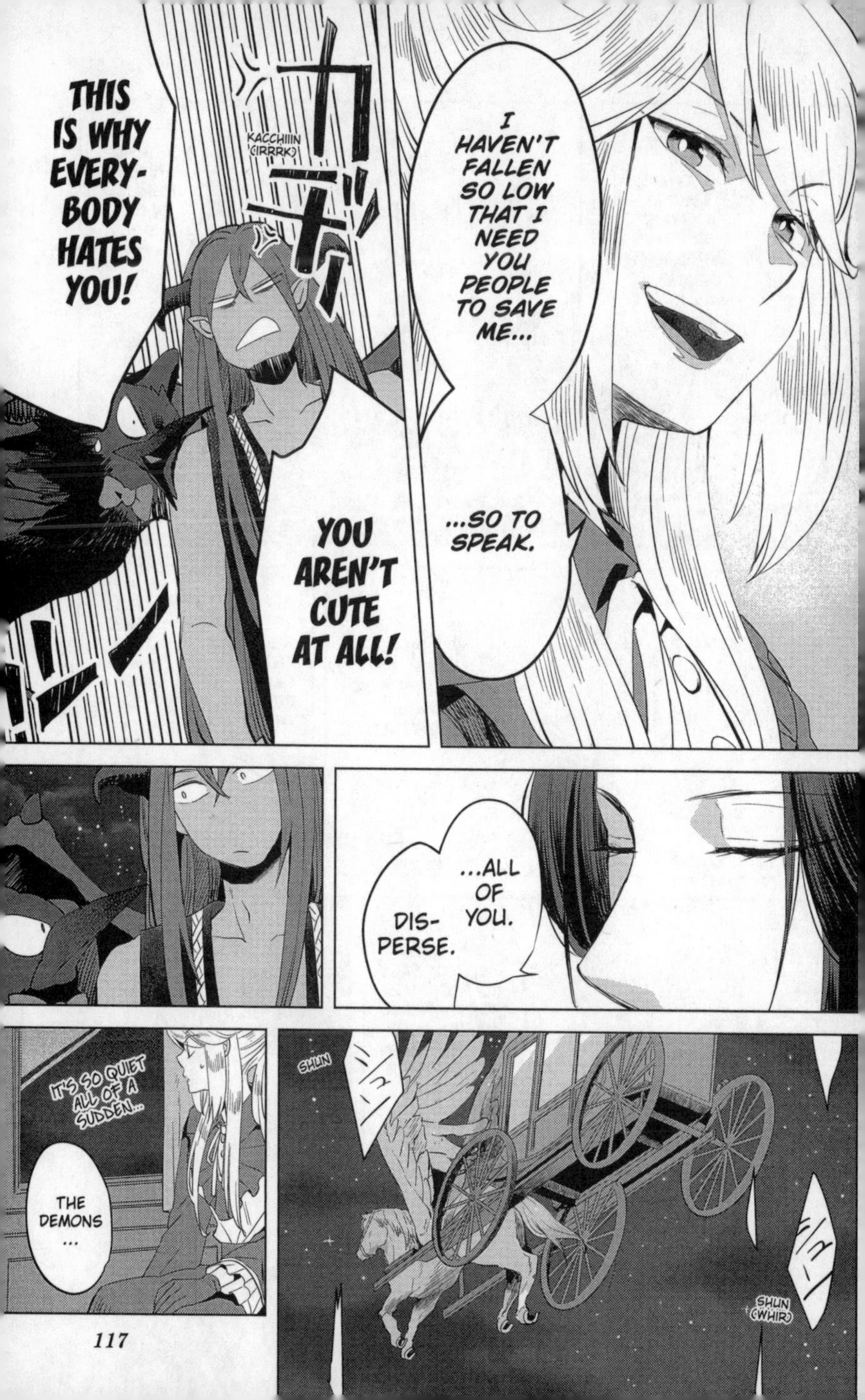
I HAVEN'T FALLEN SO LOW THAT I NEED YOU PEOPLE TO SAVE ME...
...SO TO SPEAK.
YOU AREN'T CUTE AT ALL!
KACCHIIIN (IRRRK)
THIS IS WHY EVERY-BODY HATES YOU!
...ALL OF YOU.
DIS-PERSE.
SHUN
SHUN (WHIR)
IT'S SO QUIET ALL OF A SUDDEN...
THE DEMONS ...

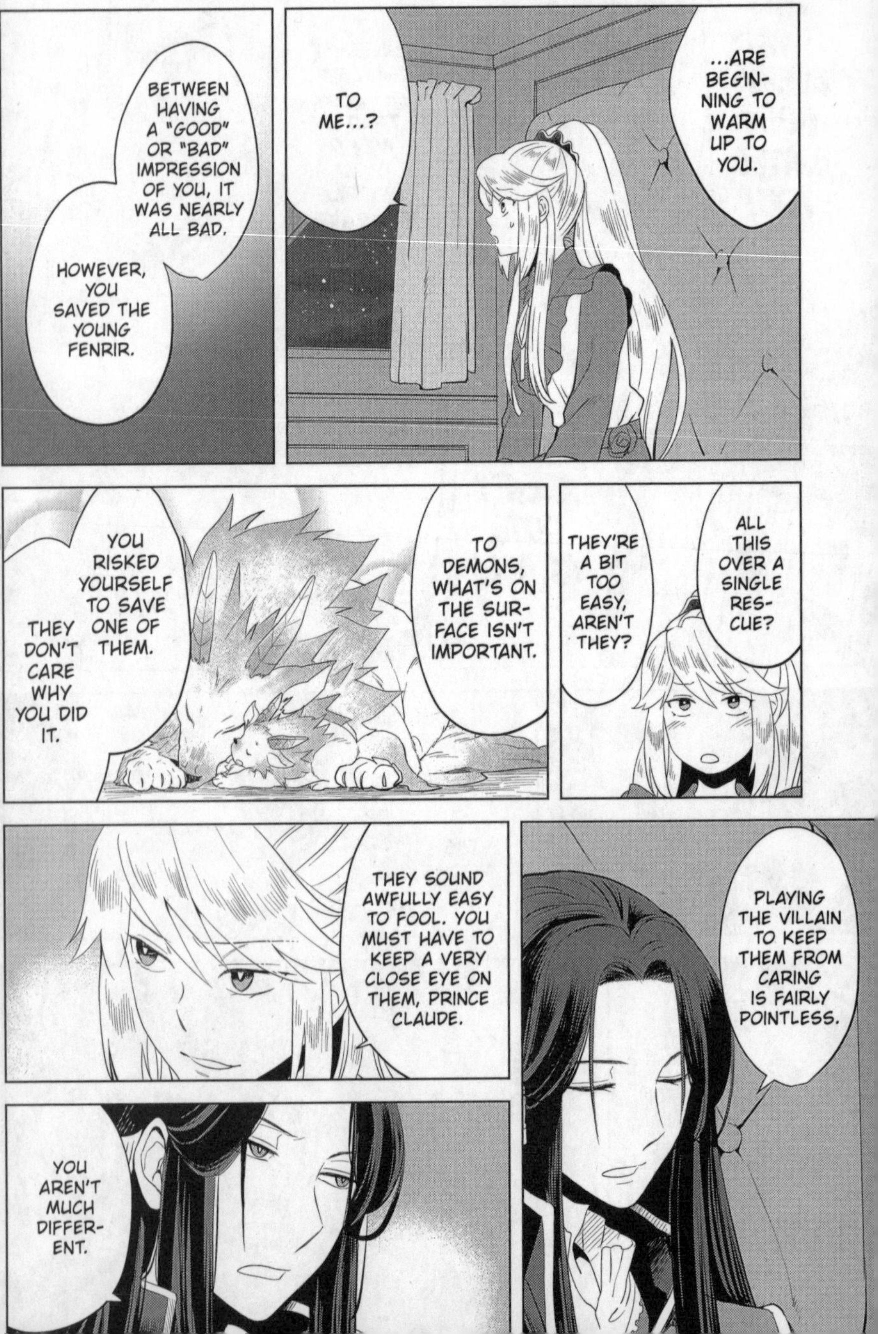
...ARE BEGINNING TO WARM UP TO YOU.
TO ME...?
BETWEEN HAVING A "GOOD" OR "BAD" IMPRESSION OF YOU, IT WAS NEARLY ALL BAD.
HOWEVER, YOU SAVED THE YOUNG FENRIR.
ALL THIS OVER A SINGLE RESCUE?
THEY'RE A BIT TOO EASY, AREN'T THEY?
TO DEMONS, WHAT'S ON THE SURFACE ISN'T IMPORTANT.
YOU RISKED YOURSELF TO SAVE ONE OF THEM.
THEY DON'T CARE WHY YOU DID IT.
PLAYING THE VILLAIN TO KEEP THEM FROM CARING IS FAIRLY POINTLESS.
THEY SOUND AWFULLY EASY TO FOOL. YOU MUST HAVE TO KEEP A VERY CLOSE EYE ON THEM, PRINCE CLAUDE.
YOU AREN'T MUCH DIFFERENT.

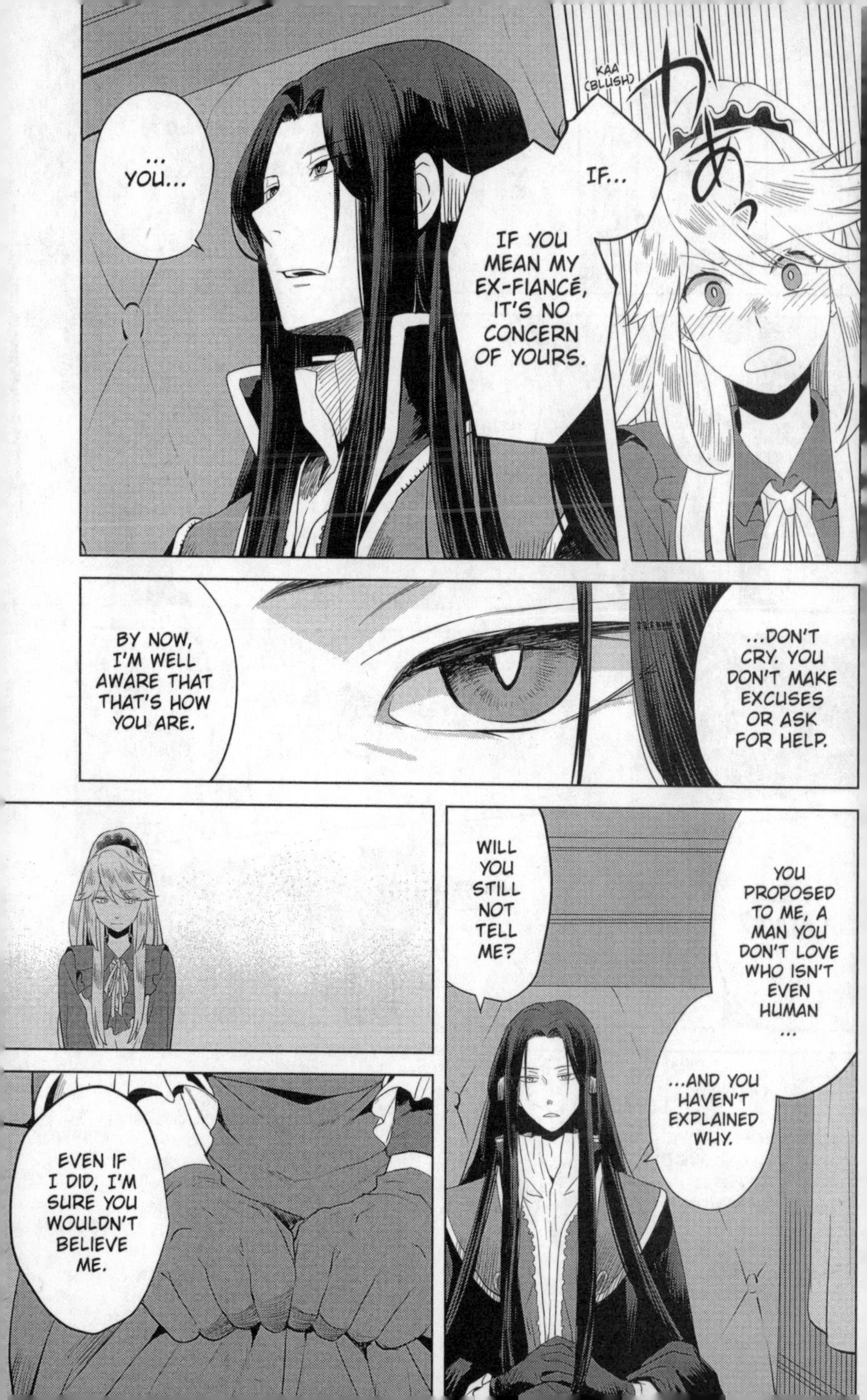
KAA (BLUSH)
IF...
IF YOU MEAN MY EX-FIANCÉ, IT'S NO CONCERN OF YOURS.
... YOU...
...DON'T CRY. YOU DON'T MAKE EXCUSES OR ASK FOR HELP.
BY NOW, I'M WELL AWARE THAT THAT'S HOW YOU ARE.
YOU PROPOSED TO ME, A MAN YOU DON'T LOVE WHO ISN'T EVEN HUMAN ...
...AND YOU HAVEN'T EXPLAINED WHY.
WILL YOU STILL NOT TELL ME?
EVEN IF I DID, I'M SURE YOU WOULDN'T BELIEVE ME.

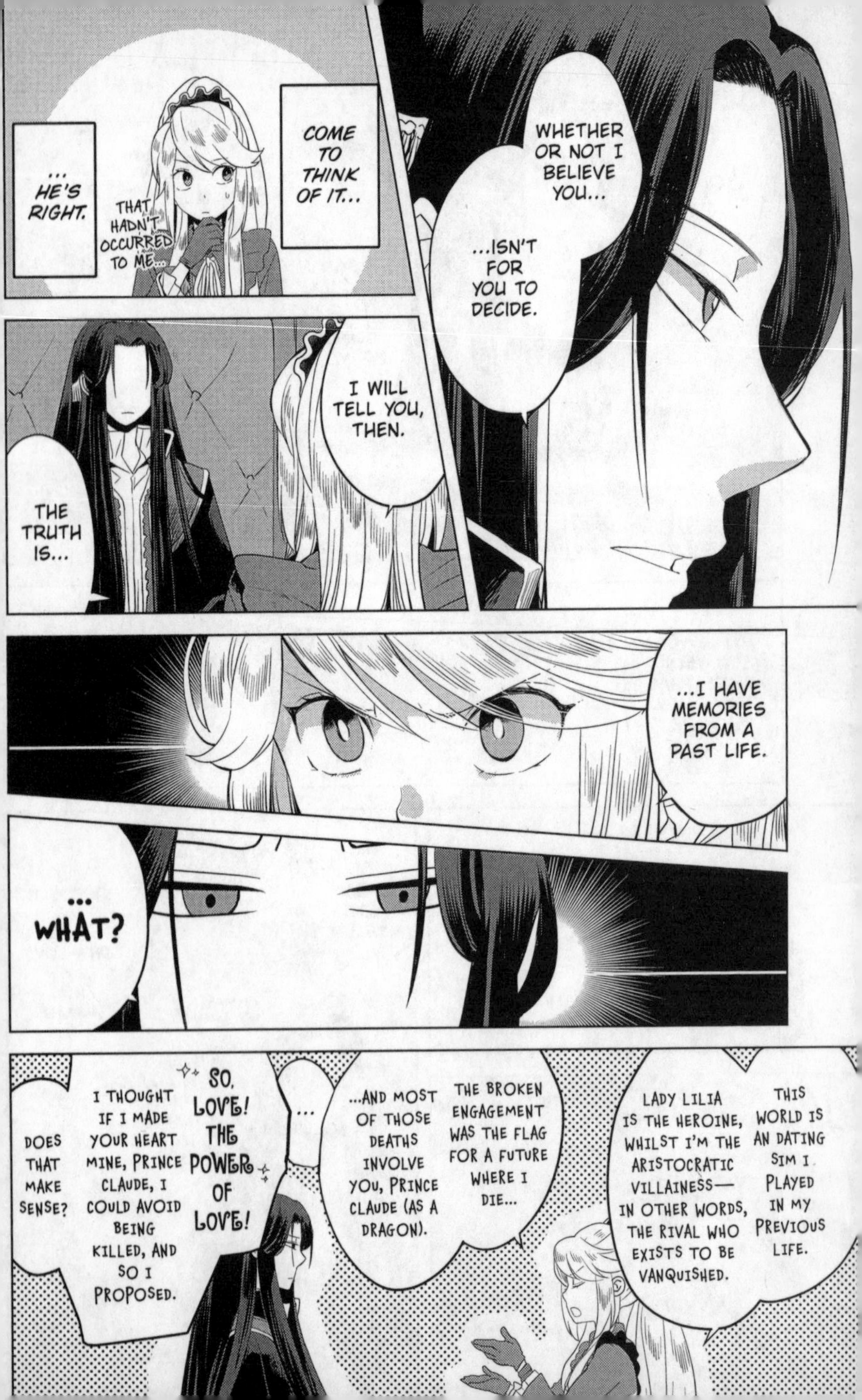
WHETHER OR NOT I BELIEVE YOU...
...ISN'T FOR YOU TO DECIDE.
COME TO THINK OF IT...
...HE'S RIGHT.
THAT HADN'T OCCURRED TO ME...
I WILL TELL YOU, THEN.
THE TRUTH IS...
...I HAVE MEMORIES FROM A PAST LIFE.
...WHAT?
THIS WORLD IS AN DATING SIM I PLAYED IN MY PREVIOUS LIFE.
LADY LILIA IS THE HEROINE, WHILST I'M THE ARISTOCRATIC VILLAINESS—IN OTHER WORDS, THE RIVAL WHO EXISTS TO BE VANQUISHED.
THE BROKEN ENGAGEMENT WAS THE FLAG FOR A FUTURE WHERE I DIE...
...AND MOST OF THOSE DEATHS INVOLVE YOU, PRINCE CLAUDE (AS A DRAGON).
...
SO, LOVE! THE POWER OF LOVE!
I THOUGHT IF I MADE YOUR HEART MINE, PRINCE CLAUDE, I COULD AVOID BEING KILLED, AND SO I PROPOSED.
DOES THAT MAKE SENSE?

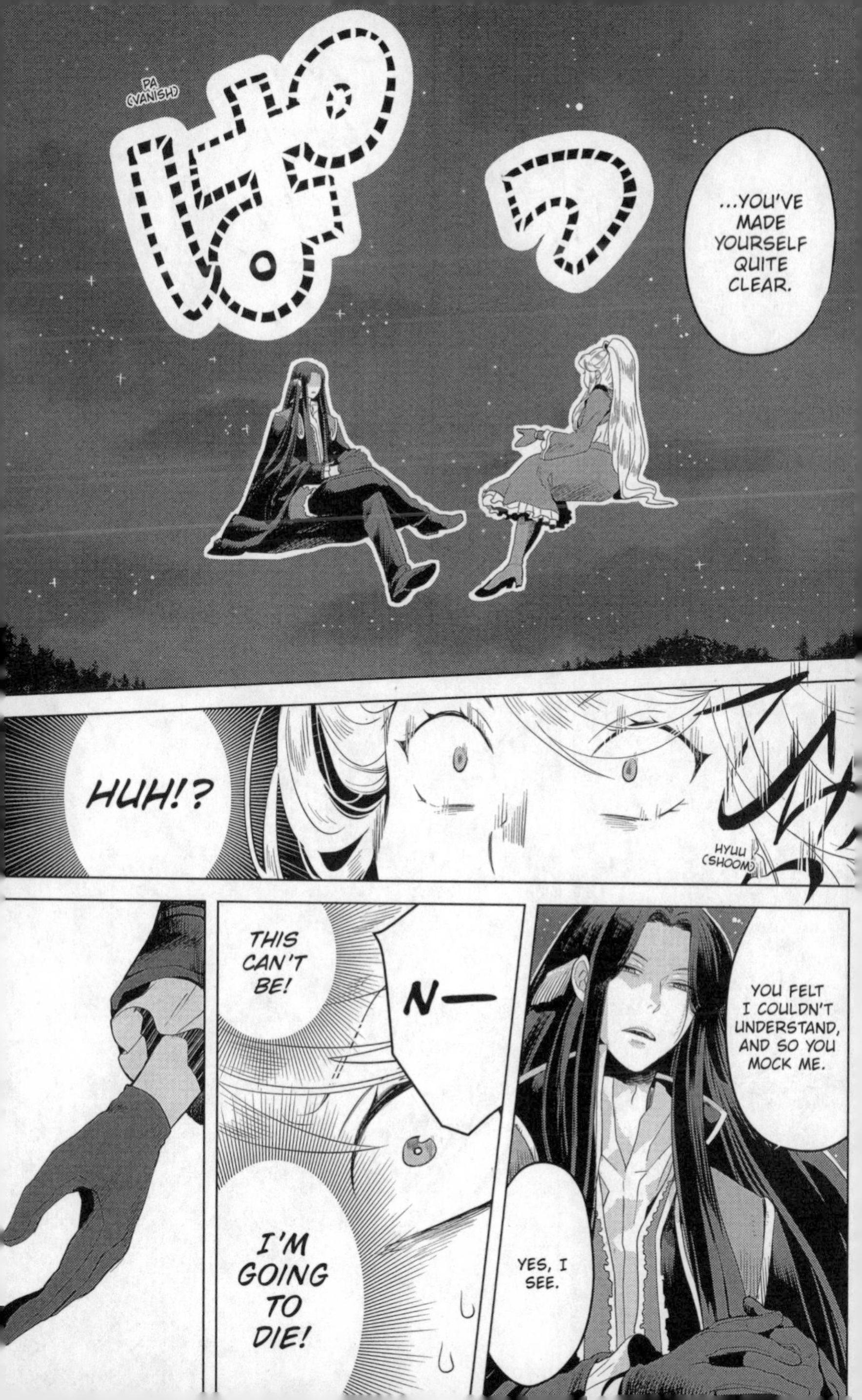
...YOU'VE MADE YOURSELF QUITE CLEAR.
PA (VANISH)
HYUU (SHOOM)
HUH!?
YOU FELT I COULDN'T UNDERSTAND, AND SO YOU MOCK ME.
YES, I SEE.
N—
THIS CAN'T BE!
I'M GOING TO DIE!

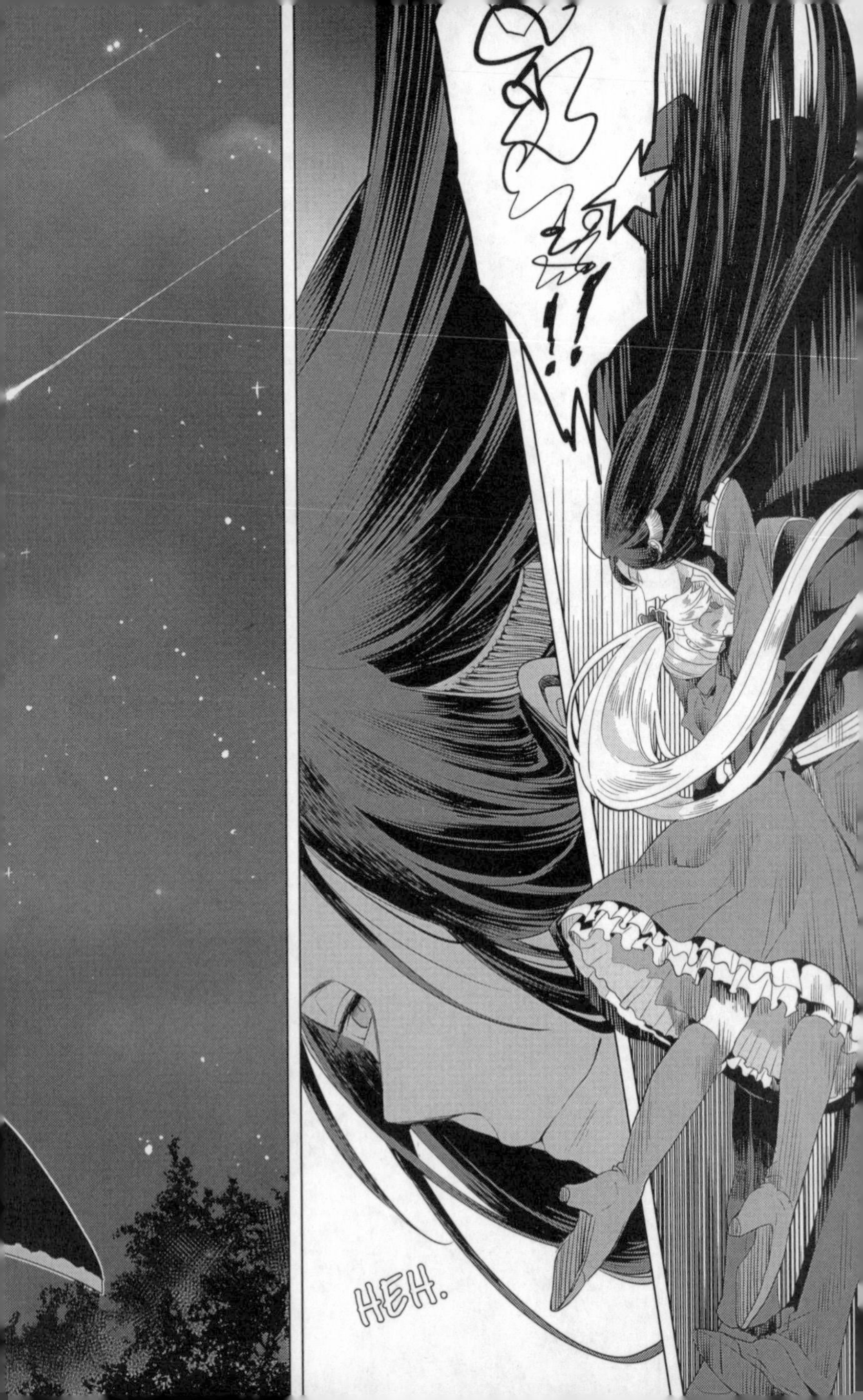
HEH.

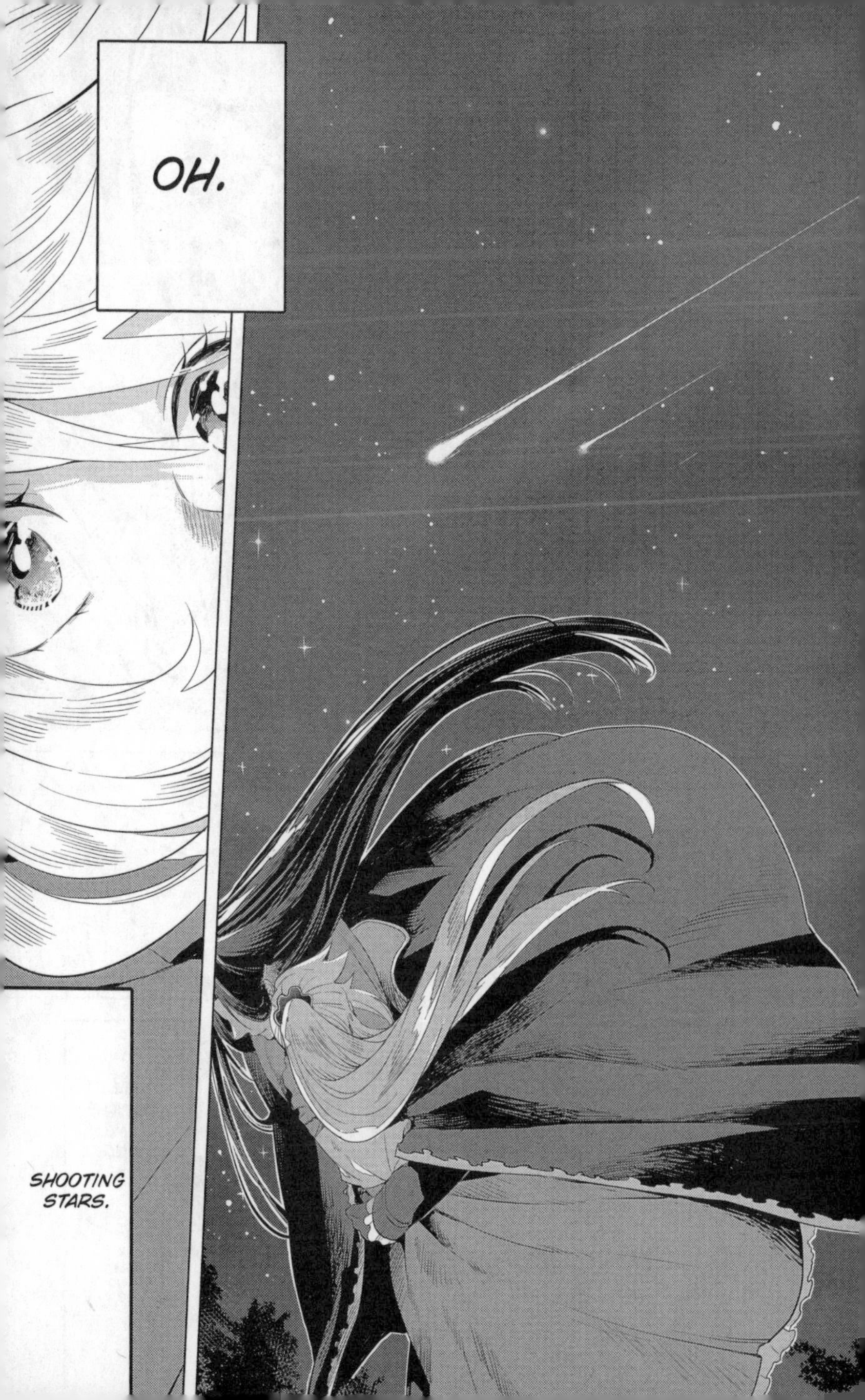
OH.
SHOOTING STARS.

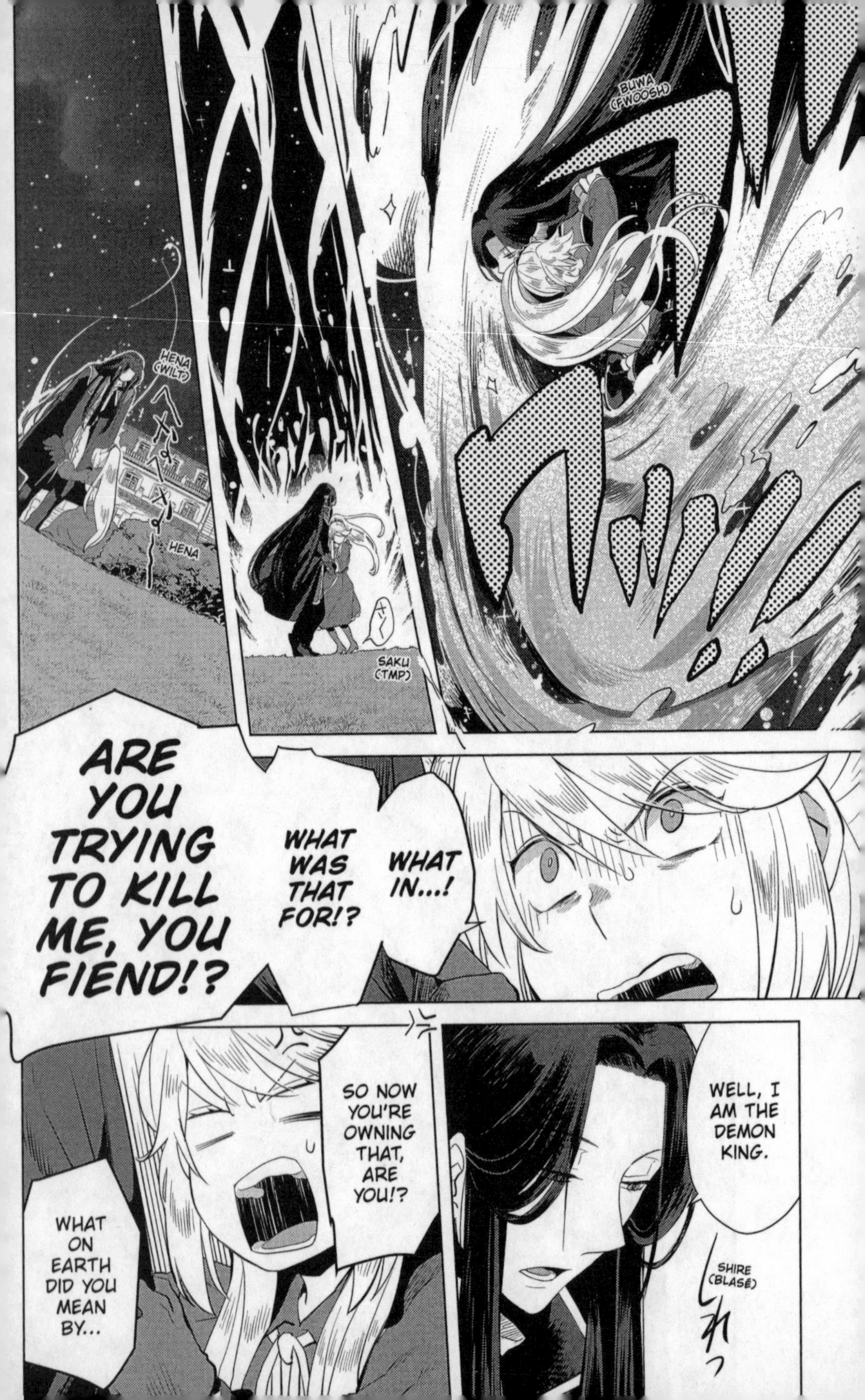
BUWA (FWOOSH)
SAKU (TMP)
HENA (WILT)
HENA
WHAT IN...!
WHAT WAS THAT FOR!?
ARE YOU TRYING TO KILL ME, YOU FIEND!?
WELL, I AM THE DEMON KING.
SHIRE (BLASÉ)
SO NOW YOU'RE OWNING THAT, ARE YOU!?
WHAT ON EARTH DID YOU MEAN BY...

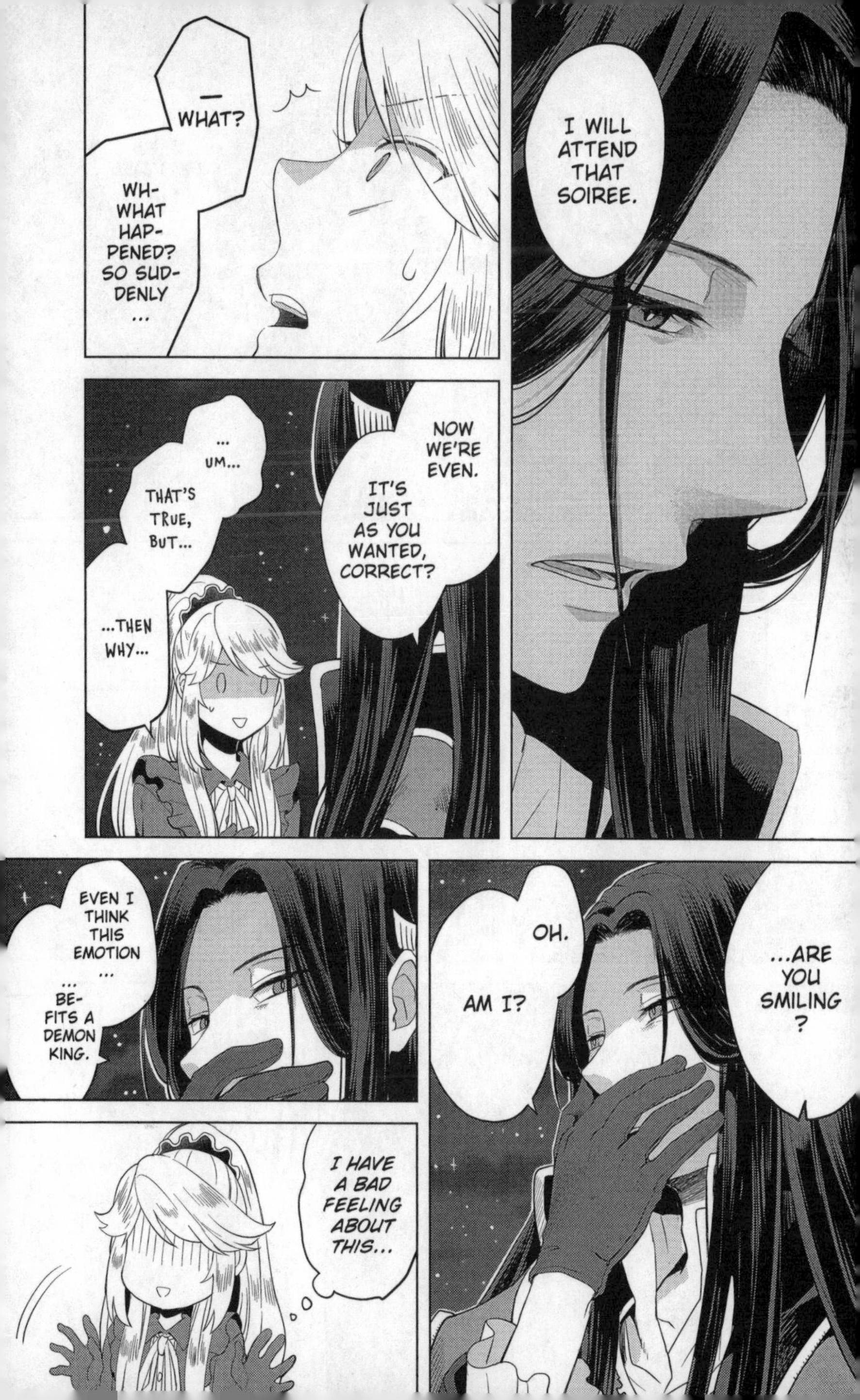
I WILL ATTEND THAT SOIREE.
—WHAT?
WH-WHAT HAPPENED? SO SUDDENLY...
NOW WE'RE EVEN.
IT'S JUST AS YOU WANTED, CORRECT?
... UM...
THAT'S TRUE, BUT...
...THEN WHY...
...ARE YOU SMILING?
OH.
AM I?
EVEN I THINK THIS EMOTION... ...BEFITS A DEMON KING.
I HAVE A BAD FEELING ABOUT THIS...

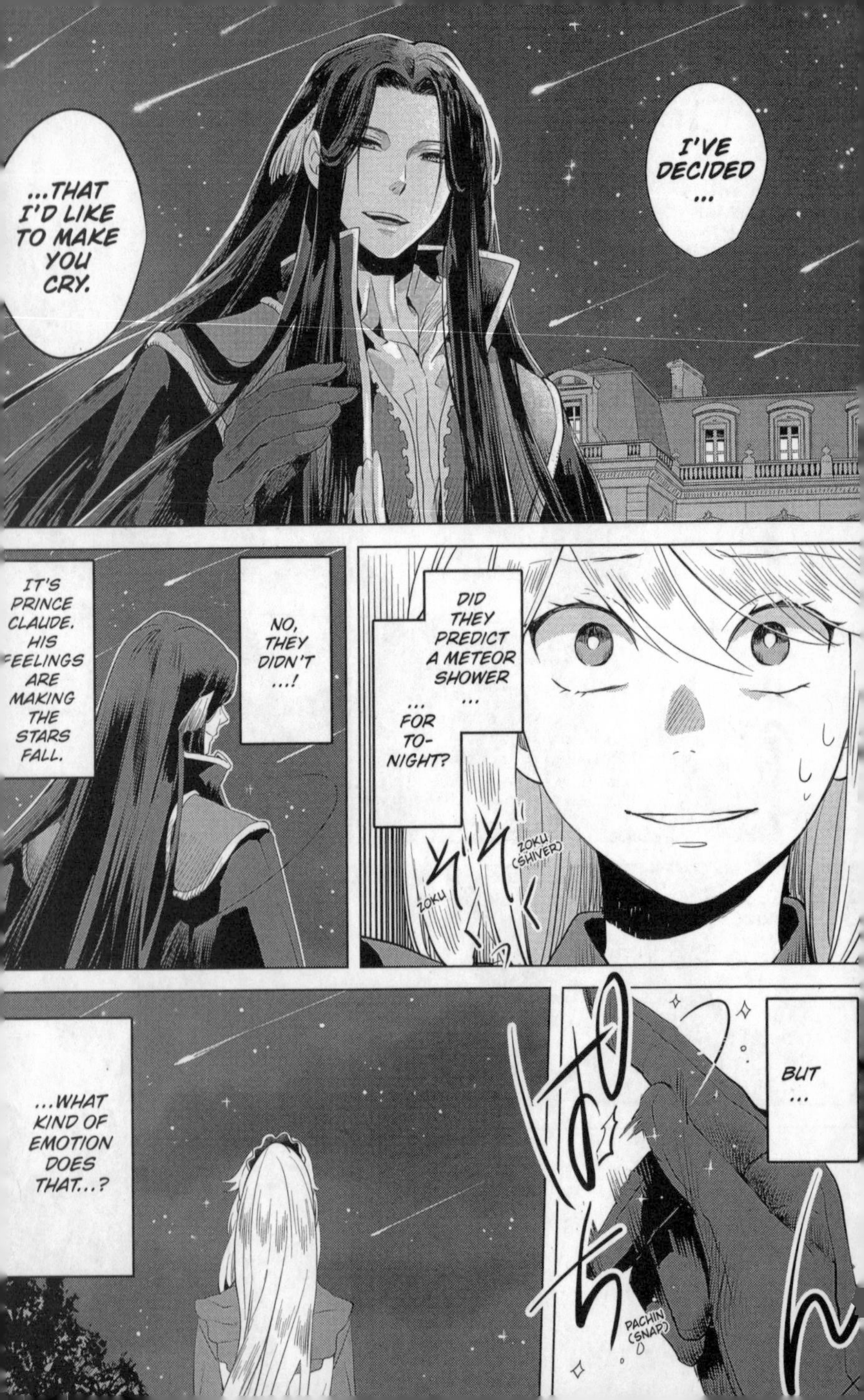
I'VE DECIDED...
...THAT I'D LIKE TO MAKE YOU CRY.
DID THEY PREDICT A METEOR SHOWER... ...FOR TO-NIGHT?
ZOKU (SHIVER)
ZOKU
NO, THEY DIDN'T...!
IT'S PRINCE CLAUDE. HIS FEELINGS ARE MAKING THE STARS FALL.
BUT...
PACHIN (SNAP)
...WHAT KIND OF EMOTION DOES THAT...?

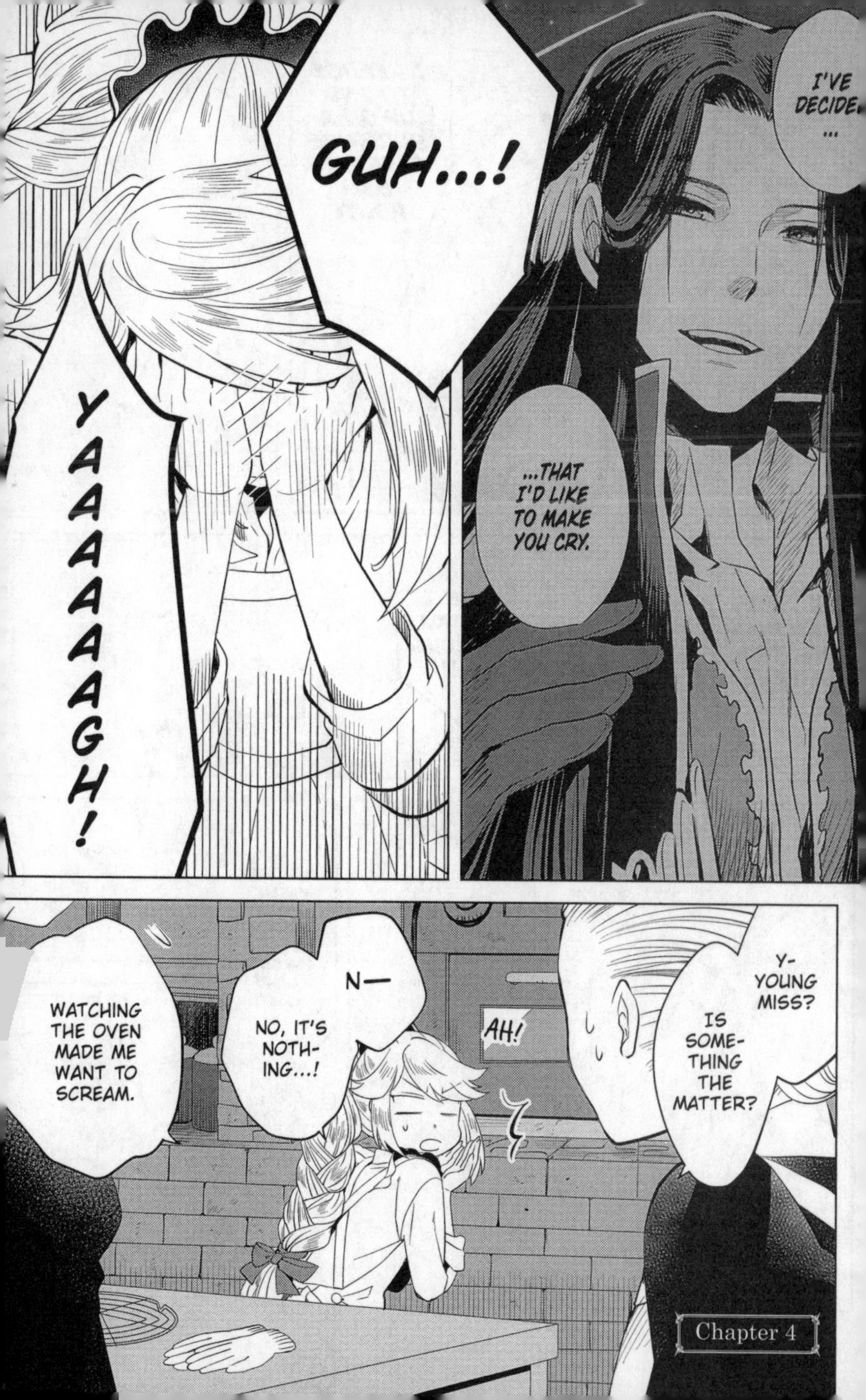
I'VE DECIDE...
...THAT I'D LIKE TO MAKE YOU CRY.
GUH...!
YAAAAAAAAGH!
Y-YOUNG MISS?
IS SOMETHING THE MATTER?
AH!
N—
NO, IT'S NOTHING...!
WATCHING THE OVEN MADE ME WANT TO SCREAM.

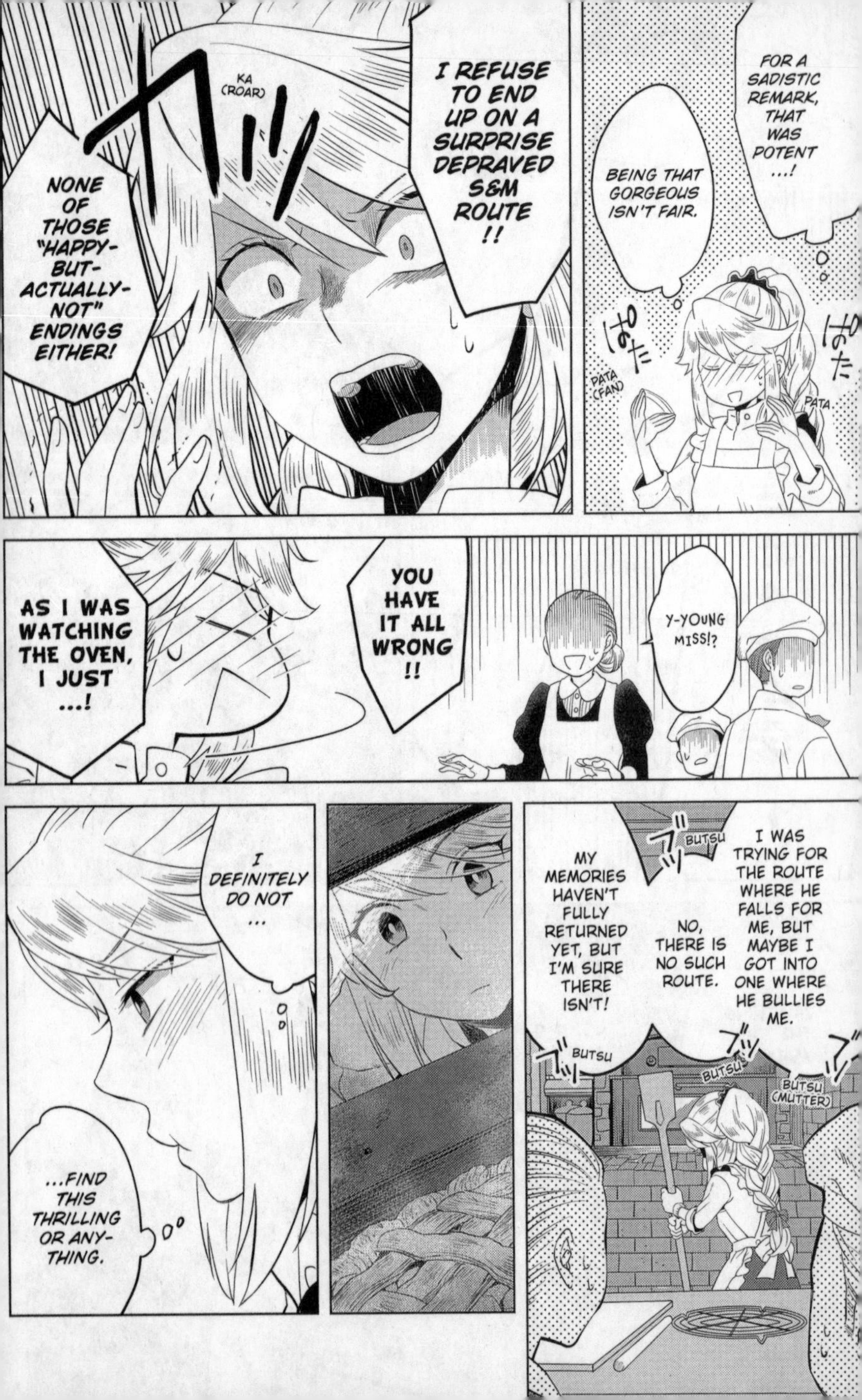
FOR A SADISTIC REMARK, THAT WAS POTENT...!
BEING THAT GORGEOUS ISN'T FAIR.
PATA (FAN)
PATA
I REFUSE TO END UP ON A SURPRISE DEPRAVED S&M ROUTE!!
KA (ROAR)
NONE OF THOSE "HAPPY-BUT-ACTUALLY-NOT" ENDINGS EITHER!
Y-YOUNG MISS!?
YOU HAVE IT ALL WRONG!!
AS I WAS WATCHING THE OVEN, I JUST...!
I WAS TRYING FOR THE ROUTE WHERE HE FALLS FOR ME, BUT MAYBE I GOT INTO ONE WHERE HE BULLIES ME.
BUTSU
NO, THERE IS NO SUCH ROUTE.
MY MEMORIES HAVEN'T FULLY RETURNED YET, BUT I'M SURE THERE ISN'T!
BUTSU
BUTSU
BUTSU (MUTTER)
I DEFINITELY DO NOT...
...FIND THIS THRILLING OR ANYTHING.

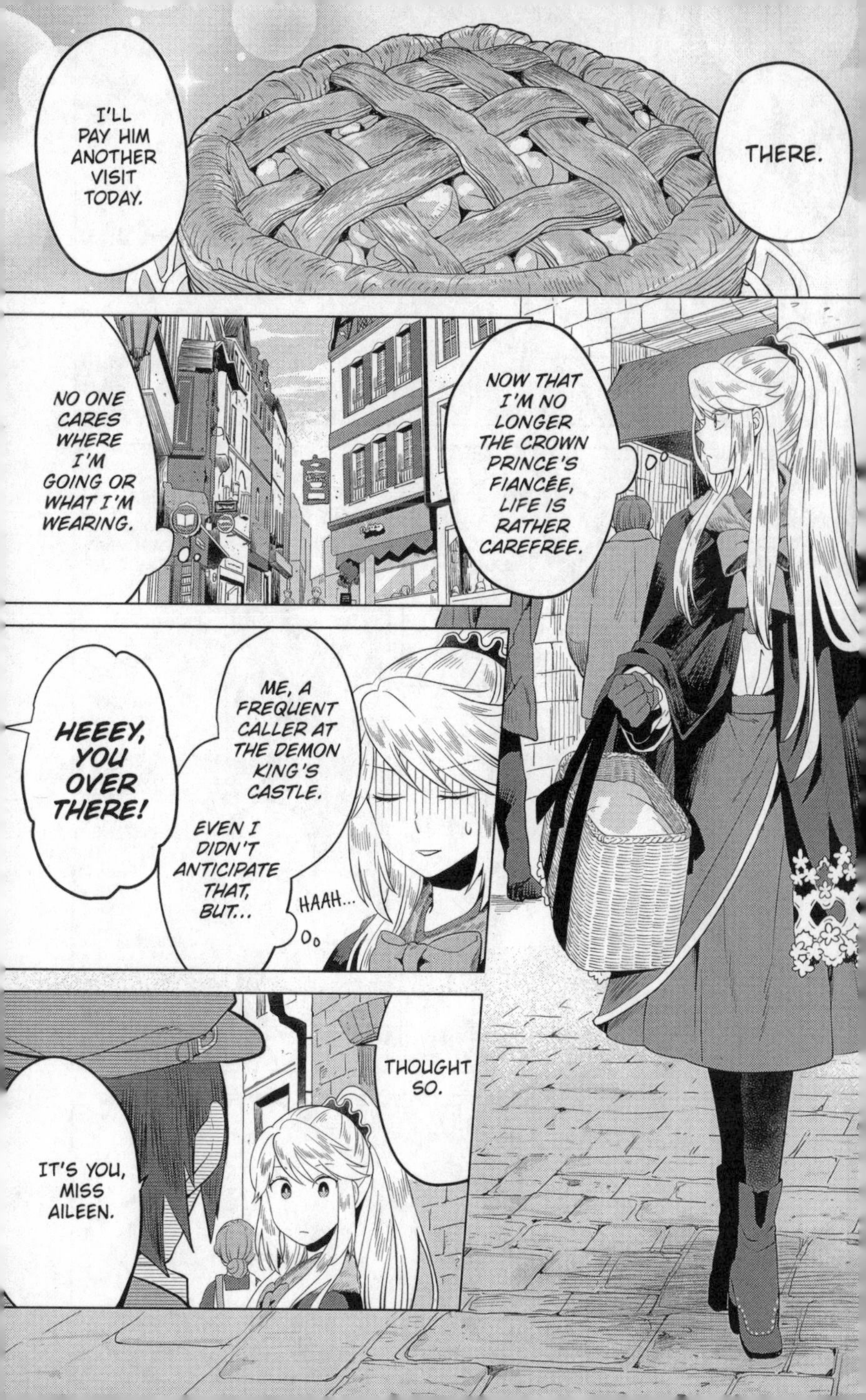
THERE.
I'LL PAY HIM ANOTHER VISIT TODAY.
NOW THAT I'M NO LONGER THE CROWN PRINCE'S FIANCÉE, LIFE IS RATHER CAREFREE.
NO ONE CARES WHERE I'M GOING OR WHAT I'M WEARING.
ME, A FREQUENT CALLER AT THE DEMON KING'S CASTLE.
EVEN I DIDN'T ANTICIPATE THAT, BUT...
HAAH...
HEEEY, YOU OVER THERE!
THOUGHT SO.
IT'S YOU, MISS AILEEN.

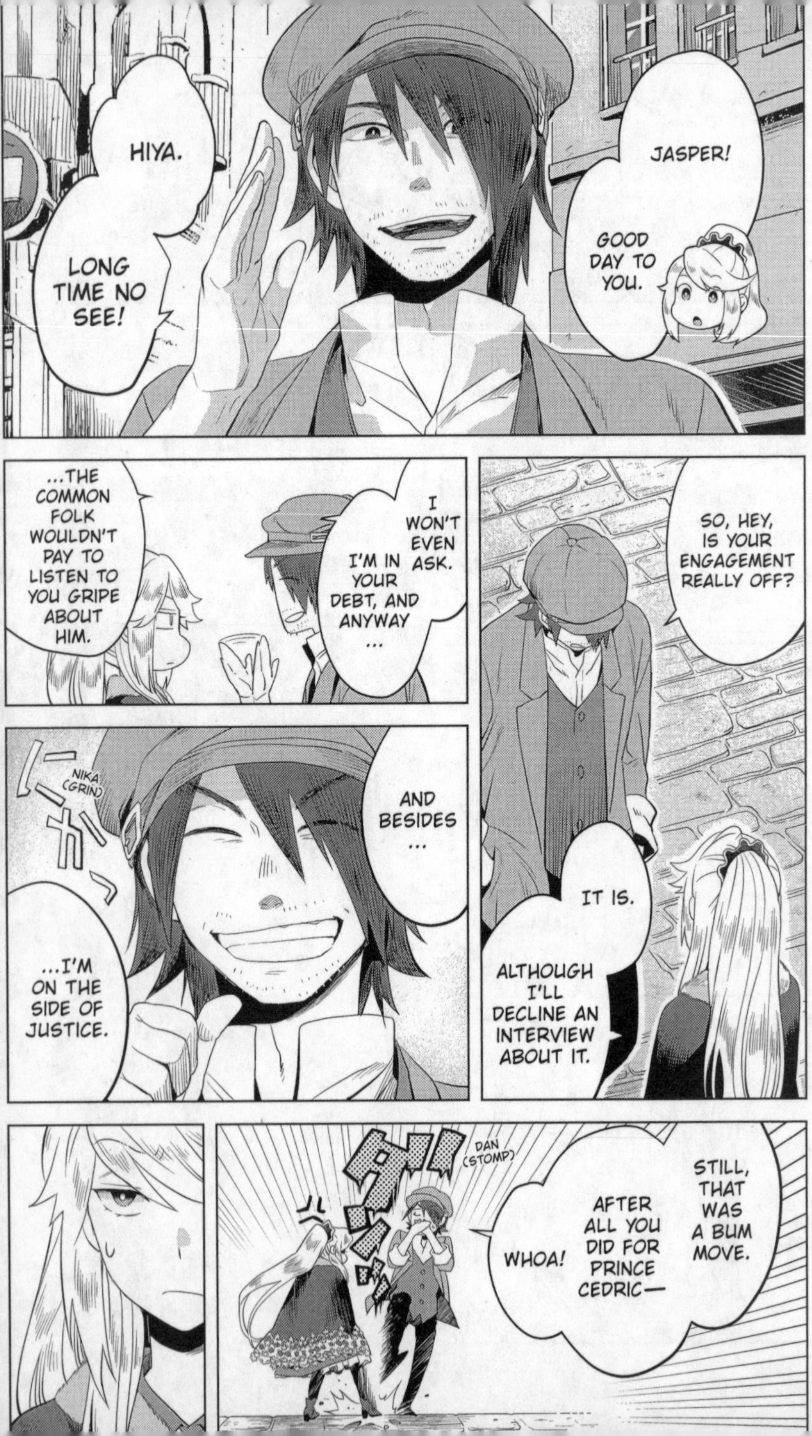
JASPER!
GOOD DAY TO YOU.
HIYA.
LONG TIME NO SEE!
SO, HEY, IS YOUR ENGAGEMENT REALLY OFF?
IT IS.
ALTHOUGH I'LL DECLINE AN INTERVIEW ABOUT IT.
I WON'T EVEN ASK. I'M IN YOUR DEBT, AND ANYWAY ...
...THE COMMON FOLK WOULDN'T PAY TO LISTEN TO YOU GRIPE ABOUT HIM.
AND BESIDES ...
NIKA (GRIN)
...I'M ON THE SIDE OF JUSTICE.
STILL, THAT WAS A BUM MOVE.
AFTER ALL YOU DID FOR PRINCE CEDRIC—
DAN (STOMP)
WHOA!

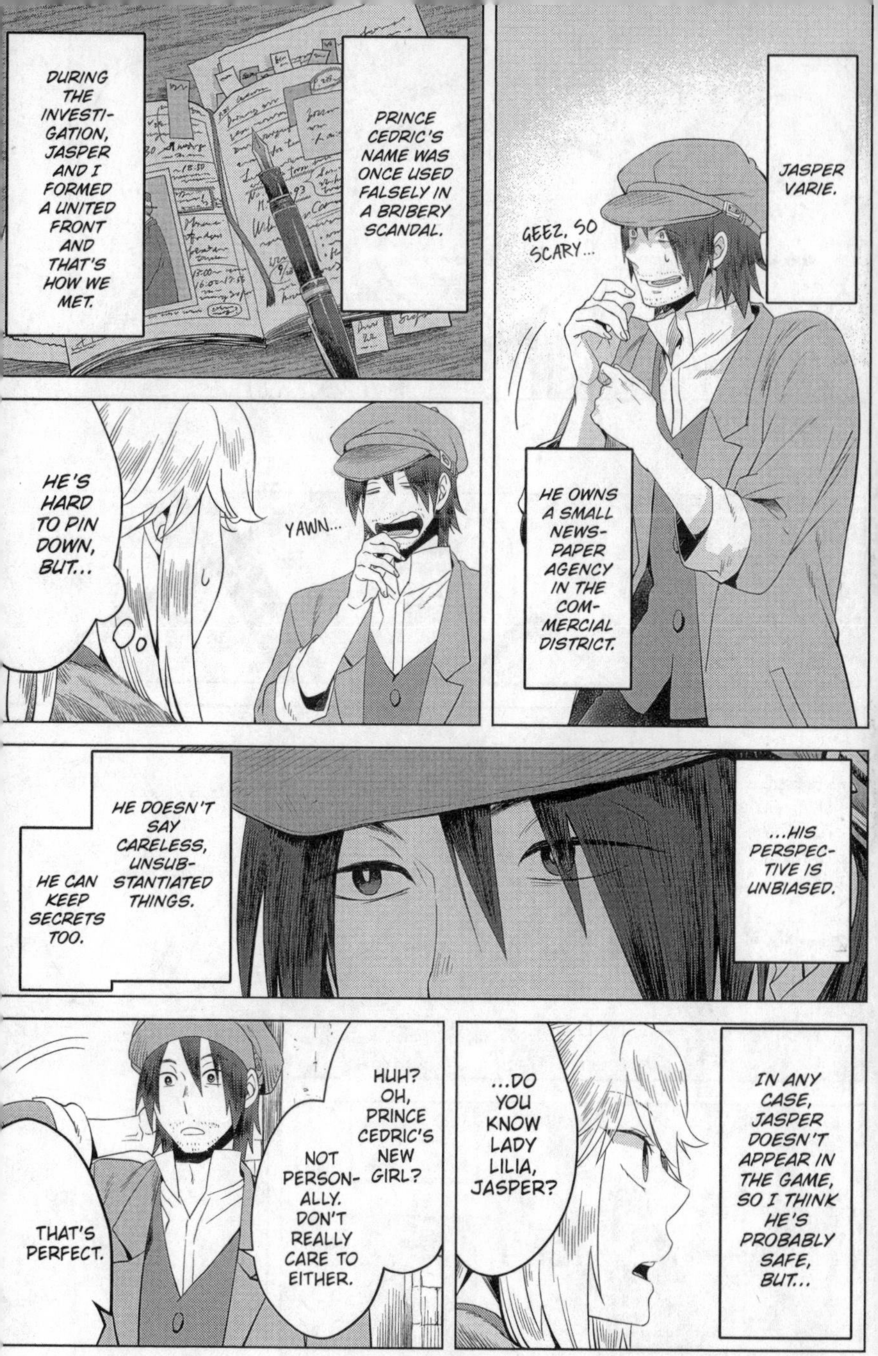

JASPER VARIE.
GEEZ, SO SCARY...
HE OWNS A SMALL NEWSPAPER AGENCY IN THE COMMERCIAL DISTRICT.
PRINCE CEDRIC'S NAME WAS ONCE USED FALSELY IN A BRIBERY SCANDAL.
DURING THE INVESTIGATION, JASPER AND I FORMED A UNITED FRONT AND THAT'S HOW WE MET.
YAWN...
HE'S HARD TO PIN DOWN, BUT...
...HIS PERSPECTIVE IS UNBIASED.
HE DOESN'T SAY CARELESS, UNSUBSTANTIATED THINGS.
HE CAN KEEP SECRETS TOO.
IN ANY CASE, JASPER DOESN'T APPEAR IN THE GAME, SO I THINK HE'S PROBABLY SAFE, BUT...
...DO YOU KNOW LADY LILIA, JASPER?
HUH? OH, PRINCE CEDRIC'S NEW GIRL?
NOT PERSONALLY. DON'T REALLY CARE TO EITHER.
THAT'S PERFECT.

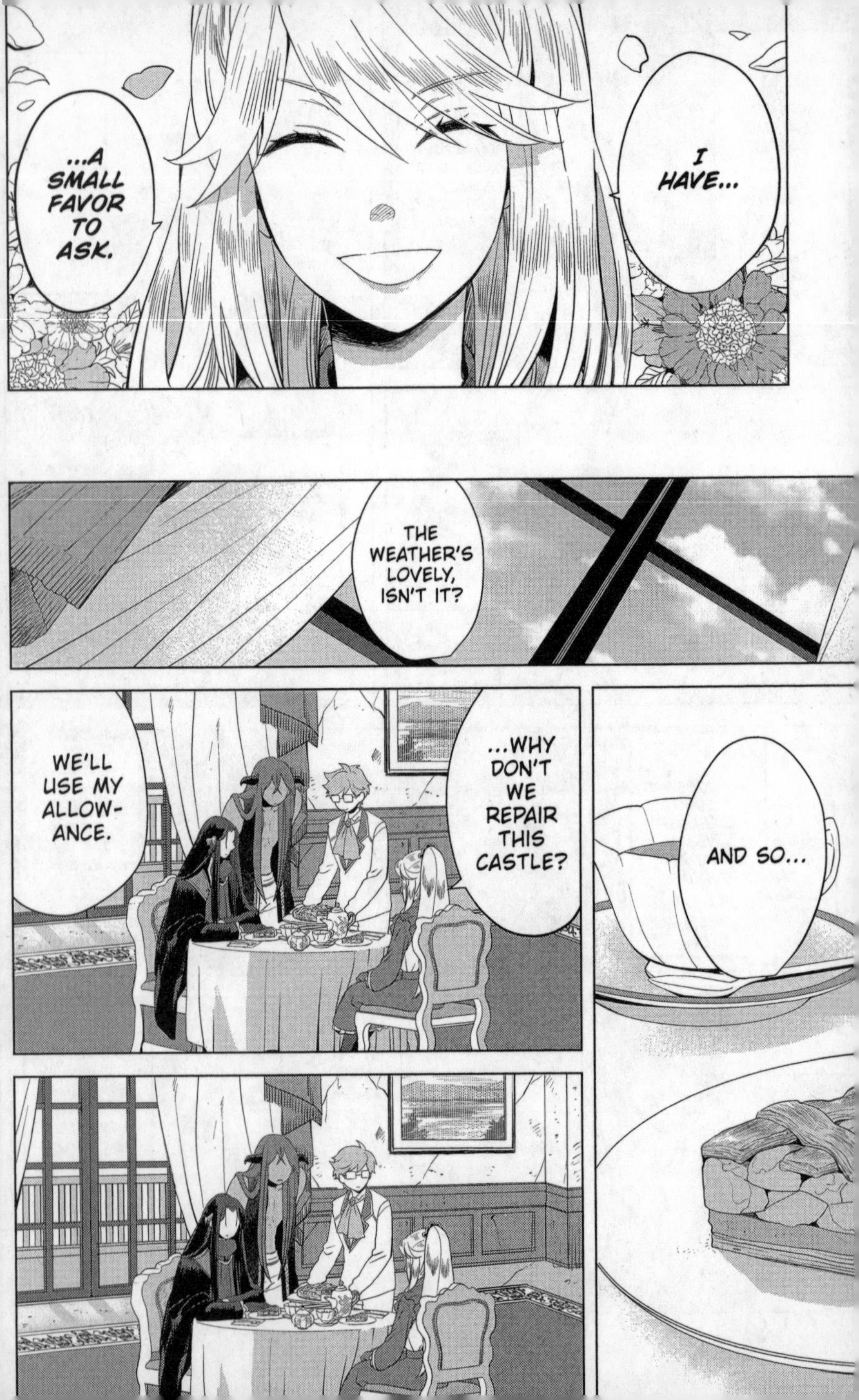
I HAVE...
...A SMALL FAVOR TO ASK.
THE WEATHER'S LOVELY, ISN'T IT?
AND SO...
...WHY DON'T WE REPAIR THIS CASTLE?
WE'LL USE MY ALLOWANCE.

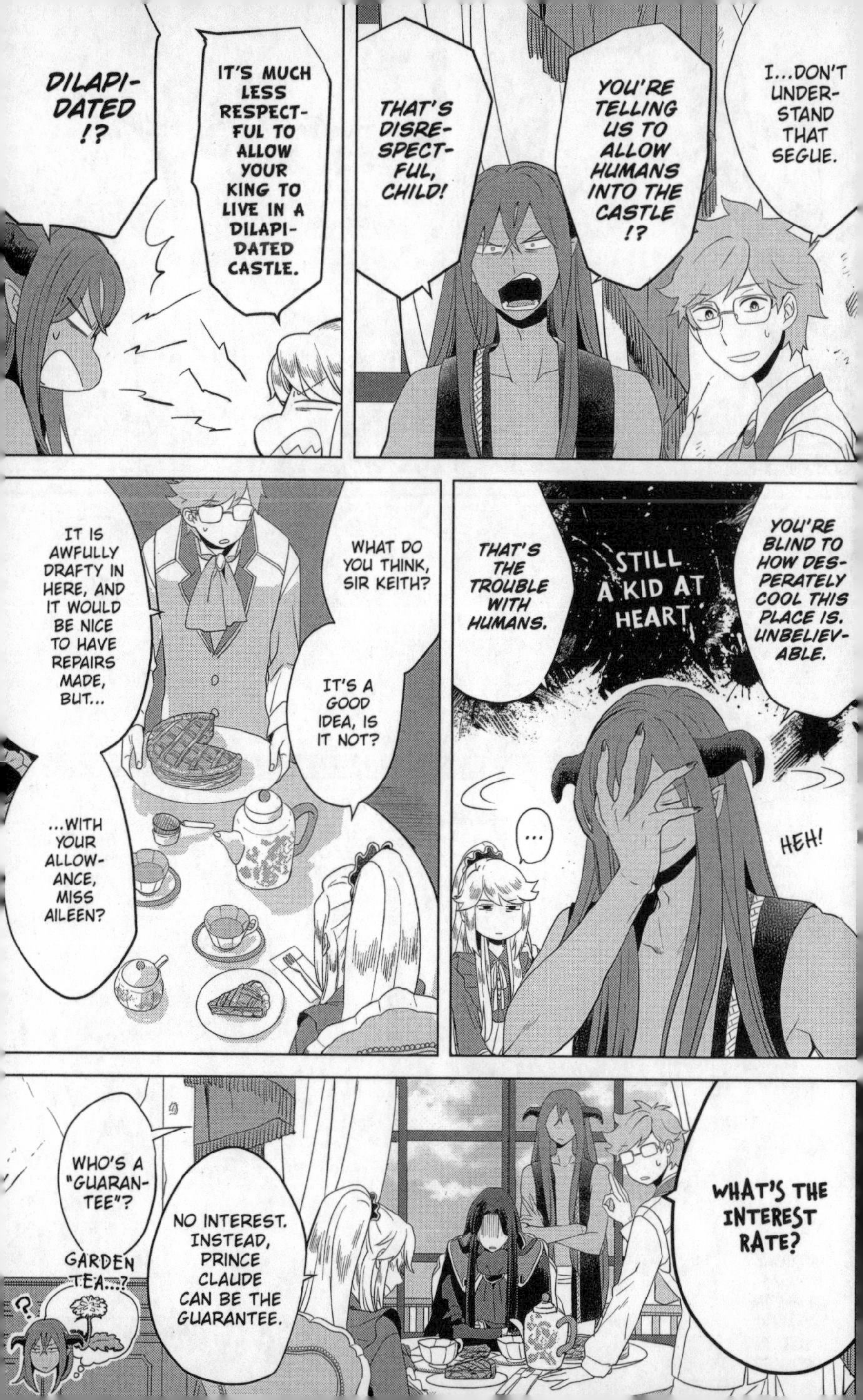
I...DON'T UNDERSTAND THAT SEGUE.
YOU'RE TELLING US TO ALLOW HUMANS INTO THE CASTLE!?
THAT'S DISRESPECTFUL, CHILD!
IT'S MUCH LESS RESPECTFUL TO ALLOW YOUR KING TO LIVE IN A DILAPIDATED CASTLE.
DILAPIDATED!?
YOU'RE BLIND TO HOW DESPERATELY COOL THIS PLACE IS. UNBELIEVABLE.
STILL A KID AT HEART
THAT'S THE TROUBLE WITH HUMANS.
HEH!
...
WHAT DO YOU THINK, SIR KEITH?
IT IS AWFULLY DRAFTY IN HERE, AND IT WOULD BE NICE TO HAVE REPAIRS MADE, BUT...
IT'S A GOOD IDEA, IS IT NOT?
...WITH YOUR ALLOWANCE, MISS AILEEN?
WHAT'S THE INTEREST RATE?
NO INTEREST. INSTEAD, PRINCE CLAUDE CAN BE THE GUARANTEE.
WHO'S A "GUARANTEE"?
GARDEN TEA...?
?

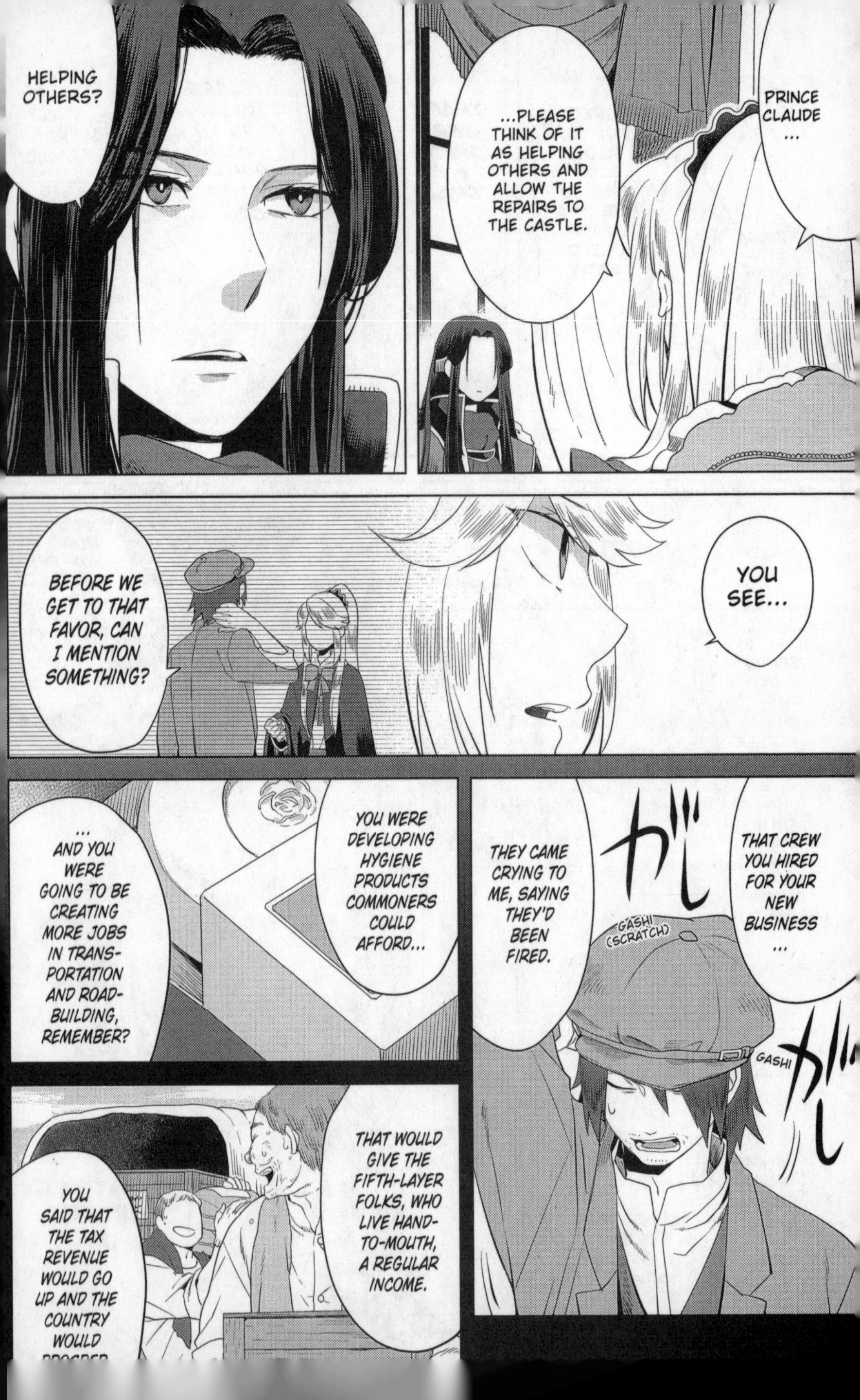
PRINCE CLAUDE...
...PLEASE THINK OF IT AS HELPING OTHERS AND ALLOW THE REPAIRS TO THE CASTLE.
HELPING OTHERS?
YOU SEE...
BEFORE WE GET TO THAT FAVOR, CAN I MENTION SOMETHING?
THAT CREW YOU HIRED FOR YOUR NEW BUSINESS...
GASHI (SCRATCH)
GASHI
THEY CAME CRYING TO ME, SAYING THEY'D BEEN FIRED.
YOU WERE DEVELOPING HYGIENE PRODUCTS COMMONERS COULD AFFORD...
...AND YOU WERE GOING TO BE CREATING MORE JOBS IN TRANS-PORTATION AND ROAD-BUILDING, REMEMBER?
THAT WOULD GIVE THE FIFTH-LAYER FOLKS, WHO LIVE HAND-TO-MOUTH, A REGULAR INCOME.
YOU SAID THAT THE TAX REVENUE WOULD GO UP AND THE COUNTRY WOULD

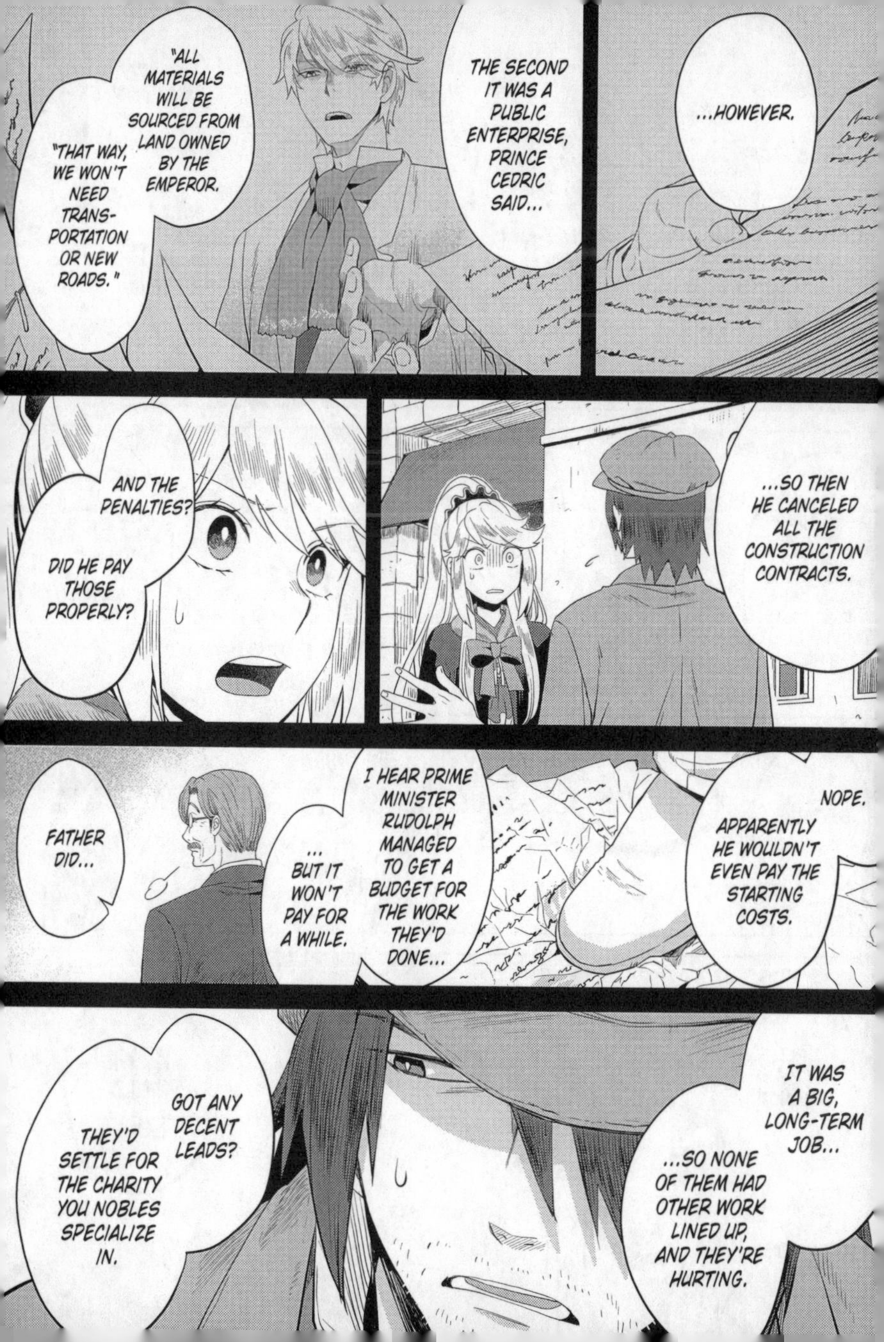
...HOWEVER.
THE SECOND IT WAS A PUBLIC ENTERPRISE, PRINCE CEDRIC SAID...
"ALL MATERIALS WILL BE SOURCED FROM LAND OWNED BY THE EMPEROR.
"THAT WAY, WE WON'T NEED TRANS-PORTATION OR NEW ROADS."
...SO THEN HE CANCELED ALL THE CONSTRUCTION CONTRACTS.
AND THE PENALTIES?
DID HE PAY THOSE PROPERLY?
NOPE.
APPARENTLY HE WOULDN'T EVEN PAY THE STARTING COSTS.
I HEAR PRIME MINISTER RUDOLPH MANAGED TO GET A BUDGET FOR THE WORK THEY'D DONE...
...BUT IT WON'T PAY FOR A WHILE.
FATHER DID...
IT WAS A BIG, LONG-TERM JOB...
...SO NONE OF THEM HAD OTHER WORK LINED UP, AND THEY'RE HURTING.
GOT ANY DECENT LEADS?
THEY'D SETTLE FOR THE CHARITY YOU NOBLES SPECIALIZE IN.

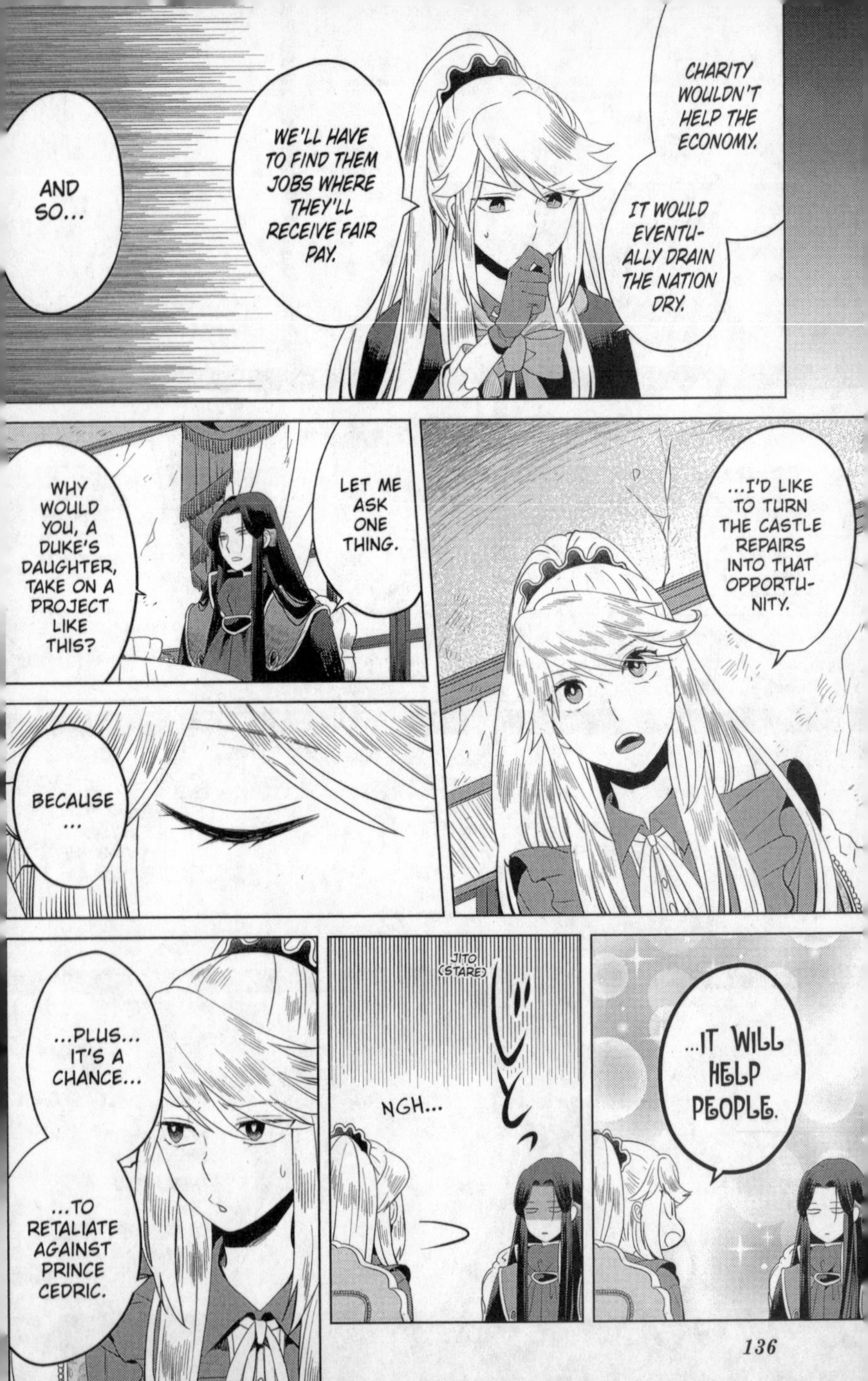
CHARITY WOULDN'T HELP THE ECONOMY.
IT WOULD EVENTU-ALLY DRAIN THE NATION DRY.
WE'LL HAVE TO FIND THEM JOBS WHERE THEY'LL RECEIVE FAIR PAY.
AND SO...
...I'D LIKE TO TURN THE CASTLE REPAIRS INTO THAT OPPORTU-NITY.
LET ME ASK ONE THING.
WHY WOULD YOU, A DUKE'S DAUGHTER, TAKE ON A PROJECT LIKE THIS?
BECAUSE ...
...IT WILL HELP PEOPLE.
JITO (STARE)
NGH...
...PLUS... IT'S A CHANCE...
...TO RETALIATE AGAINST PRINCE CEDRIC.

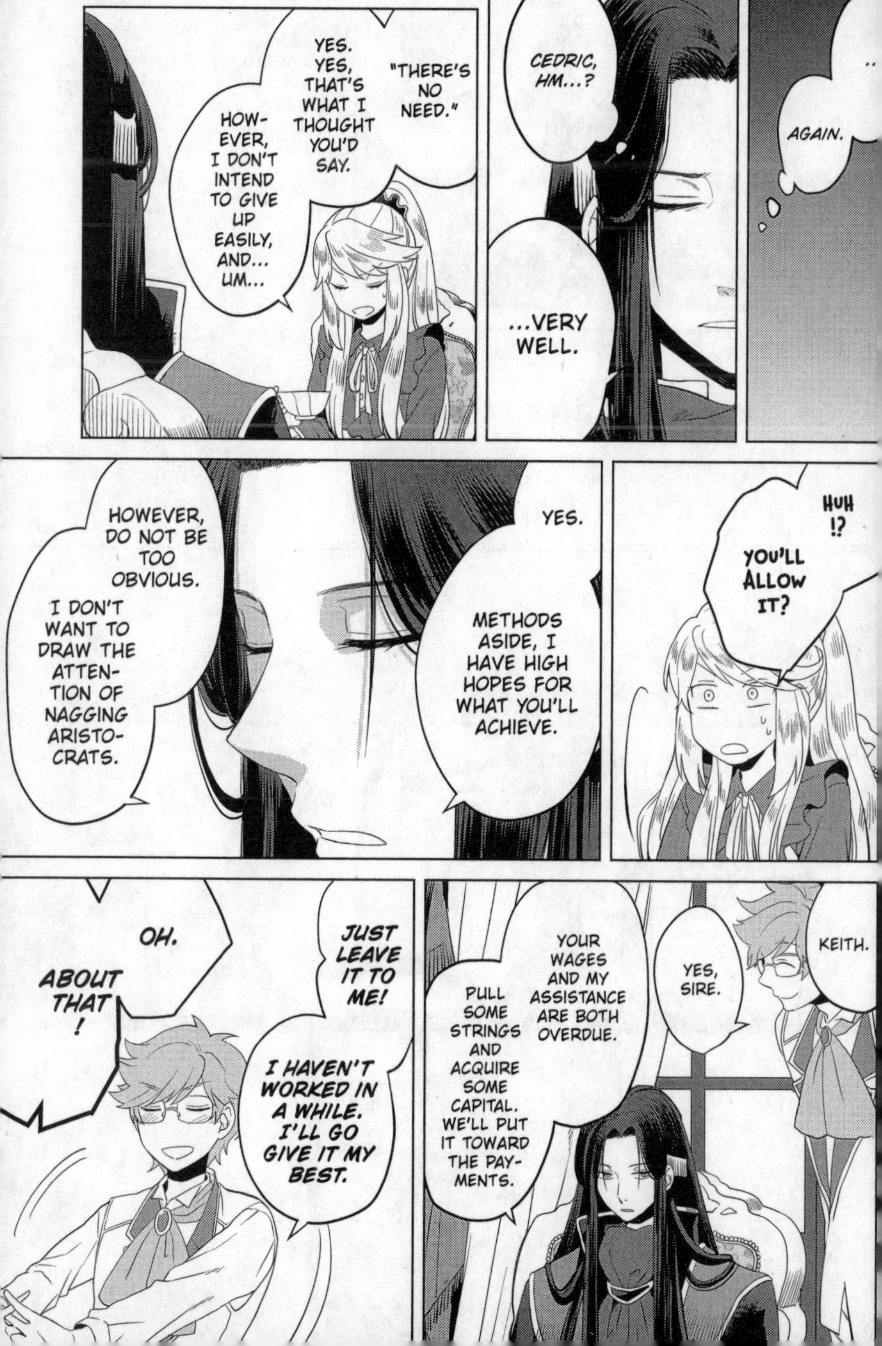

.. AGAIN.
CEDRIC, HM...?
...VERY WELL.
"THERE'S NO NEED." YES. YES, THAT'S WHAT I THOUGHT YOU'D SAY. HOW-EVER, I DON'T INTEND TO GIVE UP EASILY, AND... UM...
HUH!? YOU'LL ALLOW IT?
YES. METHODS ASIDE, I HAVE HIGH HOPES FOR WHAT YOU'LL ACHIEVE.
HOWEVER, DO NOT BE TOO OBVIOUS. I DON'T WANT TO DRAW THE ATTEN-TION OF NAGGING ARISTO-CRATS.
KEITH.
YES, SIRE.
YOUR WAGES AND MY ASSISTANCE ARE BOTH OVERDUE. PULL SOME STRINGS AND ACQUIRE SOME CAPITAL. WE'LL PUT IT TOWARD THE PAY-MENTS.
OH. ABOUT THAT!
JUST LEAVE IT TO ME! I HAVEN'T WORKED IN A WHILE. I'LL GO GIVE IT MY BEST.

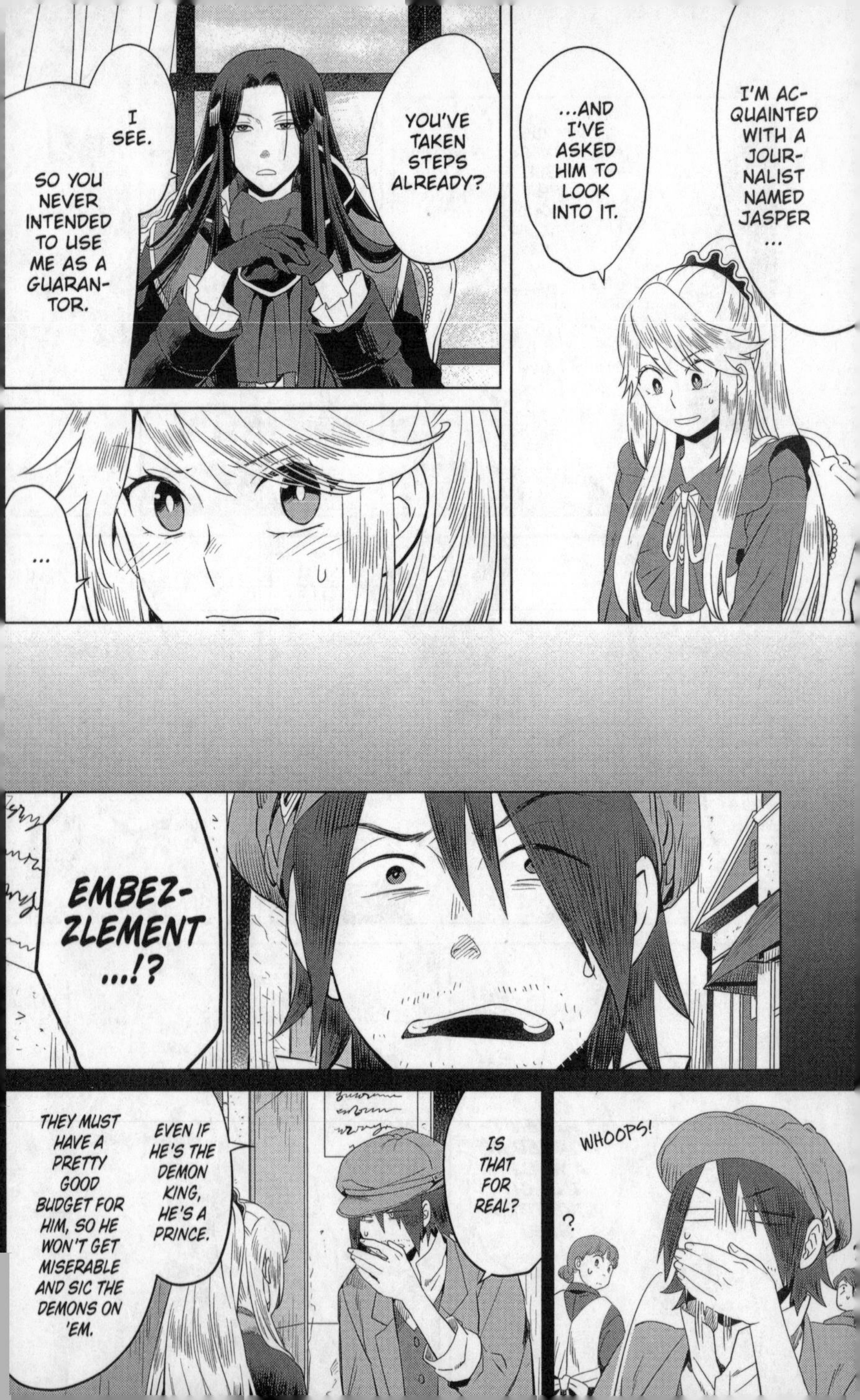
I'M ACQUAINTED WITH A JOURNALIST NAMED JASPER...
...AND I'VE ASKED HIM TO LOOK INTO IT.
YOU'VE TAKEN STEPS ALREADY?
I SEE.
SO YOU NEVER INTENDED TO USE ME AS A GUARANTOR.
...
EMBEZZLEMENT...!?
WHOOPS!
?
IS THAT FOR REAL?
EVEN IF HE'S THE DEMON KING, HE'S A PRINCE.
THEY MUST HAVE A PRETTY GOOD BUDGET FOR HIM, SO HE WON'T GET MISERABLE AND SIC THE DEMONS ON 'EM.

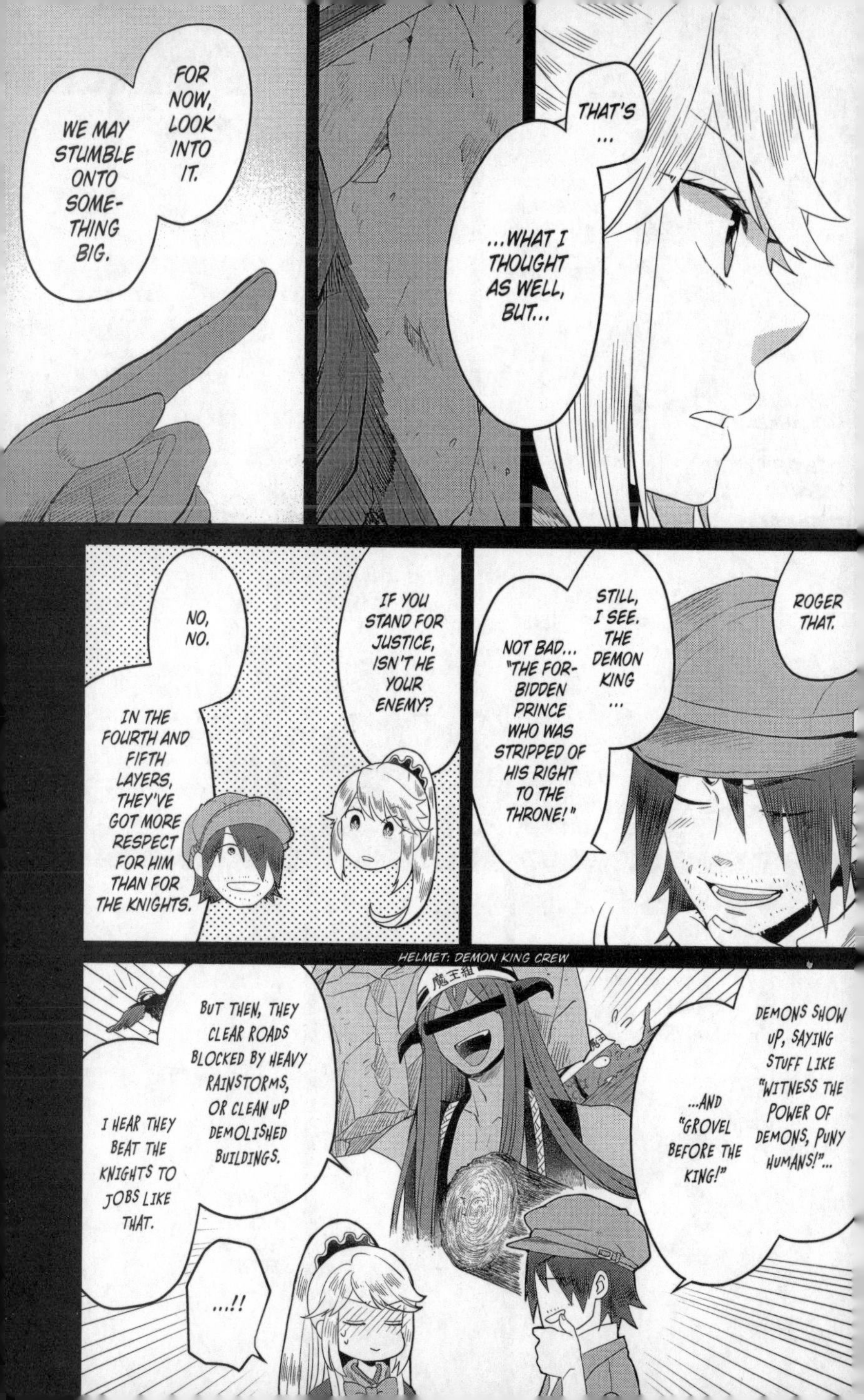
THAT'S...
...WHAT I THOUGHT AS WELL, BUT...
FOR NOW, LOOK INTO IT.
WE MAY STUMBLE ONTO SOMETHING BIG.
ROGER THAT.
STILL, I SEE. THE DEMON KING...
NOT BAD... "THE FORBIDDEN PRINCE WHO WAS STRIPPED OF HIS RIGHT TO THE THRONE!"
IF YOU STAND FOR JUSTICE, ISN'T HE YOUR ENEMY?
NO, NO.
IN THE FOURTH AND FIFTH LAYERS, THEY'VE GOT MORE RESPECT FOR HIM THAN FOR THE KNIGHTS.
HELMET: DEMON KING CREW
魔王組
DEMONS SHOW UP, SAYING STUFF LIKE "WITNESS THE POWER OF DEMONS, PUNY HUMANS!"...
...AND "GROVEL BEFORE THE KING!"
BUT THEN, THEY CLEAR ROADS BLOCKED BY HEAVY RAINSTORMS, OR CLEAN UP DEMOLISHED BUILDINGS.
I HEAR THEY BEAT THE KNIGHTS TO JOBS LIKE THAT.
...!!

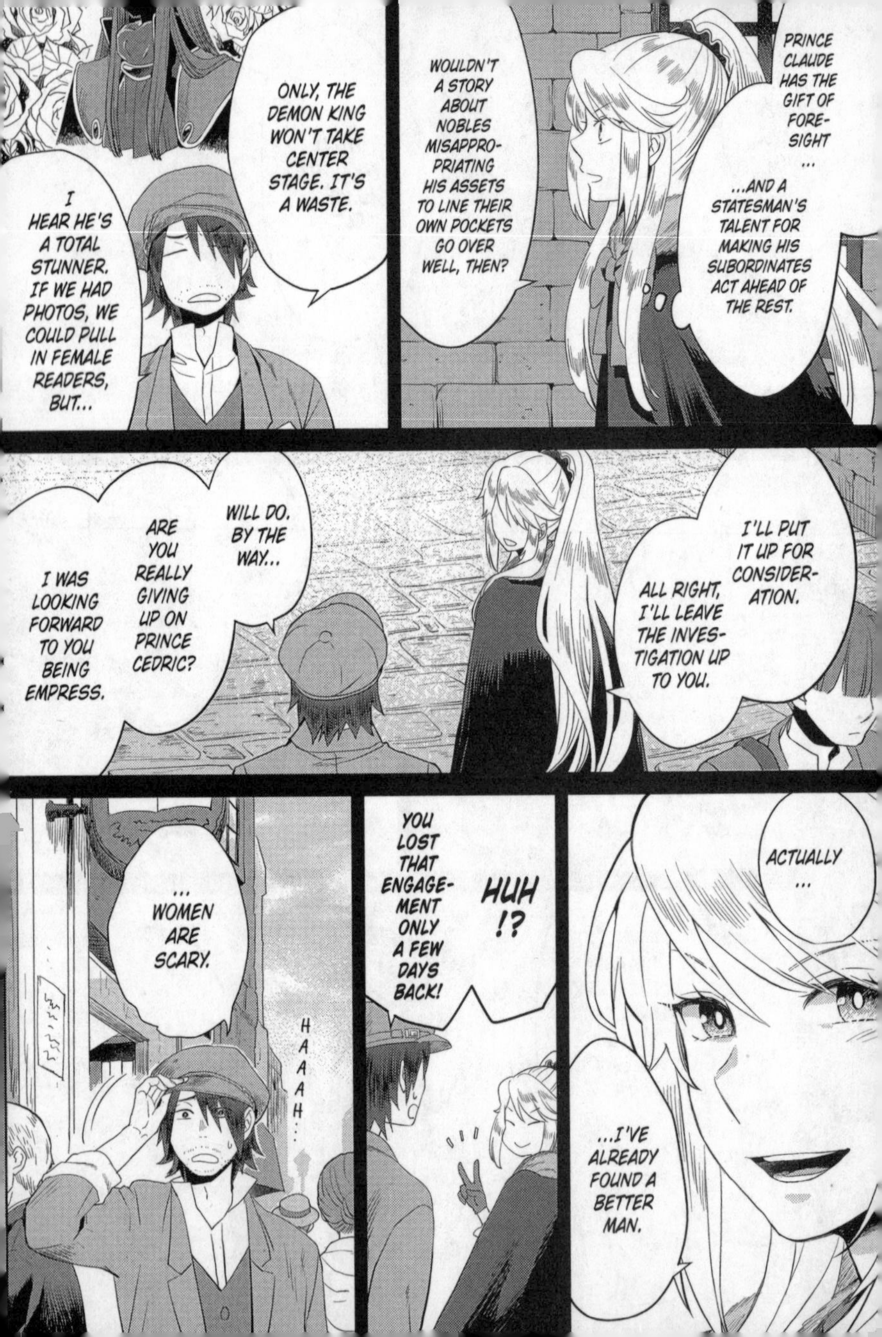
PRINCE CLAUDE HAS THE GIFT OF FORE-SIGHT...
...AND A STATESMAN'S TALENT FOR MAKING HIS SUBORDINATES ACT AHEAD OF THE REST.
WOULDN'T A STORY ABOUT NOBLES MISAPPROPRIATING HIS ASSETS TO LINE THEIR OWN POCKETS GO OVER WELL, THEN?
ONLY, THE DEMON KING WON'T TAKE CENTER STAGE. IT'S A WASTE.
I HEAR HE'S A TOTAL STUNNER. IF WE HAD PHOTOS, WE COULD PULL IN FEMALE READERS, BUT...
I'LL PUT IT UP FOR CONSIDERATION.
ALL RIGHT, I'LL LEAVE THE INVESTIGATION UP TO YOU.
WILL DO. BY THE WAY...
ARE YOU REALLY GIVING UP ON PRINCE CEDRIC?
I WAS LOOKING FORWARD TO YOU BEING EMPRESS.
ACTUALLY...
...I'VE ALREADY FOUND A BETTER MAN.
YOU LOST THAT ENGAGEMENT ONLY A FEW DAYS BACK!
HUH!?
...WOMEN ARE SCARY.
HAAAAH...

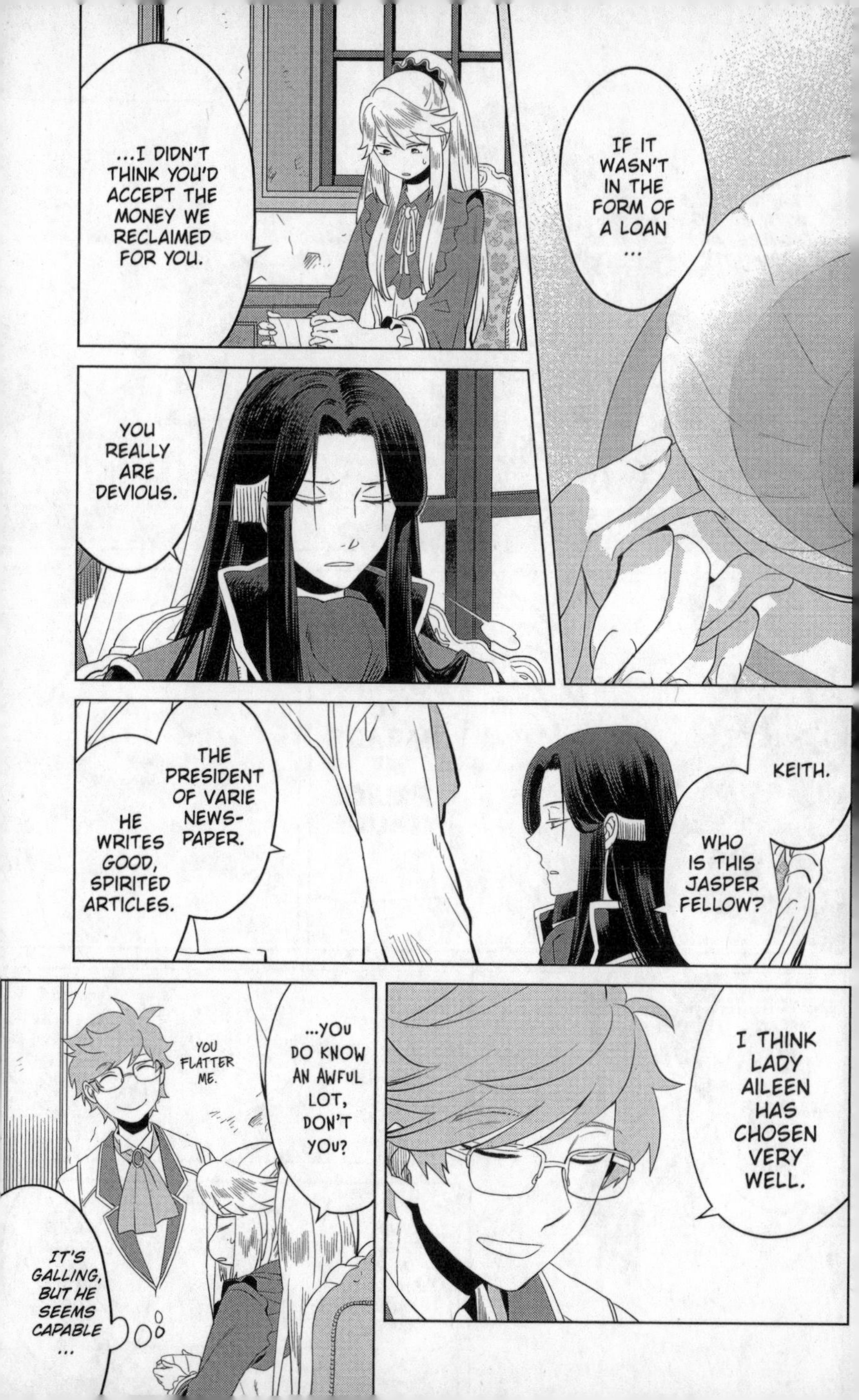
IF IT WASN'T IN THE FORM OF A LOAN...
...I DIDN'T THINK YOU'D ACCEPT THE MONEY WE RECLAIMED FOR YOU.
YOU REALLY ARE DEVIOUS.
KEITH.
WHO IS THIS JASPER FELLOW?
THE PRESIDENT OF VARIE NEWSPAPER.
HE WRITES GOOD, SPIRITED ARTICLES.
I THINK LADY AILEEN HAS CHOSEN VERY WELL.
...YOU DO KNOW AN AWFUL LOT, DON'T YOU?
YOU FLATTER ME.
IT'S GALLING, BUT HE SEEMS CAPABLE...

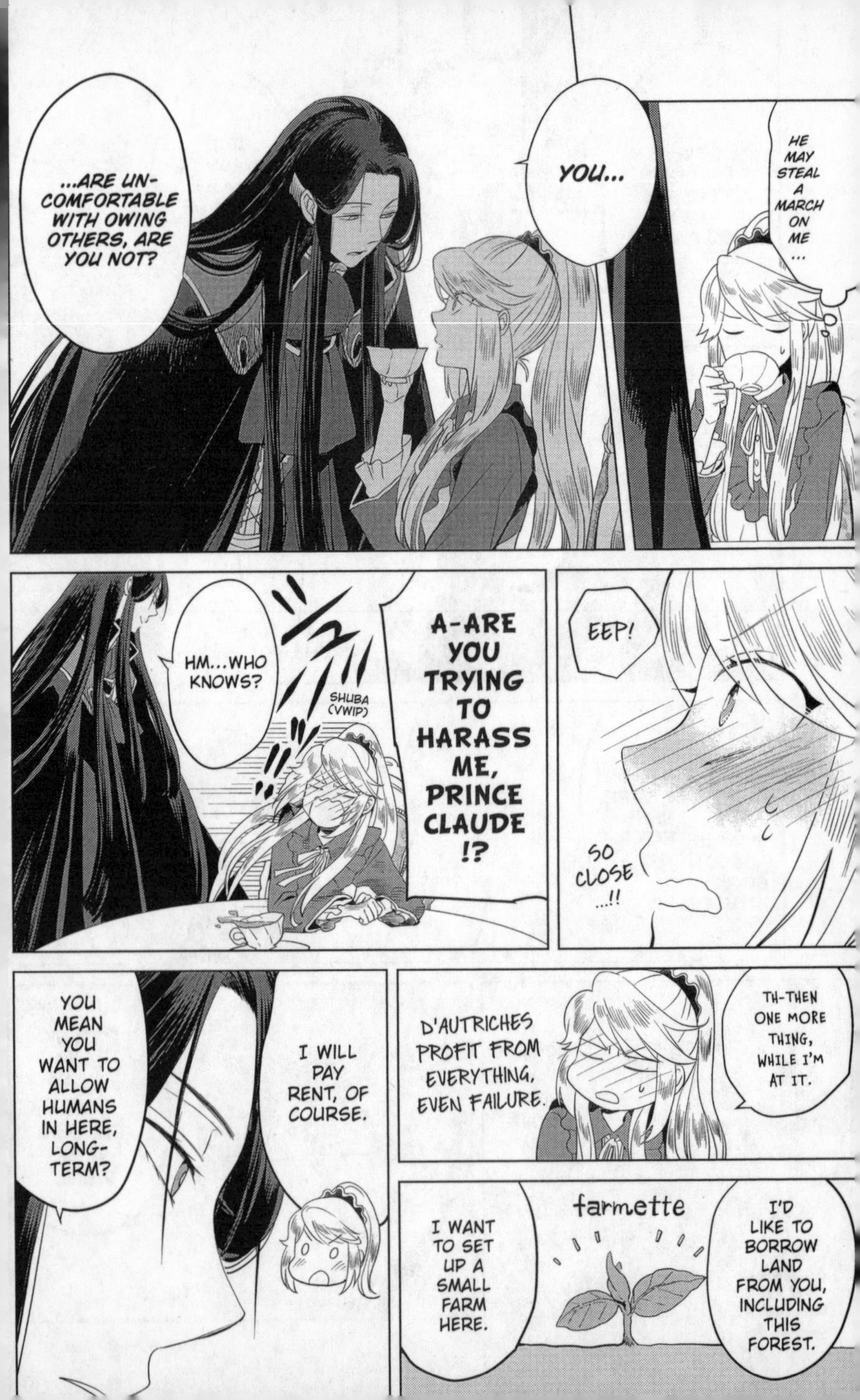
HE MAY STEAL A MARCH ON ME...
YOU...
...ARE UN-COMFORTABLE WITH OWING OTHERS, ARE YOU NOT?
EEP!
SO CLOSE...!!
A-ARE YOU TRYING TO HARASS ME, PRINCE CLAUDE!?
SHUBA (VWIP)
HM...WHO KNOWS?
TH-THEN ONE MORE THING, WHILE I'M AT IT.
D'AUTRICHES PROFIT FROM EVERYTHING, EVEN FAILURE.
I'D LIKE TO BORROW LAND FROM YOU, INCLUDING THIS FOREST.
farmette
I WANT TO SET UP A SMALL FARM HERE.
I WILL PAY RENT, OF COURSE.
YOU MEAN YOU WANT TO ALLOW HUMANS IN HERE, LONG-TERM?

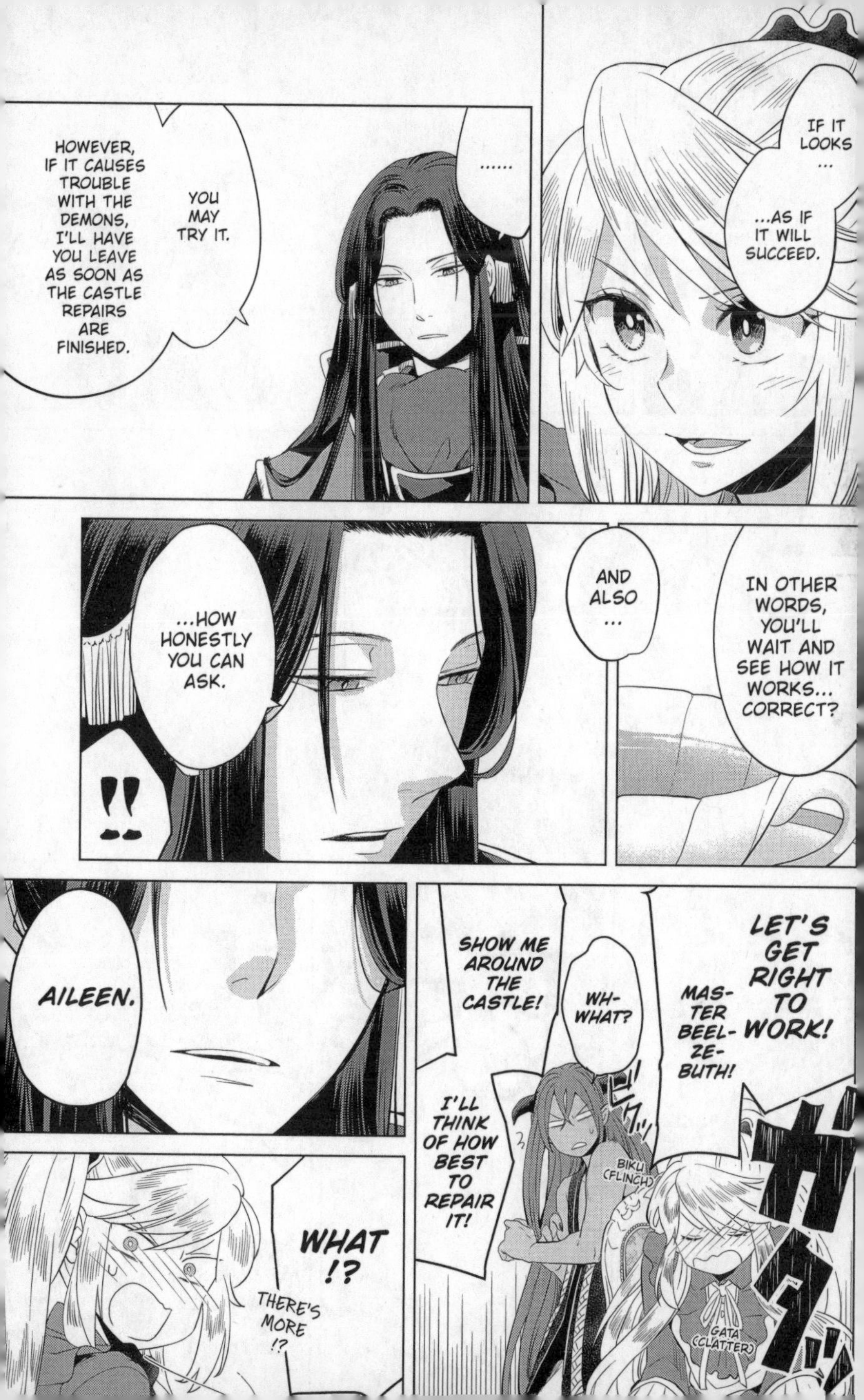
IF IT LOOKS ...
...AS IF IT WILL SUCCEED.
......
YOU MAY TRY IT.
HOWEVER, IF IT CAUSES TROUBLE WITH THE DEMONS, I'LL HAVE YOU LEAVE AS SOON AS THE CASTLE REPAIRS ARE FINISHED.
IN OTHER WORDS, YOU'LL WAIT AND SEE HOW IT WORKS... CORRECT?
AND ALSO ...
...HOW HONESTLY YOU CAN ASK.
!!
LET'S GET RIGHT TO WORK!
MAS-TER BEEL-ZE-BUTH!
SHOW ME AROUND THE CASTLE!
WH-WHAT?
I'LL THINK OF HOW BEST TO REPAIR IT!
BIKU (FLINCH)
GATA (CLATTER)
AILEEN.
WHAT!?
THERE'S MORE!?

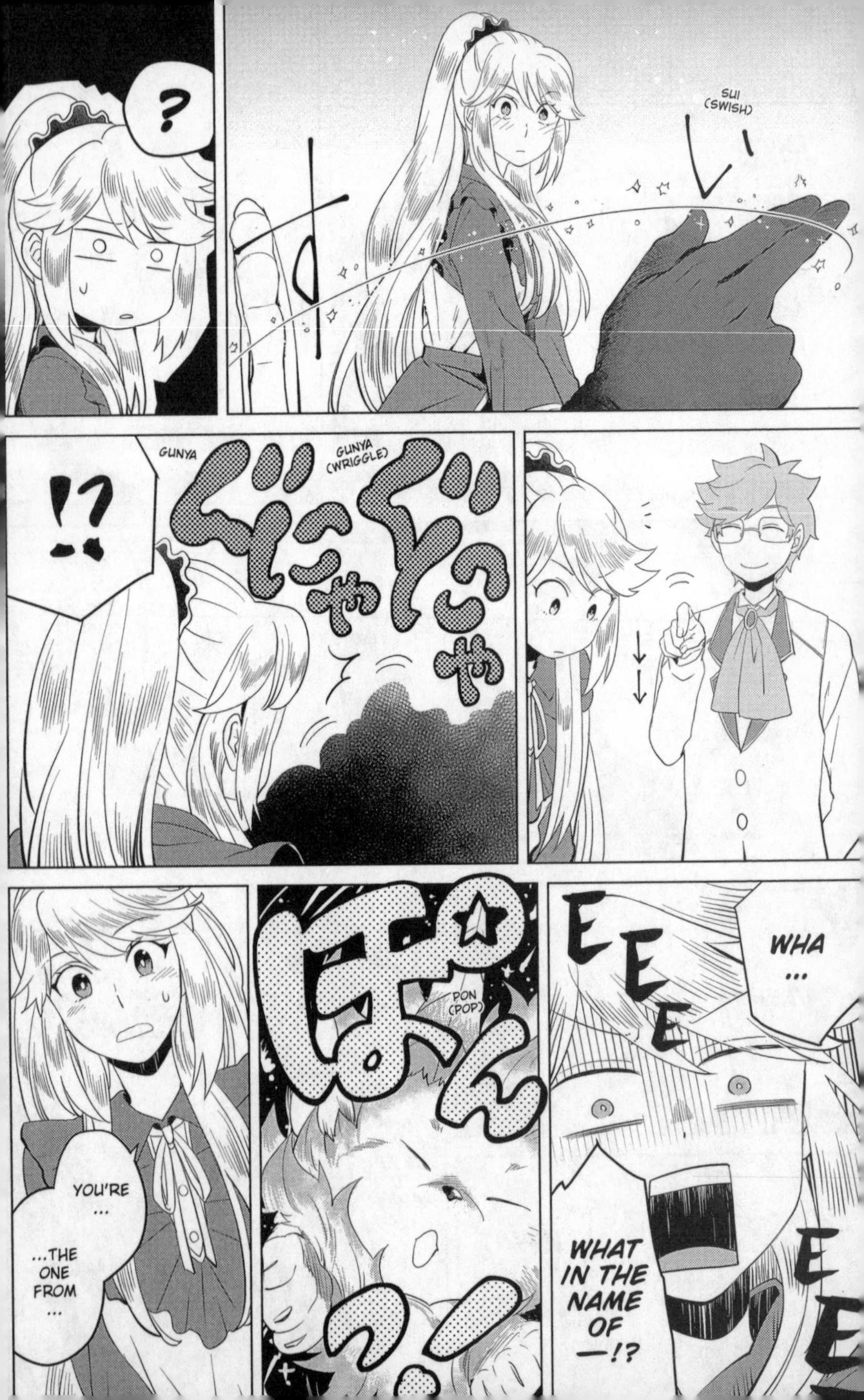

SUI (SWISH)
?
GUNYA (WRIGGLE)
GUNYA
!?
WHA ...
EEE
WHAT IN THE NAME OF —!?
EE
PON (POP)
YOU'RE ...
...THE ONE FROM ...

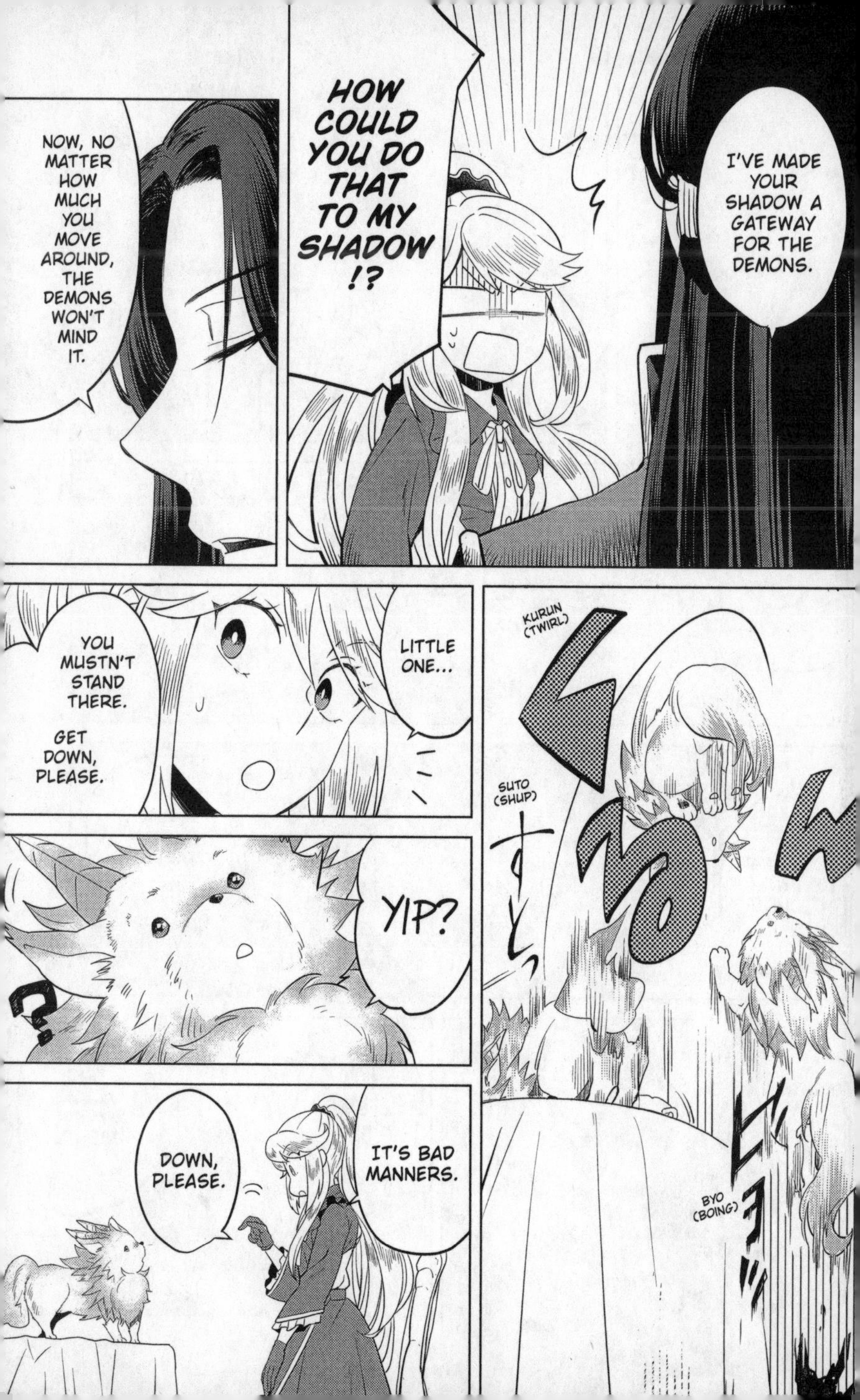
I'VE MADE YOUR SHADOW A GATEWAY FOR THE DEMONS.
HOW COULD YOU DO THAT TO MY SHADOW!?
NOW, NO MATTER HOW MUCH YOU MOVE AROUND, THE DEMONS WON'T MIND IT.
KURUN (TWIRL)
SUTO (SHUP)
BYO (BOING)
LITTLE ONE...
YOU MUSTN'T STAND THERE.
GET DOWN, PLEASE.
YIP?
IT'S BAD MANNERS.
DOWN, PLEASE.

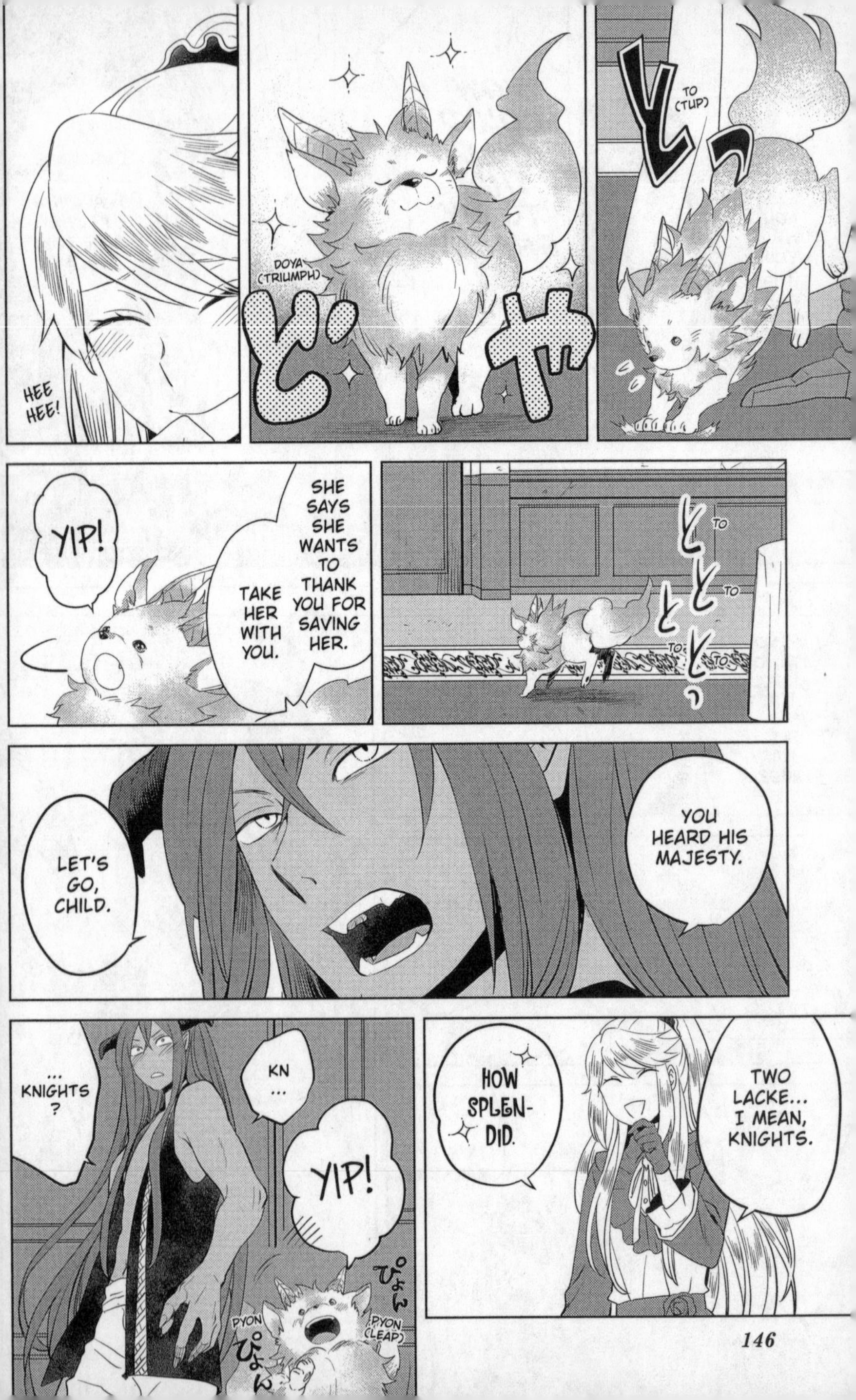
とっ
TO (TUP)
どや
DOYA (TRIUMPH)
HEE HEE!
とととと
TO TO TO TO
SHE SAYS SHE WANTS TO THANK YOU FOR SAVING HER.
TAKE HER WITH YOU.
YIP!
YOU HEARD HIS MAJESTY.
LET'S GO, CHILD.
TWO LACKE... I MEAN, KNIGHTS.
HOW SPLENDID.
KN...
YIP!
...KNIGHTS?
ぴょん
PYON (LEAP)
ぴょん
PYON

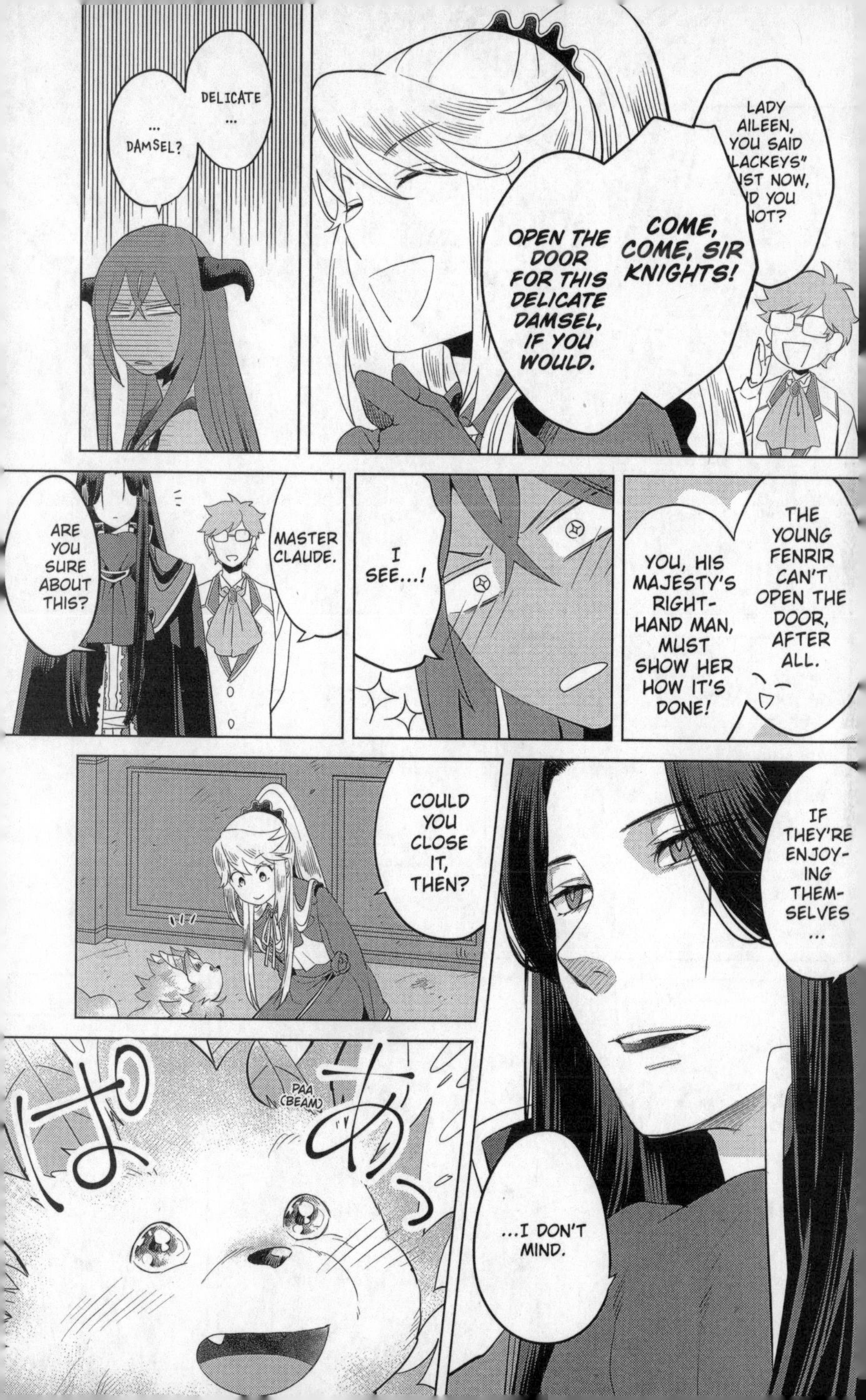

LADY AILEEN, YOU SAID LACKEYS" ST NOW, D YOU OT?
COME, COME, SIR KNIGHTS!
OPEN THE DOOR FOR THIS DELICATE DAMSEL, IF YOU WOULD.
DELICATE ... ... DAMSEL?
THE YOUNG FENRIR CAN'T OPEN THE DOOR, AFTER ALL.
YOU, HIS MAJESTY'S RIGHT-HAND MAN, MUST SHOW HER HOW IT'S DONE!
I SEE...!
MASTER CLAUDE.
ARE YOU SURE ABOUT THIS?
IF THEY'RE ENJOY-ING THEM-SELVES...
...I DON'T MIND.
COULD YOU CLOSE IT, THEN?
PAA (BEAM)

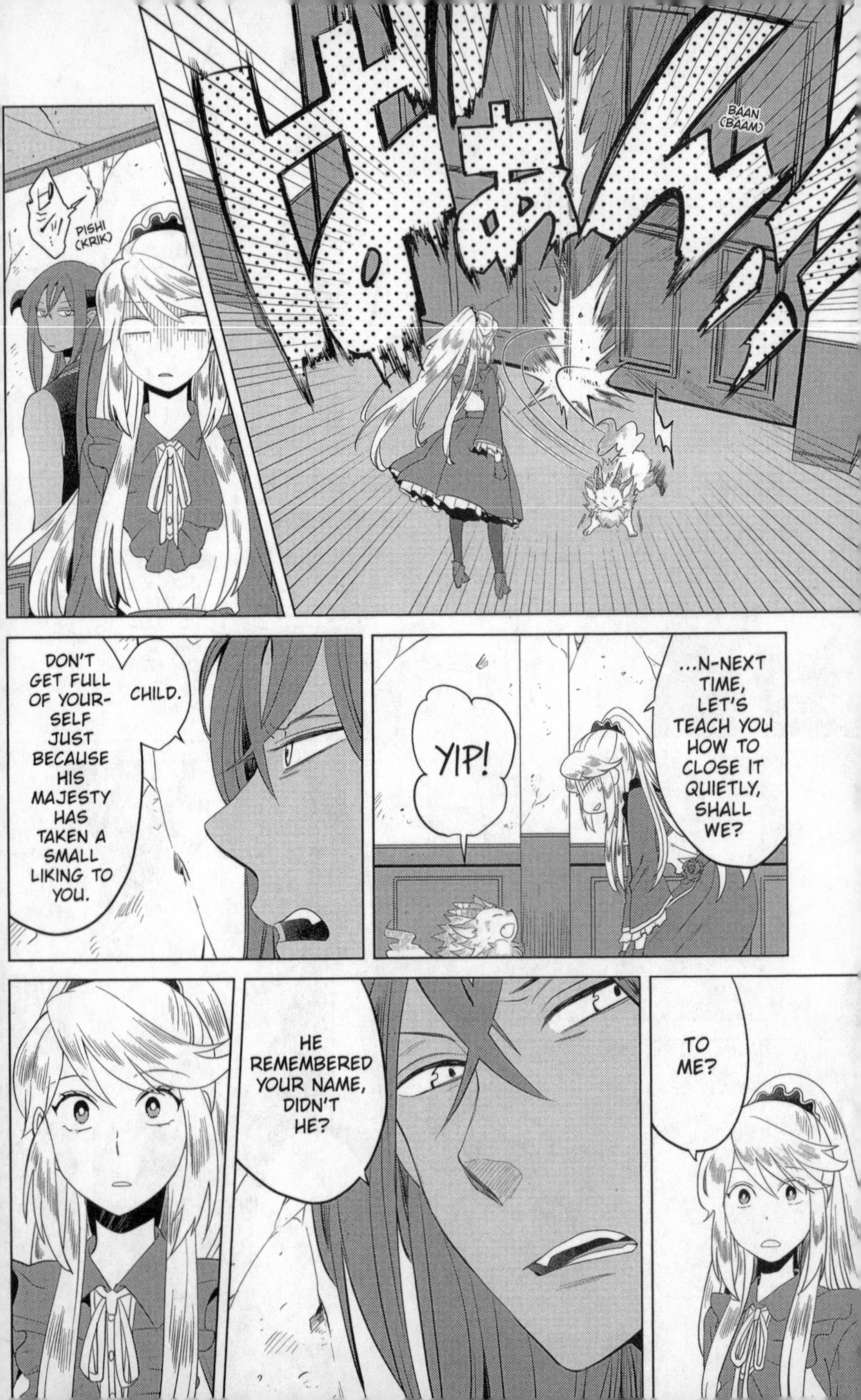
BAAN (BAAM)
PISHI (KRIK)
...N-NEXT TIME, LET'S TEACH YOU HOW TO CLOSE IT QUIETLY, SHALL WE?
YIP!
CHILD.
DON'T GET FULL OF YOURSELF JUST BECAUSE HIS MAJESTY HAS TAKEN A SMALL LIKING TO YOU.
TO ME?
HE REMEMBERED YOUR NAME, DIDN'T HE?

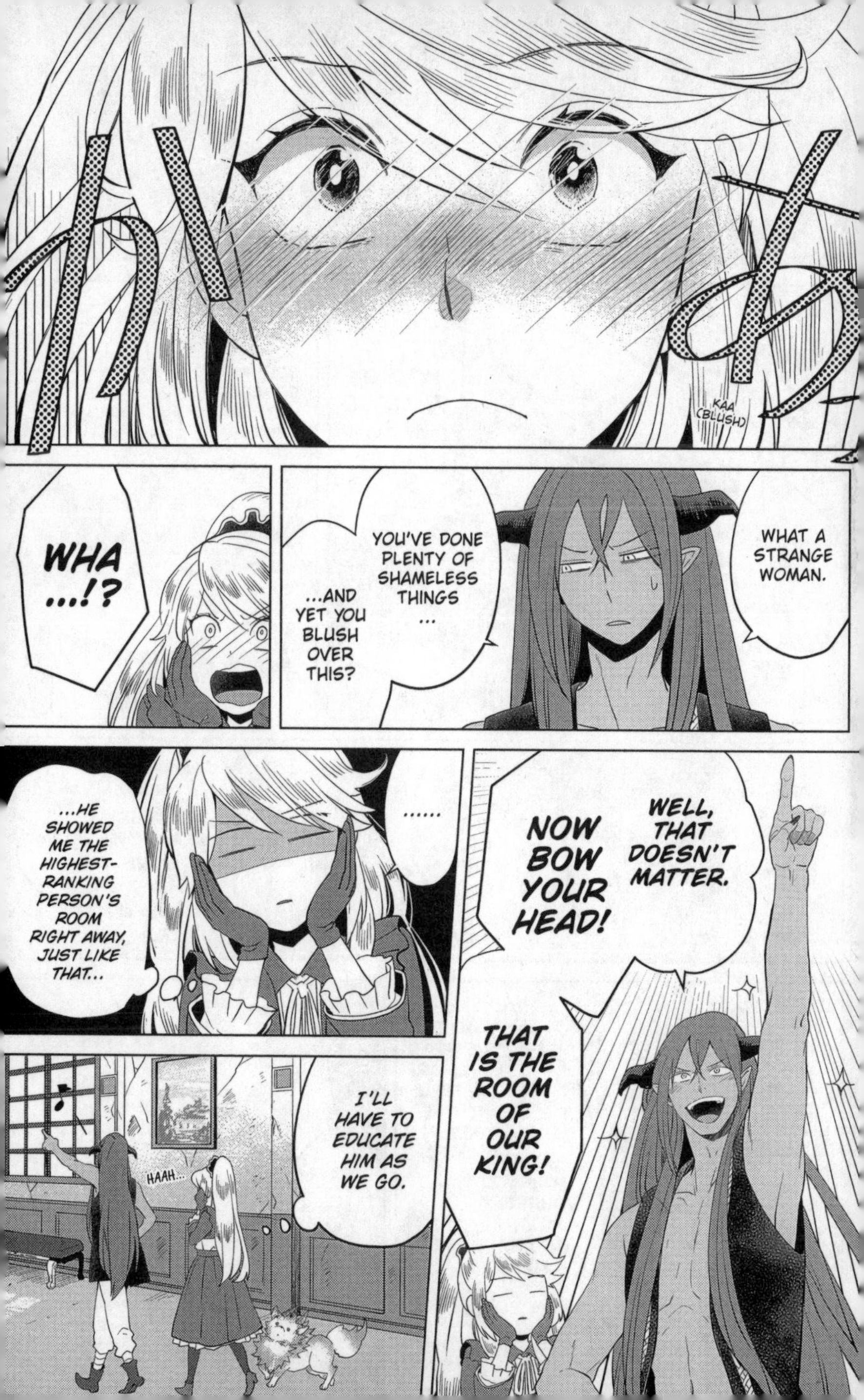
KAA (BLUSH)
WHAT A STRANGE WOMAN.
YOU'VE DONE PLENTY OF SHAMELESS THINGS ...
...AND YET YOU BLUSH OVER THIS?
WHA ...!?
WELL, THAT DOESN'T MATTER.
NOW BOW YOUR HEAD!
THAT IS THE ROOM OF OUR KING!
......
...HE SHOWED ME THE HIGHEST-RANKING PERSON'S ROOM RIGHT AWAY, JUST LIKE THAT...
I'LL HAVE TO EDUCATE HIM AS WE GO.
HAAH...

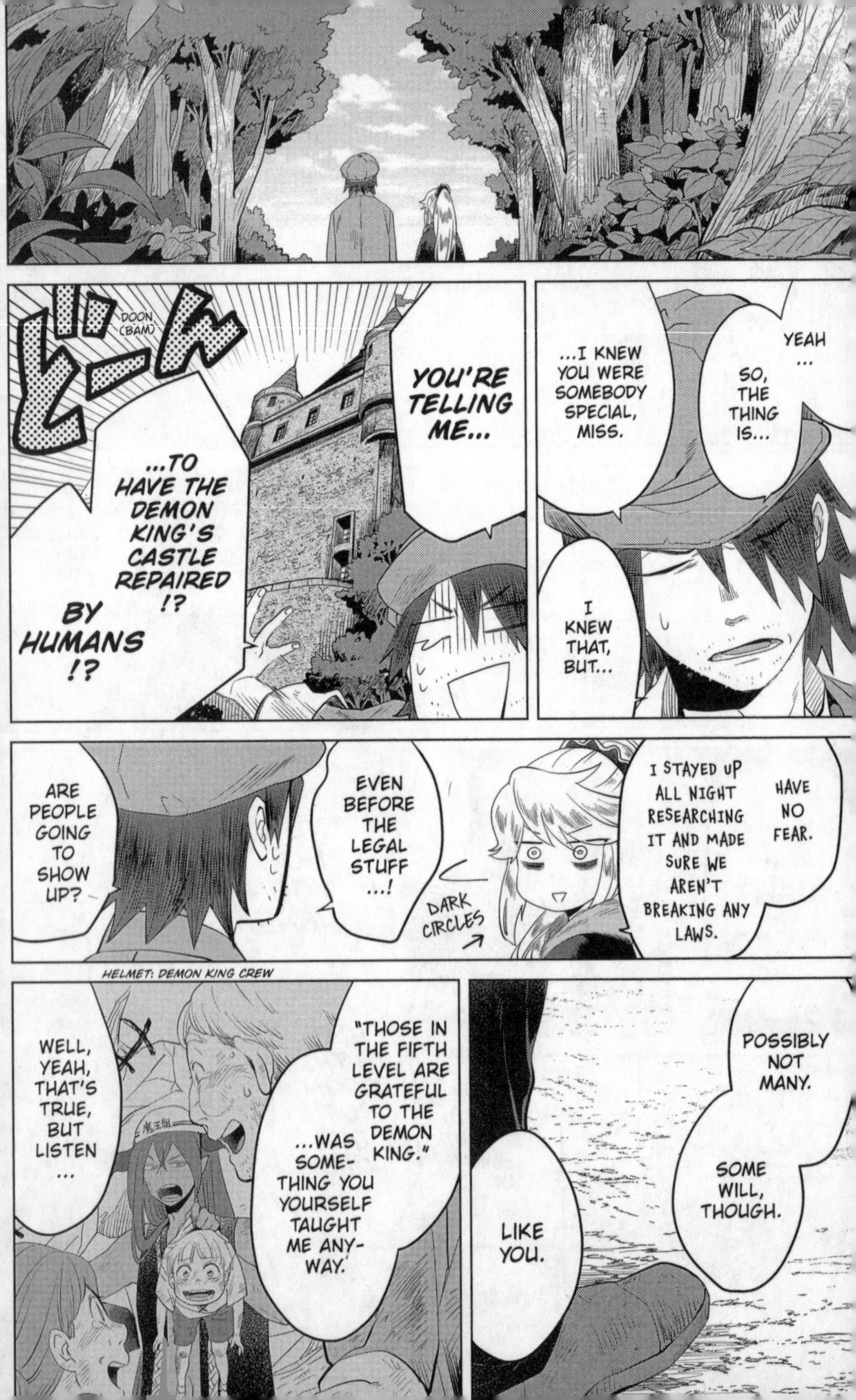
YEAH...
SO, THE THING IS...
...I KNEW YOU WERE SOMEBODY SPECIAL, MISS.
I KNEW THAT, BUT...
YOU'RE TELLING ME...
DOON (BAM)
...TO HAVE THE DEMON KING'S CASTLE REPAIRED!?
BY HUMANS!?
HAVE NO FEAR.
I STAYED UP ALL NIGHT RESEARCHING IT AND MADE SURE WE AREN'T BREAKING ANY LAWS.
DARK CIRCLES
EVEN BEFORE THE LEGAL STUFF...!
ARE PEOPLE GOING TO SHOW UP?
HELMET: DEMON KING CREW
POSSIBLY NOT MANY.
SOME WILL, THOUGH.
LIKE YOU.
"THOSE IN THE FIFTH LEVEL ARE GRATEFUL TO THE DEMON KING."
...WAS SOMETHING YOU YOURSELF TAUGHT ME ANYWAY.
WELL, YEAH, THAT'S TRUE, BUT LISTEN...

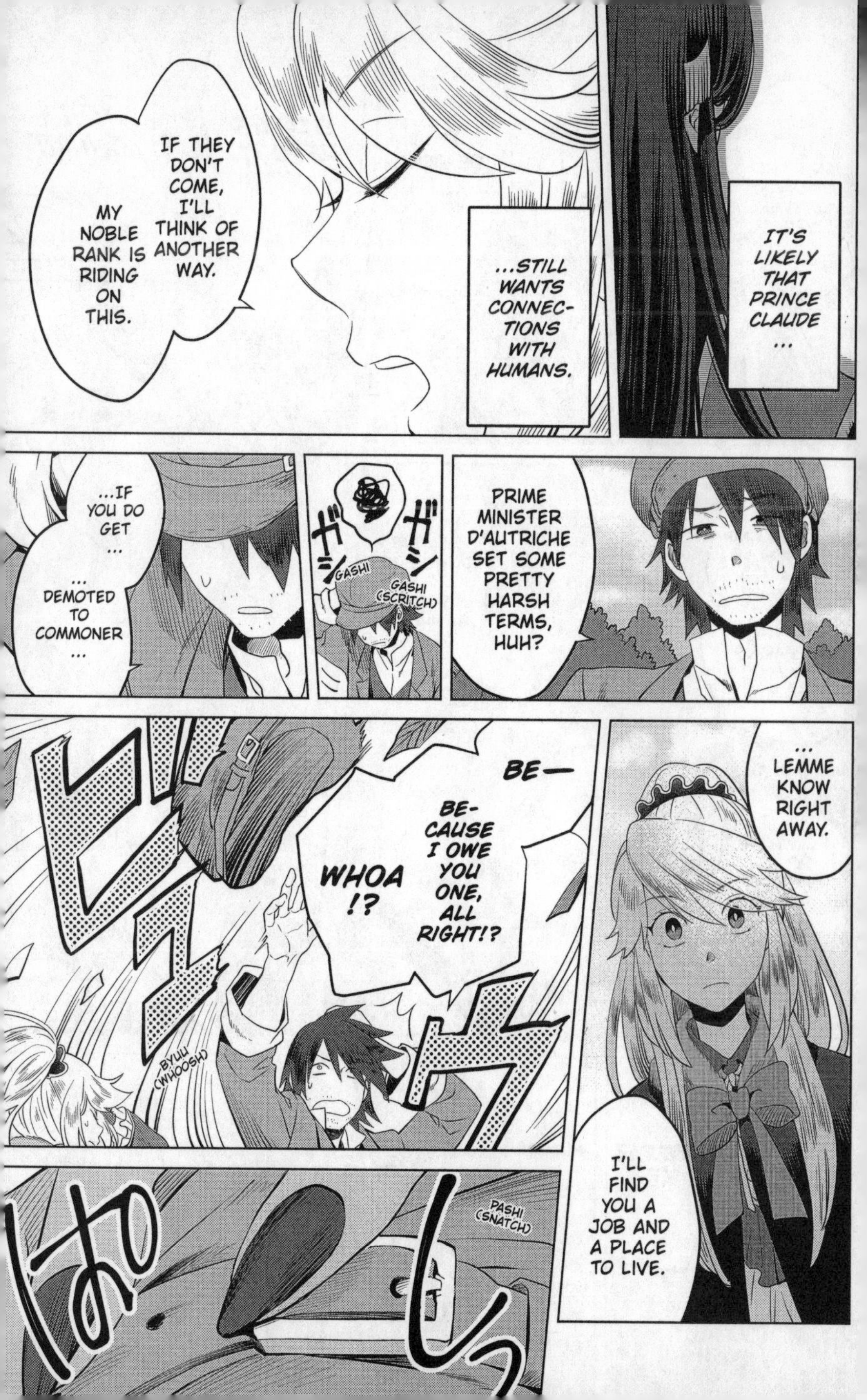
IT'S LIKELY THAT PRINCE CLAUDE ...
...STILL WANTS CONNEC-TIONS WITH HUMANS.
IF THEY DON'T COME, I'LL THINK OF ANOTHER WAY.
MY NOBLE RANK IS RIDING ON THIS.
PRIME MINISTER D'AUTRICHE SET SOME PRETTY HARSH TERMS, HUH?
GASHI GASHI (SCRITCH)
...IF YOU DO GET ...
... DEMOTED TO COMMONER ...
... LEMME KNOW RIGHT AWAY.
I'LL FIND YOU A JOB AND A PLACE TO LIVE.
BE—
BE-CAUSE I OWE YOU ONE, ALL RIGHT!?
WHOA!?
BYUU (WHOOSH)
PASHI (SNATCH)

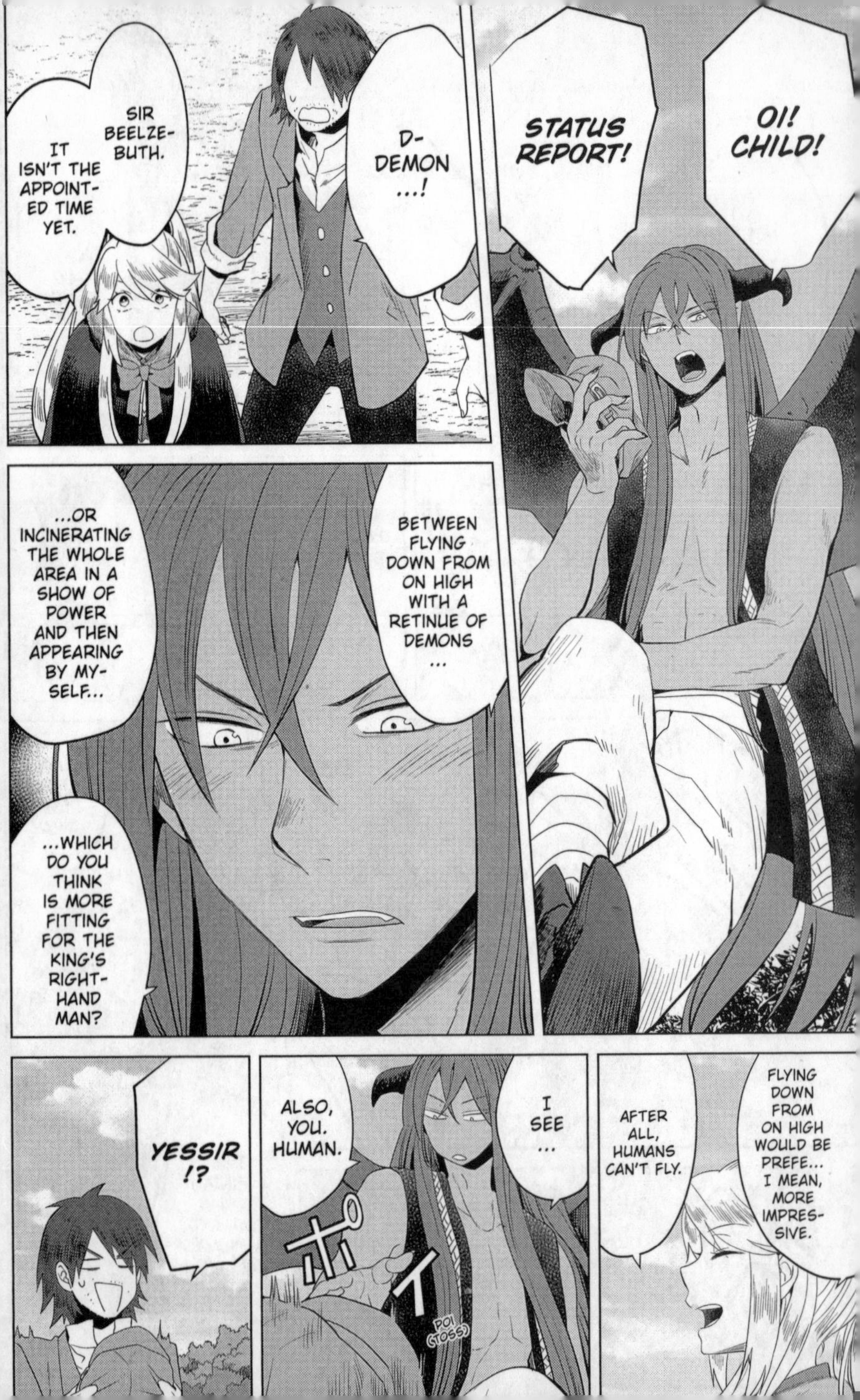
OI! CHILD!
STATUS REPORT!
D-DEMON...!
SIR BEELZEBUTH.
IT ISN'T THE APPOINTED TIME YET.
BETWEEN FLYING DOWN FROM ON HIGH WITH A RETINUE OF DEMONS...
...OR INCINERATING THE WHOLE AREA IN A SHOW OF POWER AND THEN APPEARING BY MYSELF...
...WHICH DO YOU THINK IS MORE FITTING FOR THE KING'S RIGHT-HAND MAN?
FLYING DOWN FROM ON HIGH WOULD BE PREFE... I MEAN, MORE IMPRESSIVE.
AFTER ALL, HUMANS CAN'T FLY.
I SEE...
ALSO, YOU. HUMAN.
POI (TOSS)
YESSIR!?

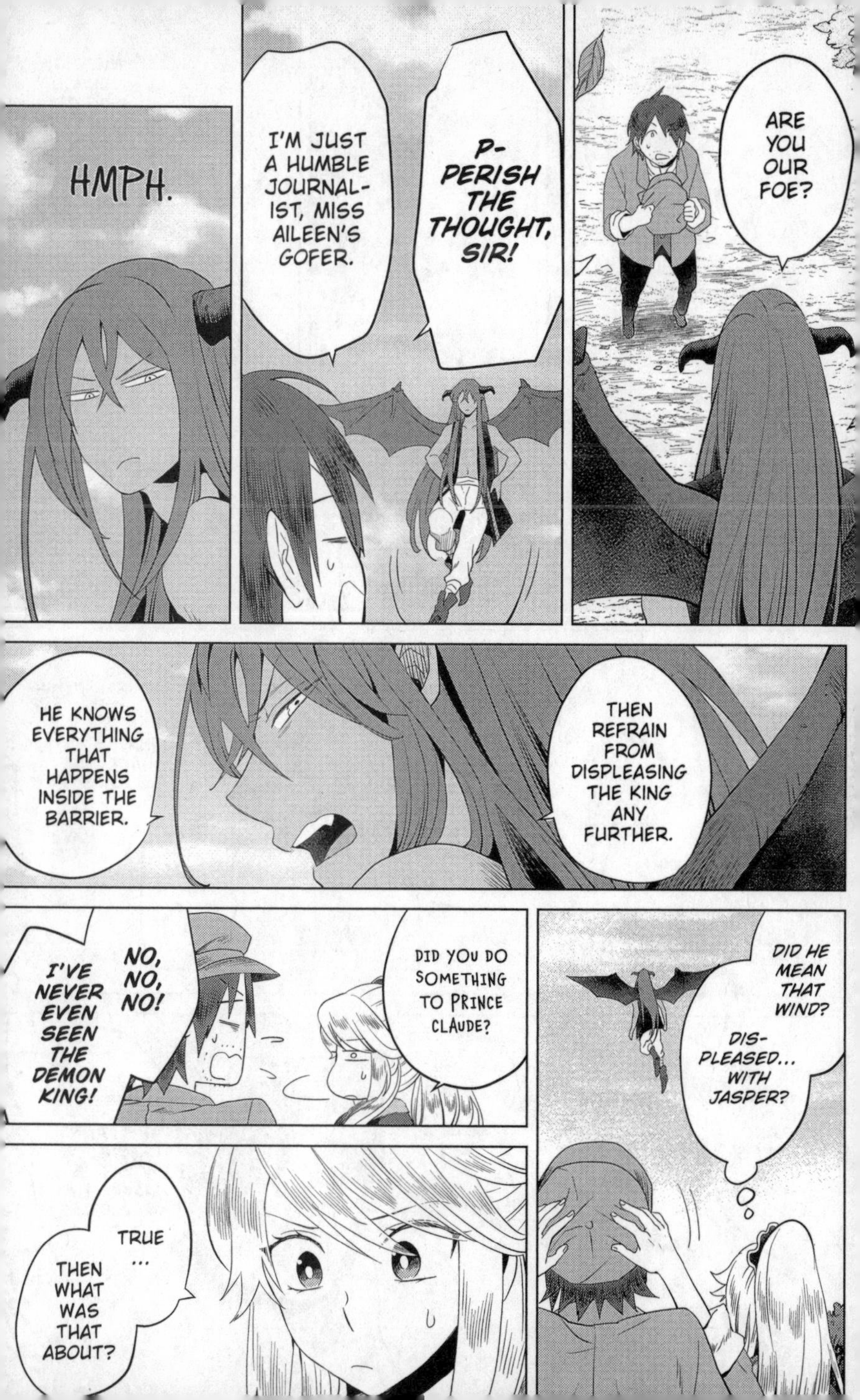
ARE YOU OUR FOE?
P-PERISH THE THOUGHT, SIR!
I'M JUST A HUMBLE JOURNAL-IST, MISS AILEEN'S GOFER.
HMPH.
THEN REFRAIN FROM DISPLEASING THE KING ANY FURTHER.
HE KNOWS EVERYTHING THAT HAPPENS INSIDE THE BARRIER.
DID HE MEAN THAT WIND?
DIS-PLEASED... WITH JASPER?
DID YOU DO SOMETHING TO PRINCE CLAUDE?
NO, NO, NO!
I'VE NEVER EVEN SEEN THE DEMON KING!
TRUE...
THEN WHAT WAS THAT ABOUT?

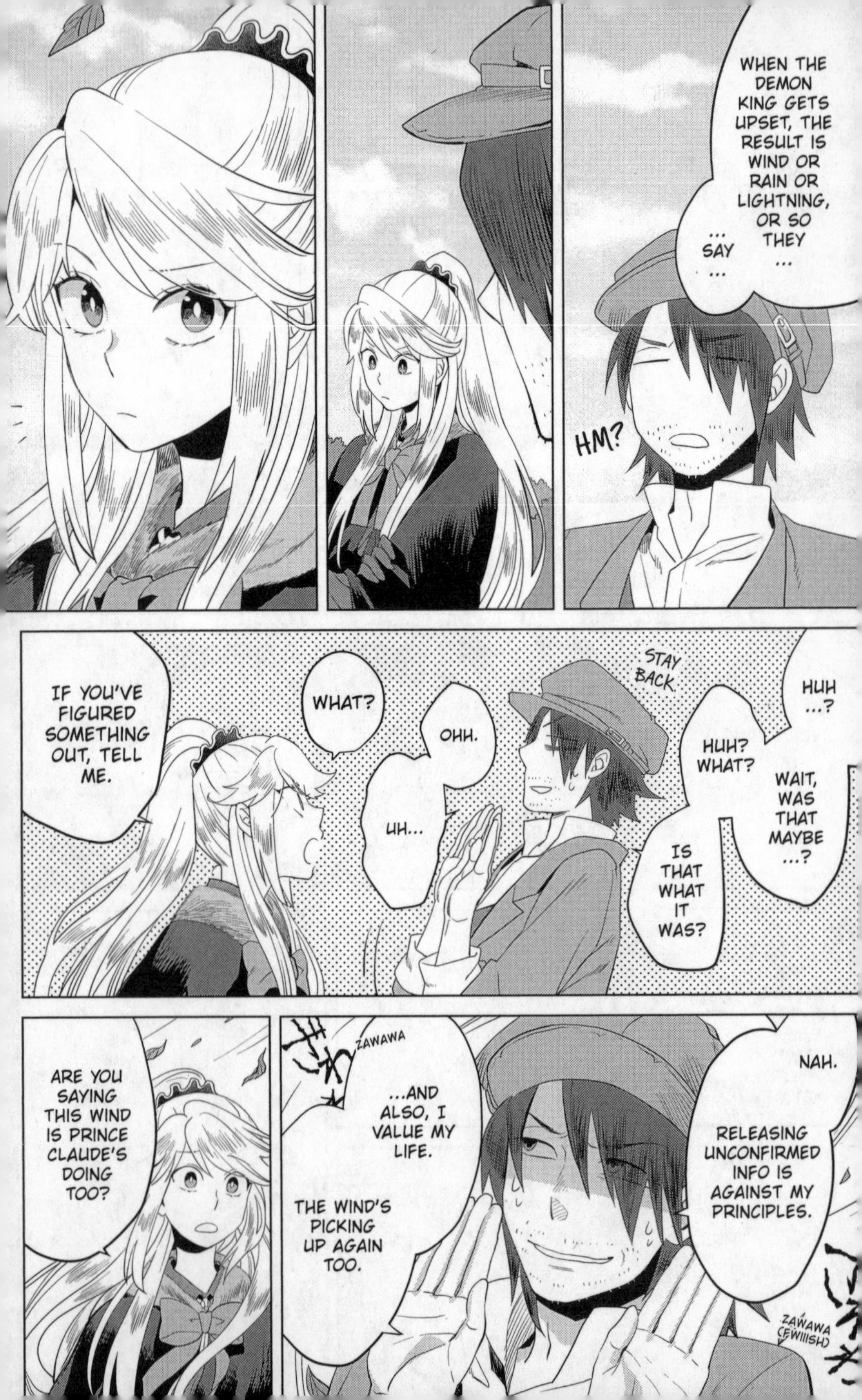
WHEN THE DEMON KING GETS UPSET, THE RESULT IS WIND OR RAIN OR LIGHTNING, OR SO THEY ... SAY ...
HM?
HUH ...?
WAIT, WAS THAT MAYBE ...?
HUH? WHAT?
IS THAT WHAT IT WAS?
STAY BACK.
OHH.
UH...
WHAT?
IF YOU'VE FIGURED SOMETHING OUT, TELL ME.
NAH.
RELEASING UNCONFIRMED INFO IS AGAINST MY PRINCIPLES.
ZAWAWA (FWIIISH)
...AND ALSO, I VALUE MY LIFE.
THE WIND'S PICKING UP AGAIN TOO.
ZAWAWA
ARE YOU SAYING THIS WIND IS PRINCE CLAUDE'S DOING TOO?

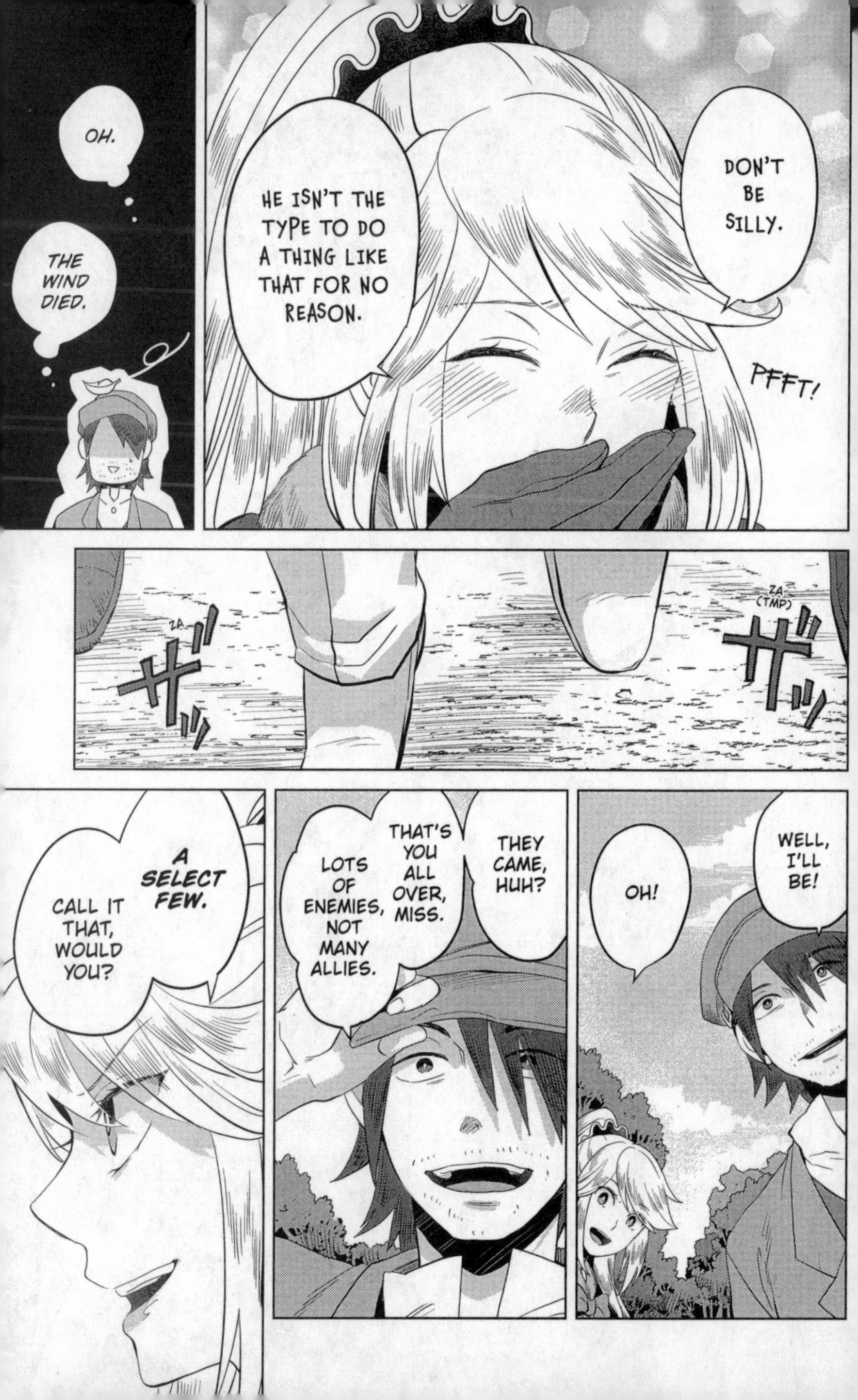
DON'T BE SILLY.
PFFT!
HE ISN'T THE TYPE TO DO A THING LIKE THAT FOR NO REASON.
OH.
THE WIND DIED.
ZA (TMP)
ZA
WELL, I'LL BE!
OH!
THEY CAME, HUH?
THAT'S YOU ALL OVER, MISS.
LOTS OF ENEMIES, NOT MANY ALLIES.
A SELECT FEW.
CALL IT THAT, WOULD YOU?

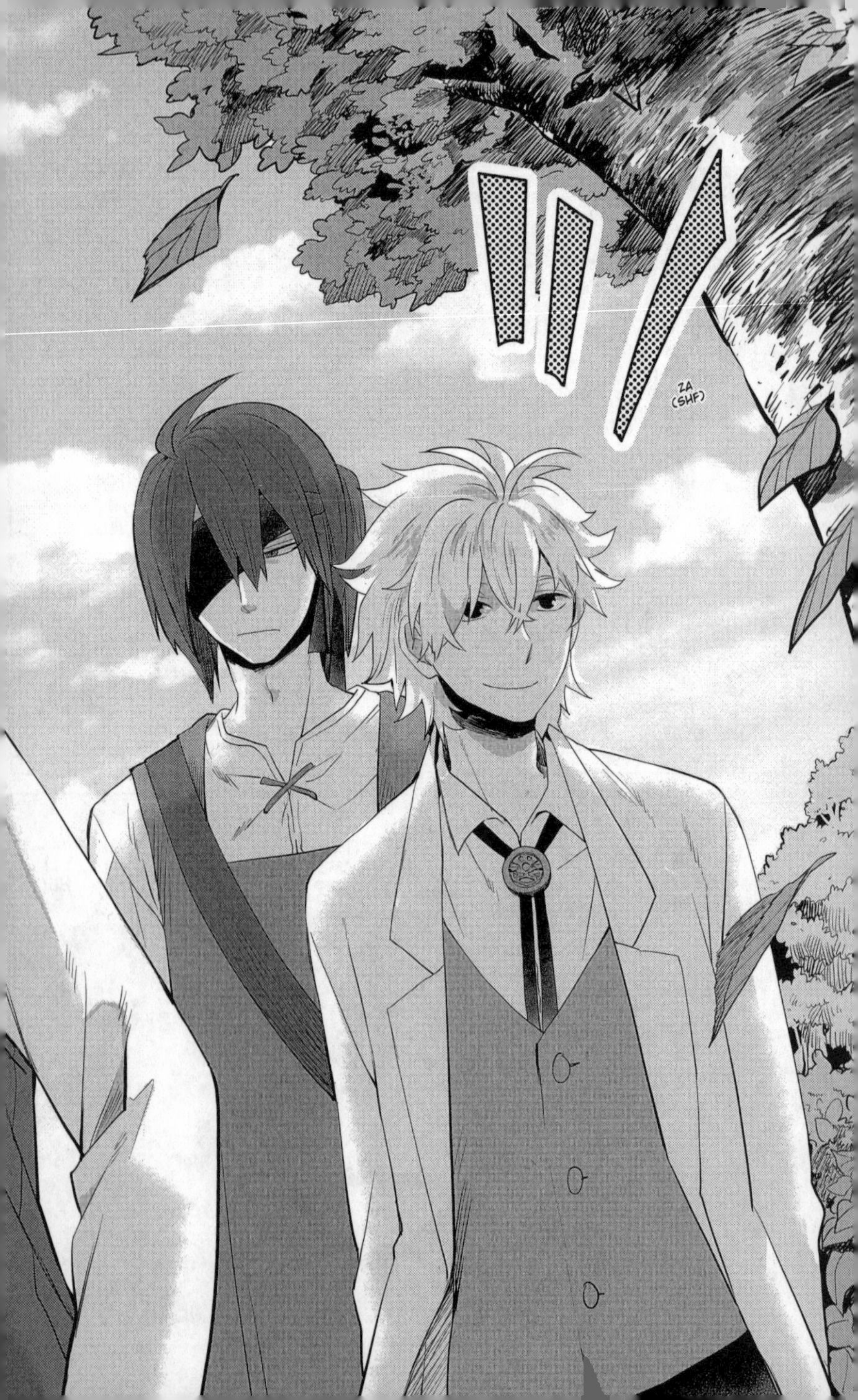
ZA
(SHF)

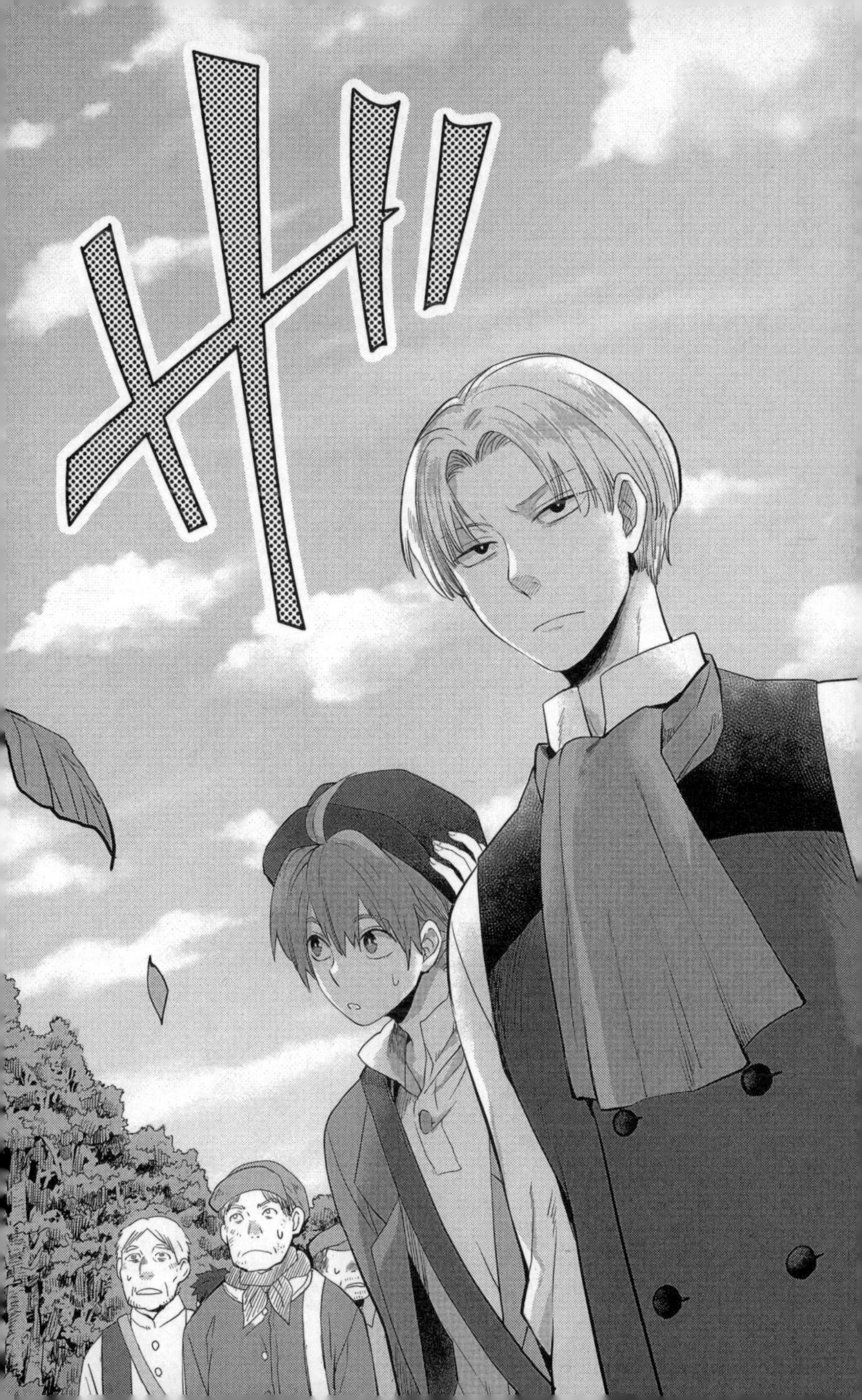
ザ

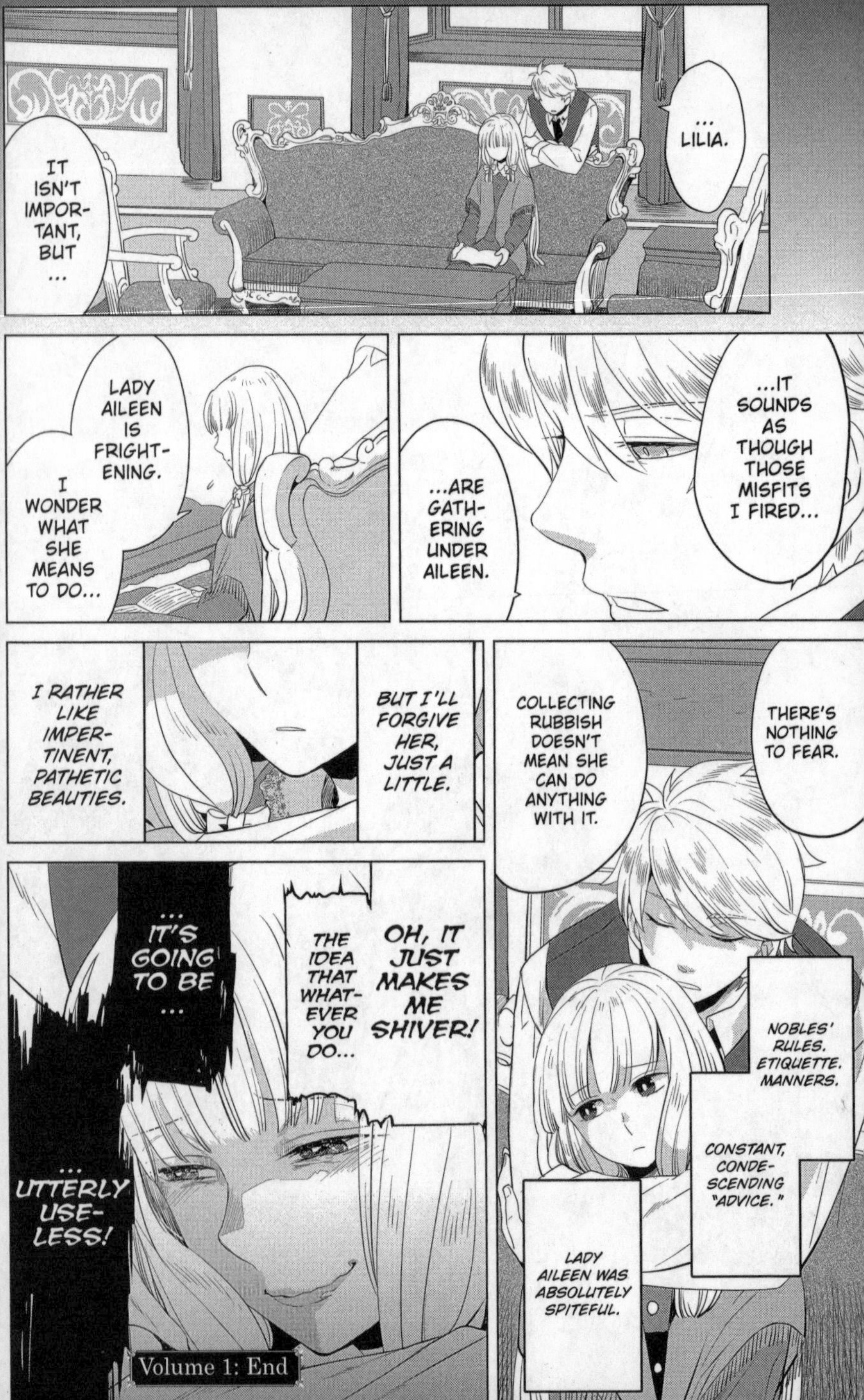
... LILIA.
IT ISN'T IMPORTANT, BUT ...
...IT SOUNDS AS THOUGH THOSE MISFITS I FIRED...
...ARE GATHERING UNDER AILEEN.
LADY AILEEN IS FRIGHTENING.
I WONDER WHAT SHE MEANS TO DO...
THERE'S NOTHING TO FEAR.
COLLECTING RUBBISH DOESN'T MEAN SHE CAN DO ANYTHING WITH IT.
NOBLES' RULES. ETIQUETTE. MANNERS.
CONSTANT, CONDESCENDING "ADVICE."
LADY AILEEN WAS ABSOLUTELY SPITEFUL.
BUT I'LL FORGIVE HER, JUST A LITTLE.
I RATHER LIKE IMPERTINENT, PATHETIC BEAUTIES.
OH, IT JUST MAKES ME SHIVER!
THE IDEA THAT WHATEVER YOU DO...
... IT'S GOING TO BE ...
... UTTERLY USELESS!
Volume 1: End

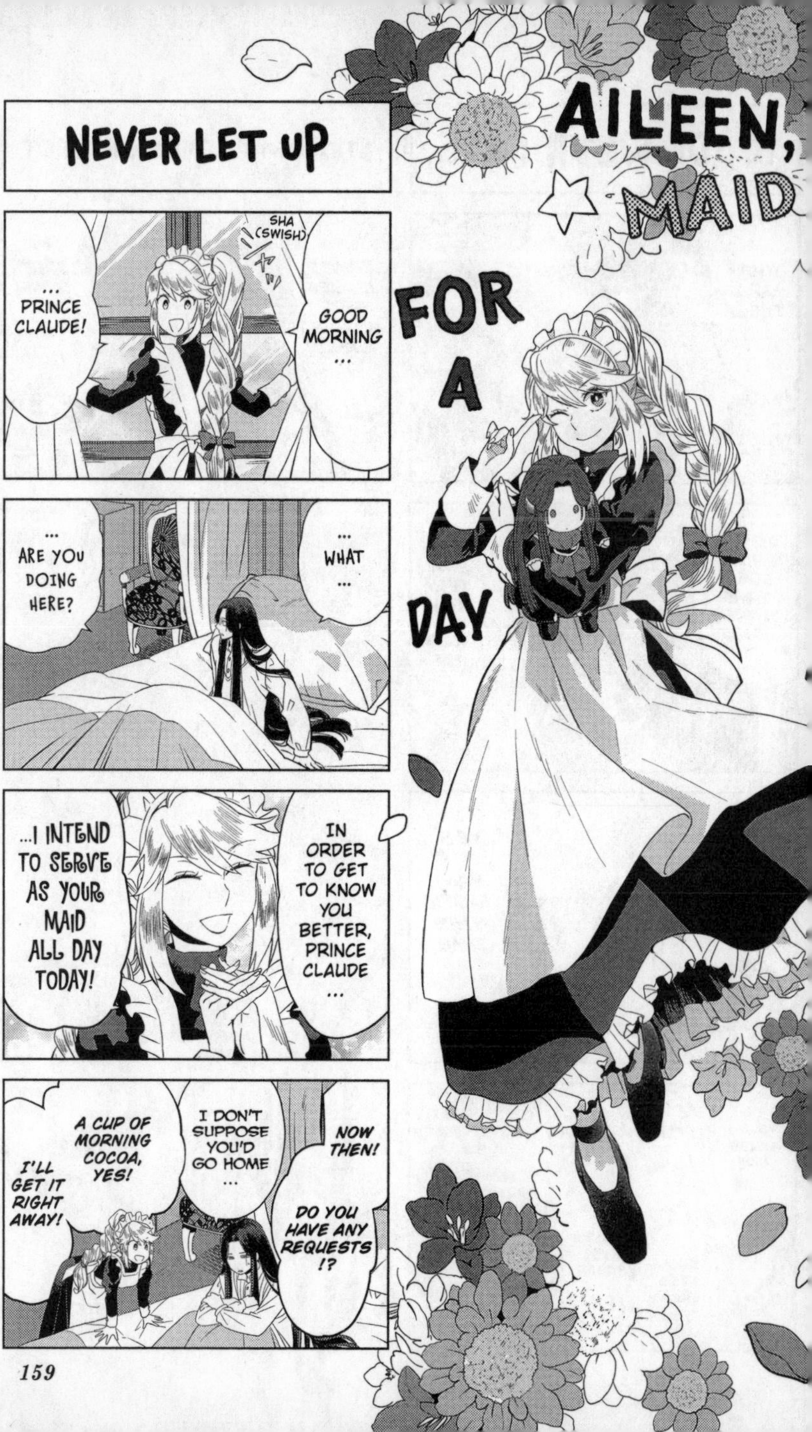
AILEEN, MAID FOR A DAY
NEVER LET UP
GOOD MORNING ...
SHA (SWISH)
... PRINCE CLAUDE!
... WHAT ...
... ARE YOU DOING HERE?
IN ORDER TO GET TO KNOW YOU BETTER, PRINCE CLAUDE ...
...I INTEND TO SERVE AS YOUR MAID ALL DAY TODAY!
NOW THEN!
DO YOU HAVE ANY REQUESTS !?
I DON'T SUPPOSE YOU'D GO HOME ...
A CUP OF MORNING COCOA, YES!
I'LL GET IT RIGHT AWAY!

STRIKE WHILE THE IRON IS HOT

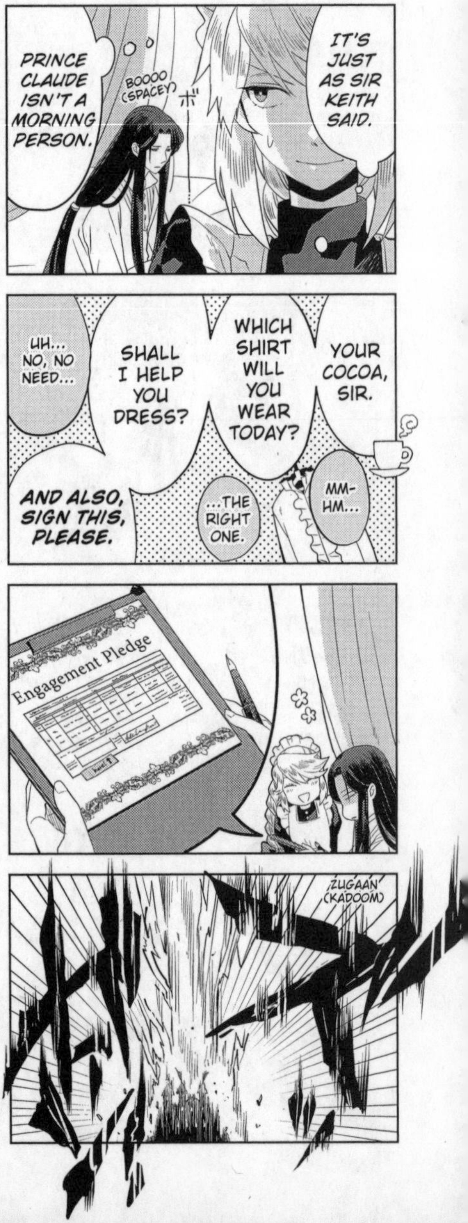
IT'S JUST AS SIR KEITH SAID.
BOOOO (SPACEY)
PRINCE CLAUDE ISN'T A MORNING PERSON.
YOUR COCOA, SIR.
MM-HM...
WHICH SHIRT WILL YOU WEAR TODAY?
...THE RIGHT ONE.
SHALL I HELP YOU DRESS?
UH... NO, NO NEED...
AND ALSO, SIGN THIS, PLEASE.
Engagement Pledge
ZUGAAN (KADOOM)

MADE WITH CARE

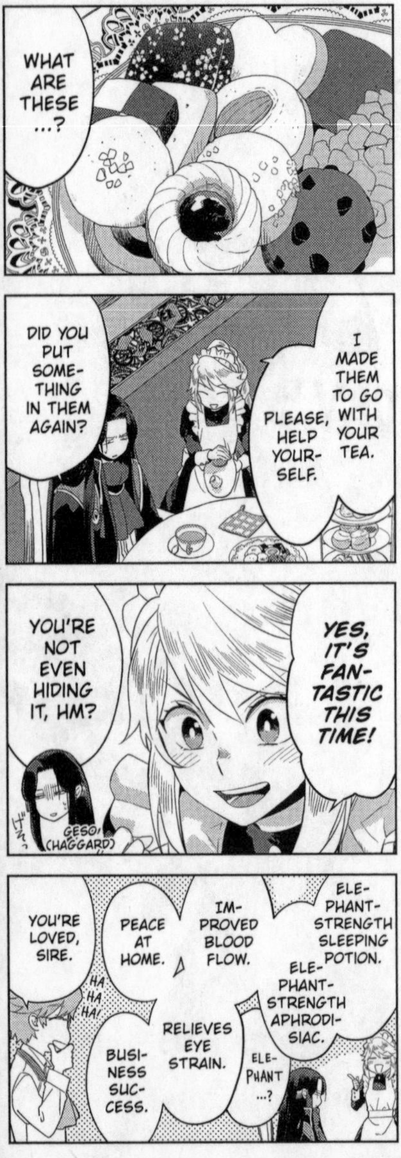
WHAT ARE THESE ...?
I MADE THEM TO GO WITH YOUR TEA.
PLEASE, HELP YOURSELF.
DID YOU PUT SOMETHING IN THEM AGAIN?
YES, IT'S FANTASTIC THIS TIME!
YOU'RE NOT EVEN HIDING IT, HM?
GESO! (HAGGARD)
ELEPHANT-STRENGTH SLEEPING POTION.
IMPROVED BLOOD FLOW.
PEACE AT HOME.
YOU'RE LOVED, SIRE.
HA HA HA!
ELEPHANT-STRENGTH APHRODISIAC.
RELIEVES EYE STRAIN.
BUSINESS SUCCESS.
ELEPHANT...?

ALL THE RAGE

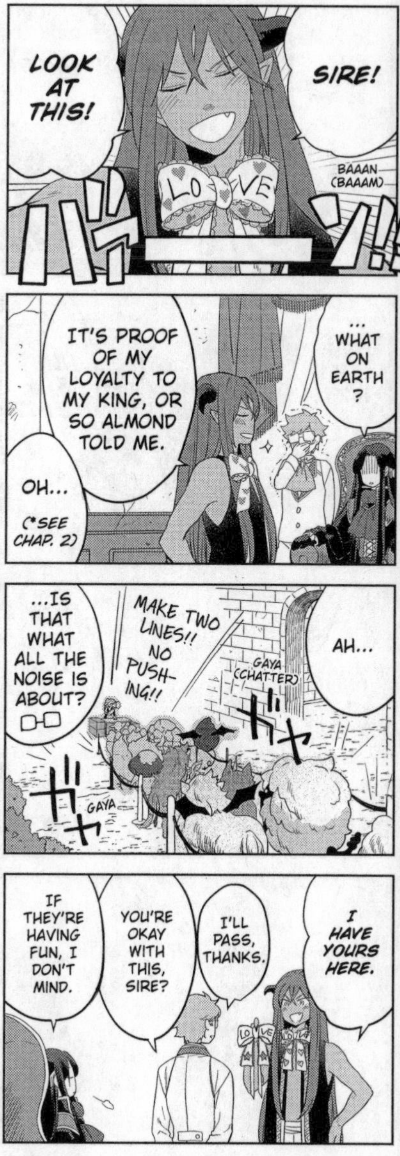
SIRE!
LOOK AT THIS!
BAAAN (BAAAM)
... WHAT ON EARTH ?
IT'S PROOF OF MY LOYALTY TO MY KING, OR SO ALMOND TOLD ME.
OH...
(*SEE CHAP. 2)
AH...
GAYA (CHATTER)
MAKE TWO LINES!! NO PUSHING!!
...IS THAT WHAT ALL THE NOISE IS ABOUT?
GAYA
I HAVE YOURS HERE.
I'LL PASS, THANKS.
YOU'RE OKAY WITH THIS, SIRE?
IF THEY'RE HAVING FUN, I DON'T MIND.

A BRIEF RESPITE

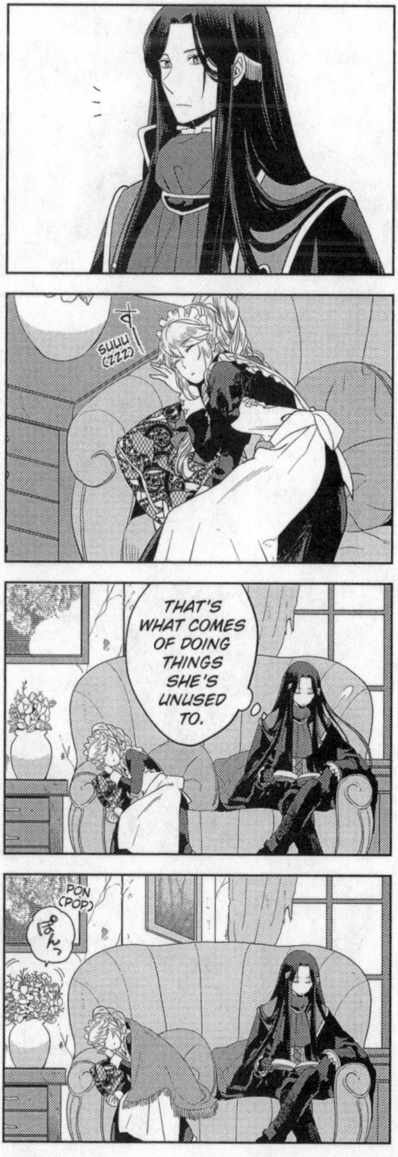
SUUU (ZZZ)
THAT'S WHAT COMES OF DOING THINGS SHE'S UNUSED TO.
PON (POP)
ぽんっ

RESULTS: DEBATABLE

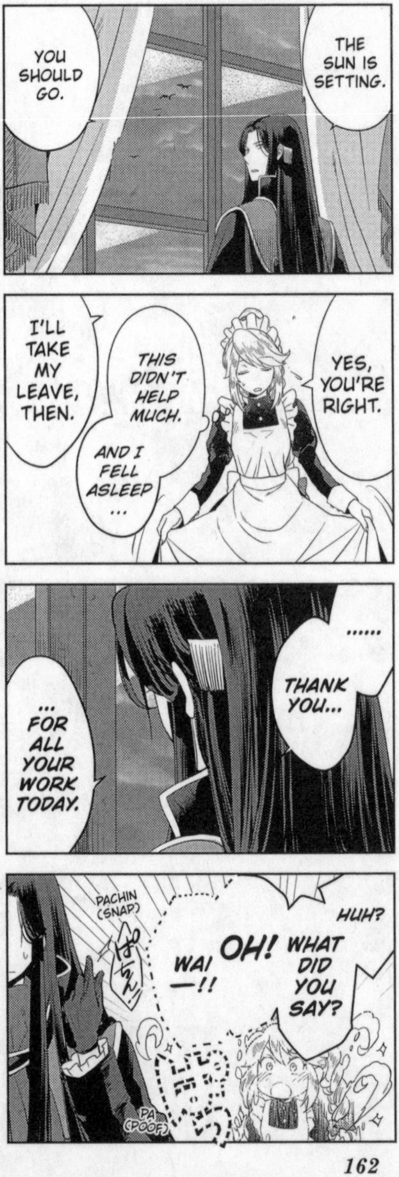
THE SUN IS SETTING.
YOU SHOULD GO.
YES, YOU'RE RIGHT.
THIS DIDN'T HELP MUCH.
AND I FELL ASLEEP...
I'LL TAKE MY LEAVE, THEN.
......
THANK YOU...
...FOR ALL YOUR WORK TODAY.
HUH? WHAT DID YOU SAY?
OH!
PACHIN (SNAP)
WAI—!!
PA (POOF)

THE PARTY'S OVER

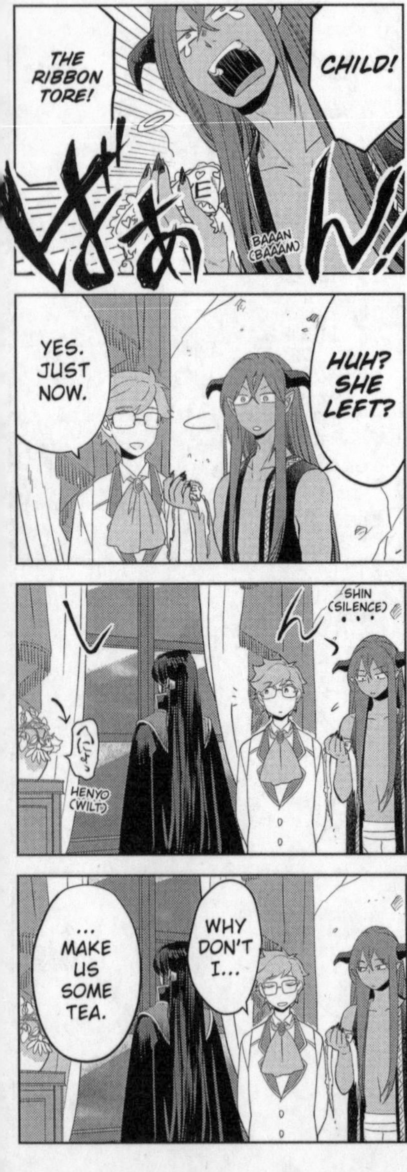
CHILD!
THE RIBBON TORE!
BAAAN (BAAAM)
HUH? SHE LEFT?
YES. JUST NOW.
SHIN (SILENCE)
HENYO (WILT)
WHY DON'T I...
...MAKE US SOME TEA.

I'm **VILLAINESS,** So I'm
the **VILLAINESS,** I'm
Taming the **Final Boss**

I'm the VILLAINESS, So I'm Taming the Final Boss 1

Anko Yuzu

ORIGINAL STORY:
Sarasa Nagase

CHARACTER DESIGN:
Mai Murasaki

Translation: Taylor Engel   Lettering: Rachel J. Pierce

This book is a work of fiction. Names, characters, places, and incidents are the product of the author's imagination or are used fictitiously. Any resemblance to actual events, locales, or persons, living or dead, is coincidental.

AKUYAKU REIJO NANODE LAST BOSS WO KATTE MIMASHITA Vol. 1
© Anko Yuzu 2018 © Sarasa Nagase 2018
© Mai Murasaki 2018
First published in Japan in 2018 by KADOKAWA CORPORATION, Tokyo.
English translation rights arranged with KADOKAWA CORPORATION, Tokyo
and Yen Press, LLC through Tuttle-Mori Agency, Inc.

English translation © 2021 by Yen Press, LLC

Yen Press
150 West 30th Street, 19th Floor
New York, NY 10001

Visit us at yenpress.com • facebook.com/yenpress
twitter.com/yenpress • yenpress.tumblr.com
instagram.com/yenpress

First Yen Press Edition: August 2021

Yen Press is an imprint of Yen Press, LLC.
The Yen Press name and logo are trademarks of Yen Press, LLC.

The publisher is not responsible for websites (or their content) that are not owned by the publisher.

Library of Congress Control Number: 2021935585

ISBNs: 978-1-9753-2120-8 (paperback)
978-1-9753-2119-2 (ebook)

10 9 8 7 6 5 4 3 2 1

BVG

Printed in the United States of America